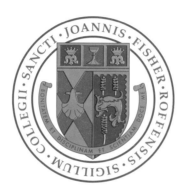

A HISTORY OF THE THIRD✠REICH

VOLUME 4: PRIMARY SOURCES

Jeff T. Hay, *Editor*

Christopher R. Browning, *Consulting Editor*

Daniel Leone, *President*

Bonnie Szumski, *Publisher*

Scott Barbour, *Managing Editor*

GREENHAVEN
PRESS®

THOMSON

GALE

San Diego • Detroit • New York • San Francisco • Cleveland • New Haven, Conn. • Waterville, Maine • London • Munich

Acknowledgments

The editor wishes to thank Professor Christopher R. Browning of the University of North Carolina, Chapel Hill, a Holocaust expert and early mentor, for his contribution to the selection of entries for these volumes. He would also like to thank the staff of Greenhaven Press, notably editor Viqi Wagner, whose hard work and resourcefulness were a great help in completing the project.

LIBRARY OF CONGRESS CATALOGING-IN-PUBLICATION DATA

A history of the Third Reich / Jeff T. Hay, book editor.
    p.   cm.
Includes bibliographical references and index.
  ISBN 0-7377-1116-7 (v. 1 : alk. paper)
  ISBN 0-7377-1118-3 (v. 2 : alk. paper)
  ISBN 0-7377-1478-6 (v. 1 and v. 2 set : alk. paper)
  ISBN 0-7377-1120-5 (v. 3 : alk. paper)
  ISBN 0-7377-1477-8 (v. 4 : alk. paper)
  1. Germany—History—1933–1945. 2. National socialism—History. I. Hay, Jeff T.
DD256.5 .H529 2003
943.086—dc21

2002033900

CONTENTS

Chapter 3: Concentration Camps and the Holocaust

Chapter 4: Everyday Life in the Third Reich

CHAPTER ONE

THE RISE OF THE THIRD REICH

The Third Reich had its beginnings in the German Workers' Party, a small political party that formed in the southern German city of Munich in 1919. Many of its early members were disgruntled veterans of World War I. Over the next twenty years, until World War II started on September 1, 1939, the German Workers' Party underwent a remarkable transformation, becoming one of the most powerful political movements on earth. Under the leadership of Adolf Hitler, it changed its name to the National Socialist German Workers' Party (NSDAP), or the Nazi Party for short.

The period from 1919 until 1933 was known within the Nazi movement as the Kampfzeit, or Days of Struggle. During those years Hitler and his comrades worked to build their movement into a strong political force in anticipation of the moment when they could take over Germany. An early highlight of the Days of Struggle was the Beer Hall Putsch of 1923, Hitler's violent first attempt to grab power. Its failure taught Hitler patience and the advantage of working within the existing political system. Over the next years he refined the Nazi message in speeches and in his book, *Mein Kampf (My Struggle)*. The Nazis' goals included restoring German strength and influence and fulfilling what Hitler saw as destiny by expanding into eastern Europe. Meanwhile the Nazis sought to differentiate themselves philosophically from other German political groups, especially their greatest enemies, the Communists.

On January 30, 1933, the Nazi Party finally took power when Adolf Hitler was named chancellor of Germany as the result of political intrigues. Over the next years the party seized total control of German life by moving Nazi officials into every office and every town through a process known as Gleichschaltung, or "coordination." After 1935, Hitler felt secure enough politically to seriously plan to put his old idea, eastward expansion, into operation. In November 1937 he announced his intentions to his military leaders, to their surprise, and in 1938 he made his first territorial moves, in Austria and Czechoslovakia. World War II was on the horizon.

The Personality of the Führer

Nazi press chief Otto Dietrich remembers certain aspects of Adolf Hitler's character and daily habits, focusing on his health and his relations with women as well as his love of movies.

Hitler was a complete vegetarian; he never ate meat or fish. He lived almost entirely on vegetables and certain cereals; even bread and butter would give him indigestion. Zwieback and knaekkebroed [crisp bread], honey, tomato ketchup, mushrooms, curds and yoghurt were for a long time the basic elements in his diet. In later years he could no longer stand coffee, and only limited amounts of milk. All his food was specially prepared; even his soups were not the same as those served to the other guests. In his last years he had a special Viennese dietetic cook who even at military headquarters would prepare the Fuehrer's meals in a special small kitchen. Incidentally, in 1932 when Hitler was living at the Hotel Kaiserhof in Berlin and suspected a plot to poison him, Frau Goebbels used frequently to prepare his meals at her home and spirit them up to his hotel room.

I have often wondered how, given his austere diet and his insomnia, Hitler managed to summon up the strength and the tremendous force of will that he manifested for so many years. His energy verged on the abnormal. The only possible biological explanation for it was that he must have been consuming his physical reserves at a pace which would surely lead to premature bodily degeneration.

Hitler exerted no pressure upon his guests with regard to vegetarianism, although he often talked with them about it and teased them about their food habits, calling them "corpse eaters." Only a few persons followed his custom at table. Among these was Bormann—although everyone knew that at home Bormann would not turn down a good steak. Hitler provided his guests with a substantial but never luxurious cuisine, and of course observed the wartime one-dish meal. Even at the greatest state banquets he never permitted at his table more than one main course, along with soup or entré, and a dessert. At one time his doctors recommended him to eat caviar for its nutritional value. It did him good, but after a while he stopped having it, saying it was "sinfully expensive."

Hitler also despised alcohol, the taste of which was repugnant to him. On ceremonial occasions when he had to drink a toast, his glass was always filled with mineral water. But in this respect also he let his guests follow their own tastes. However, they were restrained in the use of alcohol at his table. His opposition to smoking was much stronger. He considered nicotine extremely harmful, saying he would offer cigars and cigarettes only to his worst enemies, never to his friends. He forbade smoking in his rooms. There were exceptions to this rule only at important official functions in Berlin or Munich, and then separate smoking rooms were provided, which Hitler gave a wide berth. At the entrance to his bunker in Berlin there hung, toward the end of the war, a sign reading: "No Smoking."

I have already mentioned that Hitler restricted the conversation at table to nonpo-

Otto Dietrich, *The Hitler I Knew.* Trans. Richard and Clara Winston. London: Methuen, 1957.

litical topics. For this interlude at least he wanted to shake off the political and military problems with which his mind incessantly toiled. If serious matters were brought up, he curtly and angrily evaded them. If one had to listen to the table conversation fairly often, it soon became rather dull, revolving around a number of fixed topics to which he would always refer. He spoke a great deal about food and diet—an obvious subject at any dinner table; about the differences in foods and their preparation in various parts of the country; and about vitamins and caloric content. At this point Hitler would usually draw his doctors into the conversation, asking for expert opinions. He himself would argue in favor of a vegetarian diet, saying it had been the primeval diet of the human race and was to be desired as the diet of the future because it was both wholesome and economical. One of his favorite subjects of conversation—to the distress of Goering—was his vigorous condemnation of hunting unless it involved the hunter's actually risking his own life. He said he could never harm so beautiful an animal as a deer, and forbade all hunting on the Obersalzberg. He sneered at the amateur sportsmen, while he had words of praise for poachers, who at least killed for food. During the war he had poachers released from the prisons and placed in probationary battalions. During the last years of the war, irritated by some newspaper article, he suddenly forbade all mention of hunting in the press except for plain advertisements of game being sold for meat.

In peacetime he spoke often and intensely about the protection of animals and antivivisection. He vigorously opposed vivisection [the use of animals for experimentation]—which won him much applause from the ladies—unless experiments with animals served some military purpose. To animals he ascribed the ability to think, and for them he felt sympathy—not for human beings. He was sensitive to the sufferings of animals and expressed his sympathy in the most de-

cided terms. But he never wasted a word on humanitarianism except, on one occasion, to characterize it as a mixture of cowardice, stupidity and intellectual conceit. And that indeed was his fundamental view of it. He studiously avoided the subject of the concentration camps.

Hitler would brighten up the conversation by telling stories about his life and his experiences while traveling. Insofar as I had been present at some of these incidents he described, I noted his distinct tendency to exaggerate; he often adorned his tales with extravagant imagination. Music, the cinema, the theater, painting and architecture were also topics of conversation, or rather afforded him the chance to express his purely personal views. Such conversations, however, were seldom very fruitful, since there were strict limits to how far his interlocutors dared go in replying to him. Hitler made an effort to be humorous. Some of the guests, [photographer Heinrich] Hoffman in particular, had natural gifts for light, witty conversation; as long as Hitler spoke with them, all went well. However Hitler's wit was distinctly artificial, more often the product of his sarcastic disposition than of genuine humor. He would taunt certain persons at table, go out of his way to find barbed gibes, and since he kept up this banter with some obstinacy, and it was impossible to pay him back in the same coin, the result was often great embarrassment on all sides.

Hitler would rise from the table and kiss the hands of the ladies on either side of him to signify the end of the meal. He would leave the dining room after the last of the ladies, but before all the men. Immediately afterwards he would go out to the yard to feed his German police dog himself. Later he took this dog with him to his field headquarters in East Prussia and the Ukraine.

Hitler never took a nap after lunch, although this might have been expected, since he slept so little at night. During the last years of the war, when he was already very much on the decline physically, he

Adolf Hitler appeared to feel genuine affection for his Alsatian dog Blondi, but he showed no such warmth toward his human companions.

would take a rest at the rather unusual hour of nine to ten at night.

When at the Berghof, Hitler would usually hold a few brief administrative conferences after lunch. He might, for example, discuss Party matters with Bormann, with his chief of the Reich Chancery, Lammers—who maintained a branch office of the Berlin Chancery at Berchtesgaden—or have a talk with Ribbentrop, who would drive up from the Fuschlsee in response to a telephoned summons.

In the afternoon, often shortly after lunch, Hitler took his one walk of the day to the small tea pavilion, about fifteen minutes away at a leisurely strolling pace. In order to combine business with pleasure, Hitler usually took his stroll in the company of some official visitor who happened to be present. A short distance behind him followed the ladies and gentlemen of the private circle. The tail of this odd "procession," as it was often jokingly called, was formed by his bodyguard.

The party would remain for an hour or two in the pavilion. The conversation in this unvarying circle would often be on the dull side, and Hitler would frequently doze off in his chair by the big round table in front of the fireplace. As a rule an automobile would bring the party back the short distance to the Berghof. Thereafter Hitler, unless he had some special visits or conferences, would withdraw to his two private rooms on the first floor of the house—a master's sitting room with fireplace and balcony, and a bedroom. He would remain in these rooms until around 8:30 in the evening, when the same circle of guests would assemble for dinner. A new set of seating arrangements would meanwhile have been drawn up. The ladies dressed for dinner. . . .

Over the years there was a great deal of public speculation about Hitler's being a sick man. On the basis of much observation of his life and of my constant association with his doctors I do not believe that his states of violent agitation were the symptoms or the consequence of some acute physical illness. On the contrary, these outbursts of emotion were the cause of his frequent physical distress; they were his disease. Those explosive blasts of an overcharged brain, which left him in a state of exhaustion, affected the nerves of his stomach and deranged his digestive system. Then the physical disability exerted a reciprocal effect, intensifying his tendency to outbursts of rage.

Hitler's physical health was extraordinarily unstable. He was sick as often as he was well. Almost invariably his complaint was indigestion. In 1937, on the advice of

Doctor Morell [one of Hitler's personal physicians], he underwent a "mutaflor" cure for several months, taking pills to renew his destroyed intestinal flora. Afterwards he said he felt "reborn" and for several years was able to eat many foods that had previously made him ill. Later, as a result of the excitements and spiritual trials of the war years, his condition deteriorated again. He was given vitamin injections but by no means relied on intravenous feeding, as rumor had it. On the contrary, he did well on the food prepared for him by his Viennese diet cook. The rapid physical degeneration which brought him to the verge of collapse during the last year of the war was the result of his obstinately overstraining himself, and of the constant agitation which followed the attempt upon his life of July 20, 1944. One day early in 1945 his doctor was suddenly called to his bunker at the headquarters in the Forest of Rastenburg. From a remark later dropped by the doctor I gathered that Hitler had recovered from a very light cerebral stroke. Hitler himself once said in my presence that he had restrained himself during a violent dressing-down of a "criminally incompetent" general only because he feared he would bring a stroke on himself.

For a considerable time his close associates suspected that Hitler was suffering from cancer of the larynx. A stubborn growth had made it impossible for him to talk loudly. This fear, however, proved unfounded. The well-known Berlin specialist, Doctor Eicken, who operated on Hitler for this condition, told me during a train ride from the headquarters to Berlin that the growth had been benign, a typical polypus of the larynx; he had, he said, over the years twice performed relatively simple operations upon this growth and had been able to remove it completely.

The evil in Hitler's life was not the outcome of any serious physical disease. The fatal dynamism of his whole existence was conditioned by his very nature; it was a psychological phenomenon. In the end his demonic will consumed his body as well as everything else it touched. Hitler's whole mode of life was unhealthy, virtually suicidal, and he would not listen to his doctors' advice. The burden of work which he carried, and which he increased by insisting upon making all decisions himself, was not so great that it need have crushed his health. His "service to the race and the nation" need not have kept him from living reasonably. If he had only understood how to organize his time, if only he had set aside for rest and recuperation a fraction of the days and nights he wasted in boring, artificial "sociability," his physical condition would never have deteriorated as it did. During the more than ten years that I sat at his table, Hitler took his meals with grotesque irregularity, often not lunching before four or five o'clock in the afternoon, not dining before midnight. It was only under pressure from his associates that he reluctantly and very gradually began keeping to a somewhat more even schedule in the conduct of his life.

Every evening after dinner Hitler would see one or two movies. In the Chancery in Berlin there was a motion picture room; at the Berghof the main salon would be used. In a sense, movies provided contact with normal life in the world outside, which otherwise he never encountered. Occasionally it was proposed that he should disguise himself and go about among the public, seeing Berlin unattended, as a private citizen. He would not hear of it. He never had a double, as rumors abroad persistently maintained; the idea never even entered his head.

During the war Hitler deliberately gave up this pleasure. During all those years he saw only a single motion picture. That was one evening at the Berghof when Mussolini was visiting. If I remember rightly the movie was the successful comedy *Napoleon Is to Blame for Everything*. Instead of films he preferred recorded concerts of classical works or grand opera. He also frequently called in a first-rate amateur conjuror to put on a performance. These performances so captivated him that he issued a strict ban forbidding the newspapers from disillusioning the masses about the art of magic by publishing "explanatory" articles.

Around midnight—seldom earlier and often later—there began Hitler's nightly gathering around the fireplace. During the last peacetime years this would take place after the movies had been shown; during the war, after the end of the military conference. Some fifteen to twenty persons, those I have already described, would assemble round him on the fireplace side of the main salon, in the circle of light cast by the flaming logs. The walls around the room glowed with the rich colors of classical paintings by German and Italian masters. Over the mantelpiece a madonna by an unknown Italian looked down upon the company. On the left was Feuerbach's *Nana* and a portrait of King Henry, the "founder of cities," holding compass and rule; on the right a female nude by Botticelli and the sea-nymphs from Boecklin's *Play of the Waves*. In the dark background of the room the bronze bust of Richard Wagner seemed to come to life.

In the muted semidarkness it was again Hitler who held the floor, as he had done all day long; the rest of the company were largely listeners, there only to give him an excuse for talking. Yet I often had the impression that his mind was absent while he spoke, that his thoughts were elsewhere. Now and then, when the conversation lagged, Hitler would request reports from the OKW [the High Command of the armed forces], the foreign office or the press. He would then retire briefly to an adjoining room with one of his adjutants, if he thought it necessary to issue orders.

He seldom violated his basic principle that conversation here among the ladies must remain on the lighter side. This obviously feigned insouciance was a difficult attitude for many of the others to maintain during the grave crises of the latter years of the war. As a result some of them accepted invitations to the Berghof only when they were issued as express requests from Hitler, virtually command appearances. His adjutants were kept busy trying to fill the gaps in the dinner company and the fireplace gatherings whenever the ranks began to thin. Although these sessions often dragged on until dawn, Hitler never asked whether any of those present felt tired and wished to retire. This was his one failure in courtesy and consideration toward the ladies. Their time was their own only when Hitler rose and took his leave. To listen to him and stay by him until he thought he could sleep was the tribute which he unsparingly exacted of his guests.

Hitler certainly had innumerable opportunities for conversation with important and interesting people. I have never understood why he never made use of these opportunities. Instead, for years he abstained from anything which might have added to his personal experience. He remained perpetually in the same company, among the same faces, in the same atmosphere and, I may almost say, in the same state of monotony and boredom, producing eternally the same speeches and declarations. Only the abnormality of his disposition can explain this.

Sometimes, at a very late hour, Hitler would turn his attention solely to the ladies who sat close by him and would engage them alone in a quiet, intimate conversation. The other persons in the room would talk in whispers in order not to disturb him. At such times a note of real human warmth would enter his voice. Aside from Eva Braun, this favored feminine circle included Frau Goebbels and Frau Ley. Fraeulein von Laffert, who was part of his group in Berlin, and Unity Mitford, whom Hitler saw frequently in Munich, did not enter the Berghof circle.

Since Hitler's death a great deal has been written about his alleged amours with actresses, dancers and other women. If we wish to stick to the sober facts, these tales must be relegated to the realm of fable. Those so-called mistresses—whether in Berlin, Berchtesgaden, Munich or elsewhere—were ladies who happened to attend the Fuehrer's evening parties whose pattern I have just described. There was no possibility for an affair under these conditions. Except for the time he spent with the woman whom he later married, there was hardly an hour in Hitler's life when he was not surrounded with people. As for his intimacy with Eva Braun, this most personal of human relationships even the chronicler must respect; there his obligation to history stops. . . .

It is hard to imagine a more contrasting pair than Adolf Hitler and Eva Braun. The ideal woman, according to Hitler's ideas, should be tall and blonde, although he did not prize extreme slimness. Eva Braun had a very well-proportioned figure, but she was petite rather than tall, and brunette. Hitler would frequently take her to task for her passion for high-heeled shoes. Hitler's mind was obsessed with weighty ideological problems; she, on the other hand, was a creature of pure emotion and *joie de vivre*. She always dressed becomingly and in the latest fashion, whereas he cared little about his outward appearance. Even in front of others she would frequently scold Hitler for his naturally ill-fitting uniforms and suits, and his drab ties. He always accepted such criticism with forebearing courtesy. Unlike Hitler, Eva Braun did not refrain from alcohol. She smoked heavily when he was not about, and loved dancing, whereas he had a distinct aversion to social dancing and never set foot upon a dance floor. In spite of all these temperamental differences, the two apparently got along well; in the course of many years no serious disputes between them came to light. Eva Braun was not unintelligent. She belonged to no Party organizations—not actively, at any rate—and seldom or never said a word about politics. Undoubtedly she had an influence upon Hitler in social and cultural matters, especially in regard to the theater and the cinema, but none whatsoever in public and political life.

Nevertheless, I believe that Hitler paid a high price for not being married. He absolutely lacked any feeling about family life, his alienation from it extending even to the members of his own family. This went so far that, for example, his stepbrother Alois Hitler, who ran a restaurant on Wittenbergplatz in Berlin, could never even be mentioned in Hitler's presence. This absence of family ties severed him from the general run of mankind, for he could have no inner sympathy with the way normal people live. If he had been married, the influence of a wife, the raising of children and the duties and cares attendant upon family life, might have provided him with a natural counterpoise to his one-sided political fanaticism. Participation in the natural and human aspects of life might have affected his work for the national community and guided his public activities into more moderate and fruitful channels. As it was, the violent impulsiveness of his will ranged on unchecked to the final catastrophe. He chose to remain single throughout life and married only on the point of death. That act rounded out the profound human tragedy which comprehended even his personal relations with women. Of the six women who stood in a close human relationship to him in his life, five died by suicide, or had attempted suicide.

See also Berghof, Vol. 1; Dietrich, Otto; Hitler, Adolf, Vol. 3.

The Enabling Act

The following proclamation, known officially as the Law for the Removal of the Distress of People and Reich but called everywhere the Enabling Act, was passed by the Nazi-dominated Reichstag on March 24, 1933. It effectively granted Adolf Hitler the power to rule by decree and ignore the constitution of the Weimar Republic. He used it to dismantle the republic and assume absolute power.

The Reichstag has passed the following law, which is, with the approval of the Reichsrat [the largely irrelevant upper house of the German parliament], herewith promulgated, after it has been established that it satisfies the requirements for legislation altering the Constitution.

Article 1. In addition to the procedure for the passage of legislation outlined in the Constitution, the Reich Cabinet is also authorized to enact Laws. . . .

Jeremy Noakes and Geoffrey Pridham, eds., *Documents on Nazism, 1919–1945*. New York: Viking, 1974.

Article 2. The national laws enacted by the Reich Cabinet may deviate from the Constitution provided they do not affect the position of the Reichstag and the Reichsrat. The powers of the President remain unaffected.

Article 3. The national laws enacted by the Reich Cabinet shall be prepared by the Chancellor and published in the official gazette. They come into effect, unless otherwise specified, upon the day following their publication. . . .

Article 4. Treaties of the Reich with foreign states which concern matters of domestic legislation do not require the consent of the bodies participating in legislation. The Reich Cabinet is empowered to issue the necessary provisions for the implementing of these treaties.

Article 5. This law comes into effect on the day of its publication. It ceases to be valid on 1 April 1937: it also ceases to be valid if the present Reich Cabinet is replaced by another.

See also Enabling Act, Gleichschaltung, Vol. 1; Machtergreifung, Vol 2.

Goebbels Explains National Socialism

During the 1920s the Nazi Party sought to gain support among German workers. Here, Propaganda Minister Joseph Goebbels explains in a 1926 speech why the Nazis' brand of Germanic socialism is far preferable to the international socialism of Communists.

Appendix of Z.A.B. Zeman, *Nazi Propaganda*. London: Oxford University Press, 1973.

We want to stamp the German principle in a new form, in the form of the Third Reich. We desire this Third Reich with the utmost ardour of our hearts; the Third Reich of a great Germany; the Third Reich of a socialist shared destiny. That far transcends ideas of brotherhood, far transcends the primitive doctrine of envy. We approach the German people with the final, most brutal charge. But this final, most brutal charge conceals within itself a final great reconciliation. We accuse the Right and conciliate the Left. We accuse the Left and conciliate the Right. Both sides were guilty of the German collapse. But the primary guilty party was he from the Right and therefore he must atone and offer sacrifice. If he wants to desire the Left to unlearn its proletarian thinking he must first have enough spirit himself to unlearn his bourgeois thinking.

We do not want a bourgeois state [capitalist, liberal democracy]. We do not want a proletarian state [communism]. We want Germany! The nation is the ultimate and the greatest thing; the individual is as nothing beside it. But this nation is not completely unified until every individual has his place in it. It is not a shared destiny until the 30 million of the Left belong to it too, as a stable German working community.

We are National because we have realised that every great state concept has its origin in the soil of the homeland. We are National from a deep yearning for roots. We are not National because of remnants from the past, but from a purpose for the future. We want to deliver the world through Germany and not deliver Germany through the world. We are National because we know that no one will help us in our need, that only one single factor has the duty to set Germany free—we ourselves!

We are Socialist because we do not want to fight for the rights of our enslaved fellow countrymen as voluntarily or even reluctantly given gifts. We are Socialist because we want them to have their rights as a political necessity and out of popular justice.

We call ourselves 'Workers' Party' not because we cherish the delusion that only the manual labourer is called upon to save Germany. We call ourselves 'Workers' Party' because he is to belong to us, who ever is a German worker, whether by the head or the hand. Both belong to one another. To the one we say, 'You stand at the anvil and hammer out your destiny; you are nothing if the other man is not sitting in his study, making plans for the gigantic future of Germany. To the other we say, 'You sit in your study and make plans and schemes; you are nothing if the other man does not stand at the anvil, hammering your thoughts into an iron destiny.' Together you are everything; alone you are both lost.'

The fight has begun, not only in Germany but in the whole world. In the Far East hundreds of millions are on the march. They do not fight for their freedom with the cry, 'Long live the Third [Communist] International!' but with the cry, 'China for the Chinese!' The same fight has begun in India. The fires of freedom are glowing in the Colonies. Only Germany is thinking internationally. Only we are trusting in a right of mankind; are trusting in a right of love of peace which does not exist in the world.

Adolf Hitler once coined the phrase, 'Right is might!' Not until you have power will you receive the right! If you have no power then you can be right twenty times over and you will be wrong!

The 30 million of the Left and the 30 million of the Right are running up against each other. Only one thing gains advantage from it—the international scourge of the world. The 30 million of the Left and the 30 million of the Right rise up against each other. If the Right desires the freedom of Germany then the Left is ready to stab the Right from behind, and vice versa. Only when both stand together again, when from both a people of 60 million strong is formed again, can this people gain its freedom. The primary condition for German freedom is the will for freedom. To prepare this will is the task of our movement. Not until 60 million people want to become free with the deepest fervour of their hearts, will the destiny of the world, the God of history give his blessing upon it. This freedom is the last and greatest thing that we want.

Ask us our aim—freedom is our aim! Ask us our way—Socialism is the way to this freedom! Let the know-it-alls complain and cry for help; it is in vain. We shall not despair of freedom so long as one man still desires this freedom with this heart.

The Socialism that we want has nothing at all to do with the international-Marxist-Jewish levelling out process. We want Socialism as the doctrine of the community. We want Socialism as the ancient German idea of destiny. We want to make a people out of Germany, unified in a Socialist way, not only in joy but also in suffering. We want to make a people out of Germany, sharing its distress, its bread and its destiny. These are observations which do not stem from books, but rather from deep insight into the heart of things given to us by political instinct for the future.

We have lost a war. No people need succumb to that. We have lost a revolution. This lost revolution must be made good. Thus we no longer see a final division of the people into dozens of parties and dozens of organisations, but into two parts—the workers and the thieves, the hungry and the bloated. We shall have to discuss them in more detail. The bloated who before the war thought of Germany as a bundle of slaves; who turned the war itself into a business; who after the war rested comfortably on a foundation of facts. The hungry who before the war were excluded from the nation, who during the war sacrificed their health and their lives on the altar of the Fatherland out there in the trenches; who are now being pressed into a system more brutal and irresponsible than any that the history of the world has ever seen. They still rush past each other; the bloated still understanding well how to lead the will for freedom of the hungry into false paths. But the day of reckoning will come sooner or later when everyone will face the facts, that day on which the enemy will show himself in all his brutal nakedness, when the hungry will assault the bloated because they demand the concepts of Life, State, Nation, Germany.

Let them abuse and revile us. We know one thing: it brings no profit today to think and work for freedom. Let them laugh at us, this fast disappearing minority which, when the most brutal collapse comes, will unfurl the flag of freedom in a land ruled by majorities. History is only ever made by a minority conscious of its aim, led on the path to freedom and rebirth by a radical will. Let them laugh at the young who rise against the old. We are proud that youth is found in our ranks. For us youth is not an error in itself nor age in itself a virtue. We want to urge on youthful enthusiasm and know that this very youth has the great task of completing the work of freedom. We do not give a damn for the experience and clear wisdom of old age. What we are going through has nothing to do with experience or wisdom. The collapse of a great people is so monstrous and so terrible that it strikes everyone, whether young or old, with equal brutality. What we are taking part in today, no living person has ever experienced before. But youth has always stood in the centre of things. In the terrible years of our past it has grown so early to manhood. For in their youth our young ones have seen more and suffered more than any previous generation. Who dares to cast the first stone at us? We have changed our colours before and will change our colours again. We know that fighting costs blood, and also that no drop of blood is in vain, but is seed upon German fields of yearning. We are this youth, driven by missionary zeal, driven by the necessity for action, formed by the task laid upon us by the history of the world. This youth is building up a Germany of the future. It laughs at the wise experience and smart-aleck superiority of the wise and old. What we desire is greater than experience and knowledge. Thus young National Socialist Germany steps forward, men who desire only to help, to discriminate, to clarify, and to work. Supporters of a new idea which will shape the future. Deliberate fighters for the spirit of the future National-ist State in its clearest Socialist form and design. They are bound to this old State by nothing more than boundless hatred for its spirit and its supporters. They will be in the van of the fight against the Democratic-Liberal system. A movement for freedom does not have its profound origin in any cold powers of the intellect, but it is a thing of the will, of emotion, that will suddenly strike the people like a volcanic eruption and carry everything in its wake that was still half-hearted and cowardly. We are so terribly enslaved that neither intellect nor statistics can free us. Only the will for freedom can liberate us, and the final decision to subordinate all our thought and feeling and action to this single purpose.

Thus we do not fight against the International because we wanted to suppress the will for freedom of the slaves. The International recognises no will for freedom; but because we have realised the deceit of the International. An oppressed class, an oppressed people, has never freed itself through international protests, but always through national purpose for the future. The French citizen of the late eighteenth century did not wait for the solidarity possessed by the German and English citizen. He shook off his chains, unaided, with his own strength, and at the moment when they became unbearable for him. The powers of the old system tried to break his spirit but he defended himself and carried his principle, liberalism, victoriously through the whole world. It is the same today. The German worker will not become free until he frees himself, with his own strength, and he will do that when he can no longer bear the chains of slavery.

He is still enthusiastic about the International without having grasped its deepest meaning. His and our bitterest enemy, Democracy, money, is international. And money will not be overcome through Democracy, neither through money, but only through bloodshed.

The path to freedom is by way of the nation. The more unified this nation the stronger and more fervent the will for freedom. To give this passionate will for freedom its marching orders on a Nationalist and Socialist basis, that is the task of National Socialism. We desire freedom just like you, the German workers of the Left, only by other means, by means which will lead us to the goal. International solidarity is your programme. The solidarity of the nation, the community of the people is ours. They will come to believe us that our community of the people is not the pacifist slop that the middle-class supposes. The community of the people today is nothing other than the fight for the rights of the people for the sake of the nation. We desire this fight because it alone can bring us freedom.

There must be a fight for the future. You of the Left and we, we are fighting against each other without being real enemies. Forces are being divided in the process and we shall never arrive at our aim. Perhaps dire distress will lead you to us. Perhaps!— Don't shake your heads; in this question we are concerned with the future of Germany, and further still, with the future of Central Europe. The new state of ruin and chaos, either is in our hands.

We young men of Germany, we are bearers of the destiny of generations. Let us never forget that! From the Left and the Right the way will be found to us when need has become greatest. A path from us to you does not exist. Why can we not unite with the bourgeois parties? Because we come from two different worlds. You are living in the collapse; we live in a prophetic conception of the future State. You are a hindrance in our way. Bourgeois admonishers, you preach at our back and want to dampen our will for freedom and want us to act with moderation in the name of Nationalism and Socialism. But this we have learnt in the years of the collapse: revolutions are never made in Parliament even though new motions and new resolutions are introduced every day. Out among the people, there the force is working which will build the new state, that force which the bourgeoisie in its political design cannot acquire, because it does not seriously want to acquire it. Organisation of this force, that is the task of the *Workers' Party,* so often reviled by the bourgeois parties.

However terrible and insoluble German need may be, we believe in the day which will come. This day will come because it must come. Germany's youth has not suffered in vain. History cannot ignore that a whole generation of fighters bled to death on the battlefields for an idea, unconsciously perhaps, but it lived in all of them, this idea, in the farsighted as faith, in the believer as a dim presentiment. A young Germany learnt there that we are on earth to offer sacrifice for the nation. And thus its thought and action revolve around Germany, around Germany alone.

Thus we regard the problem of Russia not as a problem of the present, but as a problem of the future. Russia lies embedded in the great problem of Europe and when Russia awakes, the world will see a miracle. We young Germans foresee this miracle with the instinct of a man of the present. We are not the withdrawn visionaries who set their last hope for the future of Germany upon this miracle. It is our duty rather to stop at nothing, but nothing, so that we can face this coming miracle as equal partners, or step to its side. There will be an awakening in Russia which will be more terrible than the war. This awakening will bring about the Socialist National State for which the young generation in every land, consciously or unconsciously, is longing so fervently.

We have learnt this from the collapse of the International: from the misery and deceit of an unnatural, foul pacifism, of a class-solidarity puffed up with words, the nationalist instinct is raising its victorious colours in the crumbling systems of Europe. Almost imperceptibly, the formation of a Nationalist State of Socialist character emerges.

Socialism cannot and will not deliver the world. The world will never be saved. It

will save a people, perhaps the peoples; it is the political doctrine of the future nation.

We no longer believe in the proletariat's will for solidarity. We no longer believe in the world revolution, nor the salvation of the world. We believe in nothing more than our own strength. In this we believe all the more ardently, with the utmost fanaticism, with all the will for the future which burns within us. No one can save us except ourselves. If someone believed he could, we would not want it because we adamantly believe we can do it ourselves. We are Socialists, German Socialists. We do not want to have been such in vain. We are not satisfied with conviction. We seek to strengthen and deepen conviction through work and indefatigable striving. We demand clarity, clarity!

They do not know us yet! The docile, lukewarm and cowardly will be horrified at the radicalism of our demands, at the inexorable logic of what must be and what we intend to do just because it must be. Today they know in Germany that we allow no one to surpass us in our Nationalistic fanaticism for freedom. They will also soon come to realise that we stand just as firmly in the van in our will for Socialism. One thing still holds us firm in the fight, one thing still preserves our hope for the future and our passionate devotion to the people, to freedom and to the Fatherland: faith in the German worker, by mind and hand. In this we believe. We believe in the will for sacrifice, in the mad urge for freedom which slumbers in him and will one day awake. We believe in the Socialism in the worker, we believe in the mass rhythm. We believe in the future of history. That is our last consolation, our last hold.

If we ever have to say we no longer believe in this, then despair is our last refuge. But that cannot be, that must not be. We struggle for the soul of the German worker. It is there. Beneath distress, misery and hunger it slumbers and waits for him who will deliver it from death. Restorers to life! For this rôle has fate destined us. We are chosen for greater things than mere power. We are to bring the new State and with it the new man. That is no high-sounding statement, that is clear, sober truth. Already this new man is raising his still weary head, heavy with sleep and uttering words of universal significance. A time of such brutality that we still cannot envisage is approaching, indeed, we are already in its midst. In the face of these events all discussion turns to froth. Over all the confusion of empty words which wear us out to no purpose, over the shop keepers, literati and weaklings, the summons to action will sweep into the new Europe, a rushing tidal wave with a blood-red crest. For peace does not abide by the coward, but by the sword. Not all the fearless still lie buried beneath the ruins which engulf Germany.

That will be fulfillment. But to this fulfillment leads an unending path. We all seek it out with painful fumbling. One man is the pioneer who goes before us all—*Adolf Hitler.* The flag of freedom he unfurled again for the first time at a time of enormous cowardice, at a time of the most savage terror. He fought for this flag with the utmost passionate faith in freedom. He carried this flag at our head in the stormy days of November 1923. As leader of the idea he went before his followers into a shower of bullets from reaction. Let the Marxist decry us as bourgeois and capitalistic. Neither Marxist nor worker fired at us on 9 November 1923, but reaction. It fired at us because we did not want to take up our cowardly and comfortable position on the solid factual plane, because we set the passionate will for freedom on the march, because we did not preach as our ultimate goal, 'Maintenance of the peace is the primary civic duty', but, as a condition of freedom, the passionate demand for this freedom.

Thus we lead the way as those who still believe in Germany's future. Thus we let loose in the land the volcanic eruption of the new will for freedom and know that the volcano will one day become deed upon the barricades of revolution.

This is what we demand, this is what we are. We promise nothing other than the one thing: that we are honest fighters for what we desire.

Thus we are calling to battle. Before us flutters the flag of German revolution: a red background with a white circle and a black swastika. Under it we shall obtain by fighting what today is only empty talk and illusion: peace between mind and fist. Unity of the people!

See also Days of Struggle, Vol. 1; Nazism, Vol. 2; Goebbels, Joseph, Vol. 3.

Göring Celebrates the German-Italian Alliance

In this 1938 article, published in the Italian magazine Gerachia *during a visit to Italy by Adolf Hitler, Nazi leader Hermann Göring commemorates what he sees as the close friendship between not only Germany and Italy but between their respective leaders, the Führer, Hitler, and Il Duce, Benito Mussolini.*

ADOLF HITLER is Germany! The whole of Germany accompanies its beloved Leader with its thoughts on his tour through the beautiful Italian lands. And when, the day after to-morrow, the Leader and Reich chancellor of the Great-German Reich will stretch out the hand of friendship towards the illustrious Duce [Mussolini] of the powerful rising Italian Empire at the Ostia station of the Eternal City [Rome], there will ring in the feeling that Adolf Hitler brings to the House of Savoy [the Italian royal family], to the Italian people and its chosen government chief, the hearts of 75 million German people. Then the world will get to know of the joy of all the Germans, who live beyond the German frontiers, especially those who have found a home in Italy.

Can the comradeship of two men, which has grown out of the respect for each other and the same high ideals, find better and more explanatory expression, than in the friendship of the two great nations which they lead? Truly, the friendship of Italy and Germany is not founded on treaties which were created out of long-drawn-out parliamentarian conferences or democratic majority decisions. This friendship is no paper document of past epochs, but it is a lively reality, a comradeship which has been created by the leaders of two nations, and which has been consolidated and hardened in the storm of the times. Out of true manly comradeship grew a truly proven friendship of nations.

Unforgotten are the days when in the autumn of last year the Duce stayed in Germany; unforgotten in Germany is the wonderful speech which the Marshal of the Empire, the first Fascist of his country, made at the Mayfield in the Olympia Stadium in Berlin. Tremendous rejoicing was around the Duce, when in open, manly words he, the authorised spokesman of his nation, gave his assurance that Italy would never forget the upright and friendly attitude of the German people towards Italy during the fight in Abyssinia [Ethiopia]. Half a year later, a few weeks ago, it fell to us Germans to thank the Italian people for their understanding of our national interests in the return of Austria to the Reich, a

thanks which our Leader in his historic telegram to the Duce, expressed as the avowal of a whole nation. So we have, in the most deciding days of the early history of our nation's friendship, kept to this friendship, which Benito Mussolini and Adolf Hitler have cemented. This tie of friendship will remain. Following the will of two men who lead Italy and Germany, it shall possess eternal durability.

Fascism and national socialism stand faithfully together, not only because on the outside they have lots of things in common. The root of this union lies much deeper. In the defence against bolshevistic decay, against hatred and jealousy, against the arrogance of rank and politic of interests, after the storm of two glorious revolutions, they have grown out of the same ground, they have grown out of the feeling of the people for the homeland. Led by men—who have been chosen by destiny to be the saviours of their nations—led by men who have the same determination for people and fatherland, who have the courage of decision, the wisdom of statesmanly thinking and acting, and the unimpaired authority of their personalities in common, in both nations there awoke once more creative strength which spirits, foreign to the nation, had covered up.

Both nations have built up their economy anew, based on national ideas and have expanded it. North, as well as South of the Brenner [Pass, on the Austrian-Italian border], stand work and achievement, stand the creating working human beings with ability, as the centre pin of all economic plans. Here, as there, care is taken that the individual, with his righteous ambitions for success, is directed into the necessities of the great political unity of the nation. Therefore, Germany and Italy were able to loosen themselves from the sudden changes of opportunity and the speculation manœuvres of the world.

Courageously and decisively, they took their destiny into their own hands. Both nations exchange in peaceful economic traffic

Hermann Göring, *The Political Testament of Hermann Göring.* Arranged and translated by H.W. Blood-Ryan. London: John Long, 1939.

Benito Mussolini, the Fascist dictator of Italy, salutes beside his ally Adolf Hitler in September 1937.

their goods, and use with iron industriousness and unerring firmness the valuables of their soil for the welfare of their countries. Both nations, through the untiring application of science and technique, enlarged and intensified their agricultural space and production, have produced new raw materials, and have opened up additional production sources, thereby strengthening the economic and defensive resources of the nation.

The German-Italian economic relationship, which, after the Anschluss of Austria with the Reich, has opened up for both countries still far greater possibilities, is a warning example that international trade between two strong countries with highly developed economy and strict, national political leadership, flourishes best.

So the unshakable and firmly standing Rome-Berlin axis is a proof that national interests need not be oppositions, but that on the contrary, friendly work and understanding are together the surest guarantor of world peace.

See also Rome-Berlin Axis, Vol. 2; Mussolini, Benito, Vol. 3.

Göring Commemorates the Days of Struggle

In a speech made before a Nazi Party convention on March 3, 1933, Göring reminds the faithful that they have arisen to save Germany from the Jewish and Marxist Weimar Republic and that, now that Hitler has taken power, they can savor their triumph.

My dear German compatriots and more especially my dear comrades in the brown shirt! How much time has changed since last I stood before you, when, for the last time, I was able to shake you up with temperamental words in the fight for freedom, for which we all longed. Compatriots! When I stood to-day, just an hour before my departure, on the balcony of the Prussian Ministry of the Interior—the late Severing Palace—and when below in the Unter den Linden, thousands upon thousands in their brown shirts marched past with flying banners and ringing music, there came suddenly to me the realisation of how much God in His mercy has favoured us, how at last all this longing and hoping of the past fourteen years has now become reality.

Fourteen years we have fought—fourteen years we have suffered, so immeasurably as never a people have suffered. For fourteen years we and our movement have been oppressed by terror, for fourteen years they tried to instil into this nation a sense of serfdom, into us, a nation which can look back on a thousand-year-old history of heroism. People strange to our race believed themselves capable of remoulding this nation, a nation which fifteen years ago had resisted a world of enemies, this nation

which maintained a heroic fight for four years at the front and at home, the same nation which for four years protected its soil from the enemy, the nation whose land the enemy only saw as a prisoner but never as a conqueror. Such a nation they tried to make into serfs.

That alone, compatriots, marks the madness and frenzy which had taken hold upon these 'Celebrities'. They believed that they could draw their own conclusions from their own cowardice as example. They believed, because to them worldly goods counted for all, that the German people could live without ideals. So thought the so-called representatives of a people which has proved in a thousand years of history that it was always ready to sacrifice its last possession when its honour and freedom were in danger. Honour and freedom were stolen from us on that cursed day in November, 1918, when they stabbed the front line in the back.

They spoke so often about the 'Legend' of the stab with the dagger, and so often about the 'fairy tale' of betrayal. No, compatriots, there is nothing to hide. The betrayal was a fact. To-day we know the fruit that cursed 9th November [the day of the abdication of Kaiser Wilhelm II] brought us. We also know the criminals. We must have our revenge on these betrayers. They shall not go on poisoning the German people.

Fourteen long years this nation has trodden its path of suffering. Remember how bitter the suffering was and how it crept into the meanest and last little room, till no one knew a way out any longer. At that time people said: "The peace of Versailles will only hit the rich." But quickly enough the whole nation felt how it had been made the

Hermann Göring, *The Political Testament of Hermann Göring.* Arranged and translated by H.W. Blood-Ryan. London: John Long, 1939.

pack-mule on to which all burdens were loaded. For fourteen years, compatriots! I ask you to look back just once more before you cast your political vote on Sunday. Look back into those fourteen years for just one quarter of an hour and remember, in spite of our fast-moving times, what these years have meant to you, what Germany has lost and given up, and think how unspeakable the suffering was, how bitter the sorrow, and you will then recognise what it meant—to be governed for fourteen years by marxism!

What would have happened if destiny had not turned at last? If this movement, started by very few people, had not fought hard, in spite of all its setbacks, and had not taken hurdle after hurdle, if this movement—which went through the hardest battles and which was nearly dissolved, which has lost hundreds of dead and thousands of wounded—had not stormed again and again the marxist castle? Not out of its own inner strength (for that was at the time shattered), but out of the mission it had for the people, it always found new strength again. The movement had the leader, it grew, in spite of demolishing battles, into a steel block, and in one single daring attack which lasted a decade we (in the movement) beat the opponent, boarded the ship ourselves and, getting hold of the rudder, steered, at last, Germany away from the rocks into the straight course towards a clear endeavour.

A decade of tremendous struggle! Who does not remember the small beginnings? What was the most difficult? Not the ridiculous terror of the 'red Hoodlums' [Communists], not those clownish plays of the 'party minister', and not in the least the liquid manure that was poured over us. Not the lies and not the prohibitions. All these we pushed aside smilingly. We took it all as it came along, knowing that this was going to make us only the more stronger and greater! Not even, bitter as it may sound, the ten thousand wounded and not even our dead were in the long run the bitterest things! For

their blood was martyr blood! Their blood was seed for the harvest and the fruit. Their blood has written our programme, about which we are asked again and again and which was sealed with the blood of the fighters for German freedom.

All this was not the most heaviest thing to bear. The most difficult of all was the fight for the individual compatriot—the fight for the German soul, the fight for the German human being. In the bitter fight, with the ever-present poisoning marxism, to rescue the German, to make him individually once more into a valuable link of the nation, to plant in him, who was tired and stupified by lethargy, once again the spark of resistance—in him, who despised all and who wanted to know nothing any longer of his Germany—to plant in *him* once more the love of his own people—that was the most difficult. That was a tough fight!

We (in the movement) have worked night after night, evening upon evening, and we went from town to town, from county to county and again we whipped you up. Again and again we hammered it into your brains: again and again we planted it in your hearts. And so we grew. Only yesterday we were enemies—outsiders and knew better (in political thought), to-day we fight together. Bigger and bigger the army grew: harder and harder grew the struggle. At last we heaved against the mausoleum of a hollow state and with one push it was opened. Now we form the Germany of the future.

Compatriots! What we have seen was a ruin. Everything lies about on the ground—destroyed. Everywhere there are bare walls. German life, German economy in all its branches, German culture, wherever you look there lies only the smoking ruin. A battlefield—deserted and rotted, it lies there: nothing blooms and nothing gives promise of bud. Everything has died from the poisonous gas which has rotted and destroyed for fourteen years all living things.

That is the saddest chapter in the marxist rulership. The national economy and wealth, they once said, was to be given to the people. The people themselves were to be the owners of this economy. The people themselves were to be the owners of the goods produced by the national economy, and many other lies culled from the text-book of marxian socialism were put over on the people, all things which the marxists knew to be untrue and impossible of performance. Under this regime capitalism rose to the heights of most shameless exploitation. One trust was founded after another, destroying with it the personal responsibility of the small man. The factories, which had for centuries gone down from father to son, were swallowed up. They deprived business men of personal responsibility, and put the anonymous shareholder in their place, because by this means they could rob and overpower the people more easily. This was also the reason why the false fronts tore apart; they could not manage a united people.

No! These economic differences had to be preached. The workman was told: 'There, do you see that factory owner—he is your enemy'. Because he was a factory owner, in spite of his being, perhaps, the best man on earth or the best German, he was declared to be an enemy.

On the other hand the factory owner was told: 'That workman—he is your enemy! He is against you and you are against him'. So they tore open the fronts. So stood employee against employer—in two fronts, instead of standing together against the Jewish exploiters. The agrarian was given a death blow. Why? As long as the farmer sits on his land, as long as his feelings remain deeply rooted in the land on which he was born and raised, as long as words like fatherland, blood and earth remain to his ears holy—he was a menace to their system. On him they had to start. He had to be uprooted, made homeless, torn away from the soil on which he was born and had his home—away from his kind. They had to poison his brain, destroy his feelings and his heart, and so they made out of the once

proud farmer, however little he owned, an international proletarian, and he cried with them: "Proletarians of all lands! unite!" So the farmer was urbanised and weaned from the soil under the pressure of the fight and they pretended that they wished to help him again. They tried to place farmers on fresh lands, on which they could not establish themselves. They developed new farms and allowed the old matured ones to go to ruin instead of rescuing them. To us this seemed to be the first thing requiring attention. Adolf Hitler realised this in one of his first cabinet meetings, when he declared: "First of all the farmer, who is still fighting to eke out his existence, must be saved; then one can start with the others and work new land."

The marxists also cracked the whip over the middle classes. The middle classes were the broad masses of the people, fitting each into his allotted place and who cherished their old inherited estates, however small. So long as they owned estates they could, under certain circumstances, be a prop for good governmental thought, they could—worst of all—still have national feelings in their bosom. So they had to be uprooted and impoverished. And then came the impoverishing 'stunt', carried out in such a refined manner as no nation has ever seen it done before. The inflation came, which in a few months destroyed all that remained of estates and goods in Germany, and in so doing impoverished the whole nation. And the rest? Slowly, a few savings were made again, but they were taxed heavily—such mad taxation which had nothing to do with legitimate Government taxes. They were all out and out expropriations. It was a matter of 'Give us what you have left'. And so the proletarianisation of a people went on apace. Old families, landowners for generations, where have they got to to-day? Here and there there may yet be a family which still clings on to the old house which was once built by its ancestors, but they do not live there as free owners, if they are still there at all. They are there as unpaid porters and housekeepers.

What has become the destiny of these people?

So they (the previous regime) have broken up everything systematically. Where the little merchant had a shop, which he perhaps had inherited from his father, there now stands a big store—a chain store. The Jew has robbed him of it for himself. So, all over the place, were the rights of ownership destroyed—in just those places where it was responsible and where it was handled with that certain responsibility necessary to the people and the nation.

Thus were thrown more and more people into the great trough of international proletarianism. Thus was the great attempt at uprooting more and more people from their land and from among their kind, in order that they might be ruled easier. We have often been laughed at when we described the German as a 'slave'. But compatriots! how does one define the word slave? A man works, and through his own labour he creates something. When this creation remains his own, then he is a free man. When he has to give it away to some stranger, then he has become a slave, for then he does not work for himself any longer.

They were going to make out of one of the most industrious, most work loving and perhaps the most capable of all nations, the most industrious slaves. That was the long view of their plan. Not only was the German to be uprooted from his soil and expropriated, but his thinking and feeling were to be destroyed, culminating in tearing him away from his history—German history. History—from which always, when a nation becomes impoverished, it takes its last strength. From history which generations before us, who have lived through evil times, had made and who yet, in their turn, had strength to climb up again and get their new vigour out of history.

Therefore they said: away with German culture—it would eventually chain the one

or the other, through his feelings, to the fatherland. Therefore—away with German art! Here, too, the 'wirepullers' are the same again.

Compatriots! I wish you could look just for once behind the scenes. The mask is different, but the grimace behind it has always remained the same.

In destroying all German feelings and German ways of thinking, they had of course to destroy all conceptions of moral and ethical value which we have inherited from our fathers. Therefore corruption was given a free hand—one sink was next to the other, and out of each there trickled a poison into the German people of different classes. Immorality was lifted up and upheld as morality, and German morals were kicked aside in company with all else which we held holy, and all was smothered in dirt—everything for which we had fought for four years and for which many had lost their lives. They took all the good from us and the substitute they called: 'To live in a state of true beauty, freedom and dignity'. Look at the last years of internal politics. Internal politics of terror against everything which was still national. Internal politics of force against everything that stood up against them—internal politics of corruption and decay—against everything that was still called decency. And do you want to look at their foreign politics? Only they who are bred by cowardice can treat cowardly! Consisting of submission and fulfilment for years and years.

In this ruinous field marxism grows its most terrible, most ill-reeking marsh plant. On this ground, which is manured with immorality and traitorousness, grows communism.

When the 'Gentlemanly' social democrats tell me that they object strongly to be thrown into the same pot with the communists, my answer to them is: "The stinking steams of communism came from your pot. It was your Mr. Severing [a former leftist Prussian minister], the brave one, who declared that the communists were political

German field marshal and Luftwaffe commander in chief Hermann Göring joined the Nazi Party in 1922 and played integral roles in the party's rise through the Days of Struggle.

only out of a sense of protection. No! I give the signal for a fight on the whole front.'"

Compatriots! my measures will not be vitiated by any legal doubts. My measures will not be weakened by any bureaucracy. Here I have not to exercise righteousness; here I have only to destroy and to clear. Nothing else. This fight, compatriots, will be a fight against chaos and such a fight I do not lead with ordinary police means. That a 'state of citizens' may have done. Certainly I will also use the full powers of the state and the police to their utmost measure, my dear communists, in order that you do not draw wrong conclusions, but the fight to the death, in which I will 'put my fist in your necks', I will lead with those down there, my brownshirts! I will make it clear to the people that they have to defend themselves. I will make it clear to them that all strength has to be mobilised, and therefore I declare with full purpose: "In future, gentlemen, only those can enter the state who come from the national strength and not those who crowd around and lie." I am not disturbed when certain 'critics' get excited about these measures and cry for more 'justice'. I measure with two measures. I would not be just if I did not send the communists to hell at last. Too long have they lounged about in easy chairs and lived on our money—it is high time they went! Fourteen years long they have oppressed this national Germany, and for fourteen years not even a porter in a ministry was allowed to be a national socialist. That was 'justice' for you! For fourteen years they have suppressed it. No. He who acknowledges the state now, him the state will recognise—but he who tries to destroy the state, him the state will destroy.

Do not dare to come to me, you red and pinkish gentlemen, and say that we (the Nazis) have been enemies of the state once and that we too wanted to overthrow the state—and have done so. No, gentlemen, that is not a true bill, because there was no state, but only a system of bigwigs. There-

children. Now you are becoming excited that I see them, not as political children, but as criminals. Compatriots! I do not want to repeat what I said the day before yesterday, as a member of the Reich Government, in my wireless broadcast speech about the communist movement, about communist designs and about communist crimes. I will repeat only one thing I said then: 'The "gentlemen" must understand one thing. I do not dream of fighting them in the manner of a good citizen—with faint-heartedness and fore we had to struggle to bring about a state. We are no enemies of the state, but we have become tired of bigwigs and hoodlums. You, my gentlemanly Marxists, at one time overthrew the state by dirty means, but we have thrown out a system of swindlers by fair means.

You said that we were against the Republic! 'Gentlemen', if the German Republic had been a republic of freedom—if the German Republic had organised a passionate resistance in 1918 and 1919, we all would have been staunch republicans. You seem to have forgotten how your republic ever came about. You seem to have forgotten that it was begotten in perjury—you seem to have forgotten that you sullied this 'Republic'. When you declare to-day that we have been against the banner of the republic, against the black, yellow and red, we say, yes! we were against it, gentlemen. If you had at that time (1918) planted this flag as a banner of resistance on the towers of Strassbourg Minster declaring: 'Thus far and no further!' we, the old soldiers, would have knelt in homage and ardour beneath this flag. But you had hoisted it above treachery, disgrace and shame and therefore we thank God that He did not allow the old glorious symbol to flutter in the breeze over your 'new' Germany during the past fourteen years. We thank destiny that it rolled up the old glorious colours at the right time.

Compatriots! my first official task as the president of the new Reichstag will be to propose to the Reichstag that the old black-white-red flag, together with the shining swastika, shall from now onwards flutter as the new banner of victory over a new Germany.

We will show you (still speaking for the benefit of the Communist and Social-Democrats), and at last prove to you, that your time is absolutely over and that it will never come back again. We will prove to you that we have built a new foundation, far away from your house which you erected fourteen years ago and on which even the front has toppled in.

This foundation of ours will be cemented together by our own outlook, by the views which at last bring together Nationalism and Socialism. These two shall no longer stand opposite each other in deadly animosity—misunderstood—and shall no longer cause millions of people to fight each other. The enemy camps shall now be welded together into a whole—therefore shall this [philosophy] (of National Socialist creed) be the foundation of the new Reich. Only to those who have understood the cry of such unity—any, from among whatever profession, class or occupation—shall fall the honour to reconcile where reconciliation is needed. The union of the Reich, compatriots, remains an empty sham when the people are torn apart, therefore only through unity among the people can a unified Reich receive its true form. To bring about this unity is the life's work of Adolf Hitler, and because he wants to form this unity, because he wants to bring the people, from all classes, conditions, professions and occupations together into one faction, which will, in all great questions of (national) destiny think in unison, he has therefore declared the fight to the death with Marxism. For where Marxism holds sway, it does so only through the hate of disrupted classes. Therefore it had to sink. Therefore let them burn and murder—let them lie and lie again. We work and rebuild. And when to-day the foreign press, inspired by Marxist and Communist circles, declares that none other than Minister Göring himself started the Reichstag fire, in order to obtain (false) proof against Marxism, then I say, 'gentlemen', for that I had no need to start a fire in the Reichstag. There is sufficient proof of your crimes to get judgment against you.

Compatriots! all these things are spotlights thrown over the people like lightning so that it may recognise the danger in which it stands.

Two days hence you will once more be called upon. On the 5th March the call will ring. And the song that you so often sang with us will be heard. For the last time on the 5th March there will be a trumpet call to arms—German destiny makes an appeal! The German people will have to line up for Germany, for the fatherland is in danger. We men (the leaders) are ready to bear the responsibility before God and the people—that we will do! God will give us the strength if you will give us your faith. Then we will push aside the night and clouds. Then we will bring back the sun to you.

See also Days of Struggle, Vol. 1; Machtergreifung, Vol. 2; Göring, Hermann, Vol. 3.

Germany's Right to Living Space in the East

As the following selection from 1925's Mein Kampf *indicates, one of Adolf Hitler's goals from the earliest days of the Nazi movement was the expansion of German territory into eastern Europe. He suggests that the restoration of Germany's pre–World War I borders would still leave millions of ethnic Germans outside the Reich. Moreover, he claims, wresting territory from the Jews and Bolsheviks of Russia will be Germany's "territorial policy of the future."*

I want still briefly to take a position on the question of the extent to which the demand for soil and territory appears to be ethically and morally justified. This is necessary because, unfortunately, even in so-called folkish circles, there turn up all sorts of pathetic babblers who occupy themselves sketching for the German people a rectification of the injustice of 1918 as the goal of its foreign-policy activity, but beyond that find it necessary to assure the entire world of folkish fraternity and sympathy.

I would like, moreover, to say the following in anticipation: *The demand for the re-establishment of the frontiers of the year 1914 is political nonsense of such a degree and consequences as to look like a crime.* Entirely aside from the fact that the frontiers of the Reich in the year 1914 were everything but logical. For they were, in reality, neither complete with respect to the inclusion of people of German nationality, nor intelligent with respect to geo-military appropriateness. They were not the outcome of considered political action, but momentary frontiers of a political struggle in no way concluded, indeed, partly the result of the play of chance. With equal justice, and in many cases with greater justice, one could select any other milestone of German history to proclaim the re-establishment of the relations then prevailing as the goal of foreign-policy activity. The aforementioned demand, however, corresponds fully to our *bourgeois* [middle-class, democratic] world, which at this point too, has not a single creative political thought for the future, but rather lives in the past and in the very recent past at that; for even their backward gaze does not reach beyond their own epoch. The law of inertia ties them to a given situation, compels them to offer resistance to any alteration of the same, without, however, ever increasing their defensive activity beyond mere inertia. Thus it is a matter of course

Adolf Hitler, *Mein Kampf.* New York: Reynal and Hitchcock, 1939.

that these people's political horizon does not extend beyond the frontiers of the year 1914. But in so far as they proclaim the re-establishment of those frontiers as the political goal of their actions, they chain themselves permanently to the crumbling alliance of our opponents. This is the only explanation of why, eight years after a world struggle in which States with desires and aims, some of which were most heterogeneous in nature, participated, the coalition of the former victors can still keep itself together in a more or less tight form.

All these States were, in their time, exploiters of the German collapse. The fear of our strength then induced subordination of the mutual greed and envy of the individual powers. They saw the best protection against a coming rebellion in the most general possible inheriting of our Reich which could be managed. A bad conscience with fear of our national strength is even today still the most enduring cement holding together the individual members of this alliance.

And we do not disappoint them. In so far as our *bourgeois* world lays down as a political program for Germany the re-establishment of the frontiers of the year 1914, it scares back every partner who might want to bolt the alliance of our enemies, because he must fear being attacked in isolation and thereby forfeiting the protection of his individual allies. Every individual State feels itself disturbed and threatened by that slogan.

It is, moreover, doubly senseless:

(1) because the instruments of power with which to translate it from the smoke of club evenings to reality are lacking; and

(2) because the result, if it were realized, would still be so miserable that it would not pay, by God, to invest the blood of our nation for *that* again.

For the fact that even the re-establishment of the borders of the year 1914 could be achieved only with blood should seem questionable to hardly anybody at all. Only childishly naïve souls can lull themselves with the idea that they can bring about a rectification of [the Treaty of] Versailles by intrigue and begging. Entirely apart from the fact that such an attempt would presuppose the nature of a Talleyrand [a brilliant early-nineteenth-century diplomat], which we do not have. Half our political figures are rather cunning but equally characterless elements, who are on the whole inimically disposed towards our people, while the other half is composed of kind-hearted, harmless, and easy-going nitwits. Moreover, times have changed since the Congress of Vienna [in 1815]: *princes and the mistresses of princes do not barter and haggle about frontiers, but the implacable world Jew is struggling for dominion over the nations.* No nation can dislodge this fist from its throat except by the sword. Only the united, concentrated force of a mighty insurgent nationalist passion can defy the international enslavement of the nations. But such a development is and remains a bloody one.

If, however, one professes the conviction that the German future, one way or another, calls forth the supreme risk, one must, entirely aside from all considerations of political intelligence in itself, for the very sake of this risk, pose and fight for a goal worthy of it.

The frontiers of the year 1914 signify nothing at all for the future of the German nation. They embodied neither a protection in the past, nor would they embody strength for the future. The German nation will neither maintain its internal integrity through them, nor will its sustenance be guaranteed by them, nor do these frontiers appear appropriate or even satisfactory from a military viewpoint, nor, finally, can they improve the relation in which, at the moment, we find ourselves with respect to the other world powers, or rather, the real world powers. The distance to England will not be shortened, the size of the Union not achieved; no, France will not even experience a material decrease in her world political importance.

Only one thing would be certain: even assuming a favorable outcome, such an attempt at re-establishing the frontiers of 1914 would lead to an additional bleeding of our national body, to an extent that no worth-while blood reserve would be available for national life and for decisions and actions which would really insure the nation's future. On the contrary, in the intoxication of such a shallow success every added posing of goals would be the more readily abandoned, once the *'national honor'* had been restored and some doors re-opened, at least for a time, to commercial development.

As opposed to this, we National Socialists must cling unflinchingly to our foreign-policy aims, that is to guarantee the *German nation the soil and territory to which it is entitled on this earth.* And this is the only action which, before God and our German posterity, would seem to justify an investment of blood: *before God,* since we are placed in this world on condition of an eternal struggle for daily bread, as beings to whom nothing shall be given and who owe their position as lords of the earth only to the genius and courage with which they know how to struggle for and defend it: before our German posterity, however, in so far as we spill no citizen's blood except that out of it a thousand others are bequeathed to posterity. The soil and territory on which a race of German peasants will some day be able to beget sons sanction the investment of the sons of today, and will some day acquit the responsible statesmen of blood and guilt and national sacrifice, even though they be persecuted by their contemporaries.

I must attack most sharply those folkish scribbler souls who claim to see a 'breach of sacred human rights' in such an acquisition of territory, and who consequently direct their effusions against it. One really never knows who stands behind one of those fellows. It is only certain that the confusion which they are able to create is desired by and opportune to our national enemies. By such an attitude they wantonly aid from within in undermining and cutting the ground from under our nation's only means of properly standing up for its life necessities. For no nation possesses even a single square kilometer of soil and territory on this earth because of a superior will, let alone a superior right. Just as the German frontiers are frontiers of chance and temporary frontiers in the day's passing political struggles, so are the frontiers of other nations' domain of life. And so, just as the formation of our earth's surface can seem unalterable as granite only to the thoughtless nitwit, but in truth always amounts only to a seeming point of calm in a running development, created by the mighty forces of nature in a constant process of becoming, perhaps tomorrow already, to experience destruction and metamorphosis as a result of greater forces, such, too, are frontiers of the domain of life in the existence of nations.

State frontiers are man-made and can be altered by man.

The reality of a nation having managed a disproportionate acquisition of territory is no superior obligation for its eternal recognition. It proves at most the might of the conqueror and the weakness of the victim. And, moreover, this might alone makes right. If the German people today, penned into an impossible area, face a wretched future, this is as little Fate's command as its rejection would constitute a snub to Fate. Just as little as some superior power has promised another nation more soil and territory than the German, or would be insulted by the fact of this unjust division of territory. Just as our forefathers did not get the land on which we are living today as a gift from Heaven, but had to conquer it by risking their lives, so no folkish grace but only the might of a triumphant sword will in the future assign us territory, and with it life for our nation.

Much as we all today recognize the necessity for a reckoning with France, it will remain largely ineffective if our foreign-policy aim is restricted thereto. It has and will retain significance if it provides the rear cover for an enlargement of our national domain of life in Europe. For we will find this question's solution not in colonial acquisitions, but exclusively in the winning of land for settlement which increases the area of the motherland itself, and thereby not only keeps the new settlers in the most intimate community with the land of origin, but insures to the total area those advantages deriving from its united magnitude.

The folkish movement must be not the attorney for other nations, but the vanguard fighter of its own. Otherwise it is superfluous, and especially has no right to beef about the past. For then it is acting like the past. Much as the old German policy was improperly determined from dynastic viewpoints, equally little must the future be governed by dreamy folkish cosmopolitanism. Above all, however, we are not protective police for the well-known 'poor little nations,' but soldiers of our own nation.

We National Socialists, however, must go further: *the right to soil and territory can become a duty if decline seems to be in store for a great nation unless it extends its territory.* Even more especially if what is involved is not some little negro people or other, but the German mother of all life, which has given its cultural picture to the contemporary world. *Germany will be either a world power or will not be at all.* To be a world power, however, it requires that size which nowadays gives its necessary importance to such a power, and which gives life to its citizens.

With this, we National Socialists consciously draw a line through the foreign-policy trend of our pre-War period. We take up at the halting place of six hundred years ago. We terminate the endless German drive to the south and west of Europe, and direct our gaze towards the lands in the east. We finally terminate the colonial and trade policy of the pre-War period, and proceed to the territorial policy of the future.

But if we talk about new soil and territory in Europe today, we can think primarily only of *Russia* and its vassal border states.

Fate itself seems to seek to give us a tip at this point. In the surrender of Russia to bolshevism, the Russian people was robbed of that intelligentsia which theretofore produced and guaranteed its State stability. For the organization of a Russian State structure was not the result of Russian Slavdom's State-political capacity, but rather a wonderful example of the State-building activity of the German element in an inferior race. Thus have innumerable mighty empires of the earth been created. Inferior nations with German organizers and lords as leaders have more than once expanded into powerful State structures, and endured as long as the racial nucleus of the constructive State-race maintained itself. For centuries Russia drew nourishment from this Germanic nucleus of its superior strata of leaders. Today it is uprooted and obliterated almost without a trace. The Jew has replaced it. Impossible as it is for the Russians alone to shake off the yoke of the Jews through their own strength, it is equally impossible in the long run for the Jews to maintain the mighty empire. Jewry itself is not an organizing element, but a ferment of decomposition. The Persian Empire, once so powerful, is now ripe for collapse; and the end of Jewish dominion in Russia will also be the end of the Russian State itself. We have been chosen by Fate to be the witnesses of a catastrophe which will be the most powerful substantiation of the correctness of the folkish theory of race.

Our task, the mission of the National Socialist movement, however, is to bring our own nation to such political insight as will make it see its future goal fulfilled, not by an intoxicating impression of a new Alexandrian campaign, but rather by the industrious labor of the German plow which needs only to be given land by the sword.

See also Drive to the East, lebensraum, Vol. 1; *Mein Kampf,* Vol. 2.

Hitler Makes His Pitch to the German Army

In a bid to secure the support of important army officers in December 1932, Hitler gives this explanation of how a Nazi state could provide for Germany's military needs.

The World War ended in such a way that France was unable to achieve all her aims. In particular, her hopes of a general internal collapse of the Reich were not realized. The peace treaty of Versailles was thus dictated by France's attempt to maintain as broad as possible a community of interest of states hostile to Germany. This aim was to be secured in the first place through the territorial truncation of the Reich. By handing over German territory to almost all of the surrounding states, it was hoped to forge a ring of nations bound together by common interests. In the East, Russia, which at the time was of no consequence (and whose development furthermore was unpredictable) was to be replaced by Poland, which was dependent on France. The fact that East Prussia was separated off by the Polish corridor inevitably led to the strong desire to incorporate this province into Poland, which in any case surrounded most of it. And, in fact, the propaganda for a greater Poland began to press for this immediately after the signing of the Versailles treaty.

Presumably out of fear of the danger which was clearly looming, German foreign policy endeavoured to relieve the pressure in the East by establishing a close relationship with Russia. While appreciating the political and military reasons for this approach, I have always considered it

J. Noakes and G. Pridham, eds., *Nazism 1919–1945,* Vol. 3, *Foreign Policy, War, and Racial Extermination: A Documentary Reader.* Exeter, England: University of Exeter Press, 1988.

dubious and opposed it. The reasons for my attitude, of which General von Hammerstein, in particular, has been aware for many years, were and still are as follows:

1. Russia is not a state but an ideology which at the moment is restricted to this territory, or rather dominates it, but which maintains sections in all other countries which not only pursue the same revolutionary goal, but are also organisationally subordinate to the Moscow headquarters. A victory for these ideas in Germany must have incalculable consequences. However, the more one cooperates with the headquarters of this poisonous agency for diplomatic reasons, the more difficult it becomes to struggle against these poisonous tendencies. The German people are no more immune against Communism now than they were immune to the ideas of revolution in 1917 and 1918. Officers and statesmen can only assess this problem if they understand national psychologies. Experience shows that this is rarely the case.

2. For this reason I regard Soviet diplomacy not only as unreliable but as not comparable with the diplomatic leadership of other nations and, therefore, as ineligible to undertake negotiations and sign treaties. 'Treaties' can only be signed with combatants who are on the same ideological plane.

3. However, were we—which God forbid—to be saved by Soviet aid on some occasion, this would clearly imply the planting of the red flag in Germany.

4. In so far as the growth in Russia's military strength reduces the value to France of her Polish ally to the extent that French intentions towards Germany in

the East are seriously jeopardized, France will either endeavour to draw Russia away from Poland or, in the event of the failure of such an action, drop Poland and replace her with Russia.

5. Germany's political cooperation with Russia produces an adverse response from the rest of the world. Economic co-operation will destroy our German export industry in the future.

It is for these reasons that for the past twelve years or so I have consistently proposed a closer relationship with Italy on the one hand and England on the other as the most desirable diplomatic goal.

Following the noticeable reduction in the value of her Polish ally, France has endeavoured—and in my view successfully—to involve Russia in the Far East in order to relieve pressure on the Polish border. This far-reaching French action may be regarded as in essence successfully accomplished in the non-aggression pact between Russia and Poland which has now been signed.

The moment that a particular domestic political situation creates an international atmosphere hostile to Germany, Poland will seize the opportunity to attack and East Prussia will be lost. The declaration of a monarchy, for example, or any plan to restore the House of Hohenzollern—in whatever form —may immediately provoke this response.

The military means and possibilities open to East Prussia are, in my view, inadequate for a lengthy resistance with any prospect of success. Moreover, on the basis of the present political situation there will in my view be no military support from the Reich. I consider the impression of a speeding-up of German rearmament as the most serious danger. It is conceivable that France is no longer in a position to sabotage the granting of a theoretical equality of rights to Germany. In this case the succeeding period will be the most dangerous epoch in German history because the practical, technical, and organizational rearmament will have to follow

on from the granting of theoretical equality. If ever there was a reason for a preventive war then it would be in this case for an attack by France on Germany. Such a military act alone would create the new facts which are desired and the same world, which today bestows its theoretical benevolence upon us, would be wary of trying to correct the fait accompli by force of arms.

France cannot wish for anything better than to leave the first step in this new measure to a third party. It can devise reasons and pretexts for it at any time.

Thus, as I have already emphasized, I consider the threat of this attack to be acute and believe that it would be advisable to reckon with its onset at any moment!

However at present there is no possibility of Germany intervening in such a conflict. The reason for this does not lie in the lack of the necessary armaments but much more in the total unsuitability of the German people for such a task thanks to its intellectual, moral, and political decline.

The German nation at the present time consists of two ideological camps of which one must be excluded from any military service for the present state. According to the last Reichstag elections (November 6, 1932), the ideological breakdown of our people is as follows:

Communists [KPD]	6 million
Social Democrats [SPD]	7.4 million
Centre	4 million
State Party etc.	1 million
National Socialists	12 million
German National People's Party + Stahlhelm	3 million
German People's Party	1 million

That is to say: In the event of a war being forced on Germany, more than half of the population consists of people who are either more or less pacifist or else consciously hostile to defence and military matters. The opinion of some generals that military training (in a sudden war it could only be very brief) would eradicate ideological indoctrination by political parties is positively puerile. Even the two years military service in peacetime did not damage the SPD. To say that the SPD workers nevertheless did their duty in 1914 is wrong. For it was not the convinced Marxist who did his duty but the German in the Marxist who was stirred enough temporarily to renounce Marxism. The convinced Marxist leadership was already beginning to fight back in 1915 and, after remarkable and splendid resistance on the part of the population, finally in 1918 provoked a revolution and thereby caused the collapse of the Reich.

The Social Democracy of those days cannot be remotely compared with the KPD of today. In 1914 Marxism was a theory; today it dominates in practice an enormous part of the world. A war fought by Germany in its present state would from the start subject the whole nation to a test of nerves which, as far as the home front is concerned at any rate, would bear no comparison with similar events in the World War.

The idea that in this case one can fall back on the nationalist leagues is very flattering for these organizations which nowadays suffer such abuse and persecution, but is likely to be not only of no practical significance, but rather produce fearful consequences. For, if the nationalist elements are called up and moved to the front as more or less untrained cannon fodder, the homeland would then be simultaneously delivered into the hands of the red mob. The year 1918 was child's play compared with what would happen then.

Thus, while our political and military strategists regard German rearmament as a technical or organizational matter, I see the precondition for any rearmament as the creation of a new German national unity of mind and of will. Without the solution of this problem all talk of 'equality of rights' and 'rearmament' is superficial and idle chatter.

This creation of a unity of ideology, mind, and will among our people is the task

which I set myself fourteen years ago and which I have struggled to achieve ever since. I am not surprised that our official civil and military agencies treat this problem with a total lack of understanding not to say stupidity. It has always been thus throughout history. No great ideas and reforms of humanity have ever come from the professionals. Why should it be any different today. However, recognition of this historical truth does not relieve the person who has taken the measure of this question in all its enormous significance from the duty of working to resolve it. I must, therefore, however regretfully, make a stand against, indeed must combat, any German government which is not ready and determined to carry out this inward rearmament of the German nation. All other measures follow from it.

I consider the present cabinet of General von Schleicher to be particularly unfortunate because through the person of its leader alone it must show even less appreciation of this question than any other would do. This time, as ever in history, this problem of the intellectual rearmament of the nation cannot be solved by an army but only by an ideology. To involve the Army in the matter makes it appear prejudiced in many people's eyes just as such an involvement thereby compromises the task itself in the eyes of the masses. For, neither the police nor the military have ever destroyed ideologies even less have they been able to construct them. However, no human structure can survive in the long term without an ideology. Ideologies are the social contracts and bases on which substantial human organizations have to be built. Thus, in contrast to our present statesmen I see Germany's tasks for the future as follows:

1. Overcoming Marxism and its consequences until they have been completely exterminated. The creation of a new unity of mind and will for our people.

2. A general intellectual and moral rearma-

ment of the nation on the basis of this new ideological unity.

3. Technical rearmament.
4. The organizational mobilization of the national resources for the purpose of national defence.
5. Once this has been achieved, the securing of the legal recognition of the new situation by the rest of the world.

Only a deep-rooted process of regeneration instead of the present experimentation and continual seeking after new and petty palliatives can bring about a final and clear-cut solution to the German crisis. I would be grateful, Colonel, if you would judge my behaviour in the light of this view.

See also Machtergreifung, Reichswehr, Vol. 2.

Hitler Threatens Czechoslovakia

In the following speech made by Hitler on September 26, 1938, the Führer challenges Edouard Beneš, the president of Czechoslovakia, to act in the best interests of peace and his nation by giving in to German demands.

"In the Reichstag on 20 February of this year [1938] I stated that in the life of the ten million Germans beyond our frontiers there must come a change. Mr. Beneš [Czechoslovakian president Edouard Beneš] now taken a different course. He instituted a still more ruthless oppression. He set on foot a still greater terrorism. There began a period of disbanding of associations, of vetos, confiscations, and the like. This continued until at last 21 May came. And you cannot deny, my fellow-countrymen, that we have exhibited a truly unexampled patience. This 21 May was intolerable. I have given its history at the Parteitag of the Reich. In Czechoslovakia at last an election was to take place which could not be postponed any longer. Then Mr. Beneš invented a way to intimidate the Germans in Czechoslovakia: the military occupation of the [Sudeten] districts."

"This military occupation even now he intends to continue for the future in the hope that no one will venture to oppose him so long as his myrmidons are in the country. It was that insolent lie of 21 May—that Germany had mobilized—that now had to serve to cover the Czech mobilization, to excuse it, and to supply a motive. What followed you know: an infamous international world-wide agitation."

"Germany had not called a man to the colours: it never thought for a moment to solve this problem by military intervention. Still I always hoped that the Czechs at the last minute would realize that this tyranny could not be maintained any longer. But Mr. Beneš adopted the standpoint that, protected by France and by England, one could do anything with Germany with impunity—nothing could happen to him. And above all: when all other strings failed, behind him stood Soviet Russia."

"And so the answer of this man was now more than before: Shoot down, arrest, imprison—the fate of all those who in any way failed to please him. Thus it was that there came my demand in Nuremberg. This demand was quite clear: for the first time I there expressed the claim that now at last—

Adolf Hitler, *My New Order.* Ed. Raoul de Roussy de Sales. New York: Reynal and Hitchcock, 1941.

almost twenty years since the statements of [U.S.] President Wilson [in his Fourteen Points]—for these three and a half millions the right of self-determination must come into force. And once again Mr. Beneš gave his answer: more deaths, more imprisonments, more arrests. The Germans began perforce to flee."

"And then came England. I have told Mr. Chamberlain [British prime minister] quite distinctly what we regard now as the sole possibility of a solution. It is the most natural solution that there can be. I know that *all* nationalities no longer wish to remain with Dr. Beneš, but I am in the first place spokesman of the Germans, and for these Germans I have now spoken and asserted that I am no longer willing to look on calm and inactive and see how this madman in Prague thinks that he can undisturbed ill-treat three and a half million human beings."

"And I have left him in no doubt that now at last German patience has really come to an end: I have left him in no doubt that, though it is a characteristic of our German mentality to bear something for a long time and again and again to raise no protest, yet one day the moment comes when it has to stop! And now England and France have sent to Czechoslovakia the only possible demand—to set free the German area and to surrender it to the Reich."

"We are now accurately informed on the conversations which Dr. Beneš conducted at that time. Faced by the declaration of England and of France that they would no longer support Czechoslovakia if at last the fate of these peoples was not changed and the areas liberated Mr. Beneš found a way of escape. He conceded that these districts must be surrendered. That was what he stated, but what did he do? He did not surrender the area but the Germans he now drives out! And that is now the point at which the game comes to an end. Mr. Beneš had hardly spoken when he began his military subjugation afresh—only with still greater violence. We see the appalling figures: on one day 10,000 fugitives,

on the next 20,000, a day later, already 37,000, again two days later 41,000, then 62,000, then 78,000: now 90,000, 107,000, 137,000 and to-day 214,000. Whole stretches of country were depopulated, villages are burned down, attempts are made to smoke out the Germans with hand-grenades and gas. Mr. Beneš, however, sits in Prague and is convinced: 'Nothing can happen to me: in the end England and France stand behind me.'"

"And now, my fellow-countrymen, I believe that the time has come when one must mince matters no longer. If anyone for twenty years has borne such a shame, such a disgrace, such a misfortune as we have done, then in very truth it cannot be denied that he is a lover of peace. When anyone has the patience which we have shown then in very truth it cannot be said that he is bellicose. For in the last resort Mr. Beneš has seven million Czechs, but here there stands a people of over seventy-five millions."

"I have now placed a memorandum containing a last and final German proposal in the hands of the British Government. This memorandum contains nothing save the putting into effect of what Mr. Beneš has already promised. The content of this proposal is very simple:"

"That area which in its people is German and has the wish to be German comes to Germany and that, too, not only when Mr. Beneš has succeeded in driving out perhaps one or two million Germans, but now, and that immediately! I have here chosen that frontier which on the basis of the material which has existed for decades on the division of people and language in Czechoslovakia is the just frontier-line. But in spite of this I am more just than Mr. Beneš and I have no wish to exploit the power which we possess. I have therefore laid it down from the outset that this area will be placed under German supremacy because it is essentially settled by Germans, the final delimitation of the frontier, however, I then leave to the vote of our fellow-countrymen themselves who are in the area! I have therefore laid down

German-speaking children line the streets to cheer Hitler's arrival in the Sudetenland in Czechoslovakia in October 1938, when the region was ceded to Germany under the threat of German invasion.

that in this area there must then be held a plebiscite. And in order that no one can say that the procedure of the plebiscite [a vote among inhabitants] might be unjust, I have chosen as the basis for this plebiscite the Statute that governed the Saar Plebiscite [of 1935, which guaranteed the Saarland would remain in Germany rather than France]."

"Now I am and was prepared, so far as I am concerned, to allow a plebiscite to be held throughout the area. But Mr. Beneš and his friends objected. They wished that a plebiscite should be allowed only in certain parts of the area. Good, I have yielded the point. I was even prepared to allow the plebiscite to be subject to the inspection of international Commissions of Control."

"I went even further and agreed to leave the delimitation of the frontier to a German-Czech Commission. Mr. Chamberlain suggested: might it not be an international Commission? To this, too, I agreed. I even wished during this period of the plebiscite to

withdraw again the troops, and I have to-day declared my readiness to invite for this period the British Legion, which offered me its services, to go into these districts and there maintain calm and order. And I was further ready to allow the international Commission to fix the final frontier and to hand over all details of procedure to a Commission composed of Germans and Czechs."

"The content of this memorandum is nothing else than the practical execution of what Mr. Beneš has already promised and that too under the most complete international guarantees. Mr. Beneš now says that this memorandum is 'a new situation'. And in what in fact does this 'new situation' consist? It consists in this: that this time—exceptionally—the promise made by Mr. Beneš must also be kept! That is for Mr. Beneš the 'new situation'. What is there that Mr. Beneš has not promised at some time in his life? And no promise has been kept! Now for the first time he has got to keep to something."

"Mr. Beneš says: 'We cannot go back from this area'. Mr. Beneš has then understood the transfer of this area to mean that the legal title is recognized as belonging to the German Reich but the area is still to be subject to the violence of the Czechs. That is now past!"

"I have demanded that now after twenty years Mr. Beneš should at last be compelled to come to terms with the truth. On 1 October he will have to hand over to us this area."

"Mr. Beneš now places his hopes on the world! And he and his diplomats make no secret of the fact. They state: it is our hope that Chamberlain will be overthrown, that Daladier will be removed, that on every hand revolutions are on the way. They place their hope on Soviet Russia. He still thinks then that he will be able to evade the fulfilment of his obligations."

"And then I can say only one thing: now two men stand arrayed one against the other: there is Mr. Beneš and here stand I. We are two men of a different makeup. In the great struggle of the peoples while Mr. Beneš was sneaking about through the world, I as a decent German soldier did my duty. And now to-day I stand over against this man as the soldier of my people!"

"I have only a few statements still to make: I am grateful to Mr. Chamberlain for all his efforts. I have assured him that the German people desires nothing else than peace, but I have also told him that I cannot go back behind the limits set to our patience. I have further assured him, and I repeat it here, that when this problem is solved there is for Germany no further territorial problem in Europe. And I have further assured him that at the moment when Czechoslovakia solves her problems, that means when the Czechs have come to terms with their other minorities, and that peaceably and not through oppression, then I have no further interest in the Czech State. And that is guaranteed to him! We want no Czechs!"

"But in the same way I desire to state before the German people that with regard to the problem of the Sudeten Germans my patience is now at an end! I have made Mr. Beneš an offer which is nothing but the carrying into effect of what he himself has promised. The decision now lies in his hands: Peace or War! He will either accept this offer and now at last give to the Germans their freedom or we will go and fetch this freedom for ourselves. The world must take note that in four and a half years of war and through the long years of my political life there is one thing which no one could ever cast in my teeth: I have never been a coward!"

"Now I go before my people as its first soldier and behind me—that the world should know—there marches a people and a different people from that of 1918!"

"If at that time a wandering scholar was able to inject into our people the poison of democratic catchwords—the people of to-day is no longer the people that it was then. Such catchwords are for us like wasp-stings: they cannot hurt us: we are now immune."

"In this hour the whole German people will unite with me! It will feel my will to be its will. Just as in my eyes it is its future and its fate which give me the commission for my action."

"And we wish now to make our will as strong as it was in the time of our fight, the time when I, as a simple unknown soldier, went forth to conquer a Reich and never doubted of success and final victory."

"Then there gathered close about me a band of brave men and brave women, and they went with me. And so I ask you my German people to take your stand behind me, man by man, and woman by woman."

"In this hour we all wish to form a common will and that will must be stronger than every hardship and every danger."

"And if this will is stronger than hardship and danger then one day it will break down hardship and danger."

"We are determined!"

"Now let Mr. Beneš make his choice!"

See also appeasement, Vol. 1; Munich Conference, Sudetenland, Vol. 2; Beneš, Edouard, Vol. 3.

Training the
National Socialist

In Mein Kampf, *Hitler describes how to train servants of the state by focusing on such qualities as strength, determination, devotion, and the "proper" perspective on history.*

In the folkish State the folkish view of life has finally to succeed in bringing about that nobler era when men see their care no longer in the better breeding of dogs, horses and cats, but rather in the uplifting of mankind itself, an era in which the one knowingly and silently renounces, and the other gladly gives and sacrifices.

That this is possible must not be denied in a world in which hundreds and hundreds of thousands of men voluntarily impose celibacy upon themselves, obliged and bound by nothing but a command of the Church.

Should not the same renunciation be possible if it is replaced by the admonition finally to put an end to the permanently continuous original sin of a race poisoning and to give the Almighty Creator beings as He Himself created them?

Of course, the miserable host of our present petty *bourgeois* [lower-middle class] will never understand this. They will laugh at it or shrug their crooked shoulders and moaningly they will bring forth their eternal excuse: 'That would be very nice in itself, but one will never be able to do this!' —with you, of course, one can no longer do this, your world is not suitable for this. You know only *one* care: your personal lives; and *one* god: your money! However, it is not to you that we appeal, but we turn to the great

army of those who are so poor that their personal lives could not mean the highest fortune of the world, to those who do not see the ruling principle of their lives in gold but who believe in other gods. Above all we turn to the powerful host of our German youth. They grow up into a great turn of the time, and what the inertia and the indifference of their fathers have sinned will force them to fight. German youth will one day be either the builder of a new national State or it will, as the last witness, experience the complete collapse, the end of the *bourgeois* world.

For if a generation suffers from faults which it realizes, even admits, but nevertheless, as today in our *bourgeois* world, is satisfied with the cheap explanation that nothing can be done against it, then such a society is doomed to destruction. But the characteristic of our *bourgeois* world is just the fact that it is no longer able to deny the diseases. It has to admit that many things are foul and evil, but it no longer finds the determination to stand up against the evil, to integrate through frantic energy the force of a people of sixty or seventy millions and thus to set it up firmly against the danger. On the contrary: if this is done elsewhere, then one even makes silly remarks about it, and tries to point out, at least from a distance, the theoretical impossibility of the procedure and to declare success unthinkable. Thereby no reason is stupid enough in order to serve as a support for their own dwarfishness and their mental attitude. If for instance an entire continent today at last takes up the fight against liquor poisoning in order to free a people from the grip of this devastating vice, then our European *bourgeois* world has no other comment about

---

Adolf Hitler, *Mein Kampf.* New York: Reynal and Hitch-cock, 1939.

this than an empty stare and headshaking, a superior ridicule—something that suits this ridiculous society superbly. But if nothing helps and if nevertheless in some place in this world someone steps up against the sublime, inviolable accustomed routine and that even with success, then, as pointed out before, at least the *latter* is doubted and derided, whereby one does not refrain from bringing up bourgeois moral viewpoints against a struggle that tries to do away with the greatest immorality.

No, we all must not deceive ourselves about this: our present *bourgeoisie* has already become useless for every sublime task of humanity, simply because it has no quality, and is too evil; and it is too evil—if you will—less because of *willful* viciousness, but rather in consequence of an unbelievable indolence and of everything that springs from it. Therefore also those political clubs which are found under the collective name of '*bourgeois* parties' have long ceased to be anything but associations of interests of certain vocational groups and class estates, and their most sublime task is nothing but the best possible egoistic representation of their interests. It is obvious that such a political '*bourgeois*' guild is suitable for anything rather than for fighting; but especially if the opposition does not consist of pepper sacks [i.e., small tradesmen], but of masses of proletarians who have been incited towards the extreme and are determined for the ultimate.

If as the State's first task in the service and for the welfare of its nationality we recognize the preservation, care and development of the racially best elements, it is natural that this care has to extend not only to the time of birth of the young member of people and race, but that it has to educate the young offspring towards becoming a valuable member in view of later propagation.

Just as in general the presumptions for spiritual achievements lies in the racial quality of the given human material, thus also the individual's education has to focus

upon and to promote first of all physical health; for, within the masses, a healthy, vigorous spirit will be found only in a healthy and powerful body. The fact that geniuses are sometimes physically badly formed, even sick beings, is no objection. They are the exceptions which—as everywhere—prove the rule. But if the mass of a people consists of physical degenerates, then out of this swamp a really great spirit will arise only very rarely. His activity will in no case be rewarded with great success. The degraded rabble will either not understand him at all, or it will be so weakened in its will power that it will be unable to follow the soaring flight of such an eagle.

The folkish State, through this realization, has to direct its entire education primarily not at pumping in mere knowledge, but at the breeding of absolutely healthy bodies. Of secondary importance is the training of the mental abilities. But here again first of all the development of the character, especially the promotion of will power and determination, connected with education for joyfully assuming responsibility, and only as the last thing, scientific schooling.

Thereby the folkish State has to start from the presumption *that a man, though scientifically little educated but physically healthy, who has a sound, firm character, filled with joyful determination and will power, is of greater value to the national community than an ingenious weakling.* A people of scholars, when they are physically degenerated, irresolute and cowardly pacifists, will not conquer heaven, nay it will not even be able to assure its existence on this globe. In the hard struggle of fate he who knows little succumbs most rarely, but always he who draws from his knowledge the weakest consequences and puts them into activity in the poorest manner. Finally, here also a certain harmony must exist. *A rotten body is not in the least made more aesthetic by a brilliant mind,* nay, highest training of the mind could not at all be justified if its bearers were at the same time physically degenerated and crippled beings, irresolute and weak in character, hesitating and cowardly. What makes the Greek ideal of beauty immortal is the wonderful combination of the most glorious physical beauty with a brilliant mind and the noblest soul.

If [nineteenth-century general] Moltke's words 'In the long run only the efficient one is lucky' are valid, then it is certainly so for the relation between body and mind: The mind also, if healthy, will as a rule and at length only dwell in a healthy body.

In the folkish State physical training therefore is not the concern of the individual, and also not an affair that concerns primarily the parents and the community only in the second or third instance, but a requirement of the self-preservation of the nationality, represented and protected by the State. Just as the State, as far as the purely scientific training is concerned, intervenes even today in the right of self-determination of the individual and represents towards him the right of the community by subjecting the child, without asking for the agreement or non-agreement of the parents, to compulsory schooling, thus, in questions of the nationality's preservation, the national State will some day, to a much higher degree, enforce its authority against the ignorance or the non-understanding of the individual. It has to arrange its educational work in such manner that the young bodies, in their earliest childhood, are treated according to the purpose and that they receive the necessary steeling for later days. But above all it has to care that not a generation of stay-at-homes is brought up.

This work of care and education has to start even with the young mother. Just as it became possible, in the course of decades of work, to attain aseptic cleanliness during delivery and to limit puerperal fever to a few cases, thus it must and will be possible, by a thorough training of nurses and mothers, to bring about, even during the first years of the child, a treatment that serves as the most excellent basis for the later development.

School as such, in a folkish State, has to set apart infinitely more time for physical training. It won't do to burden the young brains with a ballast which they retain, according to experience, only to a fraction, whereby in most cases instead of the essential the unnecessary trifles remain, as the young child is not in a position to carry out a sensible selection of the material that has been infiltrated in him. If today, even in the curriculum of the middle schools, only two hours per week are devoted to gymnastics and the participation in it is optional with the individual, not compulsory, then this is, compared with the purely intellectual training, a gross disparity. Not a day should pass during which the young man is not trained physically for at least one hour in the morning and again in the evening, in every kind of sport and gymnastics. Here especially one kind of sport must not be forgotten which in the eyes of many 'nationals' is considered as brutal and undignified: boxing. It is incredible what erroneous opinions are current about this in the circles of the 'educated.' That the young man learns to fence and then goes about fighting duels is looked upon as natural and honorable, but that he boxes is supposed to be brutal! Why? There is no sport that, like this, promotes the spirit of aggression in the same measure, demands determination quick as lightning, educates the body for steel-like versatility. If two young people fight out a difference of opinion with their fists, it is no more brutal than if they do so with a piece of ground iron. Also, it is not less noble if one who has been attacked wards off his attacker with his fists instead of running away and calling for a policeman. But above all, the young and healthy boy has to learn to be beaten. This, of course, may appear wild in the eyes of our present spiritual fighters. But the folkish State has not the task of breeding a colony of peaceful aesthetes and physical degenerates. Not in the honest petty *bourgeois* or in the virtuous old maid does it see its ideal of humanity, but in the robust incorporation of manly forces and in women who in their turn are able to bring men into the world.

Thus the meaning of sports is not only to make the individual strong, versatile and bold, but it has also to harden him and to teach him how to bear inclemencies.

If our entire intellectual upper class had not been educated so exclusively in teaching refined manners, and if instead of this it had learned boxing thoroughly, then a German revolution by pimps, deserters and similar rabble would never have been possible; for what gave the latter its success was not the bold, courageous energy of those making the Revolution, but the cowardly, miserable lack of determination by those who ruled the State and were responsible for it. However, our entire body of intellectual leaders had been educated only 'intellectually' and were bound to be defenseless in the moment when on the side

of the opponents, instead of intellectual weapons, the crowbar came into action. But all this was possible only because our higher schools, in principle, did not educate men, but officials, engineers, technicians, chemists, lawyers, journalists, and, in order to keep this mentality alive, professors.

Our intellectual leadership always showed brilliant achievements, whereas our leaders in will power remained beneath all criticism.

By education one will certainly not be able to turn one who is fundamentally a coward into a courageous man, but it is just as certain that a man who in himself is not without courage is paralyzed in the development of his qualities if, from the very beginning, his physical force and abilities, through the faults of his education, are inferior to those of the others. How far the conviction of physical efficiency promotes one's feeling of courage, even wakens the

Members of the Hitler Youth mass for group calisthenics in a field circa 1935. Physical training was stressed over academic studies in the Nazi educational system.

spirit of aggression, can best of all be seen in the army. Here, too, it was not fundamentally heroes that existed but the broad average. But the superior training of the German soldier in peace time inoculated this entire gigantic organism with this suggestive confidence in its own superiority to a degree which even our enemies had not thought possible. For the immortal spirit and the courage of aggression, demonstrated by the German armies during the months of the midsummer and fall of 1914 were the result of that untiring education which during the long, long years of peace got the most incredible achievements out of often weak bodies and thus educated for that self-confidence which was not lost even in the horror of the greatest battles.

It is precisely our German people, that today, broken down, lies defenseless against the kicks of the rest of the world, who need that suggestive force that lies in self-confidence. But this self-confidence has to be instilled into the young fellow citizen from childhood on. His entire education and development has to be directed at giving him the conviction of being absolutely superior to the others. With his physical force and skill he has again to win the belief in the invincibility of his entire nationality. For what once led the German army to victory was the sum of the confidence which the individual and all in common had in their leaders. The confidence in the possibility of regaining its freedom is what will restore the German people. But this conviction can only be the final product of the same feeling of millions of individuals.

But here we must not deceive ourselves:

Colossal was the breakdown of our people, but just as colossal will be the exertion to end this misery some day. He who believes that through our present *bourgeois* work of educating for peace and order our people will receive the force to break one day the present world order which means our doom, and to throw the shackles of slavery into the faces of our enemies, is bit-terly wrong. Only by an excess of national will power, of thirst for freedom and highest passion, can we make up for what we once lacked.

The clothes of the young people also have to be adapted to this purpose. It is truly miserable to be compelled to see that our youth also is subject to a lunacy of fashion which helped in converting the meaning of the old proverb *'Kleider machen Leute'* [clothes make people] into a detrimental one.

Particularly with youth, clothes have to be put into the service of education. The young man who during summer walks about in long pipe-like trousers, covered up to the neck, loses, merely through his clothes, a stimulant for his physical fitness. For ambition, too, and we may as well say it, vanity also, have to be applied. Not the vanity in beautiful clothes which not everyone is able to buy, but the vanity in a beautiful, well-shaped body which everyone can help in building up.

This is of use also for the future. The girl should become acquainted with her knight. If today physical beauty were not pushed completely into the background by our dandified fashionableness, the seduction of hundreds of thousands of girls by bow-legged, disgusting Jewish bastards would never be possible. Also this is in the interest of the nation, that the most beautiful bodies find one another and thus help in giving the nation new beauty.

Today, of course, this would be necessary most of all, because the military education is lacking and thus the only institution has been eliminated which during peace time made up, at least in part, for what was otherwise neglected by education. And also there the success was to be sought not only in the training of the individual, but in the influence which it exercised on the relationship between the two sexes. The young girl preferred the soldier to the civilian.

The folkish State has to carry through and to supervise the physical training not only during the official school years; it has to care also in post-school days that, as long as a boy is in physical development, this development turns into a blessing for him. It is nonsense to believe that with the end of school time the State's right for supervision of its young citizens could suddenly stop, in order to return with the military service. This right is a duty, and as such it is permanently existent. The present State that has no interest in healthy people has neglected this duty in a criminal manner. It lets the present young generation degenerate in the streets and in brothels, instead of taking them by the leash and training them physically further until one day a healthy man and a healthy woman have grown out of this.

In what form the State continues this education is beside the point today, but the point is that it should do it and seek the ways that are useful for this purpose. The folkish State has to consider it a task of State and has to carry out through State institutions the physical education of the post-school days exactly as the intellectual education. Thereby this education, in broad outlines, can be the preparation for the future service in the army. Then the army no longer has to teach the young men, as hitherto, the fundamentals of the most simple drills, nor will it receive recruits in the current meaning, but it has to turn the young man, who is already physically completely prepared, into a soldier.

In the folkish State, therefore, the army no longer has to teach the individual how to walk and to stand, but it has to be looked upon as the ultimate and highest school of patriotic education. In the army, the young recruit should receive the necessary training in arms, but at the same time he should be formed further for his future life. But at the head of the military education should stand what had to be attributed even to the old army as its highest merit: in this school the boy should be turned into a man; and in this school he should not only learn to obey, but also acquire the training for commanding later on. He has to learn to be silent, not only when he is blamed *justly,* but he has also to learn, if necessary, to bear *injustice* in silence.

Further, strengthened by the confidence in his own force, seized by the strength of the commonly experienced *esprit de corps,* he has to gain the conviction of the invincibility of his own nationality.

After terminating the service in the army, he should be given two documents: his *diploma as a State* citizen as a legal document which now permits him public activity, and his *certificate of health* as the confirmation of physical health for marriage.

Analogous with the education of the boy, the folkish State can also direct the education of the girl from the same viewpoints. Here too the main stress should be put on physical training, and only after this on the promotion of spiritual and last of all, the intellectual values. The *goal* of female education has invariably to be the future mother.

As of secondary importance the folkish State has to promote the modeling of the *character* in every way.

It is certain that the essential features of character are fundamentally formed previously in the individual: one who is egoistic is and remains so once and forever, exactly as the idealist, in the bottom of his nature, will always be an idealist. But between the completely shaped characters there are millions of a type that appear dim and unclear. The born criminal will be and remain a criminal; but numerous people in whom a certain tendency towards criminality exists can still be made valuable members of the national community by proper education; while on the other hand by bad education vacillating characters can grow into really evil elements.

How often one complained, during the War, that our people knew so little how to be *silent!* How difficult this made it to guard even important secrets from the knowledge of the enemies! But one should ask oneself the question: Before the War, what did German education do towards training the individual for secrecy? Was not unfortunately even in school the little tattle-tale preferred to his more discreet comrade? Was not and is not tale-telling looked upon as honorable 'frankness,' and discretion as disgraceful obstinacy? Did one endeavor at all to present discretion as a manly valuable virtue? No, in the eyes of our present school education these are trifles. But these trifles cost the State uncounted millions in court expenses, for ninety per cent of all libel suits and similar trials arose only from a lack of discretion. Irresponsibly dropped remarks are passed on just as light-heartedly, our economy is constantly injured by a careless giving away of important methods of production, etc., even quiet preparations for the defense of the country are made illusory as the people have not learned to be silent but spread everything. But in case of war this inclination to talk can even lead to the loss of battles and thus contribute considerably to the unfortunate end of a struggle. Here, too, one has to be convinced that what one has not practiced during youth one cannot exercise during old age. In this category belongs also the fact that in principle the teacher, for instance, ought not to try to gain information about the pranks of silly boys by encouraging evil tale-telling. Youth has a State for itself, it faces the grown-ups with a certain closed solidarity, and this is natural. The bond of a ten-year-old boy to a comrade of the same age is a natural one and greater than that to a grown-up person. A boy who gives his comrade away exercises *treason* and thus shows a mentality which, grossly expressed and enlarged, corresponds exactly to that of the traitor to his country. Such a boy can in no way be looked upon as a *'good, decent'* child, but as a boy with few valuable characteristics. To the teacher it may be convenient, for the purpose of increasing his authority, to avail himself of such evil habits, but by this the germ of a mentality is planted in the young heart which later can have a catastrophic effect. More than once

the young tattle-tale has become a great scoundrel!

This should serve as only one example for many. Today the conscious development of good and noble character qualities at school is equal to naught. This, one day, will have to be emphasized in quite a different manner. *Loyalty, willingness to sacrifice, and silence* are virtues which a great people urgently *needs,* and their inculcation by education and training in school is more important than many of the things which now fill our curriculum. Also the elimination by education of tearful complaining, of lamenting, etc., belongs in this field. If an education forgets to influence even the child to the effect that sufferings and adversities have to be borne in silence, it must not be surprised if later, in a critical hour, for example when one day the man stands at the front, the entire mail service serves the transportation of mutual letters of complaints and laments. If in our public schools one had instilled into our young people a little less knowledge and a little more self-restraint, this would have been amply rewarded in the years 1915–18.

Thus the folkish State, in its work of education, has, besides the physical training, to put the greatest emphasis on the training of the character. By an education in this direction, numerous moral defects, which our present national body harbors, can be, if not entirely abolished, at least greatly modified.

Of highest importance is the training of will power and determination, as well as the cultivation of joy in taking responsibility.

If formerly in the army the principle was valid that an order is always better than no order, for youth this must mean first of all: an answer is always better than no answer. The dread shown in giving no answer, out of fear of saying something wrong, must be more humiliating than an incorrectly given answer. Starting from this most primitive basis youth should be educated to the effect that it acquires the courage for action.

One has often complained that in the time of November and December of 1918 actually all authorities failed, that beginning from the monarchs down to the last division commander nobody was any longer able to summon the energy for an independent decision. This terrible fact is the *Mene tekel* [Mene, mene, tekel, upharsin (Aramaic), colloquially known as 'the handwriting on the wall'] of our education, because in this cruel catastrophe is expressed, in a measure expanded to gigantic size, what generally existed in little things. It is this lack of will, and not the lack of arms, that today makes us incapable of all serious resistance. It is ingrained in our entire people, it prevents every decision which involves a risk, as though the greatness of an act did not lie in the very risk. Without being aware of it, a German general succeeded in finding the classical formula for this miserable irresoluteness: 'I will act only if I can reckon with fifty-one per cent probability of success.' In this 'fifty-one per cent' lies the tragedy of the German collapse; he who first demands of Fate the guaranty of success thereby automatically renounces the significance of a heroic act. For it lies in the fact that, with the conviction of the mortal danger of a condition, one takes the step which can perhaps lead to success. A person suffering from cancer, whose death is otherwise certain, need not first figure out fifty-one per cent in order to risk an operation. And if the latter promises a cure with only half a per cent probability, a courageous man will risk it, otherwise he should not whimper for his life.

The epidemic of the present cowardly lack of will power and determination is, taken all in all, mainly the result of our fundamentally faulty education of youth, the devastating effect of which extends into the future life, and which finds its final conclusion and its ultimate crown in the lack of civil courage of the leading statesmen.

In the same line falls also the current prevailing cowardice with regard to responsibility. Here, too, the fault lies in the education of youth, permeates next the entire public life and finds its immortal completion in the parliamentary institutions of government.

Unfortunately, even at school one puts more stress upon the 'repenting' confession and the 'contrite abjuration' by the little sinner than upon a frank admission. The latter even appears to many a public educator of today the most visible symptom of an incorrigible depravity, and so many a boy, in an incredible manner, is threatened with the gallows for qualities which would be of priceless value if they were the common good of an entire nation.

As some day the folkish State has to devote its highest attention to the education of will and determination, it has to implant joy in taking responsibility and courage for confession into the hearts of the young from their early years of life. Only if it recognizes this necessity in its full importance will it finally have as a result, after hundreds of years of educational work, a national body which will no longer succumb to those weaknesses which today have so fatally contributed to our decline.

The folkish State will be able to take over, with only minor changes, the scientific school training, which today is actually the be-all and end-all of the State's whole work of education. These changes lie in three domains.

First, the youthful brains must in general not be burdened with things 95 per cent of which it does not need and therefore forgets again. Especially the curriculum of grammar and middle schools presents today a mongrel character; in many instances, in the various subjects the material of what has to be learned has swollen up to such a degree that only a fraction of it remains in the head of the individual pupil and only a fraction of this abundance can find application, while on the other hand it is not sufficient for the need of one who works in a certain field and earns his living therein. Let us take for instance the normal State official in the thirty-fifth or fortieth year of his life, who graduated from a *Gymnasium* [college preparatory high school] or an *Oberrealschule* [upper middle school], and let us examine what he once painfully crammed into his head at school. How little of all that which was then infiltrated is still present!

Of course one will receive the answer: 'Well, the mass of material then learned had not only the purpose of supplying a great deal of knowledge later, but also that of a training of the mental receptiveness, of the thinking ability and especially of the memorizing power of the brain.' This is partly true. Yet there is the danger that the youthful brain is swamped with a flood of impressions which it is able to master only in the rarest cases, and the single elements of which it neither knows how to sift nor how to evaluate, according to their greater or smaller importance; whereby, besides, not the unessential but the essential is forgotten and sacrificed in most cases. Thus the main purpose of this much-learning is again lost; for this purpose cannot mean making the brain capable of learning by an unmeasured accumulation of material; but giving for the future that treasure of knowledge which the individual needs and from which, through him, the community will benefit. But this becomes illusory if, in consequence of the superabundance of the material that was forced upon him during youth, man later either no longer possesses this material at all, or at least not the essential parts of it. One can, for instance, not see why millions of people, in the course of the years, have to learn two or three foreign languages which thereafter only a fraction of which they can use and which therefore the majority of them forget again completely, for out of a hundred thousand pupils who, for instance, learn French, hardly two thousand will later on be able to use it actually, while ninety-eight thousand, through their entire further course of life, will no longer be in a situation where they can make use of what they have learned. During their youth, therefore, they have devoted thousands of hours to a matter which

later is of no value or significance to them. Also the objection that this material is part of general education is wrong, as one could defend this opinion only if people had at their disposal during their entire lives what they had learned. Thus now for the sake of two thousand people for whom the knowledge of this language is of use, actually ninety-eight thousand have to be tortured in vain and to sacrifice valuable time.

Besides, in this case a language is involved of which one cannot even say that it means a training of sharp logical thinking, as is perhaps the case with Latin. Therefore it would be far more useful if one would impart such a language to the young student only in its general outlines, or more correctly expressed, in its inner structure, that means to give him the knowledge of the most striking features of this language, perhaps introducing him to the principles of its grammar, pronunciation, syntax, etc., through model examples. This would suffice for general need, and, because easier to survey and to remember, it would be more valuable than the present drilling of the entire language, which nevertheless he will not completely command and will forget later on.

In addition, in this way one would avoid the risk that from the overwhelming abundance of the material only single, haphazard and unconnected fragments would remain in his memory, as the young man would be made to learn only what is most remarkable, and thus the selection according to value or non-value would have been carried out beforehand.

The general foundation, imparted in this way, would suffice for most people anyway, for their future life as well, while to the others who actually need this language later on, it gives the possibility of building up on it further and of devoting themselves to learning it thoroughly according to their free choice.

Thus, in the curriculum, the necessary time is gained for physical training as well as for the increased demands in the domains previously mentioned.

A change will have to be made especially in the present method of teaching history. There is probably hardly any people that learns more history than the German people; but there can hardly be a people that applies it to less advantage than our people. If politics is history in the making, then our education in history is condemned by our kind of political activity. Here, too, it will not do to complain about the wretched results of our political achievements, if one is not determined to care for a better education for politics. The result of our present teaching in history is, in ninety-nine out of a hundred cases, a miserable one. A few dates, birth figures and names usually remain, while a great, clear line is completely missing. All essentials which would really count are not taught at all, but it is left to the more or less ingenious disposition of the individual to find the inner motives out of the flood of dates, in the order of events. One may protest against this bitter statement as much as one likes; but one has only to read the speeches, delivered by our parliamentary gentlemen, during the various sessions, on political problems, for instance questions of foreign policy; one should consider, in this connection, that there—allegedly at least—we have to deal with the choice of the German nation, and that in any case a great part of these people have warmed the benches of our high schools, partly even of our universities, and from this one will be able to see just how insufficient the historical education of these people is. If they had not studied history at all, but if they had only a sound instinct, this would be much better and of greater benefit to the nation.

Particularly in history lessons a shortening of the material has to be carried out. The main value lies in recognizing the great lines of development. The more the lessons are restricted to this, the more it is to be hoped that benefit will arise out of this for the individual later on, which, summed up, is beneficial also to the community. For one does not learn history merely in order to know what has been, but one learns history in order to make it a teacher for the future and for the continued existence of one's own nationality. This is the *end,* and the history lessons are only a *means* to it. But today here, too, the means have become the end, the end itself is completely ignored. One must not say that a thorough study of history demands the occupation with all these details as only out of them a great line can be established. To establish this line is the task of the particular science in question. The normal average man, however, is not a history professor. To him history means primarily to render him that amount of historical insight which he needs for forming his opinion on the political affairs of his nation. He who wants to become a history professor may devote himself thoroughly to this study later on. Of course, he will have to deal with all and even the smallest details. But for this purpose our present instruction in history cannot be enough; because it is too vast for the normal average man, but much too narrow for the scholar-specialist.

For the rest, it is the task of a folkish State to see to it that at last a world history is written in which the race question is raised to a predominant position.

See also education in the Third Reich, Vol. 1; *Mein Kampf,* völkisch state, Vol. 2.

The Hossbach Memorandum

In November 1937 Hitler announced his war plans to top military and diplomatic officials. Minutes of the meeting were kept by Hitler's military adjutant, Colonel Friedrich Hossbach. His record is the first definitive statement of Hitler's territorial goals. When certain generals expressed reservations, Hitler had them replaced by intrigue or outright dismissal.

*B*erlin, 10 Nov 1937

NOTES ON THE CONFERENCE
IN THE [Reichs Chancellery]
ON 5 NOV 37
FROM 1615–2030 HOURS

Present:
The Führer and Reich Chancellor

The Reichsminister for War, General Field Marshal V. BLOMBERG

The Commander in Chief Army, General Freiherr von FRITSCH

The Commander in Chief Navy, Admiral Dr. h. c. RAEDER

The Commander in Chief Luftwaffe, General GOERING

The Reich Minister for Foreign Affairs Freiherr v. NEURATH
Colonel HOSSBACH

The Führer stated initially that the subject matter of today's conference was of such high importance, that its further detailed discussion would probably take place in Cabinet sessions. However, he, the Führer, had decided NOT to discuss this matter in the larger circle of the Reich Cabinet, because

Benjamin C. Sax and Dieter Kuntz, eds., *Inside Hitler's Germany: A Documentary History of Life in the Third Reich.* Lexington, MA: D.C. Heath, 1992.

of its importance. His subsequent statements were the result of detailed deliberations and of the experiences of his $4^{1}/_{2}$ years in Government; he desired to explain to those present his fundamental ideas on the possibilities and necessities of expanding our foreign policy and in the interests of a far-sighted policy he requested that his statements be looked upon in the case of his death as his last will and testament.

The Führer then stated:

The aim of German policy is the security and the preservation of the nation, and its propagation. This is, consequently, a problem of space.

The German nation is composed of 85 million people, which, because of the number of individuals and the compactness of habitation, form a homogeneous European racial body which cannot be found in any other country. On the other hand, it justifies the demand for larger living space more than for any other nation. If no political body exists in space, corresponding to the German racial body, then that is the consequence of several centuries of historical development, and should this political condition continue to exist, it will represent the greatest danger to the preservation of the German nation at its present high level. An arrest of the deterioration of the German element in Austria and Czechoslovakia is just as little possible as the preservation of the present state in Germany itself. Instead of growth, sterility will be introduced, and as a consequence, tensions of a social nature will appear after a number of years, because political and philosophical ideas are of a permanent nature only as long as they are able to produce the basis for the realization of the actual claim of existence of a nation. The German future is therefore dependent exclusively on the solution of the need for living space. Such a solution can be sought naturally only for a limited period, about 1–3 generations. . . .

It must be considered on principle that since the World War (1914–18) an industrialization has taken place in countries which formerly exported food. We live in a period of economic empires, in which the tendency to colonize again approaches the condition which originally motivated colonization; in Japan and Italy economic motives are the basis of their will to expand, the economic need will also drive Germany to it. Countries outside the great economic empires have special difficulties in expanding economically.

The upward tendency, which has been caused in world economy, due to armament competition, can never form a permanent basis for an economic settlement, and this latter is also hampered by the economic disruption caused by Bolshevism. It is a pronounced military weakness of those States who base their existence on export. As our exports and imports are carried out over those sea lanes which are ruled by Britain, it is more a question of security of transport rather than one of foreign currency, and this explains the great weakness in our food situation in wartime. The only way out, and one which may appear imaginary, is the securing of greater living space, an endeavor which at all times has been the cause of the formation of states and of movements of nations. It is explicable that this tendency finds no interest in Geneva and in satisfied States. Should the security of our food position be our foremost thought, then the space required for this can only be sought in Europe, but we will not copy liberal capitalist policies which rely on exploiting colonies. It is NOT a case of conquering people, but of conquering agriculturally useful space. It would also be more to the purpose to seek raw material producing territory in Europe directly adjoining the Reich and not overseas, and this solution would have to be brought into effect in one or two generations. What would be required at a later date

over and above this must be left to subsequent generations. The development of great world-wide national bodies is naturally a slow process and the German people, with its strong racial root, has for this purpose the most favorable foundations in the heart of the European Continent. The history of all times—Roman Empire, British Empire—has proved that every space expansion can only be effected by breaking resistance and taking risks. Even setbacks are unavoidable; neither formerly nor today has space been found without an owner; the attacker always comes up against the proprietor.

The question for Germany is where the greatest possible conquest could be made at lowest cost.

German politics must reckon with its two hateful enemies, England and France, to whom a strong German colossus in the center of Europe would be intolerable. Both these states would oppose a further reinforcement of Germany, both in Europe and overseas, and in this opposition they would have the support of all parties. Both countries would view the building of German military strongpoints overseas as a threat to their overseas communications, as a security measure for German commerce, and retrospectively a strengthening of the German position in Europe.

England is NOT in a position to cede any of her colonial possessions to us owing to the resistance which she experiences in the Dominions. After the loss of prestige which England has suffered owing to the transfer of Abyssinia [Ethiopia] to Italian ownership, a return of East Africa can no longer be expected. Any resistance on England's part would at best consist in the readiness to satisfy our colonial claims by taking away colonies which at the present moment are NOT in British hands, e.g. Angola. French favors would probably be of the same nature.

A serious discussion regarding the return of colonies to us could be considered only at a time when England is in a state of emergency and the German Reich is strong and well-armed. The Führer does not share the opinion that the Empire is unshakable. Resistance against the Empire is to be found less in conquered territories than amongst its competitors. The British Empire and the Roman Empire cannot be compared with one another in regard to durability; since the Punic Wars the latter did not have a serious political enemy. Only the dissolving effects which originated in Christendom, and the signs of age which creep into all states, made it possible for the Ancient Germans to subjugate Ancient Rome.

Alongside the British Empire today a number of States exist which are stronger than it. The British Mother Country is able to defend its colonial possessions only allied with other States and NOT by its own power. How could England alone, for example, defend Canada against an attack by America or its Far Eastern interests against an attack by Japan?

The singling out of the British Crown as the bearer of Empire unity is in itself an admission that the universal empire cannot be maintained permanently by power politics. The following are significant pointers in this respect.

a. Ireland's tendency for independence.
b. Constitutional disputes in India where England, by her half-measures, left the door open for Indians at a later date to utilize the nonfulfillment of constitutional promises as a weapon against Britain.
c. The weakening of the British position in the Far East by Japan.
d. The opposition in the Mediterranean to Italy which—by virtue of its history, driven by necessity and led by a genius—expands its power position and must consequently infringe British interests to an increasing extent. The outcome of the Abyssinian War is a loss of prestige for Britain which Italy is endeavoring to increase by stirring up discontent in the Mohammedan world.

It must be established in conclusion that the Empire cannot be held permanently by power politics by 45 million Britons, in spite of all the solidity of her ideals. The proportion of the populations in the Empire, compared with that of the Motherland is 9:1, and it should act as a warning to us that if we expand in space, we must NOT allow the level of our population to become too low.

France's position is more favorable than that of England. The French Empire is better placed geographically, the population of its colonial possessions represents a potential military increase. But France is faced with difficulties of internal politics. At the present time only 10 percent approximately of the nations have parliamentary governments whereas 90 percent of them have totalitarian governments. Nevertheless we have to take the following into our political considerations as power factors:

Germany Must Fight to Survive

The German question can be solved only by way of force, and this is never without risk. The battles of Frederick the Great for Silesia, and Bismarck's wars against Austria and France had been a tremendous risk and the speed of Prussian action in 1870 had prevented Austria from participating in the war. If we place the decision to apply force with risk at the head of the following expositions, then we are left to reply to the questions "when" and "how." In this regard we have to decide upon three different cases.

Case 1. Period 1943–45. After this we can only expect a change for the worse. The rearming of the Army, the Navy and the Air Force, as well as the formation of the Officers' Corps, are practically concluded. Our material equipment and armaments are modern, with further delay the danger of their becoming out-of-date will increase. In particular the secrecy of "special weapons" cannot always be safeguarded. Enlistment of reserves would be limited to the current recruiting age group and an addition from older untrained groups would be no longer available.

In comparison with the re-armament, which will have been carried out at that time by the other nations, we shall decrease in relative power. Should we not act until 1943/45, then, dependent on the absence of reserves, any year could bring about the food crisis, for the countering of which we do NOT possess the necessary foreign currency. This must be considered as a "point of weakness in the regime." Over and above that, the world will anticipate our action and will increase counter-measures yearly. Whilst other nations isolate themselves we should be forced on the offensive.

What the actual position would be in the years 1943–45 no one knows today. It is certain, however, that we can wait no longer.

On the one side the large armed forces, with the necessity for securing their upkeep, the aging of the Nazi movement and of its leaders, and on the other side the prospect of a lowering of the standard of living and a drop in the birth rate, leaves us no other choice than to act. If the Führer is still living, then it will be his irrevocable decision to solve the German space problem no later than 1943–45. The necessity for action before 1943–45 will come under consideration in cases 2 and 3.

Case 2. Should the social tensions in France lead to an internal political crisis of such dimensions that it absorbs the French Army and thus renders it incapable for employment in war against Germany, then the time for action against Czechoslovakia has come.

Case 3. It would be equally possible to act against Czechoslovakia if France should be so tied up by a war against another State, that it cannot "proceed" against Germany.

For the improvement of our military political position it must be our first aim, in every case of entanglement by war, to conquer Czechoslovakia and Austria simultaneously, in order to remove any threat from the flanks in case of a possible advance Westwards. In the case of a conflict with France it would hardly be necessary to assume that Czechoslovakia would declare war on the same day as France. However, Czechoslovakia's desire to participate in the war will increase proportionally to the degree to which we are being weakened. Its actual participation could make itself felt by an attack on Silesia, either towards the North or the West.

Once Czechoslovakia is conquered—and a mutual frontier, Germany-Hungary is obtained—then a neutral attitude by Poland in a German-French conflict could more easily be relied upon. Our agreements with Poland remain valid only as long as Germany's strength remains unshakeable; should Germany have any setbacks then an attack by Poland against East Prussia, perhaps also against Pomerania, and Silesia, must be taken into account.

Assuming a development of the situation, which would lead to a planned attack on our part in the years 1943–45, then the behavior of France, Poland and Russia would probably have to be judged in the following manner:

The Führer believes personally that in all probability England and perhaps also France have already silently written off Czechoslovakia, and that they have got used to the idea that this question would one day be cleaned up by Germany. The difficulties in the British Empire and the prospect of being entangled in another long-drawn-out European War, were decisive factors in the non-participation of England in a war against Germany. The British attitude would certainly NOT remain without influence on France's attitude. An attack by France without British support is hardly probable assuming that its offensive would stagnate along our Western fortifications. Without England's support, it would also NOT be necessary to take into consideration a march by France through Belgium and Holland, and this would also not have to be reckoned with by us in case of a conflict with France, as in every case it would have as consequence the enmity of Great Britain. Naturally, we should in every case have to bar our frontier during the operation of our attacks against

Czechoslovakia and Austria. It must be taken into consideration here that Czechoslovakia's defense measures will increase in strength from year to year, and that a consolidation of the inside values of the Austrian army will also be effected in the course of years. Although the population of Czechoslovakia in the first place is not a thin one, the embodiment of Czechoslovakia and Austria would nevertheless constitute the conquest of food for 5–6 million people, on the basis that a compulsory emigration of 2 million from Czechoslovakia and of 1 million from Austria could be carried out. The annexation of the two States to Germany militarily and politically would constitute a considerable relief, owing to shorter and better frontiers, the freeing of fighting personnel for other purposes and the possibility of re-constituting new armies up to a strength of about 12 Divisions, representing a new division per 1 million population.

No opposition to the removal of Czechoslovakia is expected on the part of Italy; however, it cannot be judged today what would be her attitude in the Austrian question since it would depend largely on whether the Duce [Mussolini] was alive at the time or not.

The measure and speed of our action would decide Poland's attitude. Poland will have little inclination to enter the war against a victorious Germany, with Russia in its rear.

Military participation by Russia must be countered by the speed of our operations; it is a question whether this need be taken into consideration at all in view of Japan's attitude.

Should Case 2 occur—paralyzation of France by a Civil War—then the situation should be utilized *at any time* for operations against Czechoslovakia, as Germany's most dangerous enemy would be eliminated.

The Führer sees Case 3 looming nearer; it could develop from the existing tensions in the Mediterranean, and should it occur he has firmly decided to make use of it any time, perhaps even as early as 1938.

Following recent experiences in the course of the events of the war in Spain, the Führer does NOT see an early end to hostilities there. Taking into consideration the time required for past offensives by Franco, a further three years duration of war is within the bounds of possibility. On the other hand, from the German point of view a 100 per cent victory by Franco is not desirable; we are more interested in a continuation of the war and preservation of the tensions in the Mediterranean. Should Franco be in sole possession of the Spanish Peninsula it would mean the end of Italian intervention and the presence of Italy on the Balearic Isles. As our interests are directed towards continuing the war in Spain, it must be the task of our future policy to strengthen Italy in her fight to hold on to the Balearic Isles. However, a solidification of Italian positions on the Balearic Isles can NOT be tolerated either by France or by England and could lead to a war by France and England against Italy, in which case Spain, if entirely in white (i.e. Franco's) hands, could participate on the side of Italy's enemies. A subjugation of Italy in such a war appears very unlikely. Additional raw materials could be brought to Italy via Germany. The Führer believes that Italy's military strategy would be to remain on the defensive against France on the Western frontier and carry out operations against France from Libya against North African French colonial possessions.

As a landing of French-British troops on the Italian coast can be discounted, and as a French offensive via the Alps to Upper Italy would be extremely difficult and would probably stagnate before the strong Italian fortifications, French lines of communication by the Italian fleet will to a great extent paralyze the transport of fighting personnel from North Africa to France, so that at its frontiers with Italy and Germany France will have at its disposal solely the metropolitan fighting forces.

If Germany profits from this war by disposing of the Czechoslovakian and the

Austrian questions, the probability must be assumed that England—being at war with Italy—would not decide to commence operations against Germany. Without British support a warlike action by France against Germany is not to be anticipated.

The date of our attack on Czechoslovakia and Austria must be made dependent on the course of the Italian-English-French war and would not be simultaneous with the commencement of military agreements with Italy, but of full independence and, by exploiting this unique favorable opportunity he wishes to begin to carry out operations against Czechoslovakia. The attack on Czechoslovakia would have to take place with the "speed of lightning."

Field Marshal von Blomberg and General von Fritsch in giving their estimate on the situation, repeatedly pointed out that England and France must not appear as our enemies, and they stated that the war with Italy would NOT bind the French army to such an extent that it would NOT be in a position to commence operations on our Western frontier with superior forces. General von Fritsch estimated the French forces which would presumably be employed on the Alpine frontier against Italy to be in the region of 20 divisions, so that a strong French superiority would still remain on our Western frontier. The French would, according to German reasoning, attempt to advance into the Rhineland. We should consider the lead which France has got in mobilization, and quite apart from the very small value of our then existing fortifications—which was pointed out particularly by Field Marshal von Blomberg—the four motorized divisions which had been laid down for the West would be more or less incapable of movement. With regard to our offensive in a South-Easterly direction, Field Marshal von Blomberg draws special attention to the strength of the Czechoslovakian fortifications, the building of which had assumed the character of a Maginot line and

which would present extreme difficulties to our attack.

General von Fritsch mentioned that it was the purpose of a study which he had laid on for this winter to investigate the possibilities of carrying out operations against Czechoslovakia with special consideration of the conquest of the Czechoslovakian system of fortifications; the General also stated that owing to the prevailing conditions he would have to relinquish his leave abroad, which was to begin on 10 November. This intention was countermanded by the Führer who gave as a reason that the possibility of the conflict was not to be regarded as being so imminent. In reply to the remark by the Minister for Foreign Affairs, that an Italian-English-French conflict be not as near as the Führer appeared to assume, the Führer stated that the date which appeared to him to be a possibility was summer 1938. In reply to statements by Field Marshal von Blomberg and General von Fritsch regarding England and France's attitude, the Führer repeated his previous statements and said that he was convinced of Britain's non-participation and that consequently he did not believe in military action by France against Germany. Should the Mediterranean conflict already mentioned lead to a general mobilization in Europe, then we should have to commence operations against Czechoslovakia immediately. If, however, the powers who are not participating in the war should declare their disinterestedness, then Germany would, for the time being, have to side with this attitude.

In view of the information given by the Führer, General Goering considered it imperative to think of a reduction or abandonment of our military undertaking in Spain. The Führer agreed to this in so far as he believed this decision should be postponed for a suitable date.

The second part of the discussion concerned materiel armament questions.

[signed] Hossbach

See also Blomberg-Fritsch crisis, Hossbach Conference, Vol. 1.

The Nazis Arrive
in a Small Town

An ordinary German remembers how the Nazis took control of his small Bavarian town in 1933, inspiring both uncertainty and hope.

If somewhere a situation arises which causes people to say: "There's something in the air," one talks strikingly little about this situation and about this air which brings forebodings of some ominous occurrence. Such was the case between March 5 and 6, 1933, in our little town on the lake. The mood was one of slight weariness, like the early-March cloudy sky. The elections, carried out amid the enthusiasm of January 30, were over. Some of those who never grow weary even dreamed about the possibility of a coalition. Nobody joined them in their fantasies. Something like a hangover (though no one would admit it) stuck to the remembrances of these election results of March 5 [when the Nazis took over the Reichstag]. Those who before had declared that one must give Hitler a chance—maybe he will still make it, they would say, because otherwise we will have Bolshevism —seemed to have become somewhat unsure of what was in the offing. On the side of the victors, on the Brown one that is, such a suspicious stillness prevailed that no one could see clearly what was to come.

Then, with the first announcements, the bombs exploded! There were rumors, quickly denied, spread anew, again denied, and eventually repeated as facts: there was a revolution in Munich. Now it was a matter of indifference whether [Bavarian governor Heinrich] Held had resigned or had been ar-

rested, or whether [Bavarian interior minister] Stützel defended himself or not, or whether [Nazi official Franz Ritter von] Epp had been appointed State Commissioner, whether he was already in Munich or only on the plane.

The only important thing was that the Brown revolution had begun. What would happen now?

Timid persons recalled 1918. Utterances like "arrest of hostages," "put them against the wall," "surrender arms," were heard. Threats which had been uttered during the election campaigns a hundred times now took on the shape of reality. What was in the making?

In the meanwhile, the National Socialist leaders of the town clung feverishly to the telephone. What they heard from the party offices was no more certain than the rumors that ran through the streets. Confirmation, denial, alarm, denial. Confirmation, denial, but finally a sure, hard fact: Alarm! The order was sent out all over the country.

"The swastika is to be raised above all public buildings. Resistance is to be crushed!" The public did not know about this order, but they saw the results of its execution. The twilight had not yet been wholly tinged with darkness, when the SA was already under arms.

"The SA under arms" represented not one but two conceptions. First, "the SA"! The "old fighters" were long known in the town; some were looked upon with pity, with understanding, some with tolerance, others with repulsion and disgust. The townsfolk did not know the others who had joined since January 30 and who now marched in the brown uniform. There were many young people especially. Now they were standing

George L. Mosse, ed., *Nazi Culture.* New York: Schocken, 1981.

alongside the veterans, who had many fights behind them, palpitant with a lust for action.

"Under arms"! This was the second conception. In the cities where the SA was old enough to have been trained in the handling of guns, it must have been quite a military spectacle to see the Brown army equipped with all the accouterments of war. Here in the town the spectacle was of a military character only in the first ranks of the battalion; the other ranks looked more romantic than military. The marching went well, at least as far as one could judge in the darkness. The sudden wheeling to the right or left and the about-faces were reminiscent of recruits on the parade ground. At the order "Halt!" there was a picturesque potpourri, as in some movie scenes in which masses of Bedouins gesticulate wildly with rifles. Anyone who was not afraid to keep step with the marching executive committee of the revolution could hear the battle-scarred veterans giving all sorts of coarse admonitions to the young revolutionaries, such as: "Hold your rifle up, dummox!"

The only dangerous aspect about these goings-on was that the rifles were loaded with live ammunition. All that was needed was an unfortunate accident to set off this mostly untrained horde on a wild shooting spree. But who wanted to prevent a revolution in a little town? Therefore the SA marched under arms to carry out their first deed.

The District Office peacefully submitted to the violence and capitulated before the rifles; it hung a red banner with a black swastika from the skylight. An armed guard stayed behind for the security of the fluttering revolution. The mayor was not in the City Hall, but this too was of no importance. Whether he agreed or not, the banner would have been hoisted anyway. Again two guards stepped forward and placed themselves under the raised banner. By now several hundred people had arrived on the scene. They looked around here and there, like inspectors, and they asked one another

what the name of the song was which the armed men were singing in celebration of their victory. Hardly anyone knew the song. It was the "Horst Wessel" song. One of the initiated explained: "They've just sung 'Lift high the banner.'"

So much had the will of the people been fulfilled in this revolution.

But now there were not enough banners. That is, there were enough banners to fit in windows, but no big ones such as were proper for public buildings. But an order is an order! So they took the largest of the small banners—it measured about one meter on each side—and marched off with it toward the flagpole at the railroad station.

Again: "Attention!" Again: "Lift high the banner!" And the little red cloth hastily climbed up, ten times higher than its own length. It must have been quite lonesome up there for the little emblem of the great revolution. Thus the first victory had been achieved without bloodshed. The inn near the railroad station had become supreme political headquarters. Here the fighters met to drink toasts to their victory, while the older ones had some private scores to settle. They marched to the dwellings of the Red officials and took their first prisoners without encountering resistance. But it was only on the following day that people learned who had been beaten up, who had been delivered to Munich, whose houses had been searched. Outwardly everything looked peaceful, just as everything looks peaceful today. The burghers went to their regular tables in the pubs that night, even if they were not in their usual gay mood. A club meeting was held, but its members were somewhat distracted. Housewives were late in placing dinner on the table, and workers stayed home.

But armed guards stood at attention in front of three buildings in the town. But did they really stand, so to speak? At about ten o'clock that night two lads were leaning against an apartment building next to the City Hall, the collars of their civilian coats turned up, for the olive-green uniform coats of the SA had not yet been designed at that time. On their heads they wore the SA caps, signs of their revolutionary dignity, and on their left arms was the red band bearing the swastika. They were flirting excitedly with two well-stacked young women. It was a rather cold night. A cigarette might warm them up. So each of the lads stuck a cigarette in his mouth and the girls lit the matches, holding them under the noses of their heroes.

At this moment a man passed by. He was a member of the Stahlhelm [a right-wing veterans organization], hence not especially a friend—indeed, the very opposite. He walked up to the guards, who were comfortably leaning against the wall, and stood there, his legs spread, and yelled: "You louts! Don't you know that you're not supposed to smoke and flirt while you're on guard duty?" As if a superior had reprimanded them, the heroes of the day dropped their cigarettes and went to fetch their rifles, which were leaning peacefully against the wall. And they went back to the City Hall, marching like soldiers.

The Stahlhelmer had long since disappeared. So had the ladies. The banner of the revolution waved above its guards, who were silent and tight-lipped—until a gust of wind ripped the proud banner on the roof gutter, tearing it from top to bottom. It was wounded on the first day! . . .

It was high time that something was done about culture in our little town. During the years of struggle the movement had had no time to waste on such a luxury item as culture. Now, however, overnight, a man had been appointed whose job was to foster and promote culture. He was a kind of obscure character and his name was Rücke. Up to now nobody had ever heard of him, so he had to make people talk about him. There were about 120 clubs and associations in the town, about one third of which concerned themselves with cultural matters, not only those of the body but also those of the soul. There were music and choral soci-

eties, theater groups, and modest quartets, and folklore and literary circles.

Some of them were quite active. Since the city was near, hardly a week went by without the announcement of a concert or a lecture by some famous person. In addition, a large artists' colony was being established on the shores of the lake. Thus anyone who wanted to partake of the joys of culture could help himself freely. But even a cultural guardian of a town wants to do something on occasion. So he convened sessions for the purpose of discussing how another dozen performances could be added to the already existing fifty monthly performances, and how all the clubs and societies and their work could be united in one hand (centralization was now the last word)—in a Brown hand, of course. For this purpose a new association was called into being, the National Socialist Cultural Community.

The first thing it did was to make an ass of itself.

The cultural guardian called for a public meeting and delivered a long speech. At the end of it everybody wondered: What exactly did he want?

Strangely enough, he allowed free discussion. So he was asked what his speech had been all about and just what new plans he had in mind. The cultural guardian, no lazy man he, freely admitted that this was exactly what he would like to find out from the people assembled there. He would like to get his plan, and an idea on how to launch something novel, from the discussions. The people in the audience were vastly amused by this, but they were shy with suggestions after seeing one of the local physicians being treated quite rudely. The meeting had one result at least. A sheet of paper was passed around and all those who wanted to apply for membership and were prepared to contribute fifty pfennigs monthly were invited to sign it.

Then the cultural guardian himself had some ideas. Since it seemed to him that German culture had been neglected in recent years, he started the first cultural evening with a talk on the topic: "Five Years in Rumania." His daughter sang and read Rumanian poems, which, of course, nobody understood, but everyone applauded vigorously. Later she performed a Rumanian national dance with some other girls —I don't know whether it really was Rumanian. Finally he gave a two-hour lecture, during which he projected on the wall all the postcards he had received during his five-year stay in Rumania.

When the lights in the hall were switched on again the entire assemblage woke up with a fright, rubbing the sleep out of their eyes.

On Herr Rücke's second cultural evening, someone who had been in the Far East and Java told some fantastic stories which would have made Karl May [a nineteenth-century German novelist] turn green with envy.

After this double debut of German culture the cultural guardian disappeared inglori-ously and into his place stepped a certain Doctor Zweihäuser. His first project was the elimination of the National Socialist Cultural Community, whose function was taken over by the Combat Groups for German Culture. The members reaped several advantages from this new arrangement. First, instead of paying fifty pfennigs monthly, they were now privileged to pay one mark every month. The real advantage was that the new society did not bother them with any kind of perfor-mances, save for the collection of the dues. Instead something new was being founded, the Group for German Performances, which was to bring true National Socialist theater to the people. One had merely to become a member of this organization and pay for a seat in the theater each month and everything else was in perfect order.

See also Gleichschaltung, Vol. 1; SA, swastika, Vol. 2.

The Young Hitler Reveals His Dream of Power

August Kubizek, who befriended and lodged with the young Adolf Hitler in Vi-enna as teenagers, knew the future Führer as well as anyone in the years before the start of his military and political career. Kubizek remembered Hitler as a distant and enigmatic youth with a passion for art, architecture, and music, particularly the operas of Richard Wagner. On one occa-sion, after attending a performance of Wagner's Rienzi, *the tale of a heroic, god-like leader who frees his countrymen but dies tragically, a transported Hitler con-fided to Kubizek his own dream of future greatness.*

Now he aspired to something higher, something I could not yet fully under-stand. All this surprised me, because I be-lieved that the [life] of an artist was for him the highest of all goals, the one most worth striving for. But now he was speaking of an [order] he would one day receive from the people, to lead them out of [slavery] to the heights of freedom.

See also Hitler, Adolf; Kubizek, August, Vol 3.

Excerpted from August Kubizek, *The Young Hitler I Knew.* Trans. E.V. Anderson. Boston: Houghton Mifflin, 1955.

Papen Recounts Hitler's Takeover

Papen recalls the details of January 1933 when, thanks to a complicated mix of back-room intrigues and political miscalculations, President Paul von Hindenburg agreed to accept a German government with Adolf Hitler as chancellor and Papen himself as vice-chancellor.

Hitler declined flatly to join the Schleicher Government, and insisted again and again that the only circumstances in which the Nazis would co-operate would be under his Chancellorship. He complained that our communiqué on August 13 had declared that he had demanded exclusive power for the party. That had not been true; nor did he make that demand now. It would be easy to reach agreement on a coalition with members of the bourgeois parties, providing these ministers maintained the institution of a Presidential Cabinet and did not remain responsible to their own parties. During the evening, Hitler repeated all these arguments to [Otto] Meissner and Oscar Hindenburg, on whom he seemed to make a strong impression.

I wish to make it quite clear that the actual question of forming a cabinet with Hitler as Chancellor was not discussed by Oscar Hindenburg, Meissner or myself. I had had no contact whatever with Hitler between January 4 and 22.

January 23: A decisive development. Schleicher saw the President and told him that his plan to split the Nazi Party could no longer be carried out. There was therefore no possibility of forming a Cabinet with a parliamentary majority, unless Hitler became Chancellor. The only alternative was to declare a state of emergency and dissolve the Reichstag. Schleicher asked for the powers to do this.

I had been right on December 1. Schleicher's plan was now identical with my own, but when he asked the President to countenance a breach of the Constitution, [President Paul von] Hindenburg answered: 'On December 2 you declared that such a measure would lead to civil war. The Army and the police, in your opinion, were not strong enough to deal with internal unrest on a large scale. Since then the situation has been worsening for seven weeks. The Nazis consider themselves in a stronger position, and the left wing is more radical in its intentions than ever. If civil war was likely then, it is even more so now, and the Army will be still less capable of coping with it. In these circumstances I cannot possibly accede to your request for dissolution of the Reichstag and *carte blanche* to deal with the situation.'

January 24: The public was still ignorant of Schleicher's rebuff at the hands of the President, but the German Nationalists returned to the attack on the government. They declared that Schleicher's policy meant surrender of the authoritarian principles which led to the formation of the Papen Cabinet. Some sections of the press demanded my return as Chancellor. Schleicher declared his intention of refraining from any breach of the Constitution. Yet there was no sign of any parliamentary majority to support him.

January 25: No attempt was made to organize a breathing-space for Schleicher. [German Nationalist leader Alfred] Hugenberg, presumably offended by Schleicher's

Franz von Papen, *Memoirs*. Trans. Brian Connell. New York: E.P. Dutton, 1953.

refusal on January 13 to take him into the Government, seemed to have made up his mind to oppose him at all costs.

January 26: More confusion and a new set of rumours. The Harzburger Front combination of German Nationalists and Nazis appeared to be finding common ground in their opposition to Schleicher. The possibility of a resignation of the Government was being mooted. One would have thought that the more moderate parties would press for a postponement of the opening of Parliament, to give a little more time for the settlement of the crisis.

January 27: The Reichstag Steering Committee met again, and agreed that the Reichstag should assemble, as arranged, on the 31st. The existence of the Government was now clearly threatened. Many organs of public opinion considered that everything depended on the Chancellor obtaining full powers from the President. It was still not known that this had already been refused. In view of the difficulties involved in granting power to Hitler, there were again suggestions in many quarters that I should form a new Government. The Nazis announced that they would take no part in any plan to declare a state of emergency and govern without either elections or Parliament.

In my report to Hindenburg after the meeting in [Nazi adviser Joachim von] Ribbentrop's house on the 22nd, I had recommended that Schleicher be given every opportunity to reach some agreement with the Reichstag, and that the President should allow a little more time for this. It was still possible that he might get agreement to a postponement. I had advised against my own reappointment as Chancellor, as I felt that my chances were even slimmer than they had been two months previously. I saw the President again on the 27th and told him there could be no question of my accepting the responsibility; it would simply mean a return to my plan of December 1. I asked him to let Schleicher know that I had no intention of threatening the Government's position in this way.

January 28: Schleicher played one more card. In the *Tägliche Rundschau,* the paper he controlled, an inspired article suggested that a Papen Cabinet with dictatorial powers would threaten the President's own position. The article announced that Schleicher would call on the President to make a formal request for powers to dissolve the Reichstag. If this was not granted, the Cabinet would resign and the President would have to assume sole responsibility for subsequent developments. Three possibilities would then present themselves: a coalition between the Nazis and the Zentrum [the Center parties] which was unlikely in view of Zentrum objections to the Nazis taking over the ministries of defence, transport and the interior; a Cabinet formed from the [1931 Right-Wing] Harzburger Front, in which the Nazis would meet opposition from Hugenberg to Hitler's appointment as Chancellor; or, as Hugenberg wanted it, a dictatorial Cabinet under Papen, supported by the German Nationalists and dependent on the granting of full powers by the President. The article considered that this last solution would be catastrophic; such a Cabinet would lead to a crisis in the Presidency, which should be avoided at all costs.

After this attempt to mobilize public opinion, Schleicher went to the President, but his demand for full powers for himself again met the arguments the President had used on the 23rd. Hindenburg refused to grant the dissolution of the Reichstag, and Schleicher presented the resignation of his whole Cabinet.

He had given up all hope of organizing a parliamentary majority, and had come round to the opinion that a Presidential Cabinet under Hitler was the only solution. After Schleicher's resignation, the Nazis made it clear that they would only settle for a Government with Hitler as Chancellor. During the whole of January their press had rejected in the sharpest possible terms any idea of a second Papen Government. The course of events after January 4 makes it impossible to defend the idea that my interview with Hitler on that date opened the way for his Chancellorship. In later years the Socialists have also made much play with the accusation that I prevented Schleicher from basing part of his support on the Trade Unions. Yet no less an authority than Gustav Noske, the Socialist leader, makes it quite clear in his memoirs that Leipart, the Trade Union leader, was instructed by the Social Democrats not to respond to

Schleicher's overtures. The Strasser-Leipart 'axis', on which Schleicher hoped to build the fortunes of his Government, was therefore doomed to failure.

About midday on January 28 I was called to the President. He gave me an account of Schleicher's last visit and his resignation. He had been told at an early hour of the *Tägliche Rundschau* article, with its threats of a crisis in the Presidency and the possibility of a breach of the Constitution being

Hitler shakes hands with German president Paul von Hindenburg, who reluctantly appointed Hitler chancellor in Berlin in January 1933.

regarded as treason. He would have expected such methods from a politician, he told me, but he could not forgive an officer for employing them. The possibility of my forming another Government was barely touched on, and then only in contrast to what he considered the unpleasant duty of calling on Hitler. I made what suggestions I could for keeping the Nazis within bounds. These were adopted when the new Cabinet was formed two days later. The President then asked me, as *homo regius* [king maker], to sound out the possibilities of forming a Cabinet under Hitler within the terms of the Constitution. I felt I had to carry out the President's request, because no one else seemed capable of reaching an acceptable compromise with Hitler. If the Defence and Foreign Ministries were given to people in whom the President had confidence, some of the other posts could be given with a clear conscience to the Nazis. Later in the day the Reichstag Steering Committee met again and agreed to postpone the session announced for Monday, the 31st, to give time for the formation of a new government.

I had my first interview with Hugenberg on the afternoon of January 28. He shared my opinion that Hitler would under no circumstances form a majority Government. There was no point in calling again on Schleicher, who had antagonized all the right wing parties, and only retained the confidence of the Zentrum. We had to reach some agreement with Hitler and seek to limit his prerogatives as much as possible. Hugenberg demanded the Reich and Prussian Ministries of Economics, in return for the support of the German Nationalists.

Thereupon I received Hitler. As I expected, he refused flatly to form a Government based on a parliamentary majority. If the President desired his movement to cooperate in the work of government, then he must be allowed to form a Presidential Cabinet with the same rights as those accorded to Schleicher and myself. On the other hand, he had no intention of making exaggerated ministerial demands, and was perfectly prepared to include certain men from previous Cabinets who enjoyed the President's confidence.

I told him that the mission I had undertaken on behalf of the President did not permit Hitler discretion in choosing the members of the Cabinet. He replied that the President could fill all the ministerial posts, provided the ministers regarded themselves as independent of the political parties. Hitler desired to be Chancellor and Commissioner for Prussia, and wanted a member of his party to be Minister of the Interior in both the Reich and Prussia.

Later the same evening I saw Dr. Schaeffer of the Bavarian People's Party. He told me that both he and [Heinrich] Brüning were prepared to accept ministerial posts under Hitler. I had to reply that there was no question of this. Hitler was not engaged in forming a majority Government, and wanted his Cabinet to consist of people without party affiliations. I expressed my regret that Brüning should have made up his mind to collaborate with Hitler so late in the day, at a time when co-operation was no longer possible. In reply, Schaeffer emphasized that there was no question of himself and Brüning joining a Papen Cabinet.

Dr. Schaeffer was to appear as a prosecution witness at my denazification trial in 1947. He confirmed under oath that he had expressed his own and Brüning's willingness to share in the work of a Hitler Cabinet and blamed me for not having taken up the offer. Brüning, on the other hand, has declared that he never had the least intention of joining a Hitler Cabinet. They cannot both be right.

It was late at night before I was able to report progress to the President. He seemed gratified at the moderation Hitler had displayed, and was delighted that men like [cold-school diplomats] Neurath, Schwerin-Krosigk, Guertner and Eltz would retain their posts in the new Government. He insisted once again that the Foreign and War

Ministries should be put in the hands of completely reliable people. Neurath was to remain Foreign Minister, and we ranged over the list of possible names for the War Ministry. My own suggestion was General von Fritsch, with whom I had spent my early military career and whose capabilities I admired. Hindenburg did not turn him down, but indicated that he would prefer someone with whom he was better acquainted. Finally he came out with the name of General von Blomberg, whom he had known as Commander of the East Prussian military district. Hindenburg considered him a gifted professional soldier, completely apolitical and with a pleasant personality. As head of the German military delegation at the Disarmament Commission, he had shown himself the possessor of all the qualities necessary for a minister. I had only a passing acquaintance with him, but I felt that I could rely on Hindenburg's judgment. If, as the President said, he had kept out of politics, it should be possible to rely on him to turn a deaf ear to the blandishments of the Nazis.

Hindenburg then went on to suggest that I should get Hugenberg to take over the combined Economic posts in one ministry. He also asked me to get from Hitler the names of the Nazis he wished to appoint to the Cabinet. His final request, right at the end of our conversation, was for me to take on the post of deputy Chancellor, as he particularly wished to retain my services for the time being. I must confess that this request came as no surprise, but I wish to emphasize that I had at no time made any such suggestion myself. It seemed a natural precaution for him to take, once he had finally made up his mind to take the dreaded plunge of appointing Hitler as Chancellor. I felt it was the least service I could give, and I undertook to accept the post if we succeeded in forming the Cabinet.

January 29: Another day of interviews and discussions. My first visitors were Hitler and [Hermann] Goering. They said they wished to appoint [Wilhelm] Frick as Reich Minister of the Interior, and Goering himself to the same post in Prussia. Frick was known as a senior Civil servant and a man of moderate opinions, who had been a success as head of the State Government of Thuringia. Both my visitors insisted that the Prussian police, which had been in the hands of the Social Democrats for ten years, would have to undergo certain changes in personnel. They declared that this would be necessary if the police were to be relied upon to deal effectively with the Communists, and with my experiences in the previous July in mind, I felt that this was by no means a negligible argument. I told Hitler that the President did not intend to give him powers as Reich Commissioner for Prussia, and that these would remain vested in me as Vice-Chancellor. Hitler accepted this decision with a bad grace, but did not make an issue of it.

My conversations with Hugenberg and some of his Harzburger Front colleagues were chiefly about the measures we should adopt to combat the Nazis' totalitarian tendencies, but we reached no definite plan. I told Hugenberg that the President wished him to act as a coordinator of economic affairs, and he seemed to consider this immense task well within his powers. He then introduced [Georg] Seldte and [Theodor] Duesterberg, the two leaders of the Stahlhelm organization, who undertook to give the new Government their support.

The Stahlhelm, it should be remarked, had always been a conservative and stabilizing factor in the political warfare of the day. It was a well organized association of ex-servicemen, with a very considerable membership, whose activities had always provided a contrast with the excesses of the Brownshirts and the Communist Rotfront. Stahlhelm support would be an important factor in maintaining some sort of balance against the Nazis. We decided that their cooperation should be further assured by appointing Seldte Minister of Labour. The Stahlhelm had always been renowned for the efficiency of its social insurance scheme, which had largely been built up by Seldte himself, and we felt that this was a particularly apt appointment.

My visitors were not all of such an approving turn of mind. A number of my Conservative friends begged me to take no part whatever in forming a Hitler Cabinet. I explained time and again that there was no other solution within the framework of the Constitution. The political parties, and the Socialists in particular, could have given Schleicher one last chance by postponing the meeting of the Reichstag. By failing to do so, they had tacitly acknowledged that the only alternative to Hitler was a breach of the Constitution.

Schleicher, in the meantime, found another card to play. He sent one of his private emissaries, von Alvensleben, to Goering, who immediately hurried over to me with the news. Schleicher had sent a message that my real intention was to deceive the Nazis, and that they would do very much better to combine with Schleicher, who only wished to retain the post of Minister of Defence. Alvensleben had indicated that means could be found to neutralize Hindenburg. Schleicher had apparently even gone so far as to suggest that if the 'old gentleman' should prove difficult, he, Schleicher, would mobilize the Potsdam garrison. Goering told me that he and Hitler had returned a flat negative to the plan and had immediately told Meissner and Oscar von Hindenburg.

This sequel to the *Tägliche Rundschau*'s remarks about a crisis in the Presidency seemed highly dangerous. I hurried to see Hindenburg, whose son had told him of this new development. He seemed comparatively unmoved, and declined to believe that a serving general and Chancellor, albeit a provisional one, would lend himself to such a step against the head of the State. We decided, however, that it was absolutely essential to have a new Minister of Defence, and a telegram was sent to Blomberg asking him to leave Geneva immediately and report to the President in Berlin the next day.

The rumour got about that Schleicher was planning a Reichswehr Putsch to remove the President. Whether, in fact, he ever really intended to take this step, or discussed it with General von Hammerstein, the Chief of Staff, will probably never be known. But it is interesting to record that when Blomberg arrived at the railway station next day, one of Hammerstein's staff officers was there to greet him with orders to report to the General immediately. The fact that he was returning was known to no one outside Hindenburg's official household and myself, so Schleicher must therefore have been tapping wires again. This attempt to get Blomberg to Hammerstein failed, because Oscar von Hindenburg was also at the station and escorted him to the President. The whole atmosphere had become so fantastic, with this possible threat of a coup, that I made up my mind to get the Cabinet formed as quickly as we could.

January 30: Blomberg saw the President at about 9 o'clock in the morning and was given a résumé of the situation. The President impressed upon him most particularly the necessity of reversing Schleicher's course and keeping the Army out of politics. At about half-past ten the members of the proposed Cabinet met in my house and walked across the garden to the Presidential palace, where we waited in Meissner's office. Hitler immediately renewed his complaints about not being appointed Commissioner for Prussia. He felt that this severely restricted his power. I told him that the President still wished to be convinced that we were all going to co-operate harmoniously, and that the question of the Prussian appointment could be left until later. To this, Hitler replied that if his powers were to be thus limited, he must insist on new Reichstag elections. To our surprise he produced the argument that the new combination between the Nazi movement and the right wing groups did not command a parliamentary majority, but if they now went to the country, their position would be assured.

This produced a completely new situation and the debate became heated. Hugenberg, in particular, objected to the idea, and Hitler tried to pacify him by stating that he would make no changes in the Cabinet, whatever the result might be. We all took this with a pinch of salt, but Neurath, Schwerin-Krosigk and Eltz did not raise any objections to the idea of new elections. By this time it was long past eleven o'clock, the time that had been appointed for our interview with the President, and Meissner asked me to end our discussion, as Hindenburg was not prepared to wait any longer.

We had had such a sudden clash of opinions that I was afraid our new coalition would break up before it was born. My immediate reaction to the election idea was that it should be possible to organize a strong group of Conservative candidates to provide some counterweight to the Nazis. I still believed that an electoral bloc of this type would appeal to the voters, and begged Hugenberg to withdraw his objections. We decided to ask the President for a dissolution decree, and extracted from Hitler a promise that he would contact the Zentrum and the Bavarian People's Party, in order to ensure the widest possible basis for a parliamentary majority. At last we were shown in to the President and I made the necessary formal introductions. Hindenburg made a short speech about the necessity for full cooperation in the interests of the nation, and we were then sworn in. The Hitler Cabinet had been formed.

See also Machtergreifung, Vol. 2; Papen, Franz von, Vol. 3.

Germany Needs Simple Soldiers

Ernst Röhm, leader of the SA, or storm troopers, until Hitler had him murdered in 1934, argues in a 1928 tract that what Germany requires is soldierly comradeship and "hate" rather than "maturity" or "diplomacy." These latter qualities, he implies, only made the nation weak.

I have opened here the book of my life to the understanding friend as well as to the nagging philistine.

The narrow-minded petit bourgeois may find my attitude injudicious, but that does not bother me.

Many books have been written, but few with such reckless frankness.

Even my political friends may have found some of my opinions objectionable; my soldier's sensibility compelled me, in spite of the prevalent onesidedness of thought and feeling, to recognize the merits of the enemy no less than the shortcomings of the friend.

I am a believer in plain talk and have not hid my heart like a skeleton in the closet.

I must write without fear, with defiance —just as it comes from my soul.

And yet nothing was further from my intention than to offend or to injure anyone. Soldiers' talk is rough and direct, but we soldiers all speak the same language and understand each other.

The "soldiers' emperor," Napoleon, is reported to have said on one occasion during his exile: "Soldiers will never be able to

George L. Mosse, ed., *Nazi Culture.* New York: Schocken, 1981.

SA commander Ernst Röhm forswore "peace and order" and instead advocated hatred and soldierly comradeship "cemented with blood."

hate me, even if they have faced me on the battlefield."

The wife of a soldier in my company, whose political convictions were far removed from mine, said to me on one occasion: "In the heart of my husband, his captain takes the first place; there is nobody to outrank him. Only then come his mother and I."

And another of my soldiers, a Communist, during the period of the soldiers' councils, jumped up in a meeting at which the officers were being denounced, and shouted: "I don't know whether what you are saying about the officers is true, but I know that as far as my captain is concerned, it's not true."

This is the way in which the hand of a soldier reaches out beyond all differences of class, rank, and political philosophy. Soldierly comradeship, cemented with blood, can perhaps temporarily relax, but it can never be torn out of the heart, it cannot be exterminated.

Still, all of Germany has not been awakened yet—despite National Socialism. My words shall be a trumpet call to those who are still asleep.

I am not appealing to the hustling and sneaky trader who has made accursed gold his God, but to the warrior who is struggling in the battle of life, who wants to win freedom and with it the kingdom of heaven.

I approve of whatever serves the purpose of German freedom. I oppose whatever runs counter to it. Europe, aye, the whole world, may go down in flames—what concern is it of ours? Germany must live and be free.

One may call me a bigoted fool—I can't help that. I am opposed to sport in its present form and to its effects. Moreover, I consider it a definite national danger. We cannot rebuild the Fatherland with champions and artificially nurtured "big guns of sport." Only the most careful development which provides physical strength and capability, with spiritual elasticity and ethical backbone, can be of use to the Volk community. Indeed, it is in keeping with these times of pretense and advertising: rubbish, confusion of the senses and sensation, have no enduring essence. . . .

The Germans have forgotten how to hate.

Virile hate has been replaced by feminine lamentation. But he who is unable to hate cannot love either. Fanatical love and hate—their fires kindle flames of freedom.

Passionlessness, matter-of-factness, objectivity, are impersonality, are sophistry.

Only passion gives knowledge, creates wisdom.

"Peace and order" is the battle cry of people living on pensions. In the last analysis you cannot govern a state on the basis of the needs of pensioners.

"One is being circumspect," wrote the [Munich newspaper] *Münchner Zeitung* in 1927 on the occasion of French attacks in the occupied zone [the French-occupied Ruhr in western Germany], "if one peacefully takes a punch in the ears."

Translated into German it means "peace and order," hence simply shaking at the knees.

Once more to hell with this peace and prudence, with the half-hearted, the middlings, the cowards!

"Non-circumspect" persons fought four and a half years at the front! The "circumspect" ones remained at home!

"Immature" persons fought in Upper Silesia for the preservation of the Reich. The "mature" persons locked themselves behind their doors.

"Irresponsible dreamers" for years and years have called upon the people to rise up against enslavement and oppression. The "responsible politicians" of the new Germany in these same years have sold Germany lock, stock, and barrel.

Our people and Fatherland are slowly but surely going under because of "circumspection" and "maturity."

From time immemorial Germany was not suited to "diplomacy" and "politics." The sword has always determined the greatness of its history.

"I most respectfully beg of the diplomats not to lose again what the soldier has gained with his blood." This is what [General] Blücher had to write his king, Frederick William II, after the Battle of "Belle-Alliance" [between France and Prussia during the Napoleonic Wars].

Only the soldier could lead his people and Fatherland out of wretchedness and shame to freedom and honor.

See also Days of Struggle, Vol. 1; SA, Vol. 2; Röhm, Ernst, Vol. 3.

A Participant Remembers the Beer Hall Putsch of 1923

In this selection Otto Strasser, an early Nazi leader and journalist who fell from grace and went into exile in the 1930s, recalls the events of the Beer Hall Putsch of November 1923. After political and military leaders failed to support Adolf Hitler, he staged a march through the streets ending up in a firefight. Strasser points out, as official Nazi accounts never did, that Hitler tried to escape wearing the dress of a female supporter.

Dawn was long in coming, and while the hands on the huge clock moved with maddening slowness the Nazis became increasingly restive. The hall presented a strange scene: some were sprawled across chairs, trying to get an hour's rest; others sat dumbly, staring into the distance, dreaming of tomorrow and the tomorrows that would follow; still others were gathered in excited groups about the untidy, litter-laden tables discussing the unexpected measure of their success and speculating on future developments.

The day began. Eight o'clock came, and passed. Nine o'clock—still no sign of the honor guard that was supposed to escort Hitler to the Governor's Palace for the ceremony marking the new national government. Open signs of worry began to appear on the faces of the Nazis in the hall. The men began to mutter. Was it possible that the victory that had seemed so easy the night before could be only a delusion? What made the waiting even worse was the fact that Hitler gave no news of developments, if any, to his men. More rumors filled the hall: the Communists had started a counterrevolution; [Bavarian governor Gustav] von Kahr had outlawed the Nazi Party and declared that all its members were guilty of high treason; the Bavarian authorities had appealed to Berlin for aid, and even now a powerful arm of the regular army was on its way to Munich to exterminate the insurrectionists. . . .

Now Hitler stepped out on the platform and an immediate hush fell over the men. He looked pale and haggard, his eyes red-rimmed and bloodshot from lack of sleep. There was a tired note in his hoarse voice as he called: "Fritz! Reinhart!"

Two uniformed brown-shirted men stepped smartly down to the apron of the stage. Hitler leaned over and whispered to them for a moment; only those closest to the trio heard what he said. "Go to von Kahr," he ordered. "Find out the reason for this delay and report back immediately to me." The two Nazis turned on their heels and went back up the aisle at the double.

A new feeling ran through the beer hall. This was action at last! Troopers tightened their belts, backs straightened, sleep-heavy eyes opened to take on a new sparkle. The spirit of dull, passive waiting changed to one of eager, active anticipation; the feeling of uncertainty was gone.

But another long hour passed without further news. The messengers did not return, and Hitler sent out a second pair of Brown Shirts. More dreary waiting. The dark suspicion that von Kahr did not intend to go through with the plan now became a certainty. The Governor, the men now knew, was backing out of the deal; his pleading for

sleep the night before and postponing the official ratification of the new government showed he never had intended to go through with it. He was doublecrossing Hitler: a case of the betrayer being betrayed.

Hitler was frantic. It was almost impossible for him to chart an accurate course of action without knowing what was happening on the outside. He could take for granted the fact that Governor von Kahr was against him, but he had no way of telling what form the opposition would take. There were three lines of action open to him. He might call a halt to the entire proceedings, send his men home and face the ridicule of Bavaria once more. Hitler's pride and vanity made this unthinkable—and he was keen enough to realize such a move would sound the death knell for National Socialism, fanatical though his belief in the movement might be. On the other hand, he could attempt to take over the government of Munich by force, which would lead to bloody fighting in which Hitler's poorly armed legions could only come out second-best. Consequently he rejected that course in spite of the pleadings and fiery assurances of such hell-for-leather fighters as Ludendorff, Kriebel and Gregor Strasser. The third choice—the middle course—was to march his Nazis through Munich and hope that such a parade would stir a mighty street demonstration into being; that government employees, laborers, clerks, men in the factories would leave their jobs and come flocking to his banner; that by sheer weight of numbers, by spontaneous public demand, the revolution would become an accomplished fact.

Yet Adolf Hitler must have known there was little merit in this plan; it had occurred to me, and I had at once realized it would be a stratagem of the last resort—which, indeed, is what it was used for now, since there was no other way.

At midday Hitler walked out onto the stage of the Bürgerbrau and again silence fell immediately over the crowd. He had made up his mind, and the tired lines seemed

Heinrich Himmler (holding flag) and SA storm troopers march through the streets of Munich during the Beer Hall Putsch of November 8–9, 1923.

to have been magically erased from his face. A new resolute light shone in his eyes and there was something in his manner that told the Nazis they were to see action. Almost as one man they surged forward and stood, expectant, in a closely packed mass before him. An electric moment of tension and utter quiet held the room.

Hitler raised a clenched fist in the air. "Comrades, we march!" he thundered.

A tremendous roar of exultation filled the beer hall. That spontaneous shout shook the glasses on the tables, echoed from the ceiling and reverberated from the walls. It must have been deafening even in the street outside.

Hitler motioned to Gregor [Strasser], and Gregor in turn gave the order to a squad of twelve burly storm troopers. They moved up the aisle like a human wedge and cut through the crowd of curious people jamming the entrance to the Bürgerbrau. Close-packed at their heels came the vanguard of the Brown

Shirt legions. They poured through the narrow entrance and spilled out into Marien-platz, the famous square on which the palace of the kings of Bavaria stands.

Troopers quickly formed in columns of fours. Banners went arrogantly aloft. Eyes were bright with the promise of coming excitement. Eagerness, youth and swashbuckling courage were the strongest weapons of this little army. Even the spectators lining the curbs felt a lift from this picture of men who dared.

The Nazis were following their leader!

Hitler stood proudly at the head of the parade, Goering on his left, Ludendorff on his right. The Leader's right arm rose in the air, fell, and the columns, marching smartly four abreast, set out for Ludwigstrasse, Munich's main street. Leading from Marienplatz to Ludwigstrasse was Residenzstrasse, a narrow alley into which the marching storm troopers barely fitted, and which opened into the wide main street.

Swinging forward bravely, a spontaneous song now bursting from the ranks, the men squeezed through the alley and into Ludwigstrasse; windows were thrown open on all sides as the citizens were attracted by the full-throated song and the pound of marching feet; other spectators came running to line the walks of Ludwigstrasse just ahead. At the head of the column, Hitler was the first to see the armed squad of General von Lossow's Reichswehr standing on the steps of Feldherren-Halle, the monument built following the Franco-Prussian war to honor the Bavarian unknown soldiers of all time. His face went deathly pale. Instinctively, he threw wide his arms to halt the column; then, as quickly, started forward again.

There was no cheering from the grimly absorbed spectators, who stood well back from the scene of trouble. This was no march of triumph; it was tragedy in the making. And Hitler's storm troops, still cooped in the alley, were unable to see what was going on ahead. Their challenging battle chants struck a bizarre note now, like a blind man unwittingly singing at a funeral.

Hitler had taken no more than four steps forward when Lieutenant Ernst Brown, in charge of the small detachment of some eighty Reichswehr, called ringingly for him to halt. Hitler found himself looking into the business ends of machine guns and rifles; he stopped irresolutely.

Standing there, he must have thought fast and concluded that the soldiers would never dare to carry out the threat to shoot; von Kahr couldn't possibly have given such an order. Hitler stepped forward again, his courage stemming from an inner conviction of his own safety. Goering and Ludendorff followed willingly at his heels, proud of his action.

"Halt!" the command rang out again, and now rifles snapped to the shoulder position, leveling.

Hitler kept marching.

A third time—the last—Lieutenant Brown ordered them to halt, and this time there

was no mistaking the menace in his voice. Rifles tightened against the shoulders of the troops and eyes took aim along the barrel sights. Machine-gun squads crouched more closely about their weapons. Again Hitler stopped short, his men close-packed directly behind him.

All this had happened so suddenly that he had had no opportunity to plan an escape from the trap. And it was certainly not courage that held him facing those menacing guns now; it was sheer vanity and pride. He couldn't allow himself to be faced down before all the onlookers, who were potential party followers. Hitler's fear was great, but his greater concern was that such a fear would be shown publicly—and the result passed for heroism. But his dilemma was still unsolvable: his vanity wouldn't let him retreat, his fear wouldn't let him advance further, and circumstance certainly wouldn't let him remain where he was.

Although his own men outnumbered the loyalist soldiers by more than ten to one, they were still at a serious disadvantage. Only the first four rows of marching Nazis were aware of what was happening—and, should a pitched battle break out, they would be the only ones who could return the soldiers' fire. Now those farther back in the alley, finding themselves halted, started pushing forward.

Hitler faced Lieutenant Brown. He raised his right hand, pointed his forefinger at the officer and began to speak. All of which was simply a desperate stall for time; Hitler probably didn't even know what he was saying—anything would do—just so he could have a few seconds to form a plan of action or scheme a face-saving escape. But it didn't work—for at that moment the impatient shoves of the rear columns pushed the front ranks forward, Hitler along with them.

Lieutenant Brown would wait no more. Pivoting, he faced his troops with arm raised. "Fire!" he shouted.

There was a staccato burst of sound. Flame spurted from a score of muzzles. The chatter of a machine gun was drowned in screams of agony.

What followed is among the most tragicomic episodes of post-war history.

Hitler, of course, was in the direct line of fire, but Ulrich Graf, a Brown Shirt in the front ranks of the marchers, threw himself in front of Hitler and with his own body protected the Nazi Fuehrer. A slug caught Graf in the side and he fell bleeding—and Hitler flung himself flat on the ground, allowing Goering and the aged Ludendorff to continue marching into the hail of death. All the versions that say anything else are false. Adolf Hitler in his cowardice flung himself ignominiously to the ground. Goering, on his left, was hit in the thigh by a bullet and he staggered after Hitler, who was now crawling as fast as possible toward safety. But General Ludendorff, head held proudly erect, marched directly toward those blazing ranks of guns.

For sheer dramatic power I have never seen anything that equaled this act. There was the great and aging General, former idol of millions of troops, supreme leader of one of the finest fighting machines the world had ever seen, now marching at the head of a threadbare gang of insurrectionists—and doing it in a way that still retained every bit of nobility he had ever carried. Indeed, I think he was even more impressive in that moment.

Can you see him? He is old; the war years have added decades to his shoulders. His hair is gray and his step is not as firm as it once was. Even his proud military dress, with its ranks of beribboned decorations, is gone—for today he is dressed in a frock coat and carries a black cane instead of a bright sword. But he is a soldier still; he is a leader, a master of soldiers. He is a hero, because that is his very character. And he marches forward at the head of the last army he is ever to command—a pitiful little band of revolutionists. And he doesn't let them down.

General Ludendorff's magnificent disdain of death, his splendid courage and soldierly nobility, so disconcerted the loyalist ranks that they ceased firing as he drew close to them. What man among them, who had followed him for years, could have shot him down then? And in that very moment, Adolf Hitler and Hermann Goering had reached the sanctuary of a convenient alley—one sprinting down it, the other hobbling after as fast as his wounded leg would allow.

Still, the deadly mission of von Kahr's troops had been accomplished. The proposed revolution had been summarily broken and the ringleaders had been put to flight. Residenzplatz alley had packed the Nazis in so closely that it was impossible for von Kahr's soldiers to miss. In the fighting—which was short, sharp and one-sided—thirteen Brown Shirts were killed outright and forty were wounded. The very first blast of gunfire had disorganized the Nazi ranks and the main body of troops had turned in panic and fled back to Marienplatz. Nor was that any reflection on the fighting spirit of Hitler's men; they knew their strategic position was hopeless, funneled as they were into a concentrated blast of gunfire.

Captain [Ernst] Roehm had taken possession of the officers' club the night before and had remained there secure in the belief that the National Socialist revolution had succeeded. Being a skillful officer, the captain had been able to storm the staff officers' building and capture it and its occupants with the loss of but three men. The first he knew about the failure of the revolution was when a large detachment of regular troops surrounded the building and placed him under arrest.

Gregor succeeded in reforming a part of his Landshut contingent in Marienplatz, but without a specific objective and additional support it was useless and foolhardy to give battle. Since I was not a Nazi, I had joined none of the revolutionary groups but had remained well on the sidelines as an observer. After the sharp exchange before the Feldherren-Halle I was naturally greatly concerned about Gregor and rushed immediately to Marienplatz, where I found him with his reassembled troops. He was at that moment giving the order to return home when I joined him for the march.

It was a sullen group that tramped the miles back to Landshut; the men were in an ugly mood. Their comrades had been shot down and left dead and dying in the streets; their movement was completely smashed and beyond repair—or at least, so it seemed even to the most optimistic. What further oppressive measures Governor von Kahr would take they did not know, although they could assume that such measures would definitely be taken.

Hitler fled from Munich by himself. Not even Goering could keep up with him as he crawled to the corner, where he jumped up and took to his heels. A short distance from the scene of the shooting he commandeered a private car at gun's point and forced the driver to take him to the small town of Uffing, where lived Frau Hanfstaengel, the mother of one of his financial backers. Her son was "Putzie" Hanfstaengel, the Harvard University graduate and Americanized Nazi who later became foreign press representative for the Nazi party.

For three days Hitler remained at this house, in hiding. On the third day there came a knock at the door, an insistent knock that had the sound of authority behind it. While Hitler rushed into the bedroom, Frau Hanfstaengel ran downstairs to answer it. Four uniformed policemen stood there.

One of them said stiffly: "We have reason to believe that Herr Adolf Hitler is hiding here."

"That is not so, officer!" Frau Hanfstaengel answered quickly.

"In that case," he said, pushing past her, "you can certainly have no objection to us looking through the house."

Frau Hanfstaengel planted herself in the doorway and said angrily: "I won't have you going through this house. I forbid it!"

One of the police officers then produced a search warrant. His impatience showed in his abrupt tone. "Make way, frau!"

While one of the officers guarded the front door, three other police mounted the steps. Entering the bedroom in the course of their search, they came upon a door leading to a large wardrobe. An officer pulled the door open and saw a woman standing within, straightening dresses on the hangers. The officer seized her and spun her around. "She" had a black stubby mustache!

So Hitler was placed under arrest wearing one of Frau Hanfstaengel's dresses—the last comic touch in a comic-opera revolution.

At the time Hitler was taken, Gregor, [Heinrich] Himmler and I were seated at luncheon at my brother's house in Landshut. There was a knock at the door and my brother-in-law entered at Gregor's summons.

"You're just in time for lunch, Georg," Gregor said. "Pull up a chair and join us."

My brother-in-law appeared nervous. "I—I can't."

"What do you mean?" Gregor boomed in his hospitable way.

Georg told him somewhat apologetically, "I've come to arrest you. Orders from Munich, you know."

"Don't look so tragic about it, man," Gregor chided him, as he and Himmler got to their feet.

"How about me?" I asked. "Am I under arrest too?"

Georg shook his head. "No, Otto. Only Gregor and Heinrich."

See also Beer Hall Putsch, Vol. 1; Strasser, Otto, Vol. 3.

The Twenty-Five Points of the German Workers' Party

Adolf Hitler announced the following program in a speech in February 1920, one of his first speeches as a leader of the German Workers' Party, the precursor of the Nazi Party. The points were developed by Hitler and party founder Anton Drexler, who indicate that their movement is built around both Germanic nationalism and certain Socialist economic measures. Although Hitler later dropped the economic measures, he never repudiated the Twenty-Five Points.

"The programme of the German Workers' Party is an epochal programme. The leaders refuse to set up new aims after those mentioned in the programme have been achieved merely in order to make possible the further existence of the Party by artificially induced discontent among the masses.

"*1.* We demand the union of all Germans in a Pan German state in accordance with the right of all peoples to self-determination.

"*2.* We demand that the German people shall have equal rights with those of other nations; and that the Treaties of Versailles and St. Germain shall be abrogated.

"*3.* We demand space (colonies) for the maintenance of our people and the settlement of our surplus population.

"*4.* Only those who are our countrymen shall be citizens of our State. Only those who are of German blood can be considered as our countrymen regardless of creed. Hence no Jew can be regarded as a fellow-countryman.

"*5.* Those who are not citizens of the State must live in Germany as foreigners and must be subject to the law of aliens.

Konrad Heiden, *A History of National Socialism.* New York: Knopf, 1935.

"*6.* The right to choose the government and determine the laws of the State shall be the privilege only of the citizens. We therefore demand that no public office, of whatever nature, whether central, local or municipal, shall be held by any but a citizen of the State.

"We actively combat the demoralizing parliamentary administration whereby posts go by Party favour without regard to character and capability.

"*7.* We demand that the State shall undertake to ensure that every citizen has a fair chance of living decently and of earning his livelihood. If it proves impossible to provide food for the whole population, then aliens (non-citizens) must be expelled from the State.

"*8.* Any further immigration of non-Germans must be prevented. We demand that all non-Germans who have come into Germany since August 2, 1914, shall be forced to leave the realm immediately.

"*9.* The rights and duties of all citizens shall be the same.

"*10.* The first duty of every citizen shall be to work mentally or physically. No individual shall carry on any work that is deleterious to the community, but shall contribute to the benefit of all.

"Hence we demand:

"*11.* That all unearned incomes shall be abolished,

"*12.* In consideration of the tremendous sacrifices of property and life which every war imposes upon the people, all personal gains resulting from war must be regarded as treason to the nation. We therefore demand that the returns from all war-profiteering shall be forfeited down to the last farthing.

"*13.* We demand that the State shall take over all trusts.

"*14.* We demand that the State shall share in the profits of large industries.

"*15.* We demand that provision for the aged shall be made on a very greatly increased scale.

"*16.* We demand the creation and maintenance of a sound middle class; that the large stores shall be immediately communalized and rented cheaply to small tradespeople; that for all public supplies, whether national or local, preference shall be given to small traders.

"*17.* We demand an agrarian reform suitable to our national requirements; the enactment of a law to expropriate without compensation the owners of any land that may be needed for national purposes; the abolition of ground rents; and the prohibition of all speculation in land.

"*18.* We demand that relentless measures shall be taken against any who work to the detriment of the public weal. Traitors, usurers, profiteers, &c., are to be punished with death, regardless of race or creed.

"*19.* We demand that the Roman law which serves a materialist ordering of the world shall be replaced by German Common Law.

"*20.* In order to make it possible for every capable and industrious German to obtain higher education and thus the chance of rising to important posts, the State shall organize thoroughly the whole cultural system of the nation. The curricula of all educational establishments shall be arranged according to the requirements of practical life. The conception of the State Idea (the science of citizenship) shall be taught in the schools from the very beginning. We demand that specially talented children of poor parents, no matter what their station or occupation, shall be educated at the cost of the State.

"*21.* It is the duty of the State to help raise the standard of the nation's health by providing maternity welfare centres, by prohibiting juvenile labour, by increasing physical fitness through the introduction of compulsory games and gymnastics, and by the greatest possible encouragement of all associations concerned with the physical education of the young.

"*22.* We demand the abolition of the professional army and the formation of a national army.

"*23.* We demand that legal action be taken against those who propagate what they know to be political lies and disseminate them by means of the Press. In order to make possible the creation of a German Press, we demand that:

"*a.* All editors and their assistants on newspapers published in the German language shall be German citizens.

"*b.* Non-German newspapers shall require the express assent of the State to publication. They must not be published in the German language.

"*c.* Non-Germans shall be forbidden by law to have any financial interest in or in any way to influence German newspapers. The punishment for transgression of this law to be the immediate suppression of the newspaper in question and the deportation of the offending aliens.

"Journals transgressing against the common weal shall be suppressed. We demand that legal action be taken against any tendency in art or literature having a disruptive effect upon the life of the people, and that any organizations which offend against the foregoing requirements shall be dissolved.

"*24.* We demand freedom for all religious creeds in the State, in so far as they do not endanger its existence or offend against the moral or ethical sense of the Germanic race.

"The Party as such represents the standpoint of positive Christianity without binding itself to any one particular confession. It opposes the Jewish materialist spirit within and without, and is convinced that a lasting recovery of the nation can only be achieved from within on the principle.

"*25.* In order that all this may be carried out, we demand the creation of a strong central authority in the State; the unconditional control by the political central parliament of the whole State and all its organizations. The formation of professional committees, and committees representative of the several estates of the realm, to ensure the laws promulgated by the central authorities being carried out in the individual States in the union.

"The leaders of the Party undertake to promote the execution of the foregoing points at all costs, if necessary at the sacrifice of their own lives.

"Munich, *February* 24, 1920."

See also German Workers' Party, Vol. 1; Nazism, Twenty-Five Points, Vol. 2; Drexler, Anton; Hitler, Adolf, Vol. 3.

CHAPTER TWO

WORLD WAR II

World War II, the culmination of the Third Reich, began when Germany invaded Poland on September 1, 1939. Poland was the next step, after Austria and Czechoslovakia, in Adolf Hitler's attempt to expand Germany to the east. In support of Poland, Great Britain and France declared war on the Third Reich on September 3. But these two nations proved to be only a small hindrance to the growing power of the Third Reich over the next two years. By the summer of 1940 Nazi Germany, much to the world's surprise, had conquered most of western Europe. Hitler's true territorial goals, however, lay where they always had lain, in eastern Europe.

On June 21, 1941, World War II became an even broader conflict when the Third Reich launched Operation Barbarossa, the German invasion of the Soviet Union. Although Hitler hoped that his victory over the Soviet Union would be as rapid as his other triumphs, his armies quickly bogged down. When they failed to take the strategically important Russian city of Stalingrad over the winter of 1942–1943, the tide of war turned. Hitler's refusal to allow a German retreat from Stalingrad doomed an entire army to starvation or imprisonment, and even Hitler's generals recoiled from the magnitude of the loss. Some generals, in fact, worked with junior officers and civilian officials in planning the assassination of

the increasingly irrational Adolf Hitler and the overthrow of the Nazi regime, disgusted by what the Nazis had brought on Germany. Their efforts culminated in the plot of July 20, 1944, when an officer placed a bomb in Hitler's conference room. The bomb went off, but it failed to kill the Nazi leader. Hitler's vengeance was brutal and extreme.

The United States had entered the war on the side of Great Britain and the Soviet Union in December 1941. Hitler had long criticized U.S. president Franklin D. Roosevelt for questioning his decisions, and until 1944 he avoided dealing with the threat to his Reich represented by American power. As ever, he was preoccupied with eastern Europe. While the Soviets advanced from the east, the British and Americans attacked from the west and south. The Third Reich was finally defeated on May 8, 1945, eight days after Hitler committed suicide in his Berlin bunker.

The legacy of the Third Reich, ranging from the creation of a unified totalitarian state to the devastation of World War II to the horror of the Holocaust, has resulted in a fascination with the personalities and lives of the Nazi leaders. Adolf Hitler, particularly, has been the target of much curiosity and interest, and writings have tried to present the Nazi leader from a variety of perspectives. There are accounts of Hitler as a teenager, a rising political leader, and as one of the most powerful of world rulers. Few, however, were able to offer the same perspective as Eva Braun, the Nazi leader's longtime mistress. Eva Braun also had personal knowledge of other top Nazis such as Hermann Göring, Joseph Goebbels, and Heinrich Himmler.

Records and memoirs make it clear that, hardly from being a unified force, the top Nazi leadership was constantly riven by conflicts. It was a state of affairs, in fact, that Hitler favored, since he believed that competition would also allow the best man to rise to the top. For Göring, Goebbels, and Albert Speer, however, these conflicts re-quired them to be constantly on the alert as well as constantly ambitious. The personal differences among top Nazis, in fact, made for a dramatic soap opera.

The fall of the Third Reich was dramatically demonstrated as well at the trials held by the International Military Tribunal at Nuremberg from late 1945 to late 1946. There, the victorious Allies tried twenty-one top Nazis whom they had managed to capture alive. Hitler had committed suicide, as had Goebbels and Himmler. Nevertheless Göring, Speer, and the others survived to hear their charges and accept their sentences, which in many cases were death by hanging.

Diary Entries

Eva Braun, Adolf Hitler's mistress from 1932 to 1945 as well as, for one day, his wife, offers a unique perspective on not only Hitler but other top Nazis. Her later diary entries convey a sense of foreboding as the Third Reich collapses.

Obersalzberg, December 1937, Sunday
Yesterday we had a charming evening, quite domesticated, which was according to my taste. We ate alone, then he took his evening foot-bath—as usual, fully dressed, sitting on the edge of the bathtub. The water had all sorts of bathsalts in it to resemble seawater as much as possible. I read to him from an old book about Alexander the Great. It was so peaceful and quiet. *He* was in a good temper and patted my shoulder again and again. And his face was so relaxed, his cheeks were hanging down . . . I cannot get used to these sudden changes of his sometimes uncanny character . . .

December 1937
I don't know why Hermann [Göring] must always play the court jester. Sometimes I feel that he prepares some special turn every time he comes to visit Adi [Adolf]. Of course, under the mask of the court jester he can allow himself far more than any other man. I believe, on the whole, he is the only one whom *he* takes seriously. Of Goebbels *he* told me recently: "He is finished. Always tripping over petticoats . . . If I ever get rid of any of my old party comrades, it will be Goebbels."

Goering has the unpleasant habit of pinching my posterior. I don't know where he got the habit, probably he learned it from

his intercourse with waitresses. And then he always greets me with the same question: "Am I getting a kiss today?"—The Führer has a revulsion against baths, he only bathes once a month; at the same time he is amazingly clean, he washes himself thoroughly every day. I believe he does not like to be naked and I don't know whether anyone has ever seen him in swimming trunks. But he does not object to *my* nudity. He sits there, completely dressed and always very neat, the neatest man I know, and watches me carefully as if he wanted to memorise every movement. Because he does not like to take baths himself, he does not want to hear jokes about this subject. Goering knows that quite well. But recently Hermann has become as cheeky as if he felt himself wholly an equal.

And Adolf accepts this—to my annoyance. The joke about the Jew who forgot his undervest in the bath and discovered it only after a year when he wanted to bath again, was much too ancient and stupid; Adi looked as if he was about to become very unpleasant. But in the end he said nothing.

Winter 1937
Yesterday the house was full of guests; though most of them had to return after an early dinner to Berchtesgaden. A few stayed, among them Leni [Riefenstahl]. We did not see each other. She does not know that we are meeting here today. I don't know at all what's going on down below. I was forbidden to go down. I must wait in the bedroom, in a night-gown, until he comes. I wonder whether they are performing the nude dances down below of which they always talk and which I must never attend because I am "a little girl" and "the secret queen"? I must always think of Leni. She is always abus-

Eva Braun, *The Diary of Eva Braun*. Ed. Alan Bartlett. Bristol, England: Spectrum, 2000.

ing people, *he* told me, and that I don't like at all. But somehow he is fascinated by her and I don't know whether she won't oust me one day. He has just left me. Oh no, she won't take my place! . . .

Summer 1939
I think he has now suddenly decided that I alone shall remain his "secret queen". Naturally he told *me* nothing about it but I have noticed that for some time Leni has been eliminated as a rival. Last night he told me, while his eyes roamed over my body: "You are the only one of whom I never tire, your body will always remain a mystery for me even if I look at it every day for a thousand years." I am not the loveliest woman he knows, he told me. I knew that, too. But I am supposed to hide the "mystery of eternal fascination". I am very happy about it. I don't know why he always remains dressed. I can be as nude as I want to be. It's always the same: "Aren't you too hot in those clothes?" Naturally I understand that and take them off. But *he* always remains fully dressed as if he were at some reception. He always feels cold but that isn't of course the reason why he keeps his clothes on. He is simply shy. I was, too, at the beginning, but that passes. But *he* always turns away when he undresses. And yet I never look at his body. It is his eyes which have a hypnotic power over me; when I am with him, I am a different being altogether. Especially when he is excited and has that carnivorous look in his eyes. For the first time we spoke seriously about Leni. Until now he has always only smiled when I tried to find out something. Now he says: "But she is a great artist and an important human being." What do I care—if she only leaves him alone? "As a woman I find her uninteresting," he maintains and now I believe him. "She has some attraction which appealed to me, not erotically, but because of her artistic vitality." They couldn't have been really intimate, though he gives her an awful lot of money. I asked him whether she had a beautiful body.

"Yes," he said thoughtfully as if he had to recall it first, "she has a beautiful body, there is something Greek in her, she has a cold sensuality. She doesn't walk beautifully, she is not graceful and affectionate like you . . . it's all instinct. And that always repelled me." He was silent for a while then he said, "She always wanted something, always. She is the most ambitious woman I know. Sometimes I was actually tempted to give her more and more power, to raise her higher and higher—in order to see where she would end with her unusual temperament. But I have no time to act the Sun King. I have other tasks to fulfil." As he mentioned her "cold sensuality", I remembered the passage, the only one he had underlined in Shakespeare; the one about not wanting to become a fan or a pair of bellows to cool the lustful gypsy-girl. That could only refer to her. I am still tortured by this: did he have an affair with her or not? Am I ever going to find out? Of course he does not want to give *me* any power, and I never want anything from him, and have never asked for any favours; I am probably the most convenient mistress for him. . . .

1941 Saturday
The whole day long he was bad-tempered and angry because he broke one of his jacket-crowns at breakfast. This eternal trouble with his bad teeth really gets on my nerves. If there's something wrong with his teeth, his whole circle, the world and the war feel the result—but most of all, I. Only in the evening when he had asked me, as usual, whether I wasn't "too hot in my clothes" did I feel that his bad mood had passed. He didn't even take off his boots; he had to go on working later, he said. But then he did not do any work after all, and instead we talked for a long time. "I have been pondering since 1933," he said, "whether I should have, whether I could have, whether I must have a child. The children of great men have always been failures in history; but history might prove the rule with this

one exception. In so many ways I am outside the usual historical conception that I imagine the possibility of begetting a son who might continue my work as my successor. I know that I am going to live long, Germany needs me; thus, I would have time to educate my son. Perhaps it is my duty to give such a son to the Reich." I felt quite dizzy at the idea that *I*, Eva Braun, of all people might become the mother of such a son. I really did not have the courage to put any questions but I started to tremble. He noticed it, smiled and caressed me and said, "For years I have waited for my doctors to find some way of determining the sex of a child. I can't permit myself to produce a girl. A little she-Hitler—that would be ridiculous." I realised that nothing would come out of this. He only does things he simply has to do, all his decisions are made with lightning speed. Where he hesitates, little can be expected, both in great and small things. I could only try to trick him, keep it a secret—and then tell him if it's a boy. But I haven't the courage. "The idea of creating a dynasty of Hitlers has something fascinating for me," he said. "I don't want to make them Kaisers [the earlier German emperors]. The Kaiser-idea is too degenerate, too outdated and dusty. But one could make them princes, that sounds well: Prince of the Great German Reich. My son could have a son again and in this way there would be Hitlers who might see the full development of the Third Reich's glory. Of course, there is only one thing against it—I am a unique phenomenon which cannot be repeated; my successors could only be imitations, copies. And a copy is the more ridiculous the closer it resembles the original. A "little one" bearing my name would be a bad joke in world history." I dressed again and we went to his study, he wanted to hear *Tristan* [*and Isolde,* a Wagnerian opera]. As soon as we left, the valet rushed in and made up the bed. That is, of course, a strict order of *his.* The bed must always be tidy, he hates crushed pillows and cush-

ions. But I cannot get rid of the suspicion that Hinnes stands for hours outside the door, listening and that's terribly painful. *He* of course never thinks of such possibilities and *I* don't want to tell him. But how otherwise could this fellow come into the bedroom a minute after we have left it? . . .

1944

The notorious and fearsome Himmler I know very well now. He visits me often and he doesn't always try, like Goebbels, to worm something new out of me about Adolf. I believe he knows enough in any case. Otherwise he is the most curious man I have ever met. —But as far as A [Adolf] is concerned, perfectly discreet. What's so funny about him is his pedantry. If you enter his office, you almost feel that he has nothing to do. Not more than one file must remain on his desk at a time. Then he loves gadgets: he presses a button and the wall opens behind you and the guard becomes visible. He has built up a whole collection of complicated machinery; direct telephone lines to Rome, Budapest, Oslo and Stockholm, even to Switzerland; loudspeakers and listening apparatus. He says there is no official in the Chancellery or in the Ministries whose private conversations as well as telephone conversations he cannot overhear if he wishes to. "Shall we try?" he asked me several times. But the conversations of his officials do not interest me. He always carries at least three pince-nez in case he loses or breaks one; also, two watches. He is the most punctual man I know. He needs two watches to control one with the other. Only then has he the feeling that he always knows the *exact* time. He writes down everything he is told; he must have dozens of notebooks and A says this constant jotting-down makes him nervous, as if Himmler had no memory at all. He always writes with a tiny pencil which he produces from his trouser-pocket. And yet he has a fantastic memory. He can always produce any personal data promptly. He knows everybody's escapades, and about the people he hates, like Ley or Goebbels, he knows every tiny detail. He was the first person to know that Goebbels was running after the beautiful Hungarian wife of Anfuzo [an Italian diplomat] with his tongue hanging out. Of Anfuzo himself Himmler spoke with great sympathy. He was the first Italian, he said, whom he liked and who impressed him. For this reason alone he would prevent all intimacy between Goebbels and Frau A— "And even if my people have to force their way into the bedroom with guns in their hands, he won't get her," he said and swept his hand across the polished, empty top of his desk. It is really amazing: while Adolf suffers more and more from the pressure of war and has completely changed—he is nervous, irritable, full of depression and gloomy uneasiness—nothing is noticeable in Himmler. He is self-assured, completely calm, confident, cool and unbalanced. I believe he thinks more of his power, growing every month, his rising influence and his improved standing with the Führer than of the war and how everything is going to end. He always says that the new weapon will decide our victory. Whoever employs it first, will win the war. If we had it, the war would be over in a few weeks. If we only had it! . . .

Eva Braun remained loyal to Hitler until the end; the pair committed suicide together in Hitler's Berlin bunker on April 30, 1945.

GHQ [General Headquarters], 1944

Today the Führer told me with a dead-serious face, "I only have three people left whom I can trust: you, Goebbels and Himmler. You are the most faithful and you'll get your reward one day, I give you my solemn promise. Goebbels stands and falls with me. He has been gripped by the passion of the fight just like myself. He has grown above his own stature and reached one I would never have expected. Himmler is a chameleon. I warn you against him—I know you see him often. He is dangerous. He might become a danger even for me if he had any gift as an orator. But luckily he is dumb and practically sentenced to silence. Thus he can serve only me. But my generals are traitors and sentimental fools; they want to spare the troops. As if it weren't the most exacting and unsparing effort that always brought the biggest success. If I had any replacements, I would have three-fourths of the German generals shot. After the war they won't get the estates in the east for which they've been waiting so long—they'll be exiled or executed." More than ever *he* suffers from insomnia, I find him changed, his slim figure has acquired something buffalo-like and he walks with a little stoop, as if the burden of the whole of Germany rested upon him. Every evening he suffers terrible neuralgic pains which must be almost unbearable. These depressions, occasionally interrupted by brief exaltation and terrible excitement, show me that he is at the end of his tether. I also discovered that he can no longer make love—I believe he himself was the most deeply shattered by it. He probably thinks I haven't noticed anything. In such things he is so touchingly näive. What woman wouldn't notice such a thing? But of course I left him with his faith undisturbed. He has now other and greater things to think about than me. I hope that he'll quickly forget the sad and humiliating experience of last night. In any case, it is probably a passing phase—I don't know . . . perhaps there is no such thing? I have just figured out how old he is. It can only be a passing nervous weakness. But it shows that his psychological and physical state must really be causing anxiety . . .

GHQ [General headquarters or OKW] 1944, Tuesday

Dr Morell [one of Hitler's personal physicians] came and I used the opportunity to ask him about the Führer's health. M shrugged his shoulders and said that a different man would have collapsed long ago. But as *he* cannot be measured by normal standards, nothing could be said. I feel that he is evading my questions. He must feel that I, too, have changed; for he suddenly became serious and said, in his best professional manner: "Physically there is nothing to be noticed except a certain additional strain. But he lives in a condition of mental exaltation that is sometimes accompanied by hallucinations. He also has attacks of partial blindness, the cause of which I was unable to discover. That's the diagnosis *and* symptoms, my dear, in all sober truth." My tears rolled down my cheeks. M isn't at all sentimental, he nudged me and said, "Come on, get hold of yourself, we can't have any weeping virgins here in GHQ." I shook myself and it was over. We must stick it out, the new weapons are coming and then God have mercy upon our enemies!

Summer 1944

I always think: perhaps you will see him for the last time today. He won't be killed, I am sure, providence must hold its protecting hand over him. What would happen to Germany now if he died? That's unthinkable. But with me it's different. I am not afraid, I would never go into a shelter but defy the bombs. But *he* gave orders and so I obey. "The bombs don't enquire whether you are afraid or not," he said and as usual he was right. Just now we went for a walk in the summer fields and then lay in the grass. Yes, there is no doubt any more—our love has become platonic, I must accept the fact. I read about it, too. Perhaps after years of peace and relaxation it will be different again. But who thinks of such things now when everything is at stake?

See also Braun, Eva; Hitler, Adolf, Vol. 3.

Doomed German Soldiers Write Home from Stalingrad

The following are samples from the last mailbag that left German lines in Stalingrad over the winter of 1942–1943. Like soldiers in every time and conflict, the Germans remembered their families more than their duty to Hitler's Reich.

You are the wife of a German officer; so you will take what I have to tell you, upright and unflinching, as upright as you stood on the station platform the day I left for the East. I am no letter-writer and my letters have never been longer than a page.

Today there would be a great deal to say, but I will save it for later, i.e., six weeks if all goes well and a hundred years if it doesn't. You will have to reckon with the latter possibility. If all goes well, we shall be able to talk about it for a long time, so why should I attempt to write much now, since it comes hard to me. If things turn out badly, words won't do much good anyhow.

You know how I feel about you, Augusta. We have never talked much about our feelings. I love you very much and you love me, so you shall know the truth. It is in this letter. The truth is the knowledge that this is the grimmest of struggles in a hopeless situation. Misery, hunger, cold, renunciation, doubt, despair and horrible death. I will say no more about it. I did not talk about it during my leave either, and there's nothing about it in my letters. When we were together (and I mean through our letters as well), we were man and wife, and the war, however necessary, was an ugly accompaniment to our lives. But the truth is also the knowledge that what I wrote above is no complaint or lament but a statement of objective fact.

I cannot deny my share of personal guilt in all this. But it is in a ratio of 1 to 70 millions. The ratio is small; still, it is there. I wouldn't think of evading my responsibility; I tell myself that, by giving my life, I have paid my debt. One cannot argue about questions of honor.

Augusta, in the hour in which you must be strong, you will feel this also. Don't be bitter and do not suffer too much from my absence. I am not cowardly, only sad that I cannot give greater proof of my courage than to die for this useless, not to say criminal, cause. You know the family motto of the von H—'s: "Guilt recognized is guilt expiated."

Don't forget me too quickly. . . .

. . . The time has come for me to send you greetings once more, and to ask you to greet once more all the loved ones at home.

Last Letters from Stalingrad. Trans. Franz Schneider and Charles Gullans. New York: William Morrow, 1962.

German soldiers in Stalingrad in October 1942 were unprepared for the Russian winter. After months of bitter fighting and extreme hardship, the Germans surrendered to the Soviets in January 1943.

The Russians have broken through everywhere. Our troops, weakened by long periods of hunger without possibility of *(illegible),* engaged in the heaviest fighting since the beginning of this battle, without a day's relief, and in a state of complete physical exhaustion, have performed heroically. None of them surrenders! When bread, ammunition, gasoline and manpower give out, it is, God knows, no victory for the enemy to crush us!

We are aware that we are the victims of serious mistakes in leadership; also, the wearing down of the fortress Stalingrad will cause most severe damage to Germany and her people. But in spite of it, we still believe in a happy resurrection of our nation. True-hearted men will see to that! You will have to do a thorough job in putting all madmen, fools, and criminals out of business. And those who will return home will sweep them away like chaff before the wind. We are Prussian officers and know what we have to do when the time comes.

In thinking over my life once more, I can look back on it with thankfulness. It has been beautiful, very beautiful. It was like climbing a ladder, and even this last rung is beautiful, a crowning of it, I might almost say a harmonious completion.

You must tell my parents that they should not be sad; they must remember me with happy hearts. No halo, please; I have never been an angel! Nor do I want to confront my God as one; I'll manage it as a soldier, with the free, proud soul of a cavalryman, as a *Herr* [gentleman]! I am not afraid of death; my faith gives me this beautiful independence of spirit. For this I am especially thankful.

Hand my legacy to those who come after us: raise them to be *Herren!* Severe simplicity of thought and action! No squandering of energies!

Be especially loving with my parents and so help them get over the first grief. Put up a wooden cross for me in the park cemetery, as simple and beautiful as Uncle X's.

Maintain Sch— as the family seat of the X's. That is my great wish. In my writing desk is a letter in which I recorded my wishes during my last leave.

So, once more, I turn to all of you, dear ones. My thanks once more, for everything, and hold your heads high! Keep on!

I embrace all of you! . . .

. . . Nobody knows what will happen to us now, but I think this is the end. Those are hard words, but you must understand them the way they are meant. Times are different now from the day when I said good-bye and became a soldier. Then we still lived in an atmosphere which was nourished by a thousand hopes and expectations of everything turning out well in the end. But even then we were hiding a paralyzing fear beneath the words of farewell which were to console us for our two months of happiness as man and wife. I still remember one of your letters in which you wrote that you just wanted to bury your face in your hands in order to forget. And I told you then that all this had to be and that the nights in the East were much darker and more difficult than those at home.

The dark nights of the East have remained, and they have turned much darker than I had ever anticipated. In such nights one often listens for the deeper meaning of life. And sometimes there is an answer. Now space and time stand between us; and I am about to step over the threshold which will separate us eternally from our own little world and lead into that greater one which is more dangerous, yes, even devastating. If I could have made it through this war safely, I would have understood for the first time what it means to be man and wife in its true and deepest sense. I also know it now—now that these last lines are going to you.

See also Battle of Stalingrad, Vol 1.

The Legacy of the Nuremberg Trials

Nazi radio broadcaster Hans Fritzsche was one of the top Nazis tried for war crimes by the International Military Tribunal in Nuremberg in 1945 and 1946. Fritzsche was acquitted of all charges. Here he recounts the last days in the courtroom and the fates of some of the convicted. He also criticizes the tribunal for, in effect, exercising "winner's justice."

As we were taken to our places in the dock we could see that the hall was full to the last seat. Press, radio and newsreels were represented even more numerously than usual; but there was none of the usual bustle of conversation, and even before the Marshal of the Court made his customary plea for silence there was utter quiet.

First came the general summing up which was to precede the verdicts, and in which the entire course of the trial with the main points argued was reviewed. This summary made it fairly clear that on the whole the court had allowed the arguments of the Prosecution, and accepted the evidence of many documents to which the Defence had raised serious and well-founded objections.

That night we returned to our prison cells in a very subdued mood. Next morning we were to learn our fate.

On Tuesday we found the court room strangely changed. While there was the same overcrowding and the same respectful silence, the bright lights which for over ten months had shone into every nook and corner of the hall were considerably dimmed. The Tribunal did not wish the prisoners to

be photographed at the moment of listening to the verdict.

We were both surprised by such an unexpected show of tact and at the same time somewhat astonished by such a lack of reliance in our composure. As a matter of fact the gaps left by the absent photographers were well filled by the radio reporters who were all over the place in their little glass cages, broadcasting in every conceivable language. These men carefully watched our every gesture and reported our expressions down to the flutter of an eyelid; which meant that we had each of us to, as it were, put on a mask, for we felt we must on no account betray the frightful excitement that had gripped us.

First came the verdict on the indicted organisations which certainly produced some surprise. The Reich Government, the S.A., the General Staff, the Supreme Command of the Army and various other bodies were declared not to be criminal. Could that mean, we asked ourselves, that on at any rate some points, the court had after all disregarded the arguments of the Prosecution?

Then it was our turn. We were to remain together in the dock to hear the general judgment of the court as well as the verdict Guilty or Not Guilty, on the four counts preferred against each of us; then the sentences would be passed separately, each man who had been found guilty standing alone to hear the nature of his punishment. The eight judges took turns in reading the judgment and verdict on each case.

There was dead silence in the overcrowded hall, as the words Guilty or Not Guilty were announced on count after count. Most of the defendants, as soon as they had heard what concerned them personally,

Hans Fritzsche and Hildegard Springer, *The Sword in the Scales*. Trans. Diana Pyke and Heinrich Fraenkel. London: Allan Wingate, 1953.

took off their earphones so as not to be distracted while they pondered the meaning of the verdict, in which nothing had been said about the sentence to come.

In the midst of all these verdicts there came the total acquittal of Dr. Schacht who accepted it nonchalantly, as his due. When Papen heard the redeeming word his face flushed for a moment.

As far as my own case was concerned I had deliberately refrained from speculation. I had tried very hard to suppress all emotion, simply registering what was being said. In fact I suppressed my receptivity to such a degree that I even failed to notice when the staff of the court changed shifts and for once neglected my customary nod to one or the other of these long familiar faces.

Suddenly I felt I was being stared at by one of them and looking up I saw an electrician forming a word with his lips which could not be anything but "Freispruch" (acquittal). I shook my head and shrugged my shoulders. The gesture was repeated and I became worried that it might be observed. I looked around and my glance rested on one of the leading prosecutors who evidently *had* observed the little incident, for he nodded his head as if he wished to confirm the message and moved his lips to form the same German word.

At precisely this moment I heard the court's verdict on my neighbour Neurath who was found guilty on all four counts. The old gentleman was very excited, and I feared he might suffer a stroke so that owing to this temporary preoccupation I heard little of Lord Lawrence's initial remarks about my own case. I only recovered my full capacity of attention when he reached the passage " . . . not guilty in the meaning of the indictment and to be dismissed by the Marshal of the Court upon the adjournment. . . ."

The interpreter who translated these words sat little more than a yard away from me, separated only by a pane of glass. He spoke so softly that I could not hear him except through the earphones, yet, his voice and the voice of the British judge may well have seemed to me to sound like those trumpets which made the walls of Jericho crumble.

At that moment my thoughts raced back down the years to the day almost exactly a quarter of a century before on which I had embarked on a political career. Then too (it was soon after 1918) the world was full of atrocity stories, but none of them had tempted me to desert my plan for a quiet life of historical research. It was only when in the course of one of the current riots I saw a maddened crowd lynch a venerable old gentleman who was certainly in no way responsible for their troubles—it was then only that I turned away from the quiet and more congenial contemplation of past history and considered whether it was not my duty to take a hand in the politics of the day. I had looked down into the hell of passions unloosed, and I decided to help discipline and organise those passions. Never for a day had I forgotten from what had sprung that first impulse to enter politics; and whenever friend or foe appealed to the baser instincts of human nature to make them serve his cause I had always offered resistance. And now at the end of this long road I had myself been accused of having been the servant of just such hellish forces. I gave a thought to the last stretch of the journey that had brought me from the Lubianka in Moscow to Nuremberg gaol [jail].

My acquittal came to me as a complete surprise. Not because I felt guilty of war crimes and crimes against humanity, but simply because, right from the start, I had felt that I was being indicted as a deputy for a more powerful man and I therefore expected to be sentenced as a deputy too. Why else should I have been selected as a co-defendant with Ministers, Marshals and Reich-leaders in whose sphere I had never moved? Now the change came so suddenly that the very idea of survival seemed utterly strange—I did not know what to do with it.

The court announced the adjournment for lunch and the three acquitted men were asked if they wished to leave the prison immediately. We preferred to stay for a while with those whose fate was still unknown and so were taken down to lunch in the cellar, where a cloak-room had been vacated for the purpose. The rooms where we had been used to having our mid-day meal were evidently being put to some other purpose, but we were just as strictly isolated one from another as we had been in the past—though even so some of the eighteen managed to come up to the three of us and congratulate us.

After lunch those who had to wait for their sentences were shepherded into the room next door. I was standing next to the lift shaft by which, every morning, we used to be taken up to the dock when Goering passed by alone save for the guard who escorted him into the lift. We were all dead silent.

After a little while we could again hear the banging of the lift-door above. The box descended and Goering stepped out. He was chained.

When he noticed me he made towards me, the guard who held his chains allowing himself to be dragged along. The prisoner reached for my hand, shook it as well as he could, and said in a nonchalant, friendly tone: "Very glad you've been acquitted. We had a bit of a bad conscience as far as you were concerned."

I could not utter a word of the question that was on the tip of my tongue. I just could not ask him about his sentence, and he did not refer to it by as much as a gesture. Later I learned that when he spoke to me then it was just a minute or two after he had been sentenced to be hanged.

He turned away from me, bowed to the others, and was taken back to his cell.

We three acquitted men also returned that afternoon to the prison. We vacated our cells in the basement and were given for the time being accommodation on the top floor of the gaol, where the doors of our cells were left open. There was but one guard outside and his duty was only to see that we did not venture into the lower part of the building.

We leant over the railings of the landing and watched the heavy doors of the cells downstairs being unlocked, as one after another our former companions were brought back from the court; each one in chains.

A little later, Hess, Funk, Doenitz, Raeder, Schirach, Speer, and Neurath were moved up to the first floor; the others remained in their old cells in the basement. It was now evident who had been sentenced to death: Goering, Ribbentrop, Keitel, Kaltenbrunner, Rosenberg, Frank, Frick, Sauckel, Jodl, Streicher and Seyss-Inquart.

These men never left the prison again. For a few minutes each day they came out of their cells into the corridor where they were marched up and down always handcuffed; a clergyman invariably accompanied them on this walk.

Papen, Schacht and I were taken that first afternoon of our acquittal to a press conference where we had to answer a good many questions. Unlike the other two I said there and then that having been acquitted by the enemy I now wished to explain my work and justify my motives before my fellow-countrymen. About the actual form of that justification, of course, my ideas were then rather different from those which later proved practical in the face of the new special legislation which provided for life-sentences (which they did not even dare call punishment but "penitentiary measures") for certain activities.

When we left the press conference Dr. Dix, Schacht's counsel, came to meet us. He told us that the building was surrounded by German Police and that we were to be arrested as soon as we were released by the Americans. To me the whole thing seemed like being taken out of a drama and asked to act in a farce.

We were advised not to leave the building, but to wait further developments. Colonel Andrus [an American official] offered to let us stay for the night, but requested us to sign a statement that we had decided of our own free will to remain temporarily in the gaol.

This procedure had to be repeated for three nights running, because the situation was still far from clear. By Friday morning, however, I felt that I could tolerate this game of hide and seek under American protection no longer and I therefore asked for an immediate discharge, in which Dr. Schacht joined me.

We were asked to wait another twelve hours. At about midnight two lorries drew up at the prison gate; Schacht got into one and I into the other, in which I noticed an American major sitting next to the driver. As soon as we were on board the two lorries at once dashed off in different directions.

After a few minutes rapid driving we stopped to listen for the sounds of someone following; all was quiet so we turned round and raced back the way we had come finally stopping outside the house near the Palace of Justice where my counsel lodged. On the entire surface of the globe there can hardly have been any other place where I could have spent that night, and it did not require much ingenuity on the part of the civil police to deduce that fact.

As he was about to leave the Major made a nice little speech, in which he said he had been ordered to convey to me the congratulations of the court and would himself venture personally to join in these good wishes. And would I now please consider myself a free man?

I could not help laughing: uniformed figures were already dimly visible through the darkness. The American insisted on seeing me into the house and up to my lawyer's room. "No one will ever find you here," he said as he departed, but no sooner had the door closed behind him than another opened and a swarm of reporters surrounded me.

After they had made notes of what they wanted to know I looked round the tiny furnished room which was Fritz's abode in Nuremberg. Most of it was taken up by a wonderful bed, complete with snow-white linen and real quilt and I determined then and there to deprive its rightful tenant of its use for the night.

Dr. Fritz [Fritzsche's lawyer] was just considering where *he* was going to sleep when the door-bell rang. The visitor, who was in mufti but carried a large pistol dangling from his broad leather-belt, proved to be Nuremberg's Chief of Police; in his wake came twelve of his men. With a sigh and a sad glance at the snow-white bed with its quilt I proceeded to pack my luggage into its cardboard box, when all of a sudden, an American Colonel put in an appearance. He had come post-haste, having been informed of what was happening, by the military police jeep which had been waiting outside.

Now things became lively and for a while it seemed uncertain who was going to arrest whom. However, in point of fact no one was arrested at that juncture, and after I had undertaken to appear at the office of the Chief of Police at eleven next morning Dr. Fritz's small bed-sitting room began slowly to empty. The Colonel stayed to the last and saw me into bed, having given me his personal guarantee that for that one night at least I should be undisturbed. He was as good as his word.

Next morning I found how he had managed to keep his promise. Our house was surrounded by a large cordon of civil police behind whom a considerable crowd had assembled; but in the immediate vicinity of the house and in the front garden there was a patrol of Allied military police who, though heavily armed, seemed to be on the best possible terms with the inhabitants with whom they were exchanging a good deal of banter and friendly laughter. In between the M.P.s and the German police lay neutral territory which no one could either leave or enter. In front of his shop next door stood the baker while his customers were held up out of reach beyond the outer cordon. A railway worker, trying to get home after night shift, was having his breakfast smuggled across a fence.

I dressed quickly, apologised to the tenants of the house for the trouble caused to them—fortunately no one concerned failed to see the funny side of what was happening—and then made my way to the garden gate. But the guard from the military police, in spite of all my requests and explanations, absolutely refused to let me pass. I was reduced to beckoning to some German policemen and asking them to tell their chief that I had been prevented by force majeur from coming to see him.

On the afternoon of that first day of my "freedom" an agreement was concluded between four parties; the Bavarian Government, represented by an official of the special Ministry concerned with these matters; the Chief of the Nuremberg civil police; the head of local denazification bureau, Dr. Sachs; and myself. By the terms of that agreement I was guaranteed freedom to move about Nuremberg in return for which I promised not to leave the city. I kept the bargain, the other side did not. On the very next day a plain clothes man shadowed me whenever I left the house and soon afterwards guards were posted all day by my room; at night a uniformed guard took up his position in front of the house so as to keep an eye on my goings and comings. It was captivity, without bars, but none the less very unpleasant. Whenever I protested I was informed that these measures were being taken merely for my protection, though, for the life of me I neither know nor have ever been told from whom I was supposed to be protected. It was a ludicrous business but it got on my nerves.

Meanwhile, a few hundred yards away from my temporary home, my former fellow-defendants were waiting for the final decision on their appeals and a grimmer drama was drawing to a close. Every appeal was rejected.

Even after this no one knew when the death sentences were to be carried out. On the night of 15th October I found myself gripped by irresistible restlessness; somehow I felt certain that the last hour of the doomed eleven had struck, and somehow I seemed to live through their agony with them. Once before in my life I experienced a similar sensation, when in the Lubianka prison in Moscow I gave a sick fellow-prisoner a precise description of his home and family without having ever set eyes on them.

That night, being quite unable to sleep, I got up at about five A.M. and sat down at my table fully dressed. Suddenly three American officers entered and subjected me to a regular cross-examination; they wanted to know what means of committing suicide I might have kept hidden in my cell during the course of my captivity.

Why were they asking me all these questions? They had chosen a time of day for their visit which was, to say the least, unusual and I could make no sense of their interrogation whose object seemed wrapped in mystery. I was very taciturn and had little to say in answer to their questions: when the three men left me they were evidently irritated and dissatisfied.

Half an hour later the little room was once again crowded with visitors; press correspondents. They told me that Goering had committed suicide a few hours before he was to be hanged. Half an hour before he was due to call the Field Marshal his guard, who was stationed in front of the cell, noticed the prisoner making suspicious movements and heard him groan. Without leaving his post he sent word to Colonel Andrus who arrived almost immediately and ordered the door to be unlocked. Inside he found a dying man in whose hands was clasped a letter addressed to the Commandant. Andrus took it.

The next to enter the cell were the Protestant prison pastor and two doctors, a German and an American who were present when Goering died. Between his teeth were found the remains of a phial which had contained Zyancali and a rigorous enquiry was at once put in hand to find how the prisoner could have got hold of the poison.

One of those who came to see me was the only journalist who entered Goering's cell immediately after his death. He was an Englishman and happened to be in the prison office when, just about midnight, the warder's report reached Colonel Andrus and sent him post-haste to the dying man's cell. The Englishman described to me how, with the Bavarian Prime Minister, he stood facing Goering's corpse; a spot light in the corridor outside giving the only light in the miserable little room in which Goering had managed at the last to dodge our enemy's hangman. Suddenly the Bavarian Minister, gritting his teeth, had hissed: "The scoundrel! He ought to be hanged even if he is dead!" The Englishman's answer, so he told me, was: "It's only you Germans who can hate one another that much!"

After the reporters had left me an American came to see me, the prison clergyman. What he had experienced that night seemed to have made a different man of him. He spoke very slowly and with a subdued voice.

This man had been to see every one of the doomed men in his cell and had stood next to him as he was chained. He had gone along the corridor with them, down the ten steps of the stone staircase, round a sharp turn to the left, and into the gymnasium where the gruesome scene had been prepared. Every one of them he had accompanied up to the scaffold, waiting till he had spoken his last words and then kneeling down beside him. Together the two men said the "Our Father . . ." whilst the hangman approached with cap and rope; the "Amens" were spoken by the American alone since meanwhile the trap-door had opened.

The Pastor told me a little of how some of them died; he did not tell me much, nor indeed did I ask him.

Ribbentrop had, at long last, mastered his nervousness. With Goering gone it fell to him to open the grim procession; maybe it was that which gave him strength.

Even before midnight Keitel had noticed the noise of unusual activity in the prison corridors and had asked the guard on duty before his cell whether the time had come. When the man did not contradict him he had known all he wanted to know. Quietly and carefully he dressed, made his bed and tidied his few belongings; then he asked for broom and dust-cloth and cleaned the cell thoroughly. He said to his guard: "Thank you for letting me leave things straight and tidy."

Kaltenbrunner, who had been suffering from brainstorms at the beginning of the trial, succeeded in regaining his self-control.

Streicher was the only one who went to pieces, screaming at those who witnessed his death that they would come to the same end.

Frank seemed to be yearning for the end. Sauckel at the last moment learned to master his fear. Jodl was completely relaxed and almost happy, his regrets were not for himself but for those he left behind.

It so happened that a few months later I was again in the prison and by an odd chance came across a small piece of paper. On it were two rows of rectangles drawn with blank spaces in between them, and a list of familiar names together with a few mysterious figures and crosses. It was a diagram of the cells and was evidently intended to help the guards in their duties during the night of the executions. After Goering had unexpectedly upset the routine this plan had obviously been hastily sketched so as to make plain to the staff the order in which the condemned men were to be taken to the gallows. As soon as one of them was on his way the Commandant would carefully mark the vacated cell with a cross and despatch the next escort with the plan in his hand.

The puzzle of Goering's suicide led to the strangest conjectures. There was even a theory that a journalist had smuggled himself into the empty court room and fixed the phial to Goering's seat with a piece of chewing gum.

Whoever followed the trial attentively may remember a little incident which was, to my mind, very significant. In the course of the evidence given against Bormann his counsel tried to argue that no verdict could legally be reached on an accused man whose whereabouts were not only unknown but whose very existence was doubtful. In the course of his speech the lawyer quoted the old German proverb: "Nurembergers hang no man they do not hold."

It was not a particularly well chosen remark and was received in stony silence except by Goering who laughed uproariously, slapping his thighs and repeating the words over and over again. For days afterwards he talked about Dr. Berghold's "apt" quotation, beaming every time he referred to it.

It was difficult to see what he found funny in the quotation; the Nurembergers of 1946 certainly held Goering and there appeared every reason to believe they would hang him. Can it be that even then he was sure they would not—that he already possessed the means whereby to dodge the hangman? I for one consider that his otherwise inexplicable hilarity at this incident makes such an assumption entirely reasonable.

It is quite certain that no member of the prison staff provided him with the poison; while though it is theoretically possible that the phial reached him via the dock, it would in practice have been almost impossible. I know from personal observation and the official report of the proceedings of the Tribunal that no one, including my fellow-defendants, knew anything about the glass splinters which I retained in my own possession; and I have no doubt that Goering found it just as easy to conceal his means of escape as I did mine and that the little glass capsule was in his possession before his arrest.

The Americans, incidentally, seem to have reached the same conclusion; for immediately after Goering's death they introduced a rule that anyone sentenced to death was to have his cell changed at once and was to take nothing whatsoever with him to his new quarters. Even photographs and private letters had to be left behind; and the sentenced man was X-rayed during the transfer.

Goering had hoped for a sort of state funeral in Nuremberg. But his corpse with those of the other executed men was taken out of the city by American officers who had resolved to keep absolute silence about their actions. No one therefore knows exactly where the corpses were burned, though some chance observers have claimed that the Munich crematorium was used for the purpose. The ashes of the eleven were later thrown into the river Isar but at what precise point on its course is also not known. Even the Spanish Inquisition could not have displayed a more radical determination to destroy heretics in both body and spirit.

For the anti-fascist crusade was at an end and the heresy was now to be extirpated, root and branch. The mass-psychosis of our times played worse havoc than ever before with cool and statesmanlike thinking; and the slogan "Unconditional Surrender" proved the signal for a measure of arbitrary vengeance which was to jeopardise the very basis of peace.

A trial of war-guilt and atrocities at the end of a long conflict may perhaps, in the abstract, be considered a good thing. One may welcome the effort to establish a supreme international tribunal charged with the duty of seeing right is done and pronouncing from aloft a New Law for the peoples of the world. Certainly one can understand how the unhappy and innocent victims of war, cry for vengeance against those who, in the safety of their own strongholds, pulled the wires that set civilisation ablaze.

But Nuremberg failed to live up to such lofty aims; there the victors uttered their anathema only against the vanquished. They sought to establish the guilt of various Germans, even of the entire German people; but would break off a hearing whenever they saw that the deeds of the

Allies might be measured by the same yard-stick as those of the defeated.

Yet the gravest failing of the Nuremberg trial is this: it failed to transcend the guilt of individuals and reach the deeper causes of disaster. In the complex modern world it may well be possible for one nation or even one man to initiate a war; but that can only happen when the causes of war are already evident, when the powder-box is ready for the match.

The past is irrevocable. There is no point in complaints and recriminations about what has happened and is done with. We must try instead to overcome its results.

A third world war cannot be avoided by the threat of some new International Military Tribunal at the end of it, and the fact that the letters I.M.T. are written in Latin or Cyrillic, when it is over, will make little difference to the cruelty and devastation with which it is waged.

If we really wish to learn from the past a supreme and truly unbiased tribunal must be established now; not to wait till crimes against humanity are committed, but with the power at this moment to prevent the very causes of such evil.

See also Nuremberg trials, Vol. 2; Fritzsche, Hans, Vol. 3.

A Vision for a Post-Hitler Germany

The following is the draft of a radio address the German resistance planned to broadcast following their hoped-for assassination of Hitler and takeover of the German government in July 1944. It demonstrates clearly what the rebels thought was wrong with the Third Reich as well as their hope to restore German honor.

The principles on which Government will be conducted and the aims which we are pursuing have been announced. We make the following statement on this:

(1) The first task is the restoration of the full majesty of the law. The Government itself must be careful to avoid any arbitrary action, it must therefore submit itself to orderly control by the people. During the war

Michael C. Thomsett, *The German Opposition to Hitler: The Resistance, the Underground, and Assassination Plots, 1938–1945.* Jefferson, NC: McFarland, 1997. Copyright © 1997 by Jean and Michael Thomsett. Reproduced by permission.

this control can only be organized provisionally. For the time being upright and experienced men from all classes and from every Gau [District] will be called to form a Reich Council; we will be accountable to this Reich Council and will seek its advice.

There was a time when we were proud of the integrity and honesty of our people, of the security and the excellence of German administration of justice. Our grief at seeing it destroyed must be all the greater.

No human society can exist without law, no one, not even those who think they can despise it, can live without it. For each man there comes the moment when he calls upon the law. In His ordering of the universe, in His creation and in His commandments God has given us the need for the law. He gave us insight and power to ensure human institutions within the framework of the law. Therefore the independence, irremovability and security of office of the judges must be restored. We know quite well that many of them acted as they did only under the pressure of extreme terrorization; but apart from that a strict investigation will take place to find out whether judges committed the crime of misapplying the law. Those guilty will be removed. In order to restore public confidence in the administration of the law, laymen will take part in passing sentence in penal cases. This will also apply to the courts martial which have been established temporarily.

Justice will be restored. It is not the business of the judge to make new laws. His duty is to apply the law and to do so in the most scrupulous manner. The law shall not be a rigid written code, but it must be definite and clear. It was a crime against the people and against the judge to give the latter vague ideas and so-called ideology as a guiding principle. It is intolerable that men should be condemned when they could not know that what they had done was punishable. In cases where the State has by law declared actions of its own bodies to be exempt from punishment, when in fact these actions were punishable, these exceptions will be canceled as being incompatible with the nature of the law and those responsible will be called to account.

The law will be applied to all those who have offended against it. The punishment deserved will be meted out to the offenders.

Security of person and property will again be protected against arbitrary action. According to the law only the judge can interfere in these personal rights of the individual which are essential for the existence of the State and for the happiness of men and women.

The concentration camps will be abolished as soon as possible, the innocent released and the guilty brought to justice.

But in the same way we do not expect anyone to carry out lynch justice. If we are to restore the majesty of the law we must energetically oppose personal vengeance, which, in view of the injustices suffered and the wounding of the souls of men, is only

understandable. If anyone has a grudge, let him lodge an accusation with whatever public authority he likes. His accusation will be forwarded to the proper quarter. The guilty will be pitilessly punished. But the accusation must be genuine. False accusations will be punished, anonymous accusations will find their way into the wastepaper basket.

(2) We wish to restore the principles of morality in all spheres of private and public life.

Among our people who were once so upright, corruption has been practiced by high, even by the highest, officials of the Nazi Party to an extent never known before. While our soldiers were fighting, bleeding and dying on the battlefields, men like Göring, Goebbels, Ley and company were leading a life of luxury, plundering, filling their cellars and attics, urging the people to endure, and, cowards as they were, avoiding the sacrifice going on around them, both they and their entourage. All evil-doers will be called to account before the full severity of the law, their ill-gotten gains will be taken from them and restored to those from whom they were stolen. But the chief culprits shall pay with their lives and property. All their property and that which they have assigned to their relatives will be taken from them.

The reserved occupations established for political pretexts are abolished. Every man who is fit to fight can prove his worth and his will to endure at the front. We will tolerate no more fireside heroes.

An essential part of the safeguarding of law and decency is decent treatment of human beings. The persecution of Jews which has been carried out by the most inhuman, merciless and degrading methods and for which there can be no compensation is to cease forthwith. Anyone who thought that he could enrich himself with the assets of a Jew will learn that it is a disgrace for any German to strive for such ill-gotten possessions. The German people truly wants to have nothing more to do with pillagers and hyenas among the creatures made by God.

We feel it is a deep dishonor to the German name that crimes of all kinds have been committed in the occupied countries behind the backs of the fighting soldiers and abusing their protection. The honor of our dead is thereby sullied. There, too, we will see that restitution is made.

Anyone who has taken advantage of the war in these countries to fill his pockets or has departed from the rules of honor will be severely punished.

One of our noblest tasks is to restore the family as the nucleus of the community. For this we need the influence of the home, the power of religion, the cooperation of the Churches. Pure and healthy family life can only be built up on a serious and responsible conception of marriage. Immorality must be attacked if our children are not to be demoralized; for how can parents expect their children to be pure if they themselves do not exercise self-control and show their children the best example? The life of our nation will only recover when there is once more healthy family life.

We want no split in the nation. We know that many entered the Party out of idealism, out of bitterness against the Versailles dictate [the Treaty of Versailles] and its effects and against many national degradations, and others from economic or other pressure. The nation must not be divided according to this. All Germans who feel and act as Germans belong together. The only distinction which is to be made is between crime and unscrupulousness on the one hand and decency and integrity on the other. On this basis we will strive with all our might for the inner reconciliation of the people. For only if we remain united on the basis of justice and decency can we survive the fateful struggle into which God has placed our nation.

(3) We declare war on falsehood. The sun of truth shall dispel the thick fog of untruth. Our nation has been most shamelessly deceived about its economic and financial position and about military and political events. The facts will be ascertained and made public, so that everyone can examine them. It is a great mistake to assume that it is permissible for a Government to win over the people for its own purposes by lies. In His order of things God admits no double morality. Even the lies of Governments are short-lived and are always born of cowardice. Success in asserting the position of the nation, the happiness of the people, and the peace of mind of the individual can only be founded on integrity. The truth is often hard; but a people which cannot bear the truth is lost in any case. The individual can only summon up true strength if he sees things as they are. The climber who underestimates the height of the peak to be scaled, the swimmer who misjudges the distance to be covered, will exhaust his energy too soon. All untrue propaganda shall therefore stop; that applies first and foremost to the Reich Ministry of Propaganda. The abuse of the propaganda agencies of the Wehrmacht must also cease. The living and dying of our soldiers needs no propaganda. It is deeply engraved in the heart of every German wife and mother, in the heart of every German at home.

(4) The freedom of mind, conscience and faith which has been destroyed will be restored.

The Churches will again have the right freely to work for their faith. In future they will be completely separated from the State, because only by being independent and by remaining aloof from all political activity can they fulfill their task. The life of the State will be inspired by Christian thinking in word and deed. For we owe to Christianity the rise of the white races, and also the ability to combat the evil impulses within us. No community either of race or of State can renounce this combat. But true Christianity also demands tolerance towards those of other faiths or free-thinkers. The State will again give the Churches the opportunity to engage in truly Christian activities, particularly in the sphere of welfare and education.

The press will be free again. In wartime it must accept the restrictions necessary for a country in any war. Everyone who reads a newspaper shall know who is behind that paper. The press will not again be allowed to publish lies either deliberately or through carelessness.

By strict jurisdiction the editors will ensure that the rules of decency and of duty towards the welfare of the Fatherland are also observed in the press.

(5) It is, above all, German youth which calls out for truth. If proof of the divine nature of man is needed, here it is. Even the children with their instinctive knowledge of what is true and what is false turn away ashamed and angry from the falseness of the thoughts and words expected of them. It was probably the greatest crime of all to disregard and abuse this sense of truth and with it the idealism of our young people. We will therefore protect it and strengthen it.

Youth and the education of youth is one of our main cares. First and foremost this education will be placed in the hands of the parents and the schools. All schools must implant elementary principles simply, clearly and firmly in the child. Training must again be general, embracing the emotions and the understanding. It must have its roots in the people, and there must be no gulf between educated and uneducated.

Education must again be placed deliberately on the Christian-religious basis, and the Christian laws of the utmost tolerance towards those of other faiths must not be broken. On this basis the educational and training system must again be conducted calmly and steadfastly, and must be protected against constant changes and disturbances.

(6) The administration must be reorganized. Nothing which has proved its value will be abolished. But it is essential to restore at once clear responsibility and the freedom to make independent decisions. Our once so proud administration has become a pile of machines and little machines working to no purpose. No one dares to make an independent and true decision. We will demand just the opposite from the civil servants. They will do right with the greatest simplicity and with little red tape.

The civil servant must again become an example in his whole way of life, official and private; for the people have entrusted him his public sovereign power. This power may only be exercised by those who are upright, who have acquired the technical knowledge, steeled their character and proved their ability. We will put an end to the civil servants who followed the Party rules. The civil servant shall once again obey only the law and his conscience. He must show himself conscious and worthy of the distinction of being assured of a secure livelihood by the community, while others must struggle for the barest necessities. Secure in his authority and in his rights he must proceed in the ideal endeavor to be worthy of his special position by special devotion to duty.

In order to make it possible for the civil servant to carry out his duties in this loyal way, and to spare the people from having public power exercised by unworthy persons, all appointments and promotions made since January 1, 1933, are declared to be temporary. Every individual civil servant will in the very near future be examined to find out whether he has offended against the law, against discipline or against the behavior expected of every civil servant. If this is found to be the case the proper measures will be taken, either by punishment, dismissal or transfer. The Civil Service tribunals will cooperate in this. Temporary civil servants, whose performance does not fulfill the demands of their office, will be transferred to positions for which they are fitted, or if this is not possible, they will be dismissed. Luxury is out of place in Government offices, but there must be comfort in the home of the individual. Heads of departments are instructed to take the necessary measures at once. Superfluous articles of furniture will be handed over to those who have suffered damage by bombing.

(7) The arrangement of the administration, the proper distribution and fulfillment of public duties are only possible on the basis of a Constitution. A final Constitution can only be drawn up with the agreement of the people after the end of the war. For the front-line soldiers have the right to have a special say in this. So for the time being we must all content ourselves with a temporary Constitution, which will be announced at the same time. We too are bound by this.

Prussia will be dissolved. The Prussian provinces, as well as the other German Länder [states], will be amalgamated into new Reichgaue. The Reichgau will in law again be given a life of its own. To a large extent they will be self-governing. Public duties which are in any way compatible with the unity of the Reich and the systematic conduct of the Reich will be handed over to the self-administration of these Reichgaue, Kreise and Gemeinden.

In all Reichgau [party districts] authority will be exercised on behalf of the Reich by Reichstatthalter [state governors], who are to be appointed at once. As far as possible they will grant freedom of activity to the organs of self-government, but at the same time will preserve the unity of the Reich. Elected corporations in the self-governing body will guarantee liaison with the people.

(8) In wartime, economy can only be conducted in the form of State control and of control of prices. As long as there is a shortage of essential goods, a freer economy is, as everyone will realize, impossible, unless we want to pass over cold-bloodedly the vital interests of those with smaller incomes. We know quite well how distasteful this economy is, the abuses it fosters and that it does not, as is so often maintained, serve the true interests of the small consumer. For the time being, we can only simplify it, and free it from obscurities and from the confusion of different authorities

and from the lack of a sense of responsibility. We will cancel all measures which have interfered too much with the freedom of the individual and which have destroyed livelihood in trade, handicraft, business, industry and agriculture without due consideration or where this was not absolutely necessary.

Furthermore, economy may not be unnecessarily disturbed by State interference nor may the joy of production or the possibilities of creation be stifled (economic freedom shall only be held in check by law, by the safeguarding of the integrity of competition and by decent intentions). In view of our country's poverty in raw materials and the fact that we cannot grow enough to feed ourselves, autarchy is a cowardly denial of the possibility of participating in the goods and services of the whole world by an exchange of services.

The aim of our conduct of economy is that every worker, every employee and every employer shall have a share in the benefits of our economy. It is not a question of establishing free enterprise for the employer and forcing him to struggle in competition. No, the German worker too must and will have the opportunity to take part in a creative capacity in the responsibility of economy, only we cannot free him from the effect of the natural laws governing economy.

Property is the basis of all economic and cultural progress; otherwise man gradually sinks to the level of the animal. It will therefore be protected not only in the hands of the large, but also in the hands of the small, property owner, who can only call his household goods his own. The abuse of property will be combated just as will the accumulation of capital, which is unhealthy and only increases man's dependence.

The organization of economy will be based on self-administration. The system so far employed of administration from above must cease. What must be done is to restore the beneficial functioning of independent decision and thus the responsibility of the individual. As far as possible the confidence of all, including the workers, in the justice of the organization of economy must be restored.

(9) From this arises the essence of the State policy directed towards equality—social policy. Those who through no fault of their own have fallen upon evil days or who are weak must be protected and given the opportunity of securing themselves against the accidents of this life. The State must also intervene where the interest in acquiring savings (capital) conflicts with the interest of assuring work for those now living. (Such conflicts of interest can arise in times of great political and economic tension. It would be very foolish to overcome them in such a way that only capital, i.e. savings, was destroyed. It would please the small saver just as little as it would serve the interests of the people as a whole if, for example, all farms and factories were suddenly without machinery. On the other hand, all these capital goods have no value unless they can be made to serve men living now.) Thus conscientiously and with a sense of responsibility we must find a just compromise, in which each individual knows from the outset that sacrifices must be made by him as well as by others.

In cases where the powers and responsibility of the individual branches of business and industry are not sufficient to make such compromises, all those citizens engaged in business must cooperate and in the last resort a just compromise laid on the shoulders of the people as a whole, must be assured by the State. In so far as social institutions affect the worker, they will have the right to full self-administration.

But we must realize that the State does not have inexhaustible means. Even the State can only exist on what its citizens do and give to it. It cannot give the individual citizens more than it receives from the efforts of its citizens. We therefore clearly and definitely refuse to make promises of economic well-being. Each of us knows that those who have wasted their savings

must work specially hard to regain their accustomed standard of life. Thus it is with the family, in every company and also in the State. Any other idea is foolish. Cheap promises that the State can do everything are irresponsible demagogy. You with your resources are the State. We and the organs of the State are only your trustees. Each of you must stir up his resources. It is obvious that after the enormous devastation of this war we must all make special efforts to work hard to create replacements for clothing, for bombed homes and factories and for destroyed household goods. And finally we want to give our children the possibility of a better life. But we are convinced that we are all capable of doing this if we can again work in justice, decency and freedom.

(10) The basic condition for a sound economy is the organization of public funds. Expenditure must be kept within the real income which the State, the Gau [district], the Kreis [locality], and the Gemeinde [community] can draw from their citizens. Effort, character, renunciation and struggle will be requested to restore this order; but it is the most important and essential basis of an assured currency and of all economic life. The value of all savings depends on it. Without it, foreign trade, on which we have depended for more than a hundred years, is impossible.

Taxes will be considerable; but we will watch over their careful use all the more strictly. It is more important that the citizen should have the necessities of life than that the administration should provide itself with magnificent establishments and take upon itself duties which are in contradiction to the simple way of life of the individual.

We will also demand the same care from economy, which must again realize that expenditure in the administration only serves the comfort and the needs of the individual but must be borne by all in the shape of higher prices and by workers in the form of lower wages. The cessation of the enormous expenditure of the Party is a beginning of the remedy.

Since 1933, the principle of an orderly State economy was forsaken by constant and unscrupulous wasting of funds by increasing debts. It was inconvenient to pretend to the people that the general welfare had been successfully increased by extravagance. This method was in reality contemptible, for it consisted in piling up debts. Therefore, even in wartime when each State is forced to spend enormous sums, we will restore the utmost simplicity and economy in all public services. A real leveling out generally can only take place when this war is over.

We regard the mounting debts of all belligerent and natural States as an extremely great danger. They threaten currency. After this war every State will be faced with an extremely difficult task. We hope to be able to find ways of paying off the debts if we succeed in restoring confidence and cooperation between the nations.

(11) But we are still at war. We owe all our work, sacrifice and love to the men who are defending our country at the front. We must give them all the moral and material resources which we can summon. We are with them in rank and file, but now we know that only those sacrifices will be demanded which are necessary for the defense of the Fatherland and the well-being of the people, and not those which served the lust for conquest and the need for prestige of a madman; we know too that we will carry on this war until we obtain a just peace, fighting with clean hands, in decency and with that honor which distinguishes every brave soldier. We must all give our care to those who have already suffered in this war.

In our anxiety about the front we must reconcile the necessities with clarity and simplicity. There must be an end of the welter of bombastic orders which are incapable of fulfillment and which today demand from industry impossible numbers of tanks, tomorrow aircraft and the next day weapons and equipment. We shall only demand what is necessary and expedient. In contrast to the former despotic tyranny we expect from each who is called upon to carry out an order that he will on his own account point out mistakes and discrepancies.

(12) We gave a warning against this war which has brought so much misery to mankind, and therefore we can speak boldly. If national dignity at present prevents us from making bitter accusations, we will call those responsible to account. Necessary as this is, it is more important to strive for an early peace. We know that we alone are not masters of peace or war; in this we depend on other nations. We must stand firm. But at last we will raise the voice of the true Germany.

We are deeply conscious of the fact that the world is faced with one of the most vital decisions which have ever confronted the peoples and their leaders. God Himself puts the question to us whether we wish to live in accordance with the order of justice imposed by Him and whether we wish to follow His commandments to respect freedom and human dignity and help each other or not. We know that this order and these commandments have been gravely violated ever since, in 1914, the nations forsook the blessed path of peace. Now we are faced with the question whether we are willing to turn to good use the bitter experiences we have had to undergo and to turn to reconciliation, the just settlement of interests and the healing of the terrible wounds by working together.

In this hour we must tell our people that it is our highest duty bravely and patiently to cleanse the much dishonored German name. Only we Germans can and will fulfill this task. Our future, no matter what material form it takes, depends on our doing this pitilessly, seriously and honestly. For God is not there to be appealed to as Providence on each petty occasion, but He demands and ensures that His order and His commandments are not violated. It was a fatal mistake, the origins of which can be traced to the unhappy Versailles dictate, to assume that the future can be built up on the misfortune of other nations, on suppression and disregard of human dignity.

None of us wishes to malign the honor of other nations. What we demand for ourselves we must and will grant to all others. We believe that it is in the interests of all peoples that peace should be lasting. For this international confidence in the new Germany is necessary.

Confidence cannot be won by force or by talking. But whatever the future may bring, we hate the cowardly vilification of our opponents, and we are convinced that the leaders of all States want not only the victory for their own peoples but a fruitful end to this struggle, and that they are ready to alleviate at once with us the inhuman hardships, which affect all people, of this total war which was so thoughtlessly started.

With this consciousness and relying on the inner strength of our people we shall unwaveringly take those steps which we can take towards peace without harm to our people. We know that the German people wants this.

Let us once again tread the path of justice, decency and mutual respect! In this spirit each of us will do his duty. Let us follow earnestly and in everything we do the commands of God which are engraved on our conscience even when they seem hard on us, let us do everything to heal wounded souls and to alleviate suffering. Only then can we create the basis for a sure future for our people within a family of nations filled with confidence, sound work and peaceful feelings. We owe it to our dead to do this with all our might and with sacred earnestness—whose patriotism and courage in sacrifice have been criminally abused. To how many of you who have realized this did the fulfillment of your duty become the most bitter grief of conscience? How much beautiful human happiness has been destroyed in the world!

May God grant us the insight and the strength to transform these terrible sacrifices into a blessing for generations.

See also July 1944 Plot, Vol. 1; resistance movements, Germany, Vol. 2; Beck, Ludwig; Stauffenberg, Claus Schenk Graf von, Vol. 3.

Goebbels and Göring Comment on Their Rivals

In March 1943 Propaganda Minister Goebbels met with Reichsmarschall Göring at the latter's mountaintop home. In the following journal entries they discuss ways to best protect their own interests while voicing extensive criticism of their rivals among the Nazi hierarchy, all, they suggest, in the service of Germany's war effort and for the sake of Adolf Hitler.

Joseph Goebbels, *The Goebbels Diaries 1942–1943.* Ed. and trans. Louis P. Lochner. Garden City, NY: Doubleday, 1948.

At 4 P.M. I drove up to Goering's home. His house is high up on the mountain in almost wintry quiet. Goering received me most charmingly and is very openhearted. His dress is somewhat baroque and would, if one did not know him, strike one as somewhat funny. But that's the way he is, and one must put up with his idiosyncrasies; they sometimes even have a charm about them. . . .

After the exchange of a few pleasantries we immediately got down to brass tacks. He gave a general survey of the situation which

Joseph Goebbels, Reich minister of public enlightenment and propaganda, speaks at a military gathering in about 1940.

seemed somewhat superficial to me, but which, on the whole, went to the core of things. He regards the situation in the East as essentially favorable, although he naturally realizes that we are still on somewhat uncertain ground there. He is also somewhat worried about our having pretty much stripped the West in order to bring things to a standstill in the East. One dreads to think what would happen if the English and the Americans were suddenly to attempt a landing.

Events in Tunisia have also not developed the way he expected. He wants to go to Italy for several days to look after the supply lines. The quartermasters' offices in the Army have again made a lot of mistakes, and in Goering's opinion [Field Marshal Erwin] Rommel, too, is not quite equal to his task. Goering does not think very much of Rommel; he believes that he is splendid when it comes to advancing, but unable to meet serious crises and setbacks.

That may be true. Rommel has served in North Africa under terrific conditions far too long for these years not to have done something to him. But I suppose Goering bases his opinion partly on the judgment of [Field Marshal Albert] Kesselring, who has always been opposed to Rommel. Be that as it may, Goering says we must either try to achieve a decisive success in Tunisia or else swallow the bitter pill of giving up North Africa. He believes we'll lose Africa to the Americans anyway. Should we succeed, however, in breaking through in the East, our loss of Africa would not be irreparable. Goering certainly still thinks very highly of the military power and war potential of the Anglo-Saxons. He has no illusions about those.

With regard to England he finds it difficult to understand how the British plutocracy [ruling classes] can make as close an alliance with Bolshevism as was evidenced especially on the twenty-fifth anniversary of the Red Army. Goering looks at these things somewhat naïvely and is unable to differentiate between expediency and real conviction.

He seemed to me somewhat helpless about Soviet war potential. Again and again he asked in despair where Bolshevism still gets its weapons and soldiers. In my opinion this question is unimportant. The essential thing is that it still has them and always manages to get more. But Goering has learned a lot. He, too, now believes that we must expect our enemy in the East to remain strong and that it would be decidedly unwise to take things too lightly. That means —and this is the essence of my argument— that the German war potential must be used to the limit regardless.

We still have one great opportunity with our anti-Bolshevik propaganda. Its intensity should be increased as much as possible. Great results are expected from it. My description of what I intend to do along this line impresses him very much. He is amazed at what we have already achieved on this sector and what I have scheduled for the coming weeks and months.

With regard to the Soviet potential, he agrees that we can meet it effectively only with sweeping measures.

In that connection I described the situation to him as I interpret it. I went far afield and proved my case with much assurance and great skill. He was greatly impressed. After talking to him for an hour he was completely in accord.

It seems to me that Goering has been standing aside too long from the political factors that do the real driving. As a result he has wrong ideas about a number of things. But that can be corrected easily. His advantage consists in his possessing a healthy common sense which always enables him to pick his way through the thicket of a somewhat confused situation. As he is no longer closely connected with our political leaders, he has probably become somewhat tired and apathetic. It is therefore all the more necessary to get him straightened out. For he is a first-rate factor of authority. A determined leadership can't possibly be set up without him or even against him for long. . . .

The little dissensions that have crept into our work in the course of time were not even mentioned. They seem quite unimportant compared with the historic tasks that we have to discuss. Goering evidenced no inclination whatever even to touch upon them. He knew perfectly well that everything was at stake in this meeting, and that we must come to an agreement on a long-range program. I dismiss our misunderstandings with a wave of the hand and then return to the discussion of the absence of any clear leadership in our domestic and foreign politics. With him, too, the Committee of Three [Hans Lammers, Martin Bormann, and Field Marshal Wilhelm Keitel, all close advisers to Hitler] does not sit well at all. He doesn't have any regard for any of the three "Wise Men from the East," as he calls them.

He hates Lammers from the bottom of his soul. He regards him as a bureaucrat who is attempting to get the leadership of the Reich back into the hands of the ministerial bureaucracy. Unfortunately the Fuehrer does not yet quite see through him and considers this super-jurist to be a non-jurist and this super-bureaucrat a non-bureaucrat. The Fuehrer's eyes will have to be opened about him slowly. As regards Bormann, Goering is not quite certain about his true intentions. There seems to be no doubt that he is pursuing ambitious aims. Keitel, in Goering's opinion, is an absolute zero who need not be taken seriously, but whom the other two use in order to make it look as though the Wehrmacht had a hand in their measures.

Goering judges GHQ [General Headquarters or OKW] very harshly. Jodl especially has got his goat. He tells me that Jodl has even begun to tell jokes on the Fuehrer. That certainly won't do. The Fuehrer trusts these people altogether too much. To his face they are naturally very friendly but in their hearts they think quite differently. . . .

Goering sees clearly that events on the Eastern Front the past winter led to a serious crisis of confidence. The generals are doing everything possible to unload this crisis on the Fuehrer. They are now taking revenge for the previous winter, when the measures of the Fuehrer showed them up as having been wrong. . . .

We must certainly be on our guard about the old Wehrmacht and Reichswehr generals. We have very few good friends among them. They are trying to play us off one against the other. So far as I am concerned, I won't have any part in such questionable dealings.

We also spoke at length about [Field Marshal Friedrich von] Paulus, whom Goering criticizes severely. He tells me that the Fuehrer, too, is now convinced that Paulus acted in a cowardly way in surrendering to the Soviets. Goering expects this captured field marshal soon to appear as a speaker in a Moscow broadcast. That would be just about the limit. . . .

Goering evidenced the greatest concern about the Fuehrer. To him, too, the Fuehrer seems to have aged fifteen years during three-and-a-half years of war. It is a tragic thing that the Fuehrer has become such a recluse and leads so unhealthy a life. He doesn't get out into the fresh air. He does not relax. He sits in his bunker, fusses and broods. If one could only transfer him to other surroundings! But he has made up his mind to conduct this war in his own Spartan manner, and I suppose nothing can be done about it.

But it is equally essential that we succeed somehow in making up for the lack of leadership in our domestic and foreign policy. One must not bother the Fuehrer with everything. The Fuehrer must be kept free for the military leadership. One can understand his present mood of sometimes being fed up with life and occasionally even saying that death holds no terrors for him; but for that very reason we must now become his strongest personal support. As was always the case during crises of the Party, the duty of the Fuehrer's closest friends in time of need consists in gathering about him and forming a solid phalanx around his person. What we must now suffer in the way of torture to our souls will pass; what we did to master our difficulties, however, will remain.

Goering realizes perfectly what is in store for all of us if we show any weakness in this war. He has no illusions about that. On the Jewish question, especially, we have taken a position from which there is no escape. That is a good thing. Experience teaches that a movement and a people who have burned their bridges fight with much greater determination than those who are still able to retreat.

I made it clear to Goering that war must be waged not only militarily but also politically. In this connection I spoke about the proposed proclamation for the East. Goering is as firmly convinced of its necessity as I am. He does not believe, however, that Rosenberg can be persuaded to issue it.

He has the worst possible opinion of [Nazi philosopher Alfred] Rosenberg. Like myself he is astonished that the Fuehrer continues to stick to him and clothes him with powers which he is incompetent to use. Rosenberg belongs in an ivory tower, not in a ministry that must look after almost a hundred million people. The Fuehrer thought of the Ministry of the East as a guiding and not an administrative instrument when he created it. Rosenberg, following his old inclination of fussing with things which he knows nothing about, has made a gigantic apparatus of it which he is now unable to control.

Goering also doesn't think much of [Foreign Minister Joachim von] Ribbentrop. He referred very critically to the complete and obvious lack of an active foreign policy. He especially blames Ribbentrop for not succeeding in drawing Spain over to our side. [Spanish dictator Francisco] Franco is, to be sure, cowardly and irresolute; but German foreign policy ought nevertheless to have found a way to bring him into our camp. Ribbentrop also lacks the elegant touch in the handling of people. Goering gave me several truly devastating examples by way of illustration. Goering consistently claims that this war is Ribbentrop's war, and that he never made any earnest attempt to achieve a *modus vivendi* with England, simply because he has an inferiority complex. But there's no point in brooding over this today. We must deal with facts and not with the reasons for these facts. There will be plenty of time for that after the war.

There's the same trouble about our domestic policy. Everybody does and leaves undone what he pleases, because there's no strong authority anywhere. The Party goes its own way and won't have anybody interfere.

Here's where I introduce my proposals. I express the opinion that we'd be "over the hump" if we succeeded in transferring the political leadership tasks of the Reich from the Committee of Three to the Ministerial Council for the Defense of the Reich. This Ministerial Council would then have to be composed of the strong men who assisted the Fuehrer in the Revolution. These will certainly also muster the strength to bring this war to a victorious conclusion.

I blamed Goering very seriously for having permitted the Ministerial Council for the Defense of the Reich to become inactive. He could excuse himself, however, with the fact that Lammers always torpedoed his efforts by constantly butting in and reporting to the Fuehrer. This chicanery must be stopped. If Goering can muster the strength to surround himself with courageous, upright, and loyal men, such a group would undoubtedly be able to relieve the Fuehrer of most of the chores, thus setting him free again for his high mission of leadership. The Fuehrer would certainly approve of such a solution as it would make his historic tasks much easier for him.

Goering was very much impressed with my statement that I had not come to get something from him but rather to bring something to him. I talked at him with all the persuasiveness at my command and finally succeeded in bringing him completely over to our side.

The Party must again be put on its toes and its ranks straightened out. The bothersome church question must rest for the duration of the war. The petty chicaneries still practiced here and there in public life must be done away with. We must no longer waste time on side issues, but keep our eyes fixed upon the main issue, war itself. Only thus can we succeed in concentrating the strength of the nation on a single aim.

While talking I gained the spontaneous impression that my presentation visibly pepped up Goering. He became very enthusiastic about my proposals and immediately asked how we were to proceed specifically. I suggested that he make a number of nominations and I would try to win over the rest. We won't tell any of these about our real intentions; namely, of gradually putting the Committee of Three on ice and transferring its powers to the Ministerial Council. That would only create unnecessary trouble. . . .

We have no other ambition than that of supporting each other and of forming a solid phalanx around the Fuehrer. The Fuehrer sometimes wavers in his decisions if the same matter is brought to him from different sides. Nor does he always react to people as he should. That's where he needs help.

Goering is fully conscious of his somewhat weak position today. He knows that it is decidedly to his advantage for strong men to come to his side and take upon themselves the task of relieving the Fuehrer of his worst worries. We are all determined to make a new contribution to the war by our action.

Goering himself wants to win over Himmler. [Economics Minister Walther] Funk and [Labor leader Robert] Ley have already been won over by me. [Armaments Minister Albert] Speer is entirely my man. Thus we already have a group that can be proud of itself. It certainly includes all those who today enjoy the greatest prestige and highest authority in our political life.

Goering wants to come to Berlin immediately after his trip to Italy and there meet with us again. Speer is to speak to the Fuehrer before then—and if possible I also. Questions of personnel and of division of work can, I believe, be disposed of relatively quickly. We want to show the greatest loyalty in forming this group. We shall pursue no other object save that of victory. We will stand for no intrigue whatever. The fidelity of these men to the Fuehrer is to be unparalleled.

I believe we shall render the Fuehrer the greatest possible service by our action. One just can't stand by any longer and see how he is so weighed down with worries big and small that he can hardly breathe. The cause is greater than any of us; that goes without saying. The men who helped the Fuehrer win the revolution will now have to help him win the war. They were not bureaucrats then; they must not be bureaucrats today.

We still have many an ace up our sleeves. It surely isn't true that we are playing an empty game. If we make use of every possibility, we shall be able, I believe, to effect a fundamental change in the war within a relatively short time. Our problem today is not the people but the leadership. That has been true, incidentally, nearly every war.

The Committee of Three was given a task with a time limit, as the Fuehrer's decree expressly stated. The Ministerial Council for the Defense of the Reich, on the other hand, was given a task for the entire duration.

This first talk with Goering lasted almost four hours. I then had Speer brought in so that Goering himself could reveal to him what we had agreed upon.

We improved the occasion to touch upon a number of specific questions and thus to round out the picture. At the end of our talk each of us had the feeling that all problems that in any way come within our wide radius of action had found a solution in principle. As Goering put it, we shall manage the "Three Wise Men from the East" in a jiffy, whereupon we shall go to work with a driving power and an enthusiasm that will put into the shade anything that ever existed.

I am very happy that a clear basis of mutual trust was established with Goering. I believe that the Fuehrer, too, will be very happy about this. I hope we shall render him the very greatest service possible.

See also working toward the Führer, Vol. 2; Goebbels, Joseph; Göring, Hermann, Vol. 3.

Goebbels's False Optimism in April 1945

Even as the German war effort collapsed and Berlin suffered constant Allied bombing attacks, Propaganda Minister Goebbels offered new plans and praised the efforts of military commanders.

I am now working indefatigably to give the German press clear directions on the aims of our present war policy. Now that Dr. [Otto] Dietrich is out of the way Sündermann is trying to take a hand in the direction of the press. I shall stop that, however, by canceling Sündermann's reserved occupation status so that he can be made available for the front. The German press now presents a thoroughly bellicose aspect. The gravity of the situation is not concealed; readers, however, are given the arguments with which they can come to terms with the present situation in their minds. I am myself dictating guidelines for the German press which are intended to set the standard for the immediate future. They are as follows:

"1. The entire German news and propaganda policy must now be devoted exclusively to re-establishing and increasing the power of resistance, the war effort and fighting morale both at the front and at home. To achieve this aim all resources must be harnessed to produce a direct and indirect impact on readers and audiences. Anything which can be detrimental to this aim or runs counter to it, even only passively, can have no place in press or radio in these decisive days of our fateful struggle. Anything which contributes to the achievement of this great purpose should be expressly promoted and henceforth be a central feature of our newscasting.

2. The main task of the press and radio is to make clear to the German people that our Western enemies are pursuing the same infamous purposes and the same devilish annihilation plans against the German people as are our Eastern enemies; the West is using ostensibly more civilised methods only to deceive the German people and entrap the feeble-minded. The brutal Anglo-American air war is sufficient proof of our Western enemies' bestiality and shows that all their ostensibly conciliatory phrases are mere camouflage designed to paralyse the German people in their stubborn defence of their right to exist. Our task is to point out again and again that Churchill and Roosevelt are just as merciless as Stalin and will ruthlessly carry out their plans for annihilation should the German people ever give way and submit to the enemy yoke.

3. Deeds of heroism at the front and at home should be given priority and embellished with comment. They should not be presented as isolated examples but should act as a stimulus for everybody and a challenge to the whole nation to emulate these shining examples of the struggle for our freedom.

4. The cultural section of our newspapers is not to become a little bourgeois refuge for war-weary brothers. These columns too must use every method to assist in reinforcing our national resistance and our war morale. The particular job of the cultural editor is to express in lofty varied language what has been said in the political section on the military and political struggle of the day. In these weeks superficial intellectual vapourings, divorced from the war as if it

H.R. Trevor-Roper, ed., *The Diaries of Joseph Goebbels: Final Entries 1945.* Trans. Richard Barry. New York: G.P. Putnam's Sons, 1978.

was "far away in Turkey", have no justification for appearance. A plethora of tasks and multifarious possibilities are now open to the cultural editor. Discussion of Clausewitz' writings, descriptions of the Second Punic War, comments on Mommsen's Roman History, dissertations on Frederick the Great's letters and writings, the careers of great warlike geniuses all through human history—these are only a few indications of the new tasks which will do more to promote our purpose than innocent entertaining anecdotes without political or moral content.

5. The local sections of our newspapers must subordinate themselves to these requirements. No measures of communal or local significance issuing from Party, State or Wehrmacht should be presented to the reader without simultaneously impressing upon him forcibly that our struggle for existence requires the mobilisation of all forces and the expenditure of all reserves of manpower and morale. Any sacrifice in the interests of the war, however small and mundane, serves to concentrate our forces and increase our capacity for resistance and must be explained to the reader in this sense.

6. Newspaper publishers are recommended to pay particular attention to the advertisement section. All inopportune leftovers not in consonance with the spirit of the times should be eradicated."

The Führer is very much in agreement with the wording of this directive. He is convinced that I shall now succeed in getting German press policy back on the rails.

I take leave of Fischer, hitherto Head of the German Press Section, who is going to the Wehrmacht. Fischer is most downcast over what has happened; I make clear to him, however, that I could not have acted otherwise than I actually have.

Meister Hahne, the first man to be decorated with the Knight's Cross to the War Service Cross, demonstrates to me a new gun on a captured mounting; he can assemble and make available for Berlin up to 200 of these guns from stocks available in Wehrmacht arsenals and arms production workshops. Hahne proposes that a careful check of Wehrmacht ordnance depots be made; they contain a mass of parts which could be assembled to produce new weapons. We must in fact now improvise in order even partially to make good the serious shortfall in production. That in arms production is the most important. Production at Alkett, for instance, is down by 50% and will fall even further next month. This is extraordinarily worrying and we must adopt new makeshift methods if we are to avoid the resulting calamity.

Once more a mass of new decrees and instructions issue from Bormann. Bormann has turned the Party Chancellery into a paper factory. Every day he sends out a mountain of letters and files which the Gauleiters, now involved in battle, no longer even have time to read. In some cases too it is totally useless stuff of no practical value in our struggle. Even in the Party we have no clear leadership in contact with the people.

As far as our situation in the West is concerned, we now have three major operations planned: one from Holland in the direction of Hamm under command of Colonel-General Student; General Bayerlein is to try to fight his way out of the Ruhr; an attempt is to be made to meet him with a counterattack from outside. In Thuringia a new army under command of General Schulz, well known as having been decorated with the Swords, is to be formed from the units flooding into the area. This army is to take the enemy in flank and try to cut off considerable numbers of his units. Hausser has meanwhile been relieved of his command. He has definitely not stood the test. Obergruppenführer Steiner has been despatched to the Vienna area. He is to hold on there in all circumstances. The Führer has issued the strictest orders of the whole war for the defence of Vienna. Our soldiers must hold out here man for man and anyone who leaves his post is to be shot. It is hoped in this way to get the better of the critical developments in the Vienna area.

[General Ferdinand] Schörner's stock stands very high with the Führer. He has beaten off attacks on the Mährisch-Ostrau industrial zone with the utmost courage. Schörner is our most outstanding army commander. [General Heinz] Guderian has lost a great deal of credit with the Führer. Both in the Baranov and Hungarian areas he urged offensive action prematurely and so placed our operations at great risk, in fact made them impossible. The Führer has accordingly sent him on leave.

In the Führer's view the moment of decision is now upon us in the West. The Führer is indefatigable in urging the generals to resist and leave no stone unturned in order to throw fresh units into the western battle. He calls each individual army commander almost daily and points out to them what is at stake and what their duties and obligations are. In my view it would be better if the Führer addressed the people direct since here in fact are the grass-roots of resistance. Once the people were once more ready to resist, all the others would regain their old form. What both the people and the troops lack is the stirring word to rouse both man and woman. In the nature of things this stirring word can come only from the Führer. It is wrong, therefore, for the generals to think that I should speak instead of the Führer.

The situation is such that only a word from the Führer can relieve the crisis of morale in which the people is plunged at the moment. I regard it as a great mistake that the Führer does not speak. Even if at the moment we have no victory to which we can point, the Führer could still say something; it is not only in victory that one should speak but in misfortune as well. It is at present very difficult to get decisions from the Führer. He is occupied exclusively with the situation in the West and barely finds time for other problems. If, however,

he succeeds in clearing up the situation in the West even partially, he will have done something which may decide the war.

At the daily briefing conferences the Luftwaffe comes in for the sharpest criticism from the Führer. Day after day Göring has to listen without being in a position to demur at all. Colonel-General Stumpff, for instance, refused to subordinate himself to Kesselring for the new operations planned in the West. The Führer called him sharply to order saying that the relative positions of Kesselring and Stumpff were similar to those of him and Schaub.

In the West, of course, it is now and for the immediate future a continuous process of muddling through. We are in the most critical and dangerous phase of this war and one sometimes has the impression that the German people, fighting at the height of the war crisis, has broken out in a sweat impossible for the non-expert to distinguish as the precursor of death or recovery.

The Führer has had very prolonged discussions with Obergruppenführer Kammler who now carries responsibility for the reform of the Luftwaffe. Kammler is doing excellently and great hopes are placed on him.

As far as the situation in the West this evening is concerned it has deteriorated only in Thuringia. Here the enemy has advanced as far as Gotha. At the moment we have nothing with which to oppose him since we do not wish to dissipate our offensive forces. Sauckel is working feverishly to put his Gau into a state of defence. In the Teutoburger Wald too the enemy has registered small gains of ground but they are of no great significance. Otherwise he is closing up all along the Western Front so that we must certainly reckon with further attacks in the next few weeks.

In the South-east the enemy has moved nearer Vienna. We are determined to hold here in all circumstances, cost what it may. Schörner, on the other hand, has beaten off all Soviet attacks made on his front—a really first-class heroic achievement. The

Führer is extraordinarily pleased with Schörner's methods in the field. Schörner will undoubtedly be the next Field-Marshal and he
has earned this promotion.

At this Tuesday's briefing conference the
Führer was no longer so abusive of the generals. He is doing his utmost now to pull his
military staff together, to inspire them with
fresh courage and fill them with confidence
for the future. He is tirelessly preaching a
spirit of battle and resistance, as I am now
doing in our Werwolf [a largely imaginary
last-ditch resistance effort] propaganda. My
directive to the press has given him an opportunity to show the generals how such a
job should be approached. The Führer is also
extraordinarily pleased with my work on

Werwolf. He said at the briefing conference
that this is the way things must be done if the
people are not to become a prey to despair.

This evening I dictate another call to the
Werwolf movement in language reminiscent of that used in *Angriff* [Goebbels's
newspaper] in the good old days of our
struggle.

We have two air-raid alerts in Berlin this
evening. So the enemy is not proposing to
give us time off in the Reich capital. On the
contrary the break has been only for reasons
of weather and the series of air-raid alerts
will undoubtedly not come to an end for the
present.

See also Führerbunker, Vol. 1; Goebbels,
Joseph, Vol. 3.

Declaring War on the United States

*On December 9, 1941, two days after the
Japanese attack on Pearl Harbor, Hitler upheld Germany's pact with Japan by declaring war on the United States. He also blamed
U.S. president Roosevelt for various "warlike" actions in justifying his declaration.*

A nd so the influence of the American
president began to make itself felt in
terms of creating conflicts or in deepening
existing conflicts, at any event in prevent-
ing conflicts from being peacefully resolved. For years the one desire of this man
has been to see conflict break out somewhere in the world, most of all in Europe,
to give him the opportunity of linking the
American economy with that of one of the

two opponents and thereby establishing a
political nexus which might gradually draw
America into such a conflict and thereby di-
vert attention away from an economic policy which had failed at home.

From November 1938 onwards, he began
systematically to sabotage any chance of a
policy leading to European peace . . .

From July 1940 onwards Roosevelt's
measures, whether through the entry of
American citizens into the British Air Force
or through the training of English air force
personnel in the United States, moved further and further in the direction of war. And,
already in August 1940, agreement was
reached on a common military programme
for the United States and Canada.

In September 1940, he came even closer
to war. He handed over 50 destroyers from
the US fleet, accepting in return military
bases in the British possessions in north and

J. Noakes and G. Pridham, eds., *Nazism 1919–1945,* Vol. 3,
*Foreign Policy, War, and Racial Extermination: A Documen-
tary Reader.* Exeter, England: University of Exeter Press, 1988.

Hitler and his staff examine war maps. Hitler justified Germany's declaration of war on the United States on December 9, 1941, as a necessary response to American aggression.

central America. . . . After England was no longer in a position to pay cash for American deliveries he imposed on the American people the Lend-Lease Act . . . In March (1941) occurred the expropriation of all German ships by the American authorities. . . . And, on 9 April, came the first English report that, on the basis of an order of President Roosevelt, an American warship had dropped depth charges on a German U-Boat near Greenland.

On 14 June, contrary to international law, German accounts in the United States were blocked. On 17 June, President Roosevelt demanded, on the basis of mendacious excuses, the withdrawal of German consuls and the closing of German consulates. . . . At the same time, he sent a promise of aid to the Soviet Union. On 10 July, the Navy Minister, Knox, suddenly announced that the USA had issued an order to fire on German warships. On 4 September, the US

cruiser *Greer,* following orders, operated in conjunction with English aircraft against German U-Boats in the Atlantic . . . Finally, on 11 September, Roosevelt made a speech in which he himself reiterated the order to fire on all Axis ships.

The fact that, after years of negotiations with this con man, the Japanese government finally had had enough of allowing itself to be mocked in such an undignified fashion fills us all, the German people, and I believe the other decent people throughout the world with deep satisfaction. I have, therefore, handed the American Chargé d'Affaires his passports and informed him of the following:

In pursuit of a policy aimed at unlimited world dictatorship, the United States under President Roosevelt, in conjunction with England, have shrunk from no means of threatening the basis of existence of the German, Italian, and Japanese peoples. The governments of England and the United States have for this reason not only for the present but also for the future opposed any justifiable revision with the aim of a new and better world order.

Since the beginning of the war, the American President Roosevelt has increasingly been guilty of a series of the most serious crimes against international law. Illegal attacks on ships and other property of German and Italian citizens were combined with threats against and even with the deprivation of the personal liberty of those affected through internment.

The increasingly sharp attacks of the President of the United States finally culminated in his order to the American Navy, contrary to all the rules of international law, to attack ships flying the German and Italian flag on sight, to fire upon them and sink them. American ministers proudly boasted of having sunk German U-boats in this criminal fashion. German and Italian merchant ships were attacked by American cruisers, commandeered, and their innocent crews led off to prison. Moreover, President Roosevelt's plan to launch an attack on Germany and Italy in Europe itself, by 1943 at the latest, has now been published in America without any attempt at an official denial by the American government. This has destroyed the honest efforts of Germany and Italy to prevent an extension of the war and to maintain relations with the US, efforts which have demonstrated an exemplary patience in the face of intolerable provocations by President Roosevelt which have been going on for years. Germany and Italy have now found themselves finally compelled to undertake a struggle for their defence and thereby for the maintenance of the freedom and independence of their nations and empires against the United States of America and England, side by side with Japan, in fulfilment of the provisions of the Tripartite Pact of 27 September 1940.

See also Pearl Harbor, Tripartite Pact, Vol. 2.

Hitler Promises Revenge for the July 1944 Plot

Hitler suffered only minor injuries in the unsuccessful assassination attempt of July 20, 1944, plotted by members of the German resistance. Only twelve hours after the explosion at his East Prussia headquarters, Hitler broadcast a message on national radio assuring the German people that he was alive and well and leaving no doubt that his revenge would be immediate and ruthless.

If I speak to you today it is first in order that you should hear my voice and should know that I am unhurt and well, and sec-

ondly, that you should know of a crime unparelleled in German history.

A very small clique [group] of ambitious, irresponsible, and at the same time, senseless and stupid officers had concocted a plot to eliminate me and, with me, the staff of the High Command of the *Wehrmacht*. . . . This time we shall settle accounts with them in the manner to which we National Socialists are accustomed.

See also July 1944 Plot, Vol. 1, resistance movements, Germany, Vol. 2

Excerpted from William L. Shirer, *The Rise and Fall of the Third Reich.* New York: Simon and Schuster, 1960.

Hitler Responds to the Concerns of U.S. President Franklin D. Roosevelt

After facing criticism in 1939 from Roosevelt regarding his foreign policy objectives, Hitler responded in a speech in the Reichstag by claiming that despite Germany's small size, large population, and lack of resources, he had accomplished amazing things. Roosevelt, therefore, had no right to judge him. Moreover, Hitler asserted, the president's concerns over German plans were unfounded. The Führer's subtle and sarcastic delivery of this speech inspired much laughter from the assembled delegates.

The world on the 15 April 1939 was informed of the contents of a telegram which I myself did not see until later. It is difficult to classify this document or to arrange it in any known scheme. I will therefore endeavour before you, Gentlemen, and thus before the whole German people, to analyse the necessary answers in your name and in that of the German people.

1. Mr. Roosevelt is of the opinion that I too must realize that throughout the world hundreds of millions of human beings are living in constant fear of a new war or even a series of wars. This, he says, is of concern to the people of the United States, for whom he speaks, as it must also be to the peoples of the other nations of the entire western hemisphere.

In reply to this it must be said in the first place that this fear of war has undoubtedly existed among mankind from time immemorial, and justifiably so. For instance, after the Peace Treaty of Versailles fourteen wars were waged between 1919 and 1938 alone, in none of which Germany was concerned, but in which States of the 'western hemisphere', in whose name President Roosevelt also speaks, were indeed concerned. In addition there were in the same period twenty-six violent interventions and sanctions carried through by means of bloodshed and force. Germany also played no part whatever in these. The United States alone has carried out military interventions in six cases since 1918. Since 1918 Soviet Russia has engaged in ten wars and military actions involving force and bloodshed. Again, Germany was concerned in none of these, nor was she the cause of any of these events. It would therefore be a mistake in my eyes to assume that the fear of war inspiring European and non-European nations can at this present time be directly traced back to actual wars at all. The reason for this fear lies simply and solely in an unbridled agitation on the part of the Press, an agitation as mendacious as it is base, in the circulation of vile pamphlets about the heads of foreign States, and in an artificial spreading of panic which in the end goes so far that interventions from another planet are believed possible and cause scenes of desperate alarm. I believe that as soon as the responsible Governments impose upon themselves and their journalistic organs the necessary restraint and truthfulness as regards the relations of the various countries to one another, and in particular as regards internal happenings in other countries, the fear of war will disappear at once, and the tranquillity which we all desire so much will become possible.

The Speeches of Adolf Hitler, April 1922–August 1939, Vol. 2. Trans. and ed. Norman H. Baynes. New York: Howard Fertig, 1969.

2. In his telegram Mr. Roosevelt expresses the belief that every major war, even if it were to be confined to other continents, must have serious consequences while it lasts, and also for generations to come.

Answer: No one knows this better than the German people. For the Peace Treaty of Versailles imposed burdens on the German people which could not have been paid off even in a hundred years, although it has been proved precisely by American teachers of constitutional law, historians, and professors of history that Germany was no more to blame for the outbreak of the War than any other nation. But I do not believe that every conflict must have disastrous consequences for the whole surrounding world, that is for the whole globe, provided the whole world is not systematically drawn into such conflicts by means of a network of nebulous pact obligations. For since in past centuries and—as I pointed out at the beginning of my answer—also in the course of the last decades, the world has experienced a continuous series of wars, if Mr. Roosevelt's assumption were correct, humanity would already have a burden, in the sum total of the outcome of all these wars, which it would have to bear for millions of years to come.

3. Mr. Roosevelt declared that he had already appealed to me on a former occasion on behalf of a peaceful settlement of political, economic, and social problems without resort to arms.

Answer: I myself have always been an exponent of this view and, as history proves, have settled necessary political, economic, and social problems without force of arms, i.e., without resort to arms.

Unfortunately however this peaceful settlement has been made more difficult by the agitation of politicians, statesmen and newspaper representatives who were neither directly concerned nor even affected by the problems in question.

4. Mr. Roosevelt believes that the 'tide of events' is once more bringing the threat

of arms with it, and that if this threat continues a large part of the world is condemned to a common ruin.

Answer: As far as Germany is concerned I know nothing of this kind of threat to other nations, although I read in the democratic newspapers every day lies about such a threat. Every day I read of German mobilizations, of the landing of troops, of extortions—all this in regard to States with whom we are not only living in deepest peace, but also with whom we are, in many cases, the closest friends.

5. Mr. Roosevelt believes, further, that in case of war victorious, vanquished, and neutral nations will all suffer.

Answer: As a politician I have been the exponent of this conviction for twenty years, at a time when unfortunately the responsible statesmen in America could not bring themselves to make the same admission as regards their participation in the Great War and its issue.

6. Mr. Roosevelt believes lastly that it lies with the leaders of the great nations to preserve their peoples from the impending disaster.

Answer: If that is true, then it is a punishable neglect, to use no worse word, if the leaders of nations with corresponding powers are not capable of controlling their newspapers which are agitating for war, and so to save the world from the threatening calamity of an armed conflict. I am not able to understand, further, why these responsible leaders, instead of cultivating diplomatic relations between nations, make them more difficult and indeed disturb them by recalling ambassadors, etc. without any reason.

7. Mr. Roosevelt declared finally that three nations in Europe and one in Africa have seen their independent existence terminated.

Answer: I do not know which three nations in Europe are meant. Should it be a question of the provinces reincorporated in the German Reich I must draw the attention of Mr. Roosevelt to an historical error. It is not now that these nations sacrificed their independent existence in Europe, but rather in 1918 when they, contrary to solemn promises, were separated from their communities and made into nations which they never wished to be and never were, and when they had forced upon them an independence which was no independence but at the most could only mean dependence upon an international foreign world which they hated.

As for the fact, however, that one nation in Africa is alleged to have lost its freedom—that too is but an error; for it is not a question of one nation in Africa having lost its freedom—on the contrary practically all the previous inhabitants of this continent have been made subject to the sovereignty of other nations by bloody force, thereby losing their freedom. Moroccans, Berbers, Arabs, negroes, &c., have all fallen a victim to foreign might, the swords of which, however, were not inscribed 'Made in Germany', but 'Made by democracies'.

8. Mr. Roosevelt then speaks of the reports which admittedly he does not believe to be correct, but which state that further acts of aggression are contemplated against still other independent nations.

Answer: I consider every such unfounded insinuation as an offence against the tranquillity and consequently the peace of the world. I also see therein something which tends to frighten smaller nations or at least make them nervous. If Mr. Roosevelt really has any specific instances in mind in this connexion I would ask him to name the States who are threatened with aggression and to name the aggressor in question. It will then be possible to refute these monstrous general accusations by brief statements.

9. Mr. Roosevelt states that the world is plainly moving towards the moment when this situation must end in catastrophe unless a rational way of guiding events is found.

He also declares that I have repeatedly asserted that I and the German people have no desire for war and that if this is true there need be no war.

Answer: I wish to point out firstly that I have not conducted any war, secondly that for years past I have expressed my abhorrence of war and, it is true, also my abhorrence of war-mongers, and thirdly that I am not aware for what purpose I should wage a war at all. I should be thankful to Mr. Roosevelt if he would give me some explanation in this connexion.

10. Mr. Roosevelt is finally of the opinion that the peoples of the earth could not be persuaded that any governing Power has any right or need to inflict the consequences of war on its own or any other people save in the cause of self-evident home defence.

Answer: I should think that every reasonable human being is of this opinion, but it seems to me that in almost every war both sides claim a case of unquestionable home defence, and that there is no institution in this world, including the American President himself, which could clear up this problem unequivocally. There is hardly any possibility of doubt, for example, that America's entry into the Great War was not a case of unquestionable home defence. A research committee set up by President Roosevelt himself has examined the causes of America's entry into the Great War, and reached the conclusion that the entry ensued chiefly for exclusively capitalistic reasons. Nevertheless no practical conclusions have been drawn from this fact. Let us hope then that at least the United States will in the future itself act according to this noble principle, and will not go to war against any country except in the case of unquestionable home defence.

11. Mr. Roosevelt says further that he does not speak from selfishness nor fear nor weakness, but with the voice of strength and friendship for mankind.

Answer: If this voice of strength and friendship for mankind had been raised by America at the proper time, and if above all it had possessed some practical value, then at least there could have been prevented that treaty which has become the source of the direst derangement of humanity and history, namely the Dictate of Versailles.

12. Mr. Roosevelt declares further that it is clear to him that all international problems can be solved at the council table.

Answer: Theoretically one ought to believe in this possibility, for common sense would correct demands on the one hand and show the compelling necessity of a compromise on the other.

For example, according to all common sense logic, and the general principles of a higher human justice indeed according to the laws of a Divine will, all peoples ought to have an equal share of the goods of this world. It ought not then to happen that one people needs so much living space that it cannot get along with fifteen inhabitants to the square kilometre, while others are forced to nourish 140, 150, or even 200 on the same area. But in no case should these fortunate peoples curtail the existing living space of those who are, as it is, suffering, by robbing them of their colonies, for instance. I would therefore be very happy if these problems could really find their solution at the council table. My scepticism, however, is based on the fact that it was America herself who gave sharpest expression to her mistrust in the effectiveness of conferences. For the greatest conference of all time was without any doubt the League of Nations. This authoritative body representing all the peoples of the world created in accordance with the will of an American President, was supposed to solve the problems of humanity at the council table. The first State, however, that shrank from this endeavour was the United States—the reason being that President Wilson himself even then nourished the greatest doubts of the possibility of really being able to solve decisive international problems at the conference table.

We honour your well-meant opinion, Mr. Roosevelt, but opposed to your opinion stands the actual fact that in almost twenty years of the activity of the greatest conference in the world, namely, the League of Nations, it has proved impossible to solve one single decisive international problem. Contrary to Wilson's promise Germany was hindered for many years by the Peace Treaty of Versailles from participating in this great world conference. In spite of the most bitter experience one German Government believed that there was no need to follow the example of the United States, and that they should therefore take their seat at this conference table. It was not till after years of purposeless participation that I resolved to follow the example of America and likewise leave the largest conference in the world. Since then I have solved the problems concerning my people, which like all others were, unfortunately, not solved at the conference table of the League of Nations—and also without recourse to war in any case. Apart from this, however, as already mentioned, numerous other problems have been brought before world conferences in recent years without any solution having been found. If however, Mr. Roosevelt, your belief that every problem can be solved at the conference table is true, then all nations, including the United States, have been led in the past 7,000 or 8,000 years either by blind men or by criminals. For all of them, including the statesmen of the United States and especially her greatest, did not make the chief part of their history at the conference table but with the aid of the strength of their people. The freedom of North America was not achieved at the conference table any more than the conflict between the North and the South was decided there. I will say nothing about the innumerable struggles which finally led to the subjugation of the North American continent as a whole. I mention all this only in order to show that your view, Mr. Roosevelt, although undoubtedly deserving of all honour, finds no confirmation in the history either of your own country or of the rest of the world.

13. Mr. Roosevelt continues that it is no answer to the plea for peaceful discussion

for one side to plead that, unless they receive assurances beforehand that the verdict will be theirs, they will not lay aside their arms.

Answer: Do you believe, Mr. Roosevelt, that when the final fate of nations is in the balance, a Government or the leaders of a people will lay down their arms or surrender them before a conference, simply in the blind hope that in their wisdom or, if you like, their discernment, the other members of the conference will arrive at the right conclusion? Mr. Roosevelt, there has been only one country and one government which have acted according to the recipe extolled in such glowing terms, and that country was Germany. The German nation once, trusting in the solemn assurances of President Wilson and in the confirmation of these assurances by the Allies, laid down its arms and thus went unarmed to the conference table. It is true that as soon as the German nation had laid down its arms it was not even invited to the conference table but, in violation of all assurances, was made to suffer the worst breaking of a word that had ever been known. Then one day, instead of the greatest confusion known in history being resolved around the conference table, the cruellest dictated treaty in the world brought about a still more fearful confusion. But the representatives of the German nation, who, trusting to the solemn assurances of an American President, had laid down their arms and therefore appeared unarmed, were not received, even when they came to accept the terms of the dictated treaty, as the representatives of a nation which at all events had held out with infinite heroism against a whole world for four years in the struggle for its liberty and independence; they were subjected to greater degradations than those inflicted on the chieftains of Sioux tribes. The German delegates were insulted by the mob, stones were thrown at them, and they were dragged like prisoners, not to the council table of the world, but before the tribunal of the victors; and there, at the pistol's point,

they were forced to undergo the most shameful subjection and plundering that the world had ever known. I can assure you, Mr. Roosevelt, that I am steadfastly determined to see to it that not only now, but for all future time, no German shall ever enter a conference defenceless, but that at all times and for ever every German negotiator should and shall have behind him the united strength of the German nation, so help me God.

14. The President of the United States believes that in conference rooms as in courts, it is necessary that both sides enter in good faith, assuming that substantial justice will accrue to both.

Answer: German representatives will never again enter a conference that is for them a tribunal. For who is to be the judge there? At a conference there is no accused and no prosecutor, but only two contending parties. And if their own good sense does not bring about a settlement between the two parties, they will never surrender themselves to the verdict of disinterested foreign Powers.

Incidentally the United States itself declined to enter the League of Nations and to become the victim of a Court which was able by a majority vote to give a verdict against individual interests. But I should be grateful to President Roosevelt if he would explain to the world what the new World Court is to be like. Who are the judges here, according to what procedure are they selected, and on what responsibility do they act? And above all, to whom can they be made to account for their decisions?

15. Mr. Roosevelt believes that the cause of world peace would be greatly advanced if the nations of the world were to give a frank statement relating to the present and future policy of their governments.

Answer: I have already done this, Mr. Roosevelt, in innumerable public speeches. And in the course of this present meeting of the German Reichstag I have again—as far as this is possible in the space of two hours—made a statement of this kind.

I must, however, decline to give such an explanation to anyone else than to the people for whose existence and life I am responsible, and who on the other hand alone have the right to demand that I account to them. However, I give the aims of the German policy so openly that the entire world can hear it in any case. But these explanations are without significance for the outside world as long as it is possible for the Press to falsify and suspect every statement, to question it or to cover it with fresh lying replies.

16. Mr. Roosevelt believes that, because the United States as one of the nations of the western hemisphere is not involved in the immediate controversies which have arisen in Europe, I should therefore be willing to make such a statement of policy to him, as the head of a nation so far removed from Europe.

Hitler claimed that the concerns of President Franklin D. Roosevelt (pictured signing the declaration of war against Germany and Italy) over Germany's territorial ambitions were groundless.

Answer: Mr. Roosevelt therefore seriously believes that the cause of international peace would really be furthered if I were to make to the nations of the world a public statement on the present policy of the German Government.

But how does Mr. Roosevelt come to expect of the head of the German State above all to make a statement without the other governments being invited to make such a statement of their policy as well? I certainly believe that it is not feasible to make such a statement to the head of any foreign State, but rather that such statements should preferably be made to the whole world, in accordance with the demand made at the time by President Wilson for the abolition of secret diplomacy. Hitherto I was not only always prepared to do this, but, as I have already said, I have done it only too often. Unfortunately the most important statements concerning the aims and intentions of German policy have been in many so-called democratic States either withheld from the people or distorted by the Press. If, however, President Roosevelt thinks that he is qualified to address such a request to Germany or Italy of all nations because America is so far removed from Europe, we on our side might with the same right address to the President of the American Republic the question as to what aims American foreign policy has in view in its turn, and on what intentions this policy is based—in the case of the Central and South American States for instance. In this case Mr. Roosevelt would, rightly, I must admit, refer to the Monroe Doctrine and decline to comply with such a request as interference in the internal affairs of the American Continent. We Germans support a similar doctrine for Europe—and above all for the territory and the interests of the Greater German Reich.

Moreover I would obviously never presume to address such a request to the President of the United States of America, because I assume that he would probably rightly consider such a presumption tactless.

17. The American President further declares that he would then communicate information received by him concerning the political aims of Germany to other nations now apprehensive as to the course of our policy.

Answer: How has Mr. Roosevelt learned which nations consider themselves threatened by German policy and which do not?

Or is Mr. Roosevelt in a position, in spite of the enormous amount of work which must rest upon him in his own country, to recognize of his own accord all these inner spiritual and mental impressions of other peoples and their governments?

18. Finally Mr. Roosevelt asks that assurances be given him that the German Armed Forces will not attack, and above all not invade, the territory or possessions of the following independent nations. He then names those as most likely: Finland, Latvia, Lithuania, Esthonia, Norway, Sweden, Denmark, the Netherlands, Belgium, Great Britain, Ireland, France, Portugal, Spain, Switzerland, Liechtenstein, Luxemburg, Poland, Hungary, Rumania, Yugoslavia, Russia, Bulgaria, Turkey, Iraq, the Arabias, Syria, Palestine, Egypt, and Iran.

Answer: I have first of all taken the trouble to ascertain from the States mentioned whether they feel themselves threatened, and secondly and above all, whether this inquiry by the American President was addressed to us at their suggestion or at any rate with their consent.

The reply was in all cases negative, in some instances strongly so. It is true that I could not cause inquiries to be made of certain of the States and nations mentioned because they themselves—as for example Syria—are at present not in possession of their freedom, but are occupied and consequently deprived of their rights by the military agents of democratic states.

Thirdly, apart from this fact, all States bordering on Germany have received much more binding assurances and above all suggestions than Mr. Roosevelt asked from me in his curious telegram.

Fourthly, should there be any doubt as to the value of these general and direct statements which I have so often made, then any further statement of this kind, even if addressed to the American President, would be equally worthless. For ultimately it is not the value which Mr. Roosevelt attaches to such statements which is decisive, but the value attached to these statements by the countries in question.

Fifthly, I must also draw Mr. Roosevelt's attention to one or two historical errors. He mentions Ireland, for instance, and asks for a statement to the effect that Germany will not attack Ireland. Now I have just read a speech delivered by Mr. De Valera, the Prime Minister of Eire, in which strangely enough, and contrary to Mr. Roosevelt's opinion, he does not charge Germany with oppressing Ireland, but reproaches England with subjecting Ireland to continuous aggression at her hands. With all due respect to Mr. Roosevelt's insight into the needs and cares of other countries, it may nevertheless be assumed that the Eire Prime Minister will be more familiar with the dangers which threaten his country than the President of the United States.

In the same way the fact has obviously escaped Mr. Roosevelt's notice that Palestine is at present occupied not by German troops but by the English; and that the country is having its liberty restricted by the most brutal resort to force, is being robbed of its independence and is suffering the cruellest maltreatment for the benefit of Jewish interlopers. The Arabs living in that country will therefore certainly not have complained to Mr. Roosevelt of German aggression, but they do voice a continuous appeal to the world, deploring the barbarous methods with which England is attempting to suppress a people which loves its freedom and is but defending it.

This, too, is perhaps a problem which according to the American President would have to be solved at the conference table, that is, in the presence of a just judge, and not by physical force, military means, mass executions, burning down villages, blowing up houses and so on. For one fact is undoubtedly certain: in this case England is not defending herself against a threatened Arab attack, but as an interloper, and, without being called upon to do so, is endeavouring to establish her power in a foreign territory which does not belong to her. A whole series of similar errors which Mr. Roosevelt has made might be pointed out, quite apart from the difficulty of military operations on the part of Germany in States and countries, some of which are 2,000 and 5,000 kilometres away from us. In conclusion, however, I have the following statement to make:

The German Government is nevertheless prepared to give each of the States named an assurance of the kind desired by Mr. Roosevelt on the condition of absolute reciprocity, provided that the State wishes it and itself addresses to Germany a request for such an assurance together with appropriate proposals. Regarding a number of the States included in Mr. Roosevelt's list, this question can probably be accepted as settled from the very start, since we are already either allied with them or at least united by close ties of friendship. As for the duration of these agreements, Germany is willing to make terms with each individual State in accordance with the wishes of that State.

But I should not like to let this opportunity pass without giving above all to the President of the United States an assurance regarding those territories which would, after all, give him most cause for apprehension, namely the United States itself and the other States of the American continent.

And I here solemnly declare that all the assertions which have been circulated in any way concerning an intended German attack or invasion on or in American territory are rank frauds and gross untruths. Quite apart from the fact that such assertions, as far as the military possibilities are concerned, could have their origin only in a stupid imagination.

19. The American President then goes on to declare in this connexion that he regards the discussion of the most effective and immediate manner in which the peoples of the world can obtain relief from the crushing burden of armaments as the most important factor of all.

Answer: Mr. Roosevelt perhaps does not know that this problem, in so far as it concerns Germany, has already been completely solved on one occasion. The Allied Commissions had expressly confirmed the fact that between 1919 and 1923 Germany had completely disarmed. . . . According to the solemn pledges once given Germany, pledges which found their confirmation even in the Peace Treaty of Versailles, all this was supposed to be an advance contribution which would then make it possible for the rest of the world to disarm without danger. In this point, as in all others where Germany believed that a promise would be kept, she was disgracefully deceived. All attempts to induce the other States to disarm, pursued in negotiations at the conference table over many years, came, as is well known, to nothing. This disarmament would have been but the execution of pledges already given, and at the same time just and prudent. I myself, Mr. Roosevelt, have made any number of practical proposals for consultation and tried to bring about a discussion of them in order to make possible a general limitation of armaments to the lowest possible level. I proposed a maximum strength for all armies of 200,000, similarly the abolition of all offensive weapons, of bombing planes, of poison gas, &c., &c. It was not possible, however, to carry out these plans in the face of the rest of the world, although Germany herself was at the time completely disarmed. I then proposed a maximum of 300,000 for armies. The proposal met with the same negative reception. I then submitted a great number of detailed disarmament proposals—in each case before the forum of the German Reichstag and consequently before the whole world. It never occurred to anyone even to discuss the matter. The rest of the world began instead to increase still further their already enormous armaments. And not until 1934, when the last of my comprehensive proposals—that concerning 300,000 as the maximum size of the army—was ultimately turned down, did I give the order for German rearmament, which was now to be very thorough. Nevertheless I do not want to be an obstacle in the way of disarmament discussions, at which you, Mr. Roosevelt, intend to be present. I would ask you, however, not to appeal first to me and to Germany, but rather to the others; I have a long line of practical experience behind me, and shall remain sceptically inclined until reality has taught me to know better.

20. Mr. Roosevelt gives us his pledge, finally, that he is prepared to take part in discussions to establish the most practical manner of opening up avenues of international trade so that every nation of the world may be enabled to buy and sell on equal terms in the world's market, as well as to possess assurances of obtaining the raw materials and products of peaceful economic life.

Answer: It is my belief, Mr. Roosevelt, that it is not so much a question of discussing these problems theoretically, as of removing in practice the barriers which exist in international trade. The worst barriers, however, lie in the individual States themselves. Experience so far shows at any rate that the greatest world economic conferences have come to nothing, simply because the various countries were not able to maintain order in their domestic economic systems; or else because they infected the international capital market with uncertainty by currency manipulation, and, above all, by causing continual fluctuations in the value of their currencies to one another. It is likewise an unbearable burden for world economic relations that it should be possible in some countries for some ideological reason or other to let loose a wild boycott agitation against other countries and their goods and so practically to eliminate them from the market. It is my belief, Mr. Roosevelt, that it would be a great service if you with your great influence would remove these barriers to a genuinely free world trade beginning with the United States. For it is my conviction that if the leaders of nations are not even capable of regulating production in their own countries or of removing boycotts pursued for ideological reasons which can damage trade relations between countries to so great an extent, there is much less prospect of achieving by means of international agreements any really fruitful step towards the improvement of economic relations. The equal right for all of buying and selling in the world's market can only be guaranteed in this way. Further, the German people have made in this regard very concrete claims, and I would appreciate it very much if you, Mr. Roosevelt, as one of the successors to the late President Wilson, were to devote yourself to seeing that the promises be at last redeemed, on the basis of which Germany once laid down her arms and gave herself up to the so-called victors. I am thinking less of the innumerable millions extorted from Germany as so-called reparations than of the territories stolen from Germany. In and outside Europe Germany lost approximately three million square kilometres of territory, and that in spite of the fact that the whole German Colonial Empire, in contrast to the colonies of other nations, was not acquired by way of war, but solely through treaties or purchase.

President Wilson [Woodrow, 1912–1920] solemnly pledged his word that the German colonial claims, like all others, would receive the same just examination. Instead of this, however, the German possessions were given to nations who have always had the largest colonial empires, while our people was exposed to a great anxiety, which is now—as it will continue to be in the future —particularly pressing.

It would be a noble act if President Franklin Roosevelt were to redeem the promises made by President Woodrow Wilson. This would in the first place be a practical contribution to the moral consolidation of the world and consequently to the improvement of its economic conditions.

Mr. Roosevelt also stated in conclusion that the heads of all great Governments are in this hour responsible for the fate of humanity. They cannot fail to hear the prayers of their peoples to be protected from the foreseeable chaos of war. And I, too, would be held accountable for this.

Mr. Roosevelt! I fully understand that the vastness of your nation and the immense wealth of your country allow you to feel responsible for the history of the whole world and for the history of all nations. I, Sir, am placed in a much more modest and smaller sphere. You have 130 million people on 9.5 million square kilometres. You possess a country with enormous riches in all mineral resources, fertile enough to feed half a billion people and to provide them with all necessities.

I once took over a State which was faced by complete ruin, thanks to its trust in the promises of the rest of the world and to the bad régime of democratic governments. In this State there are roughly 140 people to each square kilometre—not 15 as in America. The fertility of our country cannot be compared with that of yours. We lack numerous minerals which nature has placed at your disposal in unlimited quantities. The billions of German savings accumulated in gold and foreign exchange during many years of peace were squeezed out of us and taken from us. We lost our colonies. In 1933 I had in my country seven million unemployed, a few million workers on half time, millions of peasants sinking into poverty, destroyed trade, ruined commerce; in short, general chaos.

Since then, Mr. Roosevelt, I have only been able to fulfil one simple task. I cannot feel myself responsible for the fate of a world, as this world took no interest in the pitiful fate of my own people. I have regarded myself as called upon by Providence to serve my own people alone and to deliver them from their frightful misery. Consequently, during the past six and a half years I have lived day and night for the single task of awakening the powers of my people in view of our desertion by the whole of the rest of the world, of developing these powers to the utmost, and of utilizing them for the salvation of our community. I have conquered chaos in Germany, re-established order, enormously increased production in all branches of our national economy, by strenuous efforts produced substitutes for numerous materials which we lack, smoothed the way for new inventions, developed traffic, caused mighty roads to be built and canals to be dug, called into being gigantic new factories and at the same time endeavoured to further the education and culture of our people. I have succeeded in finding useful work once more for the whole of the seven million unemployed who so appeal to the hearts of us all, in keeping the German peasant on his soil in spite of all difficulties, and in saving the land itself for him, in once more bringing German trade to a peak and in assisting traffic to the utmost. As a precaution against the threats of another world not only have I united the German people politically, but have also rearmed them; I have also endeavoured to destroy sheet by sheet that treaty which in its 448 articles contains the vilest oppression which peoples and human beings have ever been expected to put up with. I have brought back to the Reich the provinces stolen from us in 1919, I have led back to their native country millions of Germans who were torn away from us and were in misery, I have re-established the historic unity of the German living space and, Mr. Roosevelt, have endeavoured to attain all this without spilling blood and without bringing to my people and consequently to others the misery of war. I, who twenty-one years ago was an unknown worker and sol-dier of my people, have attained this, Mr. Roosevelt, by my own energy, and can therefore in the face of history claim a place among those men who have done the utmost which can be fairly and justly demanded from a single individual. You, Mr. Roosevelt, have a much easier task in comparison. You became President of the United States in 1933 when I became Chancellor of the Reich. In other words, from the very outset you stepped to the head of one of the largest and wealthiest States in the world. You have the good fortune to have to feed scarcely fifteen people per square kilometre in your country. You have at your disposal the most unlimited mineral resources in the world. As a result of the large area covered by your country and the fertility of your fields, you are enabled to ensure for each individual American ten times the amount of commodities possible in Germany. Nature has in any case enabled you to do this. In spite of the fact that the population of your country is scarcely one third greater than the number of inhabitants in Greater Germany, you possess more than fifteen times as much living space. Conditions prevailing in your country are on such a large scale that you can find time and leisure to give your attention to universal problems. Consequently the world is undoubtedly so small for you that you perhaps believe that your intervention and action can be effective everywhere. In this sense therefore your concerns and suggestions cover a much larger and wider area than mine, because my world, Mr. Roosevelt, in which Providence has placed me and for which I am therefore obliged to work, is unfortunately much smaller, although for me it is more precious than anything else, for it is limited to my people! I believe, however, this is the way in which I can be of most service to that for which we are all concerned, namely, the justice, well-being, progress and peace of the whole human community.

Hitler's Last Will and Political Testament

Having decided to marry his longtime mistress, Eva Braun, and then commit suicide, Adolf Hitler issued his last will and political testament on April 29, 1945. The documents allowed him to settle his accounts before history, name his successors, and, as ever, blame his problems on international Jewry.

*M*y private Will and Testament
As I did not consider that during the years of struggle I could take the responsibility of contracting a marriage, I have now decided, before the closing of my earthly career, to take as my wife the girl who, after many years of loyal friendship, of her own free will, in order to share her destiny with mine, entered this town when it was almost completely besieged. At her own desire she goes as my wife with me into death. It will compensate us for what we have both lost through my work in the service of my people.

What I possess belongs, in so far as it has any value, to the Party; should that no longer exist, to the State; should the State also be destroyed, no further decision of mine is necessary.

My pictures, in the collections which I have bought over the years, have never been collected for private purposes, but only for the extension of a gallery in my home town of Linz on the Danube.

It is my most sincere wish that this bequest may be duly executed.

I nominate as my Executor my most faithful Party comrade, Martin Bormann.

He is given full legal authority to make all decisions. He is permitted to take away

everything that has sentimental value or is necessary for the maintenance of a modest simple life, for my brothers and sisters, also above all for the mother of my wife and my faithful co-workers who are well known to him, principally my old Secretaries, Frau Winter, etc., who have for many years aided me by their work.

I myself and my wife, in order to escape the disgrace of deposition or capitulation, choose death. It is our wish to be burnt immediately on the spot where I have carried out the greatest part of my daily work in the course of twelve years' service to my people.

Given in Berlin, 29 April 1945, 4 A.M.

[signed] A. HITLER

My political Testament
More than thirty years have now passed since in 1914 I made my modest contribution as a volunteer in the First World War that was forced upon the Reich.

In these three decades I have been actuated solely by love and loyalty to my people in all my thoughts, acts, and life. They gave me the strength to make the most difficult decisions which have ever confronted mortal man. In these three decades I have spent my time, my working strength, and my health.

It is untrue that I or anyone else in Germany wanted the war in 1939. It was desired and instigated exclusively by those international statesmen who were either of Jewish descent or worked for Jewish interests. I have made too many offers for the control and limitation of armaments, which posterity will not for all time be able to disregard, for the responsibility for the outbreak of this war to be laid on me. I have, moreover, never wished that after the first fatal world war a second against England,

Jeremy Noakes and Geoffrey Pridham, eds., *Documents on Nazism, 1919–1945.* New York: Viking, 1974.

or even against America, should break out. Centuries will pass away, but out of the ruins of our towns and monuments hatred will grow for those finally responsible whom we have to thank for everything, International Jewry and its accomplices.

Three days before the outbreak of the German-Polish war I proposed once more to the British ambassador in Berlin a solution to the German-Polish problem, similar to that in the case of the Saar district, under international control. Neither can this offer be denied. It was rejected only because the leading circles in English politics wanted war, partly on account of the business they hoped to gain by it and partly under the influence of propaganda organized by International Jewry.

I also made it quite plain that, if the nations of Europe are again to be regarded as mere shares to be bought and sold by these international conspirators in money and finance, then Jewry, the race which is the real criminal in this murderous struggle, will be saddled with the responsibility. I further left no one in doubt that this time millions of children of Europe's Aryan peoples would not die of hunger, millions of grown men would not suffer death, nor would hundreds of thousands of women and children be burnt and bombed to death in the towns, without the real criminal having to atone for this guilt, even if by more humane means.

After six years of war, which despite all setbacks will one day go down in history as the most glorious and valiant demonstration of the purpose of a nation's life, I cannot forsake the city which is the capital of this Reich. As our forces are too small to make any further stand against the enemy attack on this place and our resistance is gradually being weakened by men who are as deluded as they are lacking in initiative, it is my wish, by remaining in this town, to share my fate with those millions of others who have taken upon themselves to do the same. Moreover, I do not wish to fall into the hands of an enemy who is looking for a new spectacle organized by the Jews for the amusement of their hysterical masses.

I have decided therefore to remain in Berlin and there of my own free will to choose death at the moment when I believe the position of Führer and Chancellor can itself no longer be held.

I die with a happy heart, conscious of the immeasurable deeds and achievements of our soldiers at the front, our women at home, the achievements of our farmers and workers, and the work, unique in history, of our Youth who bear my name.

That from the bottom of my heart I express my thanks to you all, is just as self-evident as my wish that you should, because of that, on no account give up the struggle, but rather continue it against the enemies of the Fatherland, no matter where, true to the creed of the great Clausewitz. From the sacrifice of our soldiers and from my own unity with them unto death will in any event spring up in the history of Germany the seed of a radiant renaissance of the National Socialist movement and thus of the realization of a true community of nations.

Many of the most courageous men and women have decided to unite their lives with mine unto the very last. I have begged and finally ordered them not to do this, but to take part in the further battle of the nation. I beg the heads of the Armies, the Navy and the Air Force to strengthen by all possible means the spirit of resistance of our soldiers in the National Socialist sense, specially bearing in mind that I myself also, as founder and creator of this movement, have preferred death to cowardly abdication or even capitulation.

May it become, at some future time, part of the code of honour of the German officer, as it is already in our Navy, that the surrender of a district or of a town is impossible, and that the leaders here, above all, must march ahead as shining examples, faithfully fulfilling their duty unto death.

Second Part of the political Testament
Before my death I expel the former Reich

Marshal Hermann Göring from the Party and deprive him of all rights which he may enjoy by virtue of the decree of 29 June 1941, and also by virtue of my statement in the Reichstag on 1 September 1939. I appoint in his place Grand Admiral Doenitz, President of the Reich and Supreme Commander of the Armed Forces.

Before my death I expel the former Reichsführer SS and Minister of the Interior, Heinrich Himmler, from the Party and from all offices of State. In his stead I appoint Gauleiter Karl Hanke as Reichsführer SS and Chief of the German Police, and Gauleiter Paul Giesler as Reich Minister of the Interior.

Göring and Himmler, quite apart from their disloyalty to my person, have done immeasurable harm to the country and the whole nation by secret negotiations with the enemy, which they conducted without my knowledge and against my wishes, and by illegally attempting to seize power in the State for themselves.

In order to give the German people a Government composed of honourable men, a Government which will fulfil its pledge to continue the war by every means, I appoint the following members of the new Cabinet as leaders of the nation:

President of the Reich: Doenitz
Chancellor of the Reich: Dr Goebbels
Party Minister: Bormann
Foreign Minister: Seyss-Inquart
Minister of the Interior: Gauleiter
    Giesler
Minister for War: Doenitz
C.-in-C. of the Army: Schörner
C.-in-C. of the Navy: Doenitz
C.-in-C. of the Air Force: Greim
Reichsführer SS and Chief of the
    German Police: Gauleiter Hanke
Economics: Funk
Agriculture: Backe
Justice: Thierack
Education and Public Worship:
    Dr Scheel

Propaganda: Dr Naumann
Finance: Schwerin-Krosigk
Labour: Dr Hupfauer
Munitions: Saur
Leader of the German Labour Front
    and Member of the Reich Cabinet:
    Reich Minister Dr Ley

Although a number of these men, such as Martin Bormann, Dr Goebbels, etc., together with their wives, have joined me of their own free will and did not wish to leave the capital of the Reich under any circumstances, but were willing to perish with me here, I must nevertheless ask them to obey my request, and in this case set the interests of the nation above their own feelings. By their work and loyalty as comrades they will be just as close to me after death, as I hope that my spirit will linger among them and always go with them. Let them be hard, but never unjust, above all let them never allow fear to influence their actions, and let them set the honour of the nation above everything in the world. Finally, let them be conscious of the fact that our task, that of continuing the building of a National Socialist State, represents the work of the coming centuries, which places every single person under an obligation always to serve the common interest and to subordinate his own advantage to this end. I demand of all Germans, all National Socialists, men, women and all the men of the armed forces, that they be faithful and obedient unto death to the new Government and its President.

Above all I adjure the leaders of the nation and those under them to scrupulous observance of the laws of race and to merciless opposition to the universal poisoner of all peoples, International Jewry.

Given in Berlin, this 29th day of April 1945, 4 A.M.

ADOLF HITLER

See also Führerbunker, Vol. 1; Dönitz, Karl; Hitler, Adolf, Vol. 3.

Hitler's Rambling Discourse

Members of Adolf Hitler's inner circle frequently commented, outside of Hitler's company or after his death, on the random nature of the Führer's conversation. While on retreats to the Berghof, his home in the Alps, Hitler would hold forth, often well after midnight, on any number of topics to his bored and intimidated dinner guests. The following selection provides an example.

The Hungarians have always been *poseurs*. In war they are like the British and the Poles; war to them is an affair which concerns the Government and to which they go like oxen to the slaughter. They all wear swords, but have none of the earnest chivalry which the bearing of a sword should imply.

In a book on India which I read recently, it was said that India educated the British and gave them their feeling of superiority. The lesson begins in the street itself; anyone who wastes even a moment's compassion on a beggar is literally torn to pieces by the beggar hordes; anyone who shows a trace of human sentiment is damned for ever. From these origins springs that crushing contempt for everything that is not British, which is a characteristic of the British race. Hence the reason why the typical Briton marches ahead, superior, disdainful and oblivious to everything around him. If the British are ever driven out of India, the repercussions will be swift and terrible. In the end, the Russians will reap the benefit. However miserably the inhabitants of India may live under the British

they will certainly be no better off if the British go.

Opium and alcohol bring in twenty-two and a half million [pounds] sterling to the British Exchequer [Treasury] every year. Anyone who raises his voice in protest is regarded as a traitor to the State, and dealt with accordingly. We Germans, on the contrary, will all go on smoking our pipes, while at the same time compelling the natives of our colonies to abandon the horrors of nicotine!

Britain does not wish to see India overpopulated; it is not in her interest. On the contrary, she would rather see a somewhat sparse population. If we were to occupy India, the very first preoccupation of our administrators would be to set up countless Commissions to enquire into the conditions of every aspect of human activity with a view to their amelioration; our Universities, full of solicitude for the welfare of the natives, would immediately open sister organisations all over the country; and we should finish up by quickly proving that India has a civilisation older than our own!

The Europeans are all vaccinated and so are immune from the dangers of the various epidemics. The owner of a plantation knows that it is in his own interest to prevent the outbreak of disease among his coolies, but—well, perhaps it is, after all, better to content oneself with a little less profit and not to interfere with the normal course of nature!

I have just been reading some books which every German going abroad should be compelled to read. The first of them is Alsdorff's book, which should be read by every diplomat. According to it, it was not the British who taught Indians evil ways;

H.R. Trevor-Roper, ed., *Hitler's Secret Conversations, 1941–1944*. Trans. Norman Cameron and R.H. Stevens. New York: Farrar, Straus, and Young, 1958.

when the first white men landed in the country they found the walls surrounding many of the towns were constructed of human skulls; equally, it was not Cortez who brought cruelty to the Mexicans—it was there before he arrived. The Mexicans, indeed, indulged in extensive human sacrifice, and, when the spirit moved them, would sacrifice as many as twenty thousand human beings at a time! In comparison, Cortez was a moderate man. There is no need whatever to go rushing round the world making the native more healthy than the white man. Some people I know are indignant at the sale of shoddy cotton goods to the natives; what, pray, do they suggest—that we should give them pure silk?

In Russia, we must construct centres for the collection of grain in the vicinity of all railway stations, to facilitate transportation to the west. The Ukrainian Mark must also be tied to the Reichsmark, at a rate of exchange to be fixed later.

Rosenberg wishes to raise the cultural level of the local inhabitants by encouraging their penchant for wood-carving. I disagree. I would like [Minister for the Eastern Occupied Territories Alfred] Rosenberg to see what sort of trash is sold in my own countryside to pilgrims! And it's no good saying: "What rubbish!" Saxon industries must also live. I once knew a Saxon woman who sold printed handkerchiefs. In each corner was the picture of a famous man—Hindenburg in one corner, Ludendorff in another, myself in a third, and in the fourth —her own husband!

Every time I visit the Permanent Exhibition of German Crafts, I get angry. In the first place, the furniture exhibited is simply a bad joke; as is also the method of indicating the prices. One sees, for example, a label with RM [Reichsmarks] 800. and one assumes, naturally, that it applies to the whole suite. One then finds that the bench, the picture and the curtain are not included; and the last straw is that these trashy articles claim to represent a form of art, styled

popular—the art of our small independent craftsmen. In reality the public are not interested. When the man in the street pays twelve hundred marks for something, he expects value for his money, and he does not care a rap whether the nails have been driven in by machine or hand. Honestly, what do we mean when we say the work of a craftsman? Why buy furniture in plain unvarnished wood, when the furniture industry will give you beautiful furniture polished to perfection for the same money? In Stortz' shop, for example, I have seen excellent furniture, which modest people would be delighted to possess. Arts and Crafts? Rubbish!

If a nigger delights in wearing a pair of cuffs and nothing else, why should we interfere with him?

I have been reading tales of the burning of corpses at Benares [in India]. If we were out there, our hygiene experts would rise in their wrath and institute a crusade, backed by the most rigorous penalties, to suppress this evil practice! Every day official chemists would come and analyse the river-water, and in no time a new and gigantic Ministry of Health would be set up! The British, on the other hand, have contented themselves with forbidding the immolation of widows. The Indians can think themselves lucky that we do not rule India. We should make their lives a misery! Just think of it! Two hundred yards downstream of the place where they pitch the half-burned bodies of their dead into the Ganges, they drink the river-water! Nobody ever takes any harm from it. But would we stand for a thing like that?

The inhabitants of Budapest have remained faithful to their river, and are rightly proud of two things—the beautiful monuments and buildings which adorn the surrounding hillsides, and the marvellous bridges which span the Danube. It is a wonderful city, and one of immense wealth. Its background consisted of Croatia, Slovakia, Bosnia and Herzegovina; all the plutocratic magnates poured their wealth into Budapest. After the 1848 revolution all the main thoroughfares of the city were rebuilt, twice the width of those in Vienna.

I sent all the Berlin architects to Paris, to seek inspiration there for the improvement of their own city. Three bridges are always cheaper than fifty-five streets. I am only sorry I never saw the new bridge at Cologne. It must have been marvellous!

See also Berghof, Vol. 1; Hitler, Adolf, Vol. 3; Dietrich, The Personality of the Führer, Vol. 4.

Justifying Operation Barbarossa

On June 22, 1941, the Third Reich launched Operation Barbarossa, the invasion of the Soviet Union. Hitler justified the invasion, the largest military operation in history, with the following proclamation. He claims that he has tried diplomacy, but that has failed, and therefore military action is necessary to save German interests from Jews and Bolsheviks.

Proclamation

"German people!

"National Socialists!

"Weighted down with heavy cares, condemned to months-long silence, the hour has now come *when at last I can speak frankly.*

"When on September 3, 1939, the German Reich received the English declaration of war there was repeated anew a British attempt to render impossible every beginning of a consolidation and thereby of Europe's rise, by fighting whatever power on the Continent was strongest at any given time.

"That is how of yore England ruined Spain in many wars. That is how she conducted her wars against Holland. That is how later she fought France with the aid of all Europe and that is how at the turn of the century she began the encirclement of the then German

Reich and in 1914 the World War. Only on account of its internal dissension was Germany defeated in 1918. The consequences were terrible.

"After hypocritical declarations that the fight was solely against the Kaiser and his regime, the annihilation of the German Reich began according to plan after the German Army had laid down its arms.

"While the prophecies of the French statement, that there were 20,000,000 Germans too many—in other words, that this number would have to be exterminated by hunger, disease or emigration—were apparently being fulfilled to the letter, the National Socialist movement began its work of unifying the German people and thereby initiating resurgence of the Reich. This rise of our people from distress, misery and shameful disregard bore all the signs of a purely internal renaissance. Britain especially was not in any way affected or threatened thereby.

"Nevertheless, a new policy of encirclement against Germany, born as it was of hatred, recommended immediately. Internally and externally there resulted that plot familiar to us all between Jews and democrats, Bolshevists and reactionaries, with the sole aim of inhibiting the establishment of the new German people's State, and of plunging the Reich anew into impotence and misery.

Adolf Hitler, *My New Order.* Ed. Raoul de Roussy de Sales. New York: Reynal and Hitchcock, 1941.

"Apart from us the hatred of this international world conspiracy was directed against those peoples which like ourselves were neglected by fortune and were obliged to earn their daily bread in the hardest struggle for existence.

"Above all, the right of Italy and Japan to share in the goods of this world was contested just as much as that of Germany and in fact was formally denied.

"The coalition of these nations was, therefore, only an act of self-protection in the face of the egoistic world combination of wealth and power threatening them. As early as 1936 [British] Prime Minister Churchill, according to statements by the American General Wood before a committee of the American House of Representatives, declared Germany was once again becoming too powerful and must therefore be destroyed. In the Summer of 1939 the time seemed to have come for England to begin to realize its intended annihilation by repetition of a comprehensive policy of encirclement of Germany.

"The plan of the campaign of lies staged for this purpose consisted in declaring that other people were threatened, in tricking them with British promises of guarantees and assistance, and of making them march against Germany just as it did preceding the Great War. Thus Britain from May to August, 1939, succeeded in broadcasting to the world that Lithuania, Estonia, Latvia, Finland and Bessarabia as well as the Ukraine were being directly threatened by Germany.

"A number of these States allowed themselves to be misled into accepting the promise of guarantee proffered with these assertions, thus joining the new encirclement front against Germany. *Under these circumstances I considered myself entitled to assume responsibility before my own conscience and before the history of the German people not only of assuring these countries or their governments of the falseness of British assertions, but also of setting the strongest power in the east, by especially solemn declarations, at rest concerning the limits of our interests.*

"National Socialists! At that time you probably all felt that this step was bitter and difficult for me. Never did the German people harbor hostile feeling against the peoples of Russia. However, for over ten years Jewish Bolshevist rulers had been endeavoring from Moscow to set not only Germany but all Europe aflame. At no time ever did Germany attempt to carry her National Socialist [worldview] into Russia, but on the contrary Jewish Bolshevist rulers in Moscow unswervingly endeavored to foist their domination upon us and other European peoples, not only by ideological means but above all with military force.

"The consequences of the activity of this regime were nothing but chaos, misery and starvation in all countries. I, on the other hand, have been striving for twenty years with a minimum of intervention and without destroying our production, to arrive at a new socialist order in Germany which not only eliminates unemployment but also permits the worker to receive an ever greater share of the fruits of his labor.

"The success of this policy of economic and social reconstruction of our people, consisting of systematically eliminating differences of rank and class, has a true peoples' community as the final aim of the world.

"*It was therefore only with extreme difficulty that I brought myself in August, 1939, to send my foreign minister to Moscow in an endeavor there to oppose the British encirclement policy against Germany.* I did this only from a sense of all responsibility toward the German people, but above all in the hope after all of achieving permanent relief of tension and of being able to reduce sacrifices which might otherwise have been demanded of us.

"While Germany solemnly affirmed in Moscow that the territories and countries enumerated—with the exception of Lithuania—lay outside all German political interests, a special agreement was concluded in case

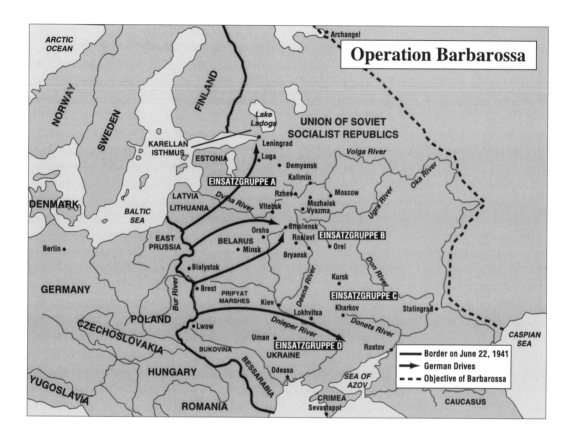

Britain were to succeed in inciting Poland actually into war with Germany. In this case, too, German claims were subject to limitations entirely out of proportion to the achievement of German forces.

"National Socialists! The consequences of this treaty which I myself desired and which was concluded in the interests of the German nation were very severe, particularly for Germans living in the countries concerned.

"Far more than 500,000 German men and women, all small farmers, artisans and workmen, were forced to leave their former homeland practically overnight in order to escape from a new regime which at first threatened them with boundless misery and sooner or later with complete extermination.

"Nevertheless, thousands of Germans disappeared. It was impossible ever to determine their fate, let alone their whereabouts. Among them were no fewer than 160 men of German citizenship. *To all this*

I remained silent because I had to. For, after all, it was my one desire to achieve final relief of tension and, if possible, a permanent settlement with this State.

"However, already during our advance in Poland, Soviet rulers suddenly, contrary to the treaty, also claimed Lithuania.

"The German Reich never had any intention of occupying Lithuania and not only failed to present any such demand to the Lithuanian Government, but on the contrary refused the request of the then Lithuania to send German troops to Lithuania for that purpose as inconsistent with the aims of German policy.

"Despite all this I complied also with this fresh Russian demand. However, this was only the beginning of continually renewed extortions which kept on repeating ever since.

"Victory in Poland which was won by German troops exclusively caused me to address yet another peace offer to the Western

Powers. It was refused owing to efforts of international and Jewish warmongers.

"At that time already the reason for such refusal lay in the fact that Britain still had hopes of being able to mobilize a European coalition against Germany which was to include the Balkans and Soviet Russia. It was therefore decided in London to send Mr. Cripps as ambassador to Moscow. He received clear instructions under all circumstances to resume relations between the English and Soviet Russia and develop them in a pro-British direction. The British press reported on the progress of this mission as long as tactical reasons did not impose silence.

"In the autumn of 1939 and spring of 1940 the first results actually made themselves felt. As Russia undertook to subjugate by armed force not only Finland but also the Baltic States she suddenly motivated this action by the assertion, as ridiculous as it was false, that she must protect these countries from an outside menace or forestall it. *This could only be meant to apply to Germany, for no other power could even gain entrance into the Baltic area, let alone go to war there. Still I had to be silent.* However, those in power in the Kremlin immediately went further.

"Whereas in the spring of 1940 Germany, in accordance with the so-called pact of friendship, withdrew her forces from the Far Eastern frontier and, in fact, for the most part cleared these areas entirely of German troops, a concentration of Russian forces at that time was already beginning in a measure which could only be regarded as a deliberate threat to Germany.

"According to a statement that Molotov personally made at that time, there were twenty-two Russian divisions in the Baltic States alone already in the spring of 1940. Since the Russian Government itself always claimed it was called in by the local population, the purpose of their presence there could only be a demonstration against Germany.

"While our soldiers from May 5, 1940, on had been breaking Franco-British power in the west, Russian military deployment on our eastern frontier was being continued to a more and more menacing extent. From August, 1940, on I therefore considered it to be in the interest of the Reich no longer to permit our eastern provinces, which moreover had already been laid waste so often, to remain unprotected in the face of this tremendous concentration of Bolshevist divisions.

"Thus there resulted British-Soviet Russian co-operation intended mainly at the tying up of such powerful forces in the east that radical conclusion of the war in the west, particularly as regards aircraft, could no longer be vouched for by the German High Command. This, however, was in line with the objects not only of the British but also of the Soviet Russian policy, for both England and Soviet Russia intended to let this war go on for as long as possible in order to weaken all Europe and render it progressively more impotent.

Russia's threatened attack on Rumania was in the last analysis equally intended to gain possession of an important base, not only of Germany's but also of Europe's, economic life, or at least destroy it. The Reich, especially since 1933, sought with unending patience to gain States in Southeast Europe as trading partners. We therefore also had the greatest interest in their internal constitutional consolidation and organization. Russia's advance into Rumania and Greece's tie-up with England threatened to turn these regions, too, within a short time into a general theater of war.

"Contrary to our principles and customs, and at the urgent request of the then Rumanian Government, which was itself responsible for this development, I advised acquiescence to the Soviet Russian demands for the sake of peace and the cession of Bessarabia. The Rumanian Government believed, however, that it could answer for this before its own people only if Germany and Italy in compensation would at least guarantee the integrity of what still remained of Rumania. *I did so with heavy heart, principally because when the German Reich gives a guarantee, that means it also abides by it.* We are neither Englishmen nor Jews.

"I still believe at this late hour to have served the cause of peace in that region, albeit by assuming serious personal obligation. In order, however, finally to solve these problems and achieve clarity concerning the Russian attitude toward Germany, as well as under pressure of continually increasing mobilization on our Eastern frontier, I invited Mr. Molotov to come to Berlin.

"The Soviet Minister for Foreign Affairs then demanded Germany's clarification of or agreement to the following four questions:

"Point one was Molotov's question: Was the German guarantee for Rumania also directed against Soviet Russia in case of attack by Soviet Russia on Rumania?

"My answer: The German guarantee is a general one and is unconditionally binding upon us. Russia, however, never declared to us that she had other interests in Rumania beyond Bessarabia. The occupation of Northern Bukovina had already been a violation of this assurance. I did not therefore think that Russia could now suddenly have more far-reaching intentions against Rumania.

"Molotov's second question: That Russia again felt menaced by Finland. Russia was determined not to tolerate this. Was Germany ready not to give any aid to Finland and above all immediately to withdraw German relief troops marching through to Kirkenes?

"My answer: Germany continued to have absolutely no political interests in Finland. A fresh war by Russia against the small Finnish people could not, however, be regarded any longer by the German Government as tolerable, all the more so as we could never believe Russia to be threatened by Finland. Under no circumstances did we want another theater of war to arise in the Baltic.

"Molotov's third question: Was Germany prepared to agree that Russia give a guarantee to Bulgaria and send Soviet Russian troops to Bulgaria for this purpose in connection with which he—Molotov—was prepared to state that the Soviets did not intend on that account, for example, to depose the King?

"My answer: Bulgaria was a sovereign State and I had no knowledge that Bulgaria had ever asked Soviet Russia for any kind of guarantee such as Rumania had requested from Germany. Moreover, I would have to discuss the matter with my allies.

"Molotov's fourth question: Soviet Russia required free passage through the Dardanelles under all circumstances and for her protection also demanded occupation of a number of important bases on the Dardanelles and Bosphorus. Was Germany in agreement with this or not?

"My answer: Germany was prepared at all times to agree to alteration of the Statute of Montreux in favor of the Black Sea States. Germany was not prepared to agree to Russia's taking possession of bases on the Straits.

"National Socialists! Here I adopted the only attitude that I could adopt *as the responsible leader of the German Reich but also as the representative of European culture and civilization and conscious of my responsibility.* The consequence was to increase in Soviet Russia the activity directed against the Reich, above all, however, the immediate commencement of undermining the new Rumanian state from within and an attempt to remove the Bulgarian Government by propaganda.

"With the help of the confused and immature leaders of the Rumanian Legion (Iron Guard) a coup d'état was staged in Rumania whose aim was to overthrow Chief of State General Antonescu and produce chaos in the country so as to remove all legal power of the government and thus the precondition for an implement of the German guarantee. *I nevertheless still believed it best to remain silent.*

"Immediately after the failure of this undertaking, renewed reinforcement of concentrations of Russian troops on Germany's eastern frontier took place. Panzer detachments and parachutists were transferred in continually increasing numbers to dangerous proximity to the German frontier. German fighting forces and the German nation know that until a few weeks ago not a single tank or mechanized division was stationed on our eastern frontier.

"If any final proof was required for the coalition meanwhile formed between England and Soviet Russia despite all diversion and camouflage, the Yugoslav conflict provided it. While I made every effort to undertake a final attempt to pacify the Balkans and in sympathetic co-operation with Il Duce invited Yugoslavia to join the Tripartite Pact, England and Soviet Russia in a joint conspiracy organized that coup d'état which in one night removed the then government which had been ready to come to agreement.

"For we can today inform the German nation that the Serb putsch against Germany did not take place merely under the British, but primarily under Soviet Russian auspices. As we remained silent on this matter also, the Soviet leaders now went still one step further. They not only organized the putsch, but a few days later also concluded that well-known friendship pact with the Serbs in their will to resist pacification of the Balkans and incite them against Germany. And this was no platonic intention: Moscow demanded mobilization of the Serb Army.

"*Since even now I still believed it better not to speak,* those in power in the Kremlin went still further: The Government of the German Reich today possesses documentary evidence which proves that Russia, in order finally to bring Serbia into the war, gave her a promise to supply her via Salonika with arms, aircraft, munitions and other war materials against Germany. And this happened almost at the very moment when I myself advised Japanese Foreign Minister Matsuoka that eased tension with Russia always was in hope, thereby to serve the cause of peace.

"Only the rapid advance of our incomparable divisions to Skoplje as well as the capture of Salonika itself frustrated the aims of this Soviet Russian-Anglo-Saxon plot. Officers of the Serb air force, however, fled to Russia and were there immediately received as allies.

"The victory of the Axis Powers in the Balkans in the first instance thwarted the plan to involve Germany this Summer in months-long battles in Southeastern Europe while meantime steadily completing the alignment of Soviet Russian armies and increasing their readiness for war in order, finally, together with England and supported by American supplies anticipated, to crush the German Reich and Italy.

"*Thus Moscow not only broke but miserably betrayed the stipulations of our friendly agreement.* All this was done while the rulers in the Kremlin, exactly as in the case of Finland and Rumania, up to the last moment pretended peace and friendship and drew up an ostensibly innocent *démenti.*

"Although until now I was forced by circumstances to keep silent again and again, *the moment has now come when to continue as a mere observer would not only be a sin of omission but a crime against the German people—yes, even against the whole of Europe.*

"Today something like 160 Russian divisions are standing at our frontiers. For weeks constant violations of this frontier have taken place, not only affecting us but from the far north down to Rumania. Russian airmen consider it sport nonchalantly to overlook these frontiers, presumably to prove to us that they already feel themselves masters of these territories. During the night of June 17 to June 18 Russian patrols again penetrated into the Reich's territory and could only be driven back after prolonged firing. This has brought us to the hour when it is necessary for us to take steps against this plot devised by the Jewish-Anglo-Saxon warmongers and equally the Jewish rulers of the Bolshevist center in Moscow.

"German people! *At this moment a march is taking place that, as regards extent, compares with the greatest the world hitherto has seen.* United with their Finnish comrades, the fighters of the victory of Narvik are standing in the Northern Arctic. German divisions commanded by the conqueror of Norway, in co-operation with the heroes of Finnish freedom, under their marshal, are protecting Finnish soil. Formations of the German eastern front extend from East Prussia to the Carpathians. German and Rumanian soldiers are united under Chief of State Antonescu from the banks of the Pruth along the lower reaches of the Danube to the shores of the Black Sea. *The task of this front, therefore, no longer is the protection of single countries, but the safeguarding of Europe and thereby the salvation of all.*

"I therefore decided today again to lay the fate and future of the German Reich and our people in the hands of our soldiers.

"May God help us especially in this fight!"

See also Barbarossa, blitzkrieg, Commissar Order, Drive to the East, Vol. 1.

The Charges Against the Surviving Nazi Leaders

The following document specifies the official charges against twenty-four surviving top Nazis made by the International Military Tribunal, which began its sessions at Nuremberg in late 1945. The tribunal considered four separate indictments: 1) conspiracy to commit crimes alleged in other counts; 2) crimes against peace; 3) war crimes; and 4) crimes against humanity. Of the twenty-four defendants listed, twenty-one were tried before the tribunal. One, Ley, committed suicide before the trial could begin and another, Krupp, was tried later. Martin Bormann was tried in absentia.

The statements hereinafter set forth following the name of each individual defendant constitute matters upon which the prosecution will rely *inter alia* [among

other things] as establishing the individual responsibility of the defendant:

GÖRING
The defendant GÖRING between 1932 and 1945 was: a member of the Nazi Party, Supreme Leader of the SA, General in the SS, a member and President of the Reichstag, Minister of the Interior of Prussia, Chief of the Prussian Police and Prussian Secret State Police, Chief of the Prussian State Council, Trustee of the Four Year Plan, Reich Minister for Air, Commander in Chief of the Air Force, President of the Council of Ministers for the Defense of the Reich, member of the Secret Cabinet Council, head of the Hermann Göring Industrial Combine, and Successor Designate to Hitler. The defendant GÖRING used the foregoing positions, his personal influence, and his intimate connection with the Führer in such a manner that: he promoted the accession to

Robert H. Jackson et. al., *The Case Against the Nazi War Criminals.* New York: Knopf, 1946.

power of the Nazi conspirators and the consolidation of their control over Germany set forth in Count One of the Indictment; he promoted the military and economic preparation for war set forth in Count One of the Indictment; he participated in the planning and preparation of the Nazi conspirators for Wars of Aggression and Wars in Violation of International Treaties, Agreements and Assurances set forth in Counts One and Two of the Indictment; and he authorized, directed and participated in the War Crimes set forth in Count Three of the Indictment, and the Crimes against Humanity set forth in Count Four of the Indictment, including a wide variety of crimes against persons and property.

RIBBENTROP

The defendant RIBBENTROP between 1932 and 1945 was: a member of the Nazi Party, a member of the Nazi Reichstag, Adviser to the Führer on matters of foreign policy, representative of the Nazi Party for matters of foreign policy, special German delegate for disarmament questions, Ambassador extraordinary, Ambassador in London, organizer and director of Dienststelle Ribbentrop, Reich Minister for Foreign Affairs, member of the Secret Cabinet Council, member of the Führer's political staff at general headquarters, and General in the SS. The defendant RIBBENTROP used the foregoing positions, his personal influence, and his intimate connection with the Führer in such a manner that: he promoted the accession to power of the Nazi conspirators as set forth in Count One of the Indictment; he promoted the preparations for war set forth in Count One of the Indictment; he participated in the political planning and preparation of the Nazi conspirators for Wars of Aggression and Wars in Violation of International Treaties, Agreements and Assurances as set forth in Counts One and Two of the Indictment; in accordance with the Führer Principle he executed and assumed responsibility for the execution of the for-

eign policy plans of the Nazi conspirators set forth in Count One of the Indictment; and he authorized, directed and participated in the War Crimes set forth in Count Three of the Indictment and the Crimes against Humanity set forth in Count Four of the Indictment, including more particularly the crimes against persons and property in occupied territories.

HESS

The defendant HESS between 1921 and 1941 was: a member of the Nazi Party, Deputy to the Führer, Reich Minister without Portfolio, member of the Reichstag, member of the Council of Ministers for the Defense of the Reich, member of the Secret Cabinet Council, Successor Designate to the Führer after the defendant Göring, a General in the SS and a General in the SA. The defendant HESS used the foregoing positions, his personal influence and his intimate connection with the Führer in such a manner that: he promoted the accession to power of the Nazi conspirators and the consolidation of their control over Germany set forth in Count One of the Indictment; he promoted the military, economic and psychological preparations for war set forth in Count One of the Indictment; he participated in the political planning and preparation for Wars of Aggression and Wars in Violation of International Treaties, Agreements and Assurances set forth in Counts One and Two of the Indictment: he participated in the preparation and planning of foreign policy plans of the Nazi conspirators set forth in Count One of the Indictment; he authorized, directed and participated in the War Crimes set forth in Count Three of the Indictment and the Crimes against Humanity set forth in Count Four of the Indictment, including a wide variety of crimes against persons and property.

KALTENBRUNNER

The defendant KALTENBRUNNER between 1932 and 1945 was: a member of the Nazi Party, a General in the SS, a member of the

Reichstag, a General of the Police, State Secretary for Security in Austria in charge of the Austrian Police, Police Leader of Vienna, Lower and Upper Austria, Head of the Reich Main Security Office and Chief of the Security Police and Security Service. The defendant KALTENBRUNNER used the foregoing positions and his personal influence in such a manner that: he promoted the consolidation of control over Austria seized by the Nazi conspirators as set forth in Count One of the Indictment; and he authorized, directed and participated in the War Crimes set forth in Count Three of the Indictment and the Crimes against Humanity set forth in Count Four of the Indictment, including particularly the Crimes against Humanity involved in the system of concentration camps.

ROSENBERG
The defendant ROSENBERG between 1920 and 1945 was: a member of the Nazi Party, Nazi member of the Reichstag, Reichsleiter in the Nazi Party for Ideology and Foreign Policy, the Editor of the Nazi newspaper "Völkischer Beobachter," and of the "NS Monatshefte," head of the Foreign Political Office of the Nazi Party, Special Delegate for the entire Spiritual and Ideological Training of the Nazi Party, Reich Minister for the Eastern Occupied Territories, organizer of the "Einsatzstab Rosenberg [task force]," a General in the SS and a General in the SA. The defendant ROSENBERG used the foregoing positions, his personal influence and his intimate connection with the Führer in such a manner that: he developed, disseminated and exploited the doctrinal techniques of the Nazi conspirators set forth in Count One of the Indictment; he promoted the accession to power of the Nazi conspirators and the consolidation of their control over Germany set forth in Count One of the Indictment; he promoted the psychological preparations for war set forth in Count One of the Indictment; he participated in the political planning and prepara-

tion for Wars of Aggression and Wars in Violation of International Treaties, Agreements and Assurances set forth in Counts One and Two of the Indictment; and he authorized, directed and participated in the War Crimes set forth in Count Three of the Indictment and the Crimes against Humanity set forth in Count Four of the Indictment, including a wide variety of crimes against persons and property.

FRANK
The defendant FRANK between 1932 and 1945 was: a member of the Nazi Party, a General in the SS, a member of the Reichstag, Reich Minister without Portfolio, Reich Commissar for the Co-ordination of Justice, President of the International Chamber of Law and Academy of German Law, Chief of the Civil Administration of Lodz, Supreme Administrative Chief of the military district of West Prussia, Poznan, Odz and Krakow and Governor General of the Occupied Polish territories. The defendant FRANK used the foregoing positions, his personal influence, and his intimate connection with the Führer in such a manner that: he promoted the accession to power of the Nazi conspirators and the consolidation of their control over Germany set forth in Count One of the Indictment; he authorized, directed and participated in the War Crimes set forth in Count Three of the Indictment and the Crimes against Humanity set forth in Count Four of the Indictment, including particularly the War Crimes and Crimes against Humanity involved in the administration of occupied territories.

BORMANN [tried in absentia]
The defendant BORMANN between 1925 and 1945 was: a member of the Nazi Party, member of the Reichstag, a member of the Staff of the Supreme Command of the SA, founder and head of the "Hilfskasse der NSDAP [Assistance Bureau of the Nazi Party]," Reichsleiter, Chief of Staff Office of the Führer's Deputy, head of the Party

Chancery, Secretary of the Führer, member of the Council of Ministers for the Defense of the Reich, organizer and head of the Volkssturm, a General in the SS and a General in the SA. The defendant BORMANN used the foregoing positions, his personal influence and his intimate connection with the Führer in such a manner that: he promoted the accession to power of the Nazi conspirators and the consolidation of their control over Germany set forth in Count One of the Indictment; he promoted the preparations for war set forth in Count One of the Indictment; and he authorized, directed and participated in the War Crimes set forth in Count Three of the Indictment and the Crimes against Humanity set forth in Count Four of the Indictment, including a wide variety of crimes against persons and property.

FRICK

The defendant FRICK between 1932 and 1945 was: a member of the Nazi Party, Reichsleiter, General in the SS, member of the Reichstag, Reich Minister of the Interior, Prussian Minister of the Interior, Reich Director of Elections, General Plenipotentiary for the Administration of the Reich, head of the Central Office for the Reunification of Austria and the German Reich, Director of the Central Office for the Incorporation of Sudetenland, Memel, Danzig, the eastern incorporated territories, Eupen, Malmedy, and Moresnot, Director of the Central Office for the protectorate of Bohemia, Moravia, the Government General, Lower Styria, Upper Carinthia, Norway, Alsace, Lorraine and all other occupied territories and Reich Protector for Bohemia and Moravia. The defendant FRICK used the foregoing positions, his personal influence, and his intimate connection with the Führer in such a manner that: he promoted the accession to power of the Nazi conspirators and the consolidation of their control over Germany set forth in Count One of the Indictment; he participated in the planning

and preparation of the Nazi conspirators for Wars of Aggression and Wars in Violation of International Treaties, Agreements and Assurances set forth in Counts One and Two of the Indictment; and he authorized, directed and participated in the War Crimes set forth in Count Three of the Indictment and the Crimes against Humanity set forth in Count Four of the Indictment, including more particularly the crimes against persons and property in occupied territories.

LEY [committed suicide before trial]

The defendant LEY between 1932 and 1945 was: a member of the Nazi Party, Reichsleiter, Nazi Party Organization Manager, member of the Reichstag, leader of the German Labor Front, a General in the SA, and Joint Organizer of the Central Inspection for the Care of Foreign Workers. The defendant LEY used the foregoing positions, his personal influence and his intimate connection with the Führer in such a manner that: he promoted the accession to power of the Nazi conspirators and the consolidation of their control over Germany as set forth in Count One of the Indictment; he promoted the preparation for war set forth in Count One of the Indictment; he authorized, directed and participated in the War Crimes set forth in Count Three of the Indictment, and in the Crimes against Humanity set forth in Count Four of the Indictment, including particularly the War Crimes and Crimes against Humanity relating to the abuse of human beings for labor in the conduct of the aggressive wars.

SAUCKEL

The defendant SAUCKEL between 1921 and 1945 was: a member of the Nazi Party, Gauleiter and Reichsstatthalter of Thuringia, a member of the Reichstag, General Plenipotentiary for the Employment of Labor under the Four Year Plan, Joint Organizer with the defendant Ley of the Central Inspection for the Care of Foreign Workers, a General in the SS and a General in the SA.

Leading Nazi defendants appear in the courtroom during the Nuremberg war crimes trial of 1945–1946: (back row, left to right) Schirach, Sauckel (partially hidden), Jodl, Papen, Seyss-Inquart, Speer, Neurath, Fritzsche; front row, Göring, Hess, Ribbentrop, Keitel, Kaltenbrunner, Rosenberg, Frank, Frick, Streicher, Funk, and Schacht. Dönitz and Raeder are not pictured.

The defendant SAUCKEL used the foregoing positions and his personal influence in such a manner that: he promoted the accession to power of the Nazi conspirators set forth in Count One of the Indictment; he participated in the economic preparations for Wars of Aggression and Wars in Violation of Treaties, Agreements and Assurances set forth in Counts One and Two of the Indictment; he authorized, directed and participated in the War Crimes set forth in Count Three of the Indictment and the Crimes against Humanity set forth in Count Four of the Indictment, including particularly the War Crimes and Crimes against Humanity involved in forcing the inhabitants of occupied countries to work as slave laborers in occupied countries and in Germany.

SPEER

The defendant SPEER between 1932 and 1945 was: a member of the Nazi Party, Reichsleiter, member of the Reichstag, Reich Minister for Armament and Munitions, Chief of the Organization Todt, General Plenipotentiary for Armaments in the Office of the Four Year Plan, and Chairman of the Armaments Council. The defendant SPEER used the foregoing positions and his personal influence in such a manner that: he participated in the military and economic planning and preparation of the Nazi conspirators for Wars of Aggression and Wars in Violation of International Treaties, Agreements and Assurances set forth in Counts One and Two of the Indictment; and he authorized, directed and participated in the War Crimes set forth in Count Three of the Indictment and the Crimes against Humanity set forth in Count Four of the Indictment, including more particularly the abuse and exploitation of human beings for forced labor in the conduct of aggressive war.

FUNK

The defendant FUNK between 1932 and 1945 was: a member of the Nazi Party, Economic Adviser of Hitler, National Socialist Deputy to the Reichstag, Press Chief of the Reich Government, State Secretary of the Reich Ministry of Public Enlightenment and Propaganda, Reich Minister of Economics, Prussian Minister of Economics, President of the German Reichsbank, Plenipotentiary for Economy, and member of the Ministerial Council for the Defense of the Reich. The defendant FUNK used the foregoing positions, his personal influence, and his close connection with the Führer in such a manner that: he promoted the accession to power of the Nazi conspirators and the consolidation of their control over Germany set forth in Count One of the Indictment; he promoted the preparations for war set forth in Count One of the Indictment; he participated in the military and economic planning and preparation of the Nazi conspirators for Wars of Aggression and Wars in Violation of International Treaties, Agreements and Assurances set forth in Counts One and Two of the Indictment; and he authorized, directed and participated in the War Crimes set forth in Count Three of the Indictment and the Crimes against Humanity set forth in Count Four of the Indictment, including more particularly crimes against persons and property in connection with the economic exploitation of occupied territories.

SCHACHT

The defendant SCHACHT between 1932 and 1945 was: a member of the Nazi Party, a member of the Reichstag, Reich Minister of Economics, Reich Minister without Portfolio and President of the German Reichs-bank. The defendant SCHACHT used the foregoing positions, his personal influence, and his connection with the Führer in such a manner that: he promoted the accession to power of the Nazi conspirators and the consolidation of their control over Germany set forth in Count One of the Indictment; he promoted the preparations for war set forth in Count One of the Indictment; and he participated in the military and economic plans and preparation of the Nazi conspirators for Wars of Aggression, and Wars in Violation of International Treaties, Agreements and Assurances set forth in Counts One and Two of the Indictment.

PAPEN

The defendant PAPEN between 1932 and 1945 was: a member of the Nazi Party, a member of the Reichstag, Reich Chancellor, Vice Chancellor under Hitler, special Plenipotentiary for the Saar, negotiator of the Concordat with the Vatican, Ambassador in Vienna and Ambassador in Turkey. The defendant PAPEN used the foregoing positions, his personal influence and his close connection with the Führer in such manner that: he promoted the accession to power of the Nazi conspirators and participated in the consolidation of their control over Germany set forth in Count One of the Indictment; he promoted the preparations for war set forth in Count One of the Indictment; and he participated in the political planning and preparation of the Nazi conspirators for Wars of Aggression and Wars in Violation of International Treaties, Agreements and Assurances set forth in Counts One and Two of the Indictment.

KRUPP [released and tried later]

The defendant KRUPP between 1932 and 1945 was: head of Friedrich KRUPP A.G., a member of the General Economic Council, President of the Reich Union of German Industry, and head of the Group for Mining and Production of Iron and Metals under the Reich Ministry of Economics. The defendant KRUPP used the foregoing positions, his personal influence, and his connection with the Führer in such a manner that: he promoted the accession to power of the Nazi conspirators and the consolidation of their control over Germany set forth in Count One of the Indictment; he promoted the preparation for war set forth in Count One of the Indictment; he participated in the military and economic planning and preparation of the Nazi conspirators for Wars of Aggression and Wars in Violation of International Treaties, Agreements and Assurances set forth in Counts One and Two of the Indictment; and he authorized, directed and participated in the War Crimes set forth in Count Three of the Indictment and the Crimes against Humanity set forth in Count Four of the Indictment, including more particularly the exploitation and abuse of human beings for labor in the conduct of aggressive wars.

NEURATH

The defendant NEURATH between 1932 and 1945 was: a member of the Nazi Party, a General in the SS, a member of the Reichstag, Reich Minister, Reich Minister of Foreign Affairs, President of the Secret Cabinet Council, and Reich Protector for Bohemia and Moravia. The defendant NEURATH used the foregoing positions, his personal influence, and his close connection with the Führer in such a manner that: he promoted the accession to power of the Nazi conspirators set forth in Count One of the Indictment; he promoted the preparations for war set forth in Count One of the Indictment; he participated in the political planning and preparation of the Nazi conspirators for Wars of Aggression and Wars in Violation of International Treaties, Agreements and Assurances set forth in Counts One and Two of the Indictment; in accordance with the Führer Principle he executed, and assumed responsibility for the execution of the foreign policy plans of the Nazi conspirators set forth in Count One of the Indict-

ment; and he authorized, directed and participated in the War Crimes set forth in Count Three of the Indictment and the Crimes against Humanity set forth in Count Four of the Indictment, including particularly the crimes against persons and property in the occupied territories.

SCHIRACH

The defendant SCHIRACH between 1924 and 1945 was: a member of the Nazi Party, a member of the Reichstag, Reich Youth Leader on the Staff of the SA Supreme Command, Reichsleiter in the Nazi Party for Youth Education, Leader of Youth of the German Reich, head of the Hitler Jugend, Reich Defense Commissioner and Reichsstatthalter and Gauleiter of Vienna. The defendant SCHIRACH used the foregoing positions, his personal influence and his intimate connection with the Führer in such a manner that: he promoted the accession to power of the Nazi conspirators and the consolidation of their control over Germany set forth in Count One of the Indictment; he promoted the psychological and educational preparations for war and the militarization of Nazi dominated organizations set forth in Count One of the Indictment; and he authorized, directed and participated in the Crimes against Humanity set forth in Count Four of the Indictment, including, particularly, anti-Jewish measures.

SEYSS-INQUART

The defendant SEYSS-INQUART between 1932 and 1945 was: a member of the Nazi Party, a General in the SS, State Councillor of Austria, Minister of the Interior and Security of Austria, Chancellor of Austria, a member of the Reichstag, a member of the Reich Cabinet, Reich Minister without Portfolio, Chief of the Civil Administration in South Poland, Deputy Governor-General of the Polish Occupied Territory, and Reich Commissar for the Occupied Netherlands. The defendant SEYSS-INQUART used the foregoing positions and his personal influence in such a manner that: he promoted the seizure and the consolidation of control over Austria by the Nazi conspirators set forth in Count One of the Indictment; he participated in the political planning and preparation of the Nazi conspirators for Wars of Aggression and Wars in Violation of International Treaties, Agreements and Assurances set forth in Counts One and Two of the Indictment; and he authorized, directed and participated in the War Crimes set forth in Count Three of the Indictment and the Crimes against Humanity set forth in Count Four of the Indictment, including a wide variety of crimes against persons and property.

STREICHER

The defendant STREICHER between 1932 and 1945 was: a member of the Nazi Party, a member of the Reichstag, a General in the SA, Gauleiter of Franconia, Editor in Chief of the anti-Semitic newspaper "Der Stürmer." The defendant STREICHER used the foregoing positions, his personal influence, and his close connection with the Führer in such a manner that: he promoted the accession to power of the Nazi conspirators and the consolidation of their control over Germany set forth in Count One of the Indictment: he authorized, directed and participated in the Crimes against Humanity set forth in Count Four of the Indictment, including particularly the incitement of the persecution of the Jews set forth in Count One and Count Four of the Indictment.

KEITEL

The defendant KEITEL between 1938 and 1945 was: Chief of the High Command of the German Armed Forces, member of the Secret Cabinet Council, member of the Council of Ministers for the Defense of the Reich, and Field Marshal. The defendant KEITEL used the foregoing positions, his personal influence and his intimate connection with the Führer in such a manner that: he promoted the military preparations for war set forth in Count One of the Indict-

ment; he participated in the political planning and preparation of the Nazi conspirators for Wars of Aggression and Wars in Violation of International Treaties, Agreements and Assurances set forth in Counts One and Two of the Indictment; he executed and assumed responsibility for the execution of the plans of the Nazi conspirators for Wars of Aggression and Wars in Violation of International Treaties, Agreements and Assurances set forth in Counts One and Two of the Indictment; he authorized, directed and participated in the War Crimes set forth in Count Three of the Indictment and the Crimes against Humanity set forth in Count Four of the Indictment, including particularly the War Crimes and Crimes against Humanity involved in the ill-treatment of prisoners of war and of the civilian population of occupied territories.

JODL

The defendant JODL between 1932 and 1945 was: Lt. Colonel, Army Operations Department of the Wehrmacht, Colonel, Chief of OKW Operations Department, Major-General and Chief of Staff OKW and Colonel-General. The defendant JODL used the foregoing positions, his personal influence, and his close connection with the Führer in such a manner that: he promoted the accession to power of the Nazi conspirators and the consolidation of their control over Germany set forth in Count One of the Indictment; he promoted the preparations for war set forth in Count One of the Indictment; he participated in the military planning and preparation of the Nazi conspirators for Wars of Aggression and Wars in Violation of International Treaties, Agreements and Assurances set forth in Counts One and Two of the Indictment; and he authorized, directed and participated in the War Crimes set forth in Count Three of the Indictment and the Crimes against Humanity set forth in Count Four of the Indictment, including a wide variety of crimes against persons and property.

RAEDER

The defendant RAEDER between 1928 and 1945 was: Commander-in-Chief of the German Navy, General-admiral, Grossadmiral, Admiralinspekteur of the German Navy, and a member of the Secret Cabinet Council. The defendant RAEDER used the foregoing positions and his personal influence in such a manner that: he promoted the preparations for war set forth in Count One of the Indictment; he participated in the political planning and preparation of the Nazi conspirators for Wars of Aggression and Wars in Violation of International Treaties, Agreements and Assurances set forth in Counts One and Two of the Indictment; he executed, and assumed responsibility for the execution of the plans of the Nazi conspirators for Wars of Aggression and Wars in Violation of International Treaties, Agreements and Assurances set forth in Counts One and Two of the Indictment; and he authorized, directed and participated in the War Crimes set forth in Count Three of the Indictment, including particularly War Crimes arising out of sea warfare.

DÖNITZ

The defendant DÖNITZ between 1932 and 1945 was: Commanding Officer of the Weddigen U-boat flotilla, Commander-in-Chief of the U-boat arm, Vice-Admiral, Admiral, Grossadmiral and Commander-in-Chief of the German Navy, Adviser to Hitler, and Successor to Hitler as head of the German Government. The defendant DÖNITZ used the foregoing positions, his personal influence, and his intimate connection with the Führer in such a manner that: he promoted the preparations for war set forth in Count One of the Indictment; he participated in the military planning and preparation of the Nazi conspirators for Wars of Aggression and Wars in Violation of International Treaties, Agreements and Assurances set forth in Counts One and Two of the Indictment; and he authorized, directed and participated in the War Crimes set forth in Count Three of the Indictment, including particularly the crimes against persons and property on the high seas.

FRITZSCHE

The defendant FRITZSCHE between 1933 and 1945 was: a member of the Nazi Party, Editor-in-Chief of the official German news agency, "Deutsche Nachrichten Büro," Head of the Wireless News Service and of the Home Press Division of the Reich Ministry of Propaganda, Ministerialdirektor of the Reich Ministry of Propaganda, head of the Radio Division of the Propaganda Department of the Nazi Party, and Plenipotentiary for the Political Organization of the Greater German Radio. The defendant FRITZSCHE used the foregoing positions and his personal influence to disseminate and exploit the principal doctrines of the Nazi conspirators set forth in Count One of the Indictment, and to advocate, encourage and incite the commission of the War Crimes set forth in Count Three of the Indictment and the Crimes against Humanity set forth in Count Four of the Indictment including, particularly, anti-Jewish measures and the ruthless exploitation of occupied territories.

See also Nuremberg trials, Vol. 2.

Accusing the Third Reich

In the opening statement of the Nuremberg war crimes trials in late 1945, American jurist Robert H. Jackson makes clear what the trials are about.

The privilege of opening the first trial in history for crimes against the peace of the world imposes a grave responsibility. The wrongs which we seek to condemn and punish have been so calculated, so malignant and so devastating, that civilization cannot tolerate their being ignored because it cannot survive their being repeated. That four great nations, flushed with victory and stung with injury stay the hand of vengeance and voluntarily submit their captive enemies to the judgment of the law is one of the most significant tributes that Power ever has paid to Reason.

This Tribunal, while it is novel and experimental, is not the product of abstract speculations nor is it created to vindicate legalistic theories. This inquest represents the practical effort of four of the most mighty of nations, with the support of fifteen more, to utilize International Law to meet the greatest menace of our times—aggressive war. The common sense of mankind demands that law shall not stop with the punishment of petty crimes by little people. It must also reach men who possess themselves of great power and make deliberate and concerted use of it to set in motion evils which leave no home in the world untouched. It is a cause of this magnitude that the United Nations will lay before Your Honors.

In the prisoners' dock sit twenty-odd broken men. Reproached by the humiliation of those they have led almost as bitterly as by the desolation of those they have attacked,

their personal capacity for evil is forever past. It is hard now to perceive in these miserable men as captives the power by which as Nazi leaders they once dominated much of the world and terrified most of it. Merely as individuals, their fate is of little consequence to the world.

What makes this inquest significant is that these prisoners represent sinister influences that will lurk in the world long after their bodies have returned to dust. They are living symbols of racial hatreds, of terrorism and violence, and of the arrogance and cruelty of power. They are symbols of fierce nationalisms and of militarism, of intrigue and war-making which have embroiled Europe generation after generation, crushing its manhood, destroying its homes, and impoverishing its life. They have so identified themselves with the philosophies they conceived and with the forces they directed that any tenderness to them is a victory and an encouragement to all the evils which are attached to their names. Civilization can afford no compromise with the social forces which would gain renewed strength if we deal ambiguously or indecisively with the men in whom those forces now precariously survive.

What these men stand for we will patiently and temperately disclose. We will give you undeniable proofs of incredible events. The catalogue of crimes will omit nothing that could be conceived by a pathological pride, cruelty, and lust for power. These men created in Germany, under the "Führerprinzip" [Führer Principle], a National Socialist despotism equaled only by the dynasties of the ancient East. They took from the German people all those dignities and freedoms that we hold natural and inalienable rights in every human being. The people were compensated by inflaming and gratifying hatreds toward those who were

---

Robert H. Jackson et al., *The Case Against the Nazi War Criminals.* New York: Knopf, 1946.

marked as "scapegoats." Against their opponents, including Jews, Catholics, and free labor, the Nazis directed such a campaign of arrogance, brutality, and annihilation as the world has not witnessed since the pre-Christian ages. They excited the German ambition to be a "master race," which of course implies serfdom for others. They led their people on a mad gamble for domination. They diverted social energies and resources to the creation of what they thought to be an invincible war machine. They overran their neighbors. To sustain the "master race" in its war-making, they enslaved millions of human beings and brought them into Germany, where these hapless creatures now wander as "displaced persons." At length bestiality and bad faith reached such excess that they aroused the sleeping strength of imperiled Civilization. Its united efforts have ground the German war machine to fragments. But the struggle has left Europe a liberated yet prostrate land where a demoralized society struggles to survive. These are the fruits of the sinister forces that sit with these defendants in the prisoners' dock.

In justice to the nations and the men associated in this prosecution, I must remind you of certain difficulties which may leave their mark on this case. Never before in legal history has an effort been made to bring within the scope of a single litigation the developments of a decade, covering a whole Continent, and involving a score of nations, countless individuals, and innumerable events. Despite the magnitude of the task, the world has demanded immediate action. This demand has had to be met, though perhaps at the cost of finished craftsmanship. In my country, established courts, following familiar procedures, applying well-thumbed precedents, and dealing with the legal consequences of local and limited events seldom commence a trial within a year of the event in litigation. Yet less than eight months ago today the courtroom in which you sit was an enemy fortress

in the hands of German SS troops. Less than eight months ago nearly all our witnesses and documents were in enemy hands. The law had not been codified, no procedures had been established, no Tribunal was in existence, no usable courthouse stood here, none of the hundreds of tons of official German documents had been examined, no prosecuting staff had been assembled, nearly all the present defendants were at large, and the four prosecuting powers had not yet joined in common cause to try them. I should be the last to deny that the case may well suffer from incomplete researches and quite likely will not be the example of professional work which any of the prosecuting nations would normally wish to sponsor. It is, however, a completely adequate case to the judgment we shall ask you to render, and its full development we shall be obliged to leave to historians.

Before I discuss particulars of evidence, some general considerations which may affect the credit of this trial in the eyes of the world should be candidly faced. There is a dramatic disparity between the circumstances of the accusers and of the accused that might discredit our work if we should falter, in even minor matters, in being fair and temperate.

Unfortunately, the nature of these crimes is such that both prosecution and judgment must be by victor nations over vanquished foes. The world-wide scope of the aggressions carried out by these men has left but few real neutrals. Either the victors must judge the vanquished or we must leave the defeated to judge themselves. After the first World War, we learned the futility of the latter course. The former high station of these defendants, the notoriety of their acts, and the adaptability of their conduct to provoke retaliation make it hard to distinguish between the demand for a just and measured retribution, and the unthinking cry for vengeance which arises from the anguish of war. It is our task, so far as humanly possible, to draw the line between the two. We must never forget that the record on which we judge these defendants today is the record on which history will judge us tomorrow. To pass these defendants a poisoned chalice is to put it to our own lips as well. We must summon such detachment and intellectual integrity to our task that this trial will commend itself to posterity as fulfilling humanity's aspirations to do justice.

At the very outset, let us dispose of the contention that to put these men to trial is to do them an injustice entitling them to some special consideration. These defendants may be hard pressed but they are not ill-used. Let us see what alternative they would have to being tried.

More than a majority of these prisoners surrendered to or were tracked down by forces of the United States. Could they expect us to make American custody a shelter for our enemies against the just wrath of our Allies? Did we spend American lives to capture them only to save them from punishment? Under the principles of the Moscow Declaration [of 1943], those suspected war criminals who are not to be tried internationally must be turned over to individual governments for trial at the scene of their outrages. Many less responsible and less culpable American-held prisoners have been and will be turned over to other United Nations for local trial. If these defendants should succeed, for any reason, in escaping the condemnation of this Tribunal, or if they obstruct or abort this trial, those who are American-held prisoners will be delivered up to our continental Allies. For these defendants, however, we have set up an International Tribunal and have undertaken the burden of participating in a complicated effort to give them fair and dispassionate hearings. That is the best-known protection to any man with a defense worthy of being heard.

If these men are the first war leaders of a defeated nation to be prosecuted in the name of the law, they are also the first to be given a chance to plead for their lives in the name of the law. Realistically, the Charter of this Tribunal, which gives them a hearing, is also the source of their only hope. It may be that these men of troubled conscience, whose only wish is that the world forget them, do not regard a trial as a favor. But they do have a fair opportunity to defend themselves—a favor which these men, when in power, rarely extended to their fellow countrymen. Despite the fact that public opinion already condemns their acts, we agree that here they must be given a presumption of innocence, and we accept the burden of proving criminal acts and the responsibility of these defendants for their commission.

When I say that we do not ask for convictions unless we prove crime, I do not mean mere technical or incidental transgression of international conventions. We charge guilt on planned and intended conduct that involves moral as well as legal wrong. And we do not mean conduct that is a natural and human, even if illegal, cutting of corners, such as many of us might well have committed had we been in the defendants' positions. It is not because they yielded to the normal frailties of human beings that we accuse them. It is their abnormal and inhuman conduct which brings them to this bar.

We will not ask you to convict these men on the testimony of their foes. There is no count of the Indictment that cannot be proved by books and records. The Germans were always meticulous record keepers, and these defendants had their share of the Teutonic passion for thoroughness in putting things on paper. Nor were they without vanity. They arranged frequently to be photographed in action. We will show you their own films. You will see their own conduct and hear their own voices as these defendants re-enact for you, from the screen, some of the events in the course of the conspiracy.

We would also make clear that we have no purpose to incriminate the whole German people. We know that the Nazi Party was not put in power by a majority of the

German vote. We know it came to power by an evil alliance between the most extreme of the Nazi revolutionists, the most unrestrained of the German reactionaries, and the most aggressive of the German militarists. If the German populace had willingly accepted the Nazi program, no Stormtroopers would have been needed in the early days of the Party and there would have been no need for concentration camps or the Gestapo, both of which institutions were inaugurated as soon as the Nazis gained control of the German state. Only after these lawless innovations proved successful at home were they taken abroad.

The German people should know by now that the people of the United States hold them in no fear, and in no hate. It is true that the Germans have taught us the horrors of modern warfare, but the ruin that lies from the Rhine to the Danube shows that we, like our Allies, have not been dull pupils. If we are not awed by German fortitude and proficiency in war, and if we are not persuaded of their political maturity, we do respect their skill in the arts of peace, their technical competence, and the sober, industrious and self-disciplined character of the masses of the German people. In 1933, we saw the German people recovering prestige in the commercial, industrial and artistic world after the setback of the last war. We beheld their progress neither with envy nor malice. The Nazi regime interrupted this advance. The recoil of the Nazi aggression has left Germany in ruins. The Nazi readiness to pledge the German word without hesitation and to break it without shame has fastened upon German diplomacy a reputation for duplicity that will handicap it for years. Nazi arrogance has made the boast of the "master race" a taunt that will be thrown at Germans the world over for generations. The Nazi nightmare

has given the German name a new and sinister significance throughout the world which will retard Germany a century. The German, no less than the non-German world, has accounts to settle with these defendants.

The fact of the war and the course of the war, which is the central theme of our case, is history. From September 1, 1939, when the German armies crossed the Polish frontiers, until September 1942, when they met epic resistance at Stalingrad, German arms seemed invincible. Denmark and Norway, The Netherlands and France, Belgium and Luxembourg, the Balkans and Africa, Poland and the Baltic States, and parts of Russia, all had been overrun and conquered by swift, powerful, well-aimed blows. That attack upon the peace of the world is the crime against international society which brings into international cognizance crimes in its aid and preparation which otherwise might be only internal concerns. It was aggressive war, which the nations of the world had renounced. It was war in violation of treaties, by which the peace of the world was sought to be safeguarded.

This war did not just happen—it was planned and prepared for over a long period of time and with no small skill and cunning. The world has perhaps never seen such a concentration and stimulation of the energies of any people as that which enabled Germany twenty years after it was defeated, disarmed, and dismembered to come so near carrying out its plan to dominate Europe. Whatever else we may say of those who were the authors of this war, they did achieve a stupendous work in organization, and our first task is to examine the means by which these defendants and their fellow conspirators prepared and incited Germany to go to war.

See also Nuremberg trials, Vol. 2.

The War's Turning Point: Germany's Loss at Stalingrad

General Erich von Manstein, a top commander in the Wehrmacht, recalls the German Sixth Army's valiant but futile attempt to take the Russian city of Stalingrad over the winter of 1942–1943.

The death-struggle of Sixth Army, which began around the turn of the year, is a tale of indescribable suffering. It was marked not only by the despair and justified bitterness of the men who had been deceived in their trust, but even more by the steadfastness they displayed in the face of an undeserved but inexorable fate, by their high degree of bravery, comradeship and devotion to duty, and by their calm resignation and humble faith in God.

If I refrain from dwelling on these things here, it is certainly not because we at Army Group Headquarters were not intensely affected by them. Respect for a heroism which may never find its equal renders me incapable of doing full justice to these happenings at Stalingrad.

There is one question, however, which I feel both impelled and qualified to answer as the former commander of Don Army Group. Was it justifiable or necessary—and if so, for how long—to demand this sacrifice of our soldiers? In other words, did Sixth Army's final battle serve any useful purpose? To answer the question properly, one must examine it against the background of the current situation, and the stern exigencies this imposed, rather than in the light of Germany's ultimate defeat.

On 26th December the commander of Sixth Army sent us the message reproduced

Rita Steinhardt Botwinick, ed., *A Holocaust Reader: From Ideology to Annihilation.* Upper Saddle River, NJ: Prentice-Hall, 1997.

below. We passed it straight on to O.K.H. [the High Command of the Army], our policy all along having been to present the Army's position in a quite unembellished form. (From this moment onwards the only reports we received on the position inside the pocket came by radio or from officers flown out as couriers. We had been unable to maintain the ultra-high-frequency radio link by which it was possible to hold teleprinter conversations over a brief period.)

The message from Colonel-General Paulus [the German commander in Stalingrad] ran as follows:

> Bloody losses, cold, and inadequate supplies have recently made serious inroads on divisions' fighting strength. I must therefore report the following:
>
> 1. Army can continue to beat off small-scale attacks and deal with local crises for some time yet, always providing that supply improves and replacements are flown in at earliest possible moment.
>
> 2. If enemy draws off forces in any strength Hoth's [Hoth commanded a separate force in support of Paulus] front and uses these or any other troops to launch mass attacks on Stalingrad fortress, latter cannot hold out for long.
>
> 3. No longer possible to execute break-out unless corridor is cut in advance and Army replenished with men and supplies.
>
> I therefore request representations at highest level to ensure energetic measures for speedy relief, unless overall situation compels sacrifice of army. Army will naturally do everything in

its power to hold out till last possible moment.

I have also to report that only 70 tons were flown in today. Some of the corps will exhaust bread supplies tomorrow, fats this evening, evening fare tomorrow. Radical measures now urgent.

The contents of this message confirmed how wrong Paulus's Chief-of-Staff had been only a week before when he asserted that the army could hold out till Easter if properly supplied.

The message also showed that when the Army Group had ordered Sixth Army to break out of the pocket one week previously, this—in view of the approach of Fourth Panzer Army—had not only been its *first* chance of being rescued but—as could be seen from the state the army was in—its *last* one, too.

Otherwise, except for local attacks, there was relative calm on the Sixth Army fronts around the end of December and beginning of January. This was either because the enemy wished to munition his artillery for a grand assault or because he was putting all the forces he could spare into an attempt to destroy Fourth Panzer Army and to score the success he was after in the large bend of the Don.

On 8th January General Hube appeared at Army Group Headquarters on his way back from seeing Hitler. The latter had had Hube flown out of Stalingrad to Lötzen to brief him on the situation of Sixth Army. Hube told me that he had given Hitler a completely unvarnished picture of things in the pocket. (This cannot, in fact, have differed in any respect from the one already available to Hitler from the Army Group's daily situation reports, but presumably he was not prepared to credit our own version without further evidence.)

Nevertheless, it was remarkable how Hube's stay in Lötzen had impressed him and to what extent he had been influenced by Hitler's display of confidence—genuine or otherwise. Hitler had declared that everything would be done to *supply Sixth Army for a long time to come* and had drawn attention to the plan for its relief at a later

German troops exchange fire with Soviet defenders amid the ruins of Stalingrad on November 26, 1942.

date. With his confidence thus restored, Hube returned into the pocket, only to be flown out again on instructions from Hitler to take over the running of the airlift from outside. Not even he was able to improve it, however, its low efficiency being due to the prevailing weather and the inadequate resources of the Luftwaffe and not to any shortcomings in the actual organization. One statement of Hube's which touched me personally concerned a rumour circulating in Sixth Army that I had sent them the signal: 'Hang on—I'll get you out: Manstein.' While I left no stone unturned to extricate Sixth Army from Stalingrad, it has never been my custom to promise the troops anything which I was not certain of fulfilling and did not rest with me alone.

General Hube, who was a fearless man, had tried to bring home to Hitler how damaging such events as the encirclement of Sixth Army must be to his prestige as Head of State. By this means he wished to suggest that Hitler should hand over command —at least on the Eastern Front—to a soldier. In view of the fact that Hube had called in to see us on his way to Lötzen, Hitler doubtless supposed that Hube's *démarche* had been inspired by me. This was in fact not the case.

When, after the fall of Stalingrad, I myself proposed a change in the supreme military command to Hitler, he was already forewarned and flatly refused to consider such a thing. Otherwise—especially as he was then still under the impression of his responsibility for the loss of Sixth Army—he might have proved more receptive to my ideas.

On 9th January the enemy called upon Sixth Army to capitulate. On Hitler's orders, the demand was rejected.

I do not think I can be reproached with ever having taken an uncritical view of Hitler's decisions or actions in the military sphere. Yet I entirely support the decision he made in this instance, for however harsh it may have been from the humanitarian point of view, it was still necessary at the time.

I do not propose to deal here with the purely soldierly viewpoint that no army may capitulate as long as it still has any strength left to fight. To abandon it would mean the very end of soldiering. Until we reach the happy era when states can do without armed might and soldiers no longer exist, this conception of soldierly honour will have to be maintained. Even the apparent hopelessness of a battle that can be avoided by capitulation does not in itself justify a surrender. If every Commander-in-Chief were to capitulate as soon as he considered his position hopeless, no one would ever win a war. Even in situations apparently quite bereft of hope it has often been possible to find a way out in the end. From General Paulus's point of view, at all events, it was his soldierly duty to refuse to capitulate. An exception could only have been made if the army had had no further role to play and could serve no useful purpose in prolonging its struggle. And this in turn brings us to the crucial point which justifies Hitler's order to refuse to capitulate and also barred the Army Group from intervening in favour of such action at that particular time. No matter how futile Sixth Army's continued resistance might be in the long run, it still had—as long as it could conceivably go on fighting—a decisive role to fulfill in the overall strategic situation. It had to try to tie down the enemy forces opposing it for the longest possible space of time.

At the beginning of December an approximate total of sixty formations (i.e. rifle divisions, armoured and mechanized brigades etc.) had been identified in the siege ring around the army. Some of them had doubtless been temporarily drawn off by the attack of Fourth Panzer Army, but new ones had been brought up to replace them. By 19th January, ninety of the 259 formations reported to be facing Don Army Group were committed around Sixth Army. What would have happened if the bulk of these ninety formations had been released through a capitulation of Sixth Army on 9th January is plain enough in the light of what has already been said about the Army Group's position and the consequent threat to the southern wing as a whole.

The army was still capable of fighting, even though this was ultimately futile from its own point of view. Yet its ability to hold out was of decisive importance for the situation on the southern wing. Every extra day Sixth Army could continue to tie down the enemy forces surrounding it was vital as far as the fate of the entire Eastern Front was concerned. It is idle to point out today that we still lost the war in the end and that its early termination would have spared us infinite misery. That is merely being wise after the event. In those days it was by no means certain that Germany was bound to lose the war in the military sense. A military stalemate, which might in turn have led to a similar state of affairs in the political field, would have been entirely within the bounds of possibility if the situation on the southern wing of the German armies could in some way have been restored. This, however, depended first and foremost on Sixth Army's continuing the struggle and holding down the enemy siege forces for as long as it possessed the slightest capacity to resist. It was the cruel necessity of war which compelled the Supreme Command to demand that one last sacrifice of the brave troops at Stalingrad. The fact that the self-same Supreme Command was responsible for the army's plight is beside the point in this context.

Following Sixth Army's refusal to capitulate on 9th January, the Soviet attack, preceded by intensive artillery preparation and supported by a large number of tanks, broke loose on all fronts. The main pressure was directed against the salient which protruded furthest west by Marinovka, and the enemy was able to break in at several points.

On 11th January the situation became even more critical, and because of the lack of ammunition and fuel the army could no longer restore it to any appreciable extent. The loss of the positions in the Karpovka Valley—and in particular of the inhabited

localities there—deprived the troops on the western front of what protection they had hitherto enjoyed against the cold. Furthermore, the state of the weather ruled out any hope of an airlift.

This aggravation of Sixth Army's plight was made clear in a special report of 12th January which the Army Group immediately forwarded to O.K.H.

'Despite the troops' heroic resistance,' the army stated, 'the heavy fighting of the last few days has resulted in deep enemy penetrations which could so far be contained only with difficulty. Reserves are no longer available; nor can any be formed. Heavy weapons now immobilised. Severe losses and inadequate supplies, together with cold, have also considerably reduced troops' powers of resistance. If enemy maintains attacks in present strength, fortress front unlikely to hold more than a few days longer. Resistance will then resolve itself into localised actions.'

On 12th January weather again stopped the airlift and also prevented the Luftwaffe from flying any sorties in support of the army's hard defensive battles.

That evening General Pickert, the man responsible for controlling the Luftwaffe's side of the airlift, came out of the pocket. He painted a shocking picture of the position and set a limit of two to four days on the army's capacity for continued resistance —an estimate that was to prove inaccurate by reason of the bravery and self-sacrifice of the troops. In Pickert's opinion not even an improvement of the airlift could make much difference from now on, as the army's resources no longer sufficed to patch up the points where the enemy had broken in.

The following information on the tactical situation inside the pocket emerged from a report brought out to us by Pickert from Paulus (who had meanwhile been promoted Colonel-General):

On the north-western front the enemy had attacked with a force of between ten and twelve divisions. Parts of 3 and 29

Motorized Infantry Divisions had been out-flanked from the north and smashed, with the result that it no longer seemed possible to rebuild a defence line here. The two gallant divisions had knocked out 100 tanks between them, but the enemy still appeared to have fifty intact.

On the southern front of the pocket, in spite of heroic resistance by 297 Infantry Division, the enemy had succeeded in breaking in after two days of intensive artillery bombardment. Here, too, there were no more forces available to close the gap. Of over 100 Soviet tanks taking part in this assault, forty had been knocked out.

The eastern front of the pocket was still holding at present, though here, too, heavy enemy pressure was being exerted.

On the north-eastern front the enemy had penetrated deeply in several places. 16 Panzer Division's fighting strength was exhausted.

Paulus further stated that the army would stand and fight to the last round. Any reduction in the size of the pocket as now suggested by Hitler to General Hube would only serve to hasten the collapse, as no heavy weapons could now be moved. Since the airlift had been inadequate all along, no improvement could help matters now. The length of time the army could continue to resist depended entirely on the intensity of the enemy's attacks.

That same day the Pitomnik airfield was lost. Henceforth the only one left to us in the Stalingrad pocket was that at Gumrak.

During the night, however, Paulus reported that there might still be some prospect of continuing to defend the city if several battalions of troops were flown in forthwith with their full scale of weapons. He had already asked us repeatedly to fly in several thousand men to make good his losses, but the Army Group had been unable to comply because it possessed neither the necessary replacements nor, indeed, a single uncommitted battalion. Nor would it in any case have acceded to these requests from Sixth Army once Fourth Panzer Army's rescue drive had become bogged down, if only because there could be no justification for dispatching any reinforcements or replacements into the pocket from then on. It was already quite bad enough to have to fly unit commanders and General Staff officers back into the pocket on their return from leave. But apart from the fact that the army urgently needed them, these officers—some of whom bore such old military names as Bismarck and Below—themselves insisted on returning to their troops, thereby proving that the tradition of self-denial and comradeship could withstand the hardest of tests.

On 13th January Colonel-General Paulus's senior aide, Captain Behr, an exemplary young officer who had already won the Knight's Cross, flew out to see us, bringing the army's war diary with him. He told us how bravely the troops were still fighting and what fortitude all ranks had shown in coming to terms with the cruelty of their fate.

See also Battle of Stalingrad, Vol. 1; Doomed German Soldiers Write Home from Stalingrad, Vol. 4.

The Nazis Invade Western Europe

American journalist William L. Shirer recounts the scene in Germany on May 10, 1940, the day Germany launched its blitzkrieg attack on the Netherlands, Belgium, Luxembourg, and France.

Berlin, May 10, 1940

The blow in the west has fallen. At dawn today the Germans marched into Holland, Belgium, Luxemburg. It is Hitler's bid for victory now or never. Apparently it was true that Germany could not outlast the economic war. So he struck while his army still had supplies and his air force a lead over the Allies'. He seems to realize he is risking all. In an order of the day to the troops he begins: "The hour of the decisive battle for the future of the German nation has come." And he concludes: "The battle beginning today will decide the future of the German nation for the next thousand years." If he loses, it certainly will.

As I see it, Hitler had three choices: to wait and fight the war out on the economic front, as was done all winter; to meet the Allies in some easy spot, say the Balkans; to seek a decision in the west by striking through neutral Holland and Belgium. He has chosen the third, and the biggest risk.

I can't boast that I was prepared for it. In fact, after broadcasting as usual last night at twelve forty-five A.M., I was sound asleep when the phone rang at seven this morning. It was one of the girls at the *Rundfunk* [broadcasting station]. She broke the news.

"When do you want to broadcast?" she asked.

"As soon as I can get there," I said.

"Ribbentrop has a press conference at the Foreign Office at eight," she offered.

"I'll skip it," I said. "Tell New York—send them an urgent—to monitor DJL [a German telegraph network]—and that I'll be on the air in an hour."

Actually it was two hours or so before I could get on the air. Time dressing, time getting out to the *Rundfunk*, time getting the whole story. There was considerable excitement at the *Rundfunk*, and it was some time before I could wrest the various communiqués from the hands of the German announcers. Fortunately, the censors, who must have been tipped during the night, were on the job and did not hold me up long. Except I could not call in my lead what the Germans were doing in Holland and Belgium "an invasion." They denied it was. I flamed up, but finally decided that since the censors had overlooked the word "invasion" three times in the script, it might be worth while to substitute "march in" in the lead in order to give radio listeners in America a story from Berlin. I didn't like the compromise. It was a question of sacrificing the whole important story for one word. And anyway, America knew an invasion when it happened.

LATER.—The people in Berlin, I must say, have taken the news of the battle which Hitler says is going to decide the future of their nation for the next thousand years with their usual calm. None of them gathered before the Chancellery as usually happens when big events occur. Few bothered to buy the noon papers which carried the news. For some reason Goebbels forbade extras.

The German memorandum "justifying" this latest aggression of Hitler's was handed to the ministers of Holland and Belgium at six A.M., about an hour and a half after German troops had violated their neutral soil. It sets up a new record, I think, for cynicism

William L. Shirer, *Berlin Diary*. New York: Knopf, 1941.

The Third Reich's New European Order

(Map legend:)
Axis nations
Axis occupation
Allied areas
Neutral nations
→ Major Axis drives
····▶ Major Allied drives
✳ Major battles

and downright impudence—even for Hitler. It requests the two governments to issue orders that no resistance be made to German troops. "Should the German forces encounter resistance in Belgium or Holland," it goes on, "it will be crushed with every means. The Belgian and Dutch governments alone would bear the responsibility for the consequences and for the bloodshed which would then become unavoidable."

The memorandum, which [Foreign Minister] Ribbentrop also read to the correspondents at the eight A.M. press conference, argues that Britain and France were about to attack Germany through the two Low

Countries and that the Reich therefore deemed it necessary to send in its own troops to "safeguard the neutrality of Belgium and Holland." This nonsensical hypocrisy is "backed up" by a spurious "document" from the High Command claiming that it has proofs that the Allied troops were about to march into Belgium and Holland in an effort to seize the Ruhr.

It's evident that the German army has struck with everything it has. The air force has gone all out and is obviously going to take full advantage of its superiority over the Allies. The High Command says that at dawn the Luftwaffe bombed scores of airfields in Holland, Belgium, and France as far south as Lyon. And then this is news: a communiqué speaks of German troops having been landed *by air* at many airports in Belgium and the Netherlands. The Germans claim they seized the airfields and occupied surrounding territory. Apparently, though the High Command censor would not let me say it in my talks today, they've been dropping thousands of parachutists. A report that the German parachutists have already occupied part of Rotterdam is not confirmed. It sounds inconceivable, but after Norway anything can happen.

First German reports claim they've crossed the river Maas (Meuse) and captured Maastricht, and have also driven through Luxemburg and into Belgium. Tonight the German army lies before Liége, which held it up for several days in 1914, and where Ludendorff first attracted attention.

War on civilians started too. The other side reported German planes had killed many. Tonight the Germans claimed three Allied planes dropped bombs in the middle of Freiburg, killing twenty-four civilians. As

a taste of what this phase of the war is going to be like, a German communiqué tonight says that "from now on, every enemy bombing of German civilians will be answered by five times as many German planes bombing English and French cities." (Note Nazi technique there. (1) The statement is part of the nerve war on the enemy. (2) It is designed to make German civilians stand up to bombings by assuring them the English and French are getting five times worse.)

That's one taste. Here's another: When the Belgian and Dutch ministers called for their passports at the Wilhelmstrasse today and at the same time lodged strong protests at the ruthless violation of their neutrality, an official statement was promptly published here saying that "an official on duty [at the Foreign Office] after reading the contents, which were arrogant and stupid, refused to accept them, and asked the two ministers to request for their passports in the usual manner"! The Germans are out of their minds.

Tired, after broadcasting all this day, and sick in the pit of the stomach.

See also Case Yellow, Vol. 1.

Hitler and Germany React to the Start of the War

Nazi insider architect, and future Minister of Armaments and War Production Albert Speer recalls that, while Hitler was certain the invasion of Poland on September 1, 1939, was necessary, the German people were not enthusiastic about the start of war.

Notes on the Polish question were exchanged with England. Out of the rush of events I particularly remember one evening in the conservatory of the Chancellor's residence. I had the impression that

Hitler looked exhausted from overwork. He spoke with deep conviction to his intimate circle: "This time the mistake of 1914 will be avoided. Everything depends on making the other side accept responsibility. In 1914 that was handled clumsily. And now again the ideas of the Foreign Office are simply useless. The best thing is for me to compose the notes myself." As he spoke he held a page of manuscript in his hand, probably the draft of a note from the Foreign Office. He hastily took his leave, not joining us for dinner, and vanished into the upper rooms. Later, in prison, I read that exchange of notes; it did not seem to me that Hitler had carried out his intent very well.

Hitler's view that the West would once more give in to his demands as it had done at Munich was supported by intelligence information: An officer on the British General Staff was said to have evaluated the strength of the Polish army and come to the conclusion that Polish resistance would soon collapse. Hitler thus had reason to hope that the British General Staff would do everything in its power to advise its government against so hopeless a war. When, on September 3, the Western powers followed up their ultimatum with declarations of war, Hitler was initially stunned, but quickly reassured himself and us by saying that England and France had obviously declared war merely as a sham, in order not to lose face before the whole world. In spite of the declarations there would be no fighting; he was convinced of that, he said. He therefore ordered the Wehrmacht to remain strictly on the defensive. He felt that this decision of his showed remarkable political acumen.

During those last days of August Hitler was in an unwonted state of nerves and at times completely lost the reassuring air of infallible leader. The hectic activities were followed by an uneasy period of quiet. For a short time Hitler resumed his customary daily routine. Even his interest in architectural plans revived. To his round table he explained: "Of course we are in a state of war with England and France, but if we on our side avoid all acts of war, the whole business will evaporate. As soon as we sink a ship and they have sizable casualties, the war party over there will gain strength." Even when German U-boats lay in a favorable position near the French battleship *Dunkerque* he refused to authorize an attack. But the British air raid on Wilhelmshaven and

the sinking of the *Athenia* soon called for a reconsideration of this policy.

He stuck unswervingly to his opinion that the West was too feeble, too worn out, and too decadent to begin the war seriously. Probably it was also embarrassing for him to admit to his entourage and above all to himself that he had made so crucial a mistake. I still remember his consternation when the news came that Churchill was going to enter the British War Cabinet as First Lord of the Admiralty. With this ill-omened press report in his hand, Goering stepped out of the door of Hitler's salon. He dropped into the nearest chair and said wearily: "Churchill in the Cabinet. That means that the war is really on. Now we shall have war with England." From these and other observations I deduced that this initiation of real war was not what Hitler had projected.

His illusions and wish-dreams were a direct outgrowth of his unrealistic mode of working and thinking. Hitler actually knew nothing about his enemies and even refused to use the information that was available to him. Instead, he trusted his inspirations, no matter how inherently contradictory they might be, and these inspirations were governed by extreme contempt for and underestimation of the others. In keeping with his classic phrase that there were always two possibilities, he wanted to have the war at the supposedly most favorable moment, while at the same time he failed to adequately prepare for it. He regarded England, as he once stressed, as "our enemy Number One," while at the same time hoping to come to an arrangement with that enemy.

I do not think that in those early days of September, Hitler was fully aware that he had irrevocably unleashed a world war. He had merely meant to move one step further. To be sure, he was ready to accept the risk associated with that step, just as he had been a year before during the Czech crisis; but he had prepared himself only for the risk, not really for the great war. His naval rearmament was obviously planned for a

Albert Speer, *Inside the Third Reich*. Trans. Richard and Clara Winston. New York: Macmillan, 1970. Copyright © 1970 by The Macmillan Company. Reproduced by permission.

later date; the battleships as well as the first large aircraft carriers were still under construction. He knew that they would not attain full military value until they could face the enemy on more or less even terms. Moreover, he had spoken so often of the neglect of the submarine arm in the First World War that he probably would not have knowingly begun the Second without preparing a strong fleet of U-boats.

But all his anxieties seemed to be scattered to the winds in early September, when the campaign in Poland yielded such successes for the German troops. Hitler seemed to recover his assurance swiftly, and later, at the climax of the war, I frequently heard him say that the Polish campaign had been a necessary thing.

> Do you think it would have been good fortune for our troops if we had taken Poland without a fight, after obtaining Austria and Czechoslovakia without fighting? Believe me, not even the best army can stand that sort of thing. Victories without loss of blood are demoralizing. Therefore it was not only fortunate there was no compromise; at the time we would have had to regard it as harmful, and I therefore would have struck in any case.

It may be, nevertheless, that by such remarks he was trying to gloss over his diplomatic miscalculations of August 1939. On the other hand, toward the end of the war Colonel General Heinrici told me about an early speech of Hitler's to the generals which points in the same direction. I noted down Heinrici's remarkable story as follows: "Hitler said that he was the first man since Charlemagne to hold unlimited power in his own hand. He did not hold this power in vain, he said, but would know how to use it in a struggle for Germany. If the war were not won, that would mean that Germany had not stood the test of strength; in that case she would deserve to be and would be doomed."

From the start the populace took a far more serious view of the situation than did Hitler and his entourage. Because of the general nervousness a false air-raid alarm was sounded in Berlin early in September. Along with many other Berliners I sat in a public shelter. The atmosphere was noticeably depressed; the people were full of fear about the future.

None of the regiments marched off to war decorated with flowers as they had done at the beginning of the First World War. The streets remained empty. There was no crowd on Wilhelmsplatz shouting for Hitler. It was in keeping with the desolate mood that Hitler had his bags packed into the cars one night to drive east, to the front. Three days after the beginning of the attack on Poland he had his adjutant summon me to the provisionally blacked-out residence in the Chancellery to bid me good-by. I found a man who lost his temper over trivialities. The cars drove up, and he tersely took his leave of the "courtiers" who were remaining behind. Not a soul on the street took notice of this historic event: Hitler driving off to the war he had staged. Obviously Goebbels could have provided a cheering crowd of any size, but he was apparently not in the mood to do it.

See also Case White, Vol. 1.

A Last Visit to Hitler

Albert Speer, the protégé of Adolf Hitler who served as Minister of Armaments and War Production from 1942 to 1945, remembers his last visit to the man who changed his life. By this time, April 1945, Hitler has retreated to his vast bunker beneath the Reichs Chancellery in Berlin to ponder his future and that of the German Reich as Allied bombs and artillery pound overhead.

Hitler's adjutant [SS General Julius Schaub] returned: "The Fuehrer is ready to see you." How often in the past twelve years had I been ushered into Hitler's presence with these words. But I was not thinking of that as I descended the fifty-odd steps into the bunker, but if I would be ascending them with a whole skin. The first person I met below was Bormann. He came forward to meet me with such unwonted politeness that I began feeling more secure. For Bormann's or Schaub's expressions had always been reliable guides to Hitler's mood. Humbly, he said to me: "When you speak with the Fuehrer . . . he'll certainly raise the question of whether we ought to stay in Berlin or fly to Berchtesgaden. But it's high time he took over the command in South Germany. . . . These are the last hours when it will be possible. . . . You'll persuade him to fly out, won't you?"

If there were anyone in the bunker attached to his life, it was obviously Bormann, who only three weeks earlier had enjoined the functionaries of the party to overcome all weaknesses, to win the victory or die at their posts. I gave a noncommittal reply, feeling a belated sense of triumph at his almost imploring manner.

Albert Speer, *Inside the Third Reich*. Trans. Richard and Clara Winston. New York: Macmillan, 1970. Copyright © 1970 by The Macmillan Company. Reproduced by permission.

Then I was led into Hitler's room in the bunker. In his welcome there was no sign of the warmth with which he had responded a few weeks before to my vow of loyalty. He showed no emotion at all. Once again I had the feeling that he was empty, burned out, lifeless. He assumed that businesslike expression which could be a mask for anything and asked me what I thought about [Grand Admiral Karl] Doenitz's approach to his job. I had the distinct feeling that he was not asking about Doenitz by chance, but that the question involved his successor. And to this day I think that Doenitz liquidated the hopeless legacy that unexpectedly became his lot with more prudence, dignity, and responsibility than Bormann or Himmler would have done. I voiced my favorable impression of the admiral, now and then enriching my account with anecdotes which I knew would please Hitler. But with the wisdom of long experience I did not try to influence him in Doenitz's favor, for fear that this would drive him in the opposite direction.

Abruptly, Hitler asked me: "What do you think? Should I stay here or fly to Berchtesgaden? Jodl has told me that tomorrow is the last chance for that."

Spontaneously, I advised him to stay in Berlin. What would he do at Obersalzberg? With Berlin gone, the war would be over in any case, I said. "It seems to me better, if it must be, that you end your life here in the capital as the Fuehrer rather than in your weekend house."

Once more I was deeply moved. At the time I thought that was a piece of good advice. Actually it was bad, for if he had flown to Obersalzberg the battle for Berlin would probably have been shortened by a week.

That day he said nothing more of an imminent turning point or that there was still hope. Rather apathetically, wearily and as if it were already a matter of course, he began speaking of his death: "I too have resolved to stay here. I only wanted to hear your view once more." Without excitement, he continued: "I shall not fight personally. There is always the danger that I would only be wounded and fall into the hands of the Russians alive. I don't want my enemies to disgrace my body either. I've given orders that I be cremated. Fräulein Braun wants to depart this life with me, and I'll shoot Blondi [his dog] beforehand. Believe me, Speer, it is easy for me to end my life. A brief moment and I'm freed of everything, liberated from this painful existence."

I felt as if I had been talking with a man already departed. The atmosphere grew increasingly uncanny; the tragedy was approaching its end.

During the last months I had hated him at times, fought him, lied to him, and deceived him, but at this moment I was confused and emotionally shaken. In this state, I confessed to him in a low voice, to my own surprise, that I had not carried out any demolitions but had actually prevented them. For a moment his eyes filled with tears. But he did not react. Such questions, so important to him only a few weeks before, were now remote. Absently, he stared at me as I faltered out my offer to stay in Berlin. He did not answer. Perhaps he sensed that I did not mean it. I have often asked myself since whether he had not always known instinctively that I had been working against him during these past months and whether he had not deduced this from my memoranda; also whether by letting me act contrary to his orders he had not provided a fresh example of the multiple strata in his mysterious personality. I shall never know.

Just then General Krebs, the army chief of staff, was announced. He had come to give the situation report. In that respect nothing had changed. The Commander in Chief of the armed forces was receiving the situation reports from the fronts as always. Only three days before the situation room in

the bunker could hardly hold the crowd of high-ranking officers, commanders of various departments of the Wehrmacht and SS, but now almost all had left in the meantime. Along with Goering, Doenitz and Himmler, Keitel and Jodl, air force Chief of Staff Koller, and the most important officers of their staffs were now outside of Berlin. Only lower-ranking liaison officers had remained. And the nature of the report had changed. Nothing but vague scraps of news were coming from outside. The chief of staff could offer little more than conjectures. The map he spread out in front of Hitler covered only the area around Berlin and Potsdam. But even here the data on the status of the Soviet advance no longer corresponded with the observations I had made a few hours before. The Soviet troops had long since come closer than the map indicated.

To my astonishment, during the conference Hitler once again tried to make a display of optimism, although he had only just finished talking with me about his impending death and the disposition of his body. On the other hand, he had lost much of his former persuasiveness. Krebs listened to him patiently and politely. Often in the past, when the situation was clearly desperate but Hitler continued undeterred to conjure up a favorable outcome, I had thought he was the captive of obsessional ideas. Now it became evident that he spoke two languages at once. How long had he been deceiving us? Since when had he realized that the struggle was lost: since the winter at the gates of Moscow, since Stalingrad, since the Allied invasion, since the Ardennes offensive of December 1944? How much was pretense, how much calculation? But perhaps it was merely that I had just witnessed another of his rapid changes of mood and that he was being as sincere with General Krebs as he had earlier been with me.

The situation conference, which ordinarily went on for hours, was quickly ended. Its very brevity revealed that this remnant of a headquarters was in its death throes. On this day Hitler even restrained from swoop-ing us off into the dream world of providen-tial miracles. We were dismissed with a few words and left the room in which so dreary a chapter of errors, omissions, and crimes had been played out. Hitler had treated me as an ordinary guest, as if I had not flown to Berlin especially for his sake. We parted without shaking hands, in the most casual manner, as if we would be seeing each other the next day.

Outside the room I met Goebbels. He an-nounced: "Yesterday the Fuehrer took a de-cision of enormous importance. He had stopped the fighting in the West so that the Anglo-American troops can enter Berlin unhindered." Here again was one of those mirages which excited the minds of these men for a few hours and aroused new hopes which as quickly as they had come would be replaced by others.

Goebbels told me that his wife and six children were now living in the bunker as Hitler's guests, in order, as he put it, to end their lives at this historic site. In contrast to Hitler, he appeared to be in fullest control of his thoughts and emotions. He showed no sign of having settled his accounts with life.

By this time it was late afternoon. An SS doctor informed me that Frau Goebbels was in bed, very weak and suffering from heart attacks. I sent word to her asking her to re-ceive me. I would have liked to talk to her alone, but Goebbels was already waiting in an anteroom and led me into the little cham-ber deep underground where she lay in a plain bed. She was pale and spoke only triv-ialities in a low voice, although I could sense that she was in deep agony over the irrevocably approaching hour when her children must die. Since Goebbels re-mained persistently at my side, our conver-sation was limited to the state of her health. Only as I was on the point of leaving did she hint at what she was really feeling: "How happy I am that at least Harald [her son by her first marriage] is alive." I too felt confined and could scarcely find words—

but what could anyone say in this situation? We said good-by in awkward silence. Her husband had not allowed us even a few minutes alone for our farewell.

Meanwhile, there was a flurry of excite-ment in the vestibule. A telegram had ar-rived from Goering, which Bormann hastily brought to Hitler. I trailed informally along after him, chiefly out of curiosity. In the telegram Goering merely asked Hitler whether, in keeping with the decree on the succession, he should assume the leader-ship of the entire Reich if Hitler remained in Fortress Berlin. But Bormann claimed that Goering had launched a coup d'état; perhaps this was Bormann's last effort to induce Hitler to fly to Berchtesgaden and take control there. At first, Hitler responded to this news with the same apathy he had shown all day long. But Bormann's theory was given fresh support when another radio message from Goering arrived. I pocketed a copy which in the general confusion lay unnoticed in the bunker. It read:

To Reich Minister von Ribbentrop:
I have asked the Fuehrer to provide me with instructions by 10 P.M. April 23. If by this time it is apparent that the Fuehrer has been deprived of his free-dom of action to conduct the affairs of the Reich, his decree of June 29, 1941, becomes effective, according to which I am heir to all his offices as his deputy. [If] by 12 midnight April 23, 1945, you receive no other word either from the Fuehrer directly or from me, you are to come to me at once by air.
(*Signed*) Goering, Reich Marshal

Here was fresh material for Bormann. "Goering is engaged in treason!" he ex-claimed excitedly. "He's already sending telegrams to members of the government and announcing that on the basis of his powers he will assume your office at twelve o'clock tonight, *mein Führer.*"

Although Hitler had remained calm when the first telegram arrived, Bormann now won his game. Hitler immediately stripped Goering of his rights of succession—Bormann himself drafted the radio message—and accused him of treason to Hitler and betrayal of National Socialism. The message to Goering went on to say that Hitler would exempt him from further punishment if the Reich Marshal would promptly resign all his offices for reasons of health.

Bormann had at last managed to rouse Hitler from his lethargy. An outburst of wild fury followed in which feelings of bitterness, helplessness, self-pity, and despair mingled. With flushed face and staring eyes, Hitler ranted as if he had forgotten the presence of his entourage: "I've known it all along. I know that Goering is lazy. He let the air force go to pot. He was corrupt. His example made corruption possible in our state. Besides he's been a drug addict for years. I've known it all along."

So Hitler had known all that but had done nothing about it.

And then, with startling abruptness, he lapsed back into his apathy: "Well, all right. Let Goering negotiate the surrender. If the war is lost anyhow, it doesn't matter who does it." That sentence expressed contempt for the German people: Goering was still good enough for the purposes of capitulation.

After this crisis, Hitler had reached the end of his strength. He dropped back into the weary tone that had been characteristic of him earlier that day. For years he had overtaxed himself; for years, mustering that immoderate will of his, he had thrust away from himself and others the growing certainty of this end. Now he no longer had the energy to conceal his condition. He was giving up.

About half an hour later Bormann brought in Goering's telegram of reply. Because of a severe heart attack Goering was resigning all his powers. How often before Hitler had removed an inconvenient associate not by dismissal, but by an allegation of illness, merely to preserve the German people's faith in the internal unity of the top leadership. Even now,

Architect Albert Speer shows Hitler plans for the grand redesign of Berlin on February 7, 1938.

when all was almost over, Hitler remained true to this habit of observing public decorum.

Only now, at the very last hour, had Bormann reached his goal. Goering was eliminated, possibly Bormann also was aware of Goering's failings; but he had hated and now overthrown the Reich Marshal solely because he had held too much power. In a way I felt sympathy for Goering at this time. I recalled the conversation in which he had assured me of his loyalty to Hitler.

The brief thunderstorm staged by Bormann was over; a few bars of [Wagner's] *Götterdämmerung* had sounded and faded. The supposed Hagen [a lead character] had left the stage. To my surprise, Hitler was amenable to a request of mine, though I made it with considerable trepidation. Several Czech managers of the Skoda Works were expecting an unpleasant fate from the Russian because of their collaboration with us. They were probably right about that. On the other hand, because of their former relations with American industry they were placing their hopes of safety on flying to American headquarters. A few days before Hitler would have strictly outlawed any such proposal. But now he was prepared to sign an order waiving all formalities so that the men could fly to safety.

While I was discussing this point with Hitler, Bormann reminded him that Ribbentrop was still waiting for an audience. Hitler reacted nervously: "I've already said several times that I don't want to see him." For some reason the idea of meeting Ribbentrop annoyed him.

Bormann insisted: "Ribbentrop has said he won't move from the threshold, that he'll wait there like a faithful dog until you call him."

This figure of speech softened Hitler; he had Ribbentrop summoned. They talked alone. Apparently Hitler told him about the escape plan of the Czech managers. But even in this desperate situation the Foreign Minister fought to defend his jurisdictional rights. In the corridor he grumbled to me: "That is a matter for the Foreign Office." In a somewhat milder tone he added: "In this particular case I have no objection if the document will say: 'At the suggestion of the Foreign Minister.'" I added these words, Ribbentrop was content, and Hitler signed the paper. This was, so far as I know, Hitler's last official dealing with his Foreign Minister.

In the meantime my paternal adviser of the past few months, Friedrich Lüschen, had arrived at the Chancellery. But all my efforts to persuade him to leave Berlin remained vain. We told each other good-by. Later, in Nuremberg, I learned that he had committed suicide after the fall of Berlin.

Toward midnight Eva Braun sent an SS orderly to invite me to the small room in the bunker that was both her bedroom and living room. It was pleasantly furnished; she had had some of the expensive furniture which I had designed for her years ago brought from her two rooms in the upper floors of the Chancellery. Neither the proportions nor the pieces selected fitted into the gloomy surroundings. To complete the irony, one of the inlays on the doors of the chest was a four-leaf clover incorporating her initials.

We were able to talk honestly, for Hitler had withdrawn. She was the only prominent candidate for death in this bunker who displayed an admirable and superior composure. While all the others were abnormal —exaltedly heroic like Goebbels, bent on saving his skin like Bormann, exhausted like Hitler, or in total collapse like Frau Goebbels—Eva Braun radiated an almost gay serenity. "How about a bottle of champagne for our farewell? And some sweets? I'm sure you haven't eaten in a long time."

I was touched by her concern; she was the first person to think that I might be hungry after my many hours in the bunker. The orderly brought a bottle of Moet et Chandon, cake, and sweets. We remained alone. "You know, it was good that you came back once more. The Fuehrer had assumed you would be working against him. But your visit has proved the opposite to him hasn't it?" I did not answer that question. "Anyhow, he liked what you said to him today. He has made up his mind to stay here, and I am staying with him. And you know the rest, too, of course. . . . He wanted to send me back to Munich. But I refused; I've come to end it here."

She was also the only person in the bunker capable of humane considerations. "Why do so many more people have to be killed?" she asked. "And it's all for nothing. . . . Incidentally, you almost came too late. Yesterday the situation was so terrible it seemed the Russians would quickly occupy all of Berlin. The Fuehrer was on the point of giving up. But Goebbels talked to him and persuaded him, and so we're still here."

She went on talking easily and informally with me, occasionally bursting out against Bormann, who was pursuing his intrigues up to the last. But again and again she came back to the declaration that she was happy here in the bunker.

By now it was about three o'clock in the morning. Hitler was awake again. I sent word that I wanted to bid him good-by. The day had worn me out, and I was afraid that I would not be able to control myself at our parting. Trembling, the prematurely aged man stood before me for the last time; the man to whom I had dedicated my life twelve years before. I was both moved and confused. For his part, he showed no emotion when we confronted one another. His words were as cold as his hand: "So, you're leaving? Good. *Auf Wiedersehen*." No regards to my family, no wishes, no thanks, no farewell. For a moment I lost my composure, said something about coming back. But he could easily see that it was a white lie, and turned his attention to something else. I was dismissed.

Ten minutes later, with hardly another word spoken to anyone, I left the Chancellor's residence. I wanted to walk once more through the neighboring Chancellery, which I had built. Since the lights were no longer functioning, I contented myself with a few farewell minutes in the Court of Honor, whose outlines could scarcely be seen against the night sky. I sensed rather than saw the architecture. There was an almost ghostly quiet about everything, like a night in the mountains. The noise of a great city, which in earlier years had penetrated to here even during the night, had totally ceased. At rather long intervals I heard the detonations of Russian shells. Such was my last visit to the Chancellery. Years ago I had built it—full of plans, prospects, and dreams for the future. Now I was leaving the ruins of my building, and of the most significant years of my life.

See also Führerbunker, Vol. 1; Hitler, Adolf; Speer, Albert, Vol. 3.

CHAPTER THREE

CONCENTRATION CAMPS AND THE HOLOCAUST

For most people, the clearest association with the Third Reich, beyond World War II, is the massive terrorist state created by Adolf Hitler and his underlings. The Nazi program of state terror and extermination began with the first concentration camps, built to house political opponents to Nazism, in 1933, and reached the extremes of inhumanity when, during World War II, SS officials massacred 6 million Jews as well as untold hundreds of thousands of other so-called enemies of the Reich.

Nazi terror had its origins in the racial beliefs of Adolf Hitler and other Nazi ideologists. They claimed from 1919, the beginning of the Nazi era, that Germans were a unique, superior race and that contact with other races, namely Jews, could only weaken Germany. Jews were, to the Nazi mind, deceitful, inferior, evil, the equivalent of a dangerous bacteria threatening the health of the German body. Soon after achieving power the Nazis began to take measures to exclude German Jews from national citizenship and to encourage their emigration from Germany. With World War II under way, however, and with most of Europe's Jews in the eastern European territories that the Nazis hoped to conquer, their tactics changed. At that point the SS, led by Heinrich Himmler and Reinhard Heydrich, took control of what the Nazis called the "Jewish Question." Their responses moved from establishing ghettos to shooting millions using special squads known as Einsatzgruppen to finally, as the January 1942 Wannsee Conference made clear, killing Jews by gassing in special death camps such as Auschwitz.

Jews were not the only targets of the Nazi terror state. Ordinary Germans too were victims. People might find themselves in concentration camps merely for uttering the wrong words or phrases. Meanwhile, and still in accordance with their racial plan to purify Germany, Nazi officials took steps to "cleanse" the German nation of those considered to be biologically unsound. The first gas chambers, in fact, were used to kill thousands of mentally and physically handicapped Germans from 1939 to 1941, a process known as euthanasia. The gas chamber techniques, of course, were in time shifted to the east for the massacre of Jews.

Not all Jews went to their deaths silently. In the Warsaw ghetto in 1943, for example, young Jews staged an armed uprising that held the Germans off for weeks. The Jews who survived the Nazis' "Final Solution to the Jewish Question," moreover, left a number of poignant accounts of their suffering and of the inhumanity of the Third Reich. So also did the records of Jews who perished, such as Anne Frank.

Major Concentration Camps in Europe 1938–1945

A General Objects to the Killings

In this official memorandum, German general Johannes Blaskowitz warns that the Nazi policy of mass killing on the eastern front may come back to haunt the regime and is, in any case, dishonorable. Urged to send the message to Hitler, Blaskowitz chose not to. Nevertheless, knowledge of his opinions among Nazi leaders slowed his promotions during World War II.

It is misguided to slaughter tens of thousands of Jews and Poles as is happening at present; because, in view of the huge population neither the concept of a Polish State nor the Jews will be eliminated by doing so. On the contrary, the way in which this slaughter is being carried out is causing great damage; it is complicating the problems and making them much more dangerous than they would have been with a considered and systematic approach. The consequences are:

(a) Enemy propaganda is provided with material which could nowhere have been more effectively devised. It is true that what the foreign radio stations have broadcast so far is only a tiny fraction of what has happened in reality. But we must reckon that the clamour of the outside world will continually increase and cause great political damage, particularly since the atrocities have actually occurred and cannot be disproved.

(b) The acts of violence against the Jews which occur in full view of the public inspire among the religious Poles not only deep disgust but also great pity for the Jewish population, to which up to now the Poles were more or less hostile. In a very short time we shall reach the point at which our arch-enemies in the eastern sphere—the Pole and the Jew, who in addition will receive the particular support of the Catholic Church—will, in their hatred against their tormentors, combine against Germany right along the line.

(c) The role of the armed forces who are compelled impotently to watch this crime and whose reputation, particularly with the Polish population, suffers irreparable harm, need not be referred to again.

(d) But the worst damage which will accrue to the German nation from the present situation is the brutalization and moral debasement which, in a very short time, will spread like a plague among valuable German manpower.

If high officials of the SS and police demand acts of violence and brutality and praise them publicly, then in a very short time we shall be faced with the rule of the thug. Like-minded people and those with warped characters will very soon come together so that, as is now the case in Poland, they can give full expression to their animal and pathological instincts. It is hardly possible to keep them any longer in check, since they can well believe themselves officially authorized and justified in committing any act of cruelty.

The only way of resisting this epidemic is to subordinate those who are guilty and their followers to the military leadership and courts as quickly as possible.

See also Commissar Order, Einsatzgruppen, Vol. 1.

Jeremy Noakes and Geoffrey Pridham, eds., *Documents on Nazism, 1919–1945*. New York: Viking, 1974.

The Last Days of the Warsaw Ghetto

Polish journalist Alexander Donat survived the Warsaw ghetto and eventually resettled in the United States. He recorded a detailed memoir of the final, chaotic days of the ghetto as Jewish defenders mounted a heroic defense.

My wife, Lena, and I thought constantly about saving our little boy. We went over and over the list of the "Aryans" we knew, trying to think which of them might be both willing and able to take him. I began to write letters to our Polish friends, telling them of our situation and begging them to save the life of an innocent child. Needless to say, these letters could not go through the mails: they had to be delivered by messenger. But even if one got hold of someone willing to deliver a letter outside the walls, the recipient was usually reluctant to accept a letter from the ghetto brought by a stranger: there was too much danger of blackmail. So I first had to alert my friends by phone, and tell them to expect a letter from me. To make these calls, I used the phone in the office of the T.O.Z. (one of the Jewish welfare agencies) at 56 Zamenhof Street, which I could get to through secret passages. The phone was in constant use: by people on errands like mine, or by smugglers contacting their confederates about conditions at the gates or arranging to receive parcels to be thrown over the wall. Each call took hours of waiting my turn. And then not everyone I wanted to reach had a phone. I would often call my former partner, Stanislaw Kapko, at his of-

fice and have him get a message to someone that he was to come to Kapko's office and await a call from me. Then I would have to call Kapko the next day to find out if the appointment had been made. When I finally spoke to the friend, I had then to persuade him to come and talk to me at the printing shop on Leszno Street. There was no danger for Gentiles in coming to the printing shop because it was located outside the ghetto, and they could always pretend to be out buying Jewish goods. Still, they were not easy to persuade. Some never came, some came and refused my request. Finally one possibility to save Wlodek began to take shape: the Maginskis.

Stefan Maginski had been a member of the group with whom I had fled Warsaw in September 1939 (whence I returned to be with my family). He was a brilliant journalist and a highly cultivated man. I loved him, and he treated me rather as if I were his younger brother. His wife, Maria, a former actress, was both a beauty and a great lady. They had no children.

Mrs. Maginski agreed to meet us in Leszno Street. She spoke of a friend in the country who, for a modest fee, would be willing to take the child. She vouched for the decency and honesty of her friend, and promised us that Wlodek would be well looked after. They themselves could not take him, because they were too old suddenly to appear with a five-year-old child, and they were, besides, working night and day with the Polish resistance. The fee was indeed modest, and happily we could afford it. Sometime earlier I had managed to increase my income by going into partnership with Izak Rubin to smuggle out some of the kerchiefs made from pillowcases in the

Excerpted from Alexander Donat, "Last Days," *Commentary*, May 1963. Copyright © 1963 by *Commentary*. Reproduced by permission.

ghetto. Thus I had the money to pay for Wlodek's care for several months in advance. By some child's instinct for self-preservation, Wlodek did everything in his power to win Mrs. Maginski, and she was much taken with him. She promised to make the necessary preparations. . . .

At the end of March, Mrs. Maginski came once more to Leszno Street—this time to tell us that all the arrangements for Wlodek had been made and we had two weeks in which to prepare him for leaving us.

Two weeks: in which we tried to memorize our five-year-old son to the look and to the touch, and in which I watched approvingly while my son's mother taught him to disavow his connection with us. "Remember, you have never lived in the ghetto. You are not a Jew. You are a Polish Catholic. Your father is a Polish army officer who was taken prisoner. Your mother is away in the country. Mrs. Maginski is your Auntie Maria."

The two weeks turned out to be only seven days. Mrs. Maginski unexpectedly returned to the printing shop one afternoon, terribly upset. The Polish Underground had received word that the liquidation of the ghetto was to take place any day now; the child must be smuggled out the next day. Next morning, Lena washed and fed her baby for the last time. At eight o'clock we joined the printers' marching column, and at eleven Mrs. Maginski came to the shop for him. Wlodek was quiet, smiling. But just as we were to say good-bye, he clutched his mother and said, "Is it true that I'll never see you again?" "What a silly boy you are!" she managed to say. "Just as soon as the war is over, I am coming to get you."

Mrs. Maginski took Wlodek's hand and walked briskly out of the building. Wlodek skipped beside her, and didn't look back once. They crossed Leszno and turned into Orla, out of sight. A Jewish policeman who was a friend of ours followed them for a little way on his bicycle. Everyone crowded around to congratulate us. We had been very lucky, they said. So, indeed, we had. . . .

On . . . Sunday (April 18) at 6 o'clock P.M., Polish police surrounded the ghetto. Within an hour the underground declared a state of emergency. The fighters were assigned to their posts. Weapons, ammunition, and food were distributed, along with supplies of potassium cyanide. By 2 A.M. the next morning (April 19) the Poles had been joined by Ukrainian, Latvian, and SS units, who ringed the ghetto walls with patrols stationed about thirty yards apart.

I had just come on guard duty at our apartment house when two boys from the Z.O.B. [a Jewish resistance organization] arrived to order us all to our shelters. They were about twenty years old, bare-headed, with rifles in their hands and grenades stuffed into their belts. It did not take long to alert everyone; by dawn the ghetto was a ghost town. I awakened Lena and the others in our flat; we put on the best clothing we could find, and took the linen bag we had filled with lump sugar and biscuits cut up into small squares. About thirty people gathered in our shelter.

We had only one weapon among us: Izak's revolver. Izak crouched at a peephole near the entrance to the shelter, from which he could see part of the courtyard. An ingenious network of tunnels connected us with the "outside" world. Through a tunnel extended to the front attic of our house, in turn connected with others, one could reach a spot just above the corner of Muranowska and Zamenhof Streets. The north side of the building, which fronted on Niska Street and the *Umschlagplatz* [this was the transfer point near the railway line which the mass deportations had made notorious], could be reached by a special passage that had been drilled through the carpenter's apartment. This same passage connected with No. 62 Zamenhof Street, where a resistance group was preparing to make its last-ditch stand. On the second floor a hole had been bored through to one of the lavatories in No. 42 Muranowska, from which we were put into connection with every building on the block.

Despite all our elaborate preparations, the German operation came upon us suddenly enough to upset all plans—those of the hundreds of people who had prepared to slip out to the "Aryan" side at the very last moment, and had documents and lodgings waiting for them, and, of course Kapko's grand scheme. That "very last moment" had come, and it was now too late for anything.

On Monday morning, the Germans marched into the ghetto through the gate at Gesia and Zamenhof Streets and took up positions in the little square opposite the *Judenrat* [Jewish council] offices. Convinced that the resistance would not fire on Jews, they sent members of the Jewish police in their front ranks. Our fighters let the Jewish police go by, and barraged the Germans who followed with bullets, hand grenades, and home-made bombs. The intersection of Zamenhof and Mila Streets, where the resistance occupied the buildings on all four corners, became the scene of a real battle. Home-made incendiary bombs, flung from an attic window, hit first one tank and then another. The tanks burst into flames and their trapped crews were burned alive. The troops panicked and scattered in disorder.

I lay on the attic floor with Izak, watching all this going on below. Izak's orders were to cover the withdrawal of our unarmed people should it become necessary for them to leave the shelter; several times I saw him point his gun and then, reluctantly, withdraw it. Below us German officers were trying to urge on their panicked "*Judenhelden*" with pistols and riding crops: the men who had been so powerful and assured when dealing with women and children and old men were now running from the fire of the resistance. Scores of German bodies lay scattered on the pavement.

When Izak and I returned to the others in the shelter to report on what we had seen, people embraced and congratulated one another, laughing and crying. Some began to chant the Psalms, and an old man recited blessings aloud.

(Later we learned from some of the fighters that the first battle of the Warsaw Ghetto resistance had occurred at the corner of Nalewki and Gesia Streets, where a German unit marching into the ghetto had been caught totally off guard and where, after several hours, this first German unit withdrew, leaving behind their dead and wounded. But replacements came, and the fighting continued at this corner off and on all day. The resistance group's meager supply of grenades and bombs finally gave out, and they then had to retreat through the back of the house at 33 Nalewki Street. Before pulling back, they set fire to the warehouse at 31 Nalewki, where the SS stored their Jewish loot. The warehouse continued to smolder and burn until the very end.) . . .

The original battle, the one at Nalewki and Gesia Streets, had not gone so well for us. There had been heavy losses on both sides; but when our boys were forced to retreat from their position, the Germans took over Gesia Street and, with it, the ghetto hospital. The SS first worked its terrible vengeance on the sick, going through ward after ward with bayonets and guns; then they shelled the building and set fire to it. Those patients and staff members who had made it to the shelters died in the fire.

All day Tuesday we watched the glow in the sky that indicated shelling in the vicinity of the Brushmakers. The Brushmakers had its own independent fighting unit, headed by Marek Edelman; and when the Germans opened attack on the district—for only twenty-eight people out of 8,000 responded to the Germans' summons to report for deportation—they walked into a mined booby-trap at the entrance to 6 Walowa Street. Stroop [the Nazi officer in charge of the Warsaw assault] then called for artillery fire on the entire Brushmakers' area. The resistance suffered very heavy losses, and house after house caught fire. Fighting was taken up again in Muranow Square. There the

Germans had set up a concentration of tanks, heavy machine guns, and flamethrowers. The resistance, on the other hand, had an underground passage to the "Aryan" side, and throughout the battle was being supplied ammunition by the Polish resistance. Muranow Square was the only Jewish position that did not suffer from an extreme shortage of weapons. In the end, some of the Jewish fighters managed to escape through their passage to the "Aryan" side. . . .

The apartment house across the street [from us] caught fire, and the sparks carried by the wind constituted a real danger to us. In accordance with a plan previously agreed upon, I made my way to the building next door where—amazingly enough—there was still a telephone in working order. I calmly reported the fire to the fire department, and within a few minutes they appeared to put it out. It took some time before the fire department, undoubtedly under German orders, ceased responding to our calls.

Tuesday evening a blood-red glow hung over the southern end of the ghetto, and here and there throughout the rest of the ghetto a building was burning: in some instances, like that of the warehouse, from a fire set by the resistance, more often from the shelling and occasional air bombardment. That night the grapevine offered sensational news: the uprising had spread from the ghetto to the whole of Warsaw. Organizations like the AK (the Home Army) and the GL (the People's Guard) were joining their Jewish comrades; an unlimited supply of arms was making its way to the ghetto; more important, we heard, the Allies had promised to parachute troops and supplies to us. We would show the bastards yet!

For the first time in two days, we lit the stove and ate cooked potatoes and kasha from our reserve stock. We then went to sleep in our own beds, full of hope for tomorrow.

But Wednesday was no different from the day before. We could hear the same

gunfire and explosions. The fires were spreading. This was the day that Stroop began to close in, using two thousand trained troops, and thirty officers, with tanks, machine guns, and air power. Ammunition was giving out. And our boys were retreating from one position to another. There was no question that we would be defeated—but everyone fought on.

For Stroop the major problem was the tens of thousands of civilian Jews holed up in their shelters. [SS leader Heinrich] Himmler's order had been categorical, but to pull the Jews individually out of their hiding places before destroying the ghetto might take months. The resistance understood this too, and after two days of street fighting, decided to save their ammunition for the defense of the bunkers. Stroop, then, was faced with the challenge of extricating Jews from the ghetto at the risk of a house-to-house skirmish for each and every one of them.

It was a challenge he was equal to. He called in the army engineers and ordered them to set fire to every building. The engineers moved methodically from house to house, drenching the ground floor with gasoline and setting off explosives in the cellars. The ghetto was to be razed to the ground. . . .

In his report of April 22, 1943, Stroop wrote: "Whole families of Jews, enveloped in flames, leaped out of windows, or slid to the ground on bedsheets tied together. Measure were taken to liquidate these Jews at once."

Then came Easter Sunday. The day was bright, and the citizenry of Warsaw, dressed in their finest, crowded into the churches. I thought, perhaps Wlodek is among them. When the mass was over, the holiday crowds pushed through the streets to catch sight of Warsaw's newest spectacle. . . . Batteries of artillery were set up in Nowiniarska Street, from which the Germans kept up a steady barrage against the ghetto. And everywhere the flame, and the stench of roasting human flesh. The sight was awesome—and exciting. From time to time a living torch would be seen crouched on a window sill and then leaping through the air. Occasionally one such figure caught on some obstruction and hung there. The spectators would shout to the German riflemen, "Hey, look over there . . . no, over there!" As each figure completed its gruesome trajectory, the crowds cheered.

Fighting of a sort was still going on inside the ghetto—scattered and disorganized, but determined. Those people who had been burned out of their shelters were roaming the streets, looking for hiding places. We allowed another ten people into our shelter.

It was now the ninth day of the uprising, Tuesday, April 27. Someone who had been sent out to reconnoiter brought us word that the Germans were coming into our street. We heard shots in the courtyard. . . .

"They are setting fire to the staircases and the ground floor apartments," Izak whispered. We could hear nothing, but in half an hour the heat became unbearable and black smoke began to fill the shelter. Our turn had come.

Izak announced that we were to evacuate the shelter. Nearly half our companions refused to budge. They had chosen to use their potassium cyanide, and with a kind of gentle indifference they sat watching the rest of us scurrying around. Below us was an inferno: our only way out was by the roof. There were five of us now, Izak, Lena, I, and two other friends; I never saw what happened to the others. We crossed the roof to the

Women and children surrender during the Warsaw ghetto uprising of 1943. After World War II, this photograph was introduced as evidence to convict the soldier holding the gun (far right).

neighboring house, not yet on fire. Then began a tortuous journey through attics, and passages and dugouts and cellars. Our plan was to get as far away from our burning house as possible, and, under cover of night, cross the pavement to the backs of the houses on Mila Street, then down Mila and across Nalewki to a certain house that still had a passageway out of the ghetto.

By late afternoon we were at the middle of the block. At dawn Izak went to scout: we had to cross the street, find a shelter, contact a fighting group. Before he returned, we heard the now-familiar sound of windows breaking and smelled the smoke. The staircases in this building were in worse condition than our own had been. We went to the roof again, and sat, dazed by the fresh air and sunshine, straddling the roof's peak. What were we to do now? The look of death had come over Lena's face and I discovered that in the scramble for the roof, the little bag she had been wearing around her neck had slipped loose and was gone. In that bag was our last refuge: cyanide. We had to decide, then, whether to remain on the roof and burn alive or to try to make our way down. One of our friends decided for us: "There is always time to die," he said. We scrambled down through the burning staircase and ran out of the doorway with our hands above our heads. We were led by a waiting German officer out into Muranowska Street. A large number of Jews from the surrounding apartment houses were already gathered there. Among them were a few of our neighbors.

One of the SS men kept staring at Lena and asked her her name. She gave him her married name, and he walked away without a word. They had been classmates together at the university.

We were lined up five across, and made our way toward the *Umschlagplatz*. As we passed Niska Street, Lena clutched my hand. A woman, holding a child by the hand, stood screaming at an upper-story window and then threw herself into the street. This was our last sight of the Warsaw Ghetto.

See also Jewish Fighting Organization, Vol 1; Warsaw ghetto uprising, Vol. 2

Eichmann Remembers

Kidnapped and brought to Israel after more than a decade of hiding in South America, SS lieutenant colonel Adolf Eichmann faced, before the Israeli state trial that condemned him to death, interrogation by Israeli police captain Avner Less. In the transcripts that follow, Less leads Eichmann to admit his involvement in the Lidice massacre of 1942, carried out in revenge for the assassination of Reinhard Heydrich, as well as his partici- *pation in the persecution of Gypsies and thousands of gassing deaths.*

LESS: Do you know what happened to most of the children?

EICHMANN: I do not know. I had nothing to do with Lidice, nothing whatever, nothing whatever . . . Not even any . . . I wasn't even informed.

LESS: Do you know anything about a shipment of children who were sent by the commander of the Security Police in Prague from Lidice to Litzmannstadt, formerly and now again the Polish city of Lodz?

Eichmann Interrogated: Transcripts from the Archives of the Israeli Police. Trans. Ralph Manheim. London: Bodley Head, 1983.

EICHMANN: No, no. I don't know anything about it.

LESS: I'm going to show you some photostats of documents concerning the treatment of eighty-eight Czech children from Lidice, who arrived in Litzmannstadt on June 13, 1942. The first is a letter signed by Krumey, who worked with you for a time, and was then head of the Relocation Center in Litzmannstadt.

EICHMANN: Yes, that's Krumey's signature.

LESS: Dated Litzmannstadt, June 17, 1942. To the Commander of the Security Police and the SD in Prague. Re: The transfer of Czech children to Litzmannstadt. The second is a telegram of June 20, 1942, from Krumey in Litzmannstadt to Reich Security Headquarters [RSHA], Bureau IV B 4. Attention: Obersturmbannführer Eichmann, Berlin. Re: Transfer of 88 Czech children from the town of Lidice to Litzmannstadt. Reference: Conference with Obersturmbannführer Eichmann. Do you wish to comment?

EICHMANN: Yes. In the first place, I must say that I absolutely don't remember any such thing. In the second place: If—I see that the matter was somehow handled by my bureau . . . it refers to a conference with me—I imagine that it must have been handled in a purely transportational sense and that . . . I see that the Race and Settlement Office passed on seven children as . . . as susceptible to re-Germanization.

LESS: What happened to the children who were not found susceptible to re-Germanization?

EICHMANN: I don't know that either. If they were shipped to Litzmannstadt . . . After all, these things weren't handled by me, by my bureau, I mean. This Lidice business was decided at the top. What they ordered, I don't know.

LESS: Were those children sent to Kulmhof concentration camp [Chelmno] for special treatment [gassing]?

EICHMANN: I don't know, Herr Hauptmann [captain, sir]. I don't know. By that I mean that maybe they were and maybe they weren't. I don't know.

LESS: Were non-Jews as well as Jews liquidated in Kulmhof?

EICHMANN: I don't . . . Except for those first two times I've told . . . I never went to Kulmhof after that. I don't know. But this whole Lidice business must . . . must have been handled by some central headquarters. But I don't know which.

LESS: But why did Krumey write to you, rather than someone else, about those eighty-eight children?

EICHMANN: Maybe they got mixed up with us for transportational reasons. Maybe they were attached to a deportation train, a Jewish deportation train. Conceivably, I got orders to attach them to some deportation train. It's possible.

LESS: Was it up to you to—

EICHMANN: No, no, it was not up to me.

LESS: . . . decide what was to be done with them? To make arrangements?

EICHMANN: No, no. Certainly not.

LESS: In this telegram of June 22, 1942, Krumey writes to Reich Security Headquarters: "On June 13, 1942, 88 Czech children from the village of Lidice, orphaned by the action there, have arrived in Litzmannstadt. Since thus far no instructions concerning the disposition of these children have reached here, I request pertinent orders. I have notified IV B 4 of the transfer of these children on the assumption that they have been earmarked for special treatment. In the meantime, the Race and Settlement Office has removed seven children susceptible to re-Germanization."

EICHMANN: Hmm. Yes, that's another one of those . . . things. The whole business must have been ordered by a higher authority . . . Seeing it was a measure of retaliation for the assassination of Heydrich, I imagine the Reichsführer [Heinrich Himmler] himself must have given the necessary orders.

LESS: In this letter to you, Krumey refers to a conversation with you. The second letter shows that he assumed these children were marked for special treatment, in other words, extermination. Doesn't it seem likely that this point came up in his conversation with you and that he wrote you this letter on the basis of said conversation?

EICHMANN: It is certainly possible that Krumey said that to himself and asked: How about it, should they be given special treatment or not? And I must have answered: It's not in my department. Jews are in my department, not Czech children. What orders were given after that, I don't know.

LESS: In this connection, I'm going to show you some more photostats. One is a letter of July 9, 1942, to Reich Security Headquarters IV B 4 [the branch of the Gestapo responsible for "Jewish Affairs" and headed by Eichmann]. Attention: Obersturmbannführer Eichmann. "Re: Czech children. The SS Race and Settlement Office has sent us twelve un-Germanizable children, aged one to fifteen, from the districts of Lidice and Lesaki. Further instructions are requested."

The next is a telegram dated July 14, 1942, from Berlin. "To the Central Relocation Office, Litzmannstadt. Attention: Obersturmbannführer Krumey. Re: Czech children. Reference: Your telegram of July 9, 1942. Request you turn over the twelve un-Germanizable children immediately to Litzmannstadt Gestapo, which has received further instructions." Signed RSHA IV B 4. per proc. Günther. Do you wish to comment?

EICHMANN: I do. I've said I couldn't remember, and I must now repeat that none of this is known to me. As I told you, I did not handle the matter. My deputy signed.

LESS: Günther's telegram is signed IV B 4.

EICHMANN: Oh, well, telegrams . . . That is . . . anyway, the telegram is signed. That can't be denied. It makes no difference that it wasn't signed by me. Obviously, it was sent by the bureau . . . by my bureau. That's clear. But it was certainly signed and drafted by someone else, not by me. But . . .

turn over Czech children immediately to the Litzmannstadt Gestapo, which has received further instructions . . . ?

LESS: Can't we gather that the further instructions to the Litzmannstadt Gestapo were sent by your department?

EICHMANN: I could not, I mean Bureau IV B 4 could not have given instructions in this matter. At the most, it could have relayed them. The bureau had no authority to give orders in this matter. If it gave any definitive instructions, they must have come from higher up. Lidice was not handled by Bureau IV B 4. Lidice was handled from higher up, on the basis of a . . . of a general order.

LESS: Do these documents I have shown you indicate that you had something to do with the fate of these children?

EICHMANN: Something . . . that we shared the responsibility . . .

LESS: Yes.

EICHMANN: I'd put it this way. They definitely indicate . . . I won't say that I . . . but the bureau, yes, that's clear to me . . .

LESS: But in 1942 you were the bureau head!

EICHMANN: I was the bureau head, unquestionably. But Lidice was an affair which no bureau head, no department head or Gruppenleiter [SS group leader] could decisively decide; it was handled higher . . . higher up . . . it . . .

LESS: Was the deportation of the gypsies to the death camps also handled by your Bureau IV B 4?

EICHMANN: Yes. But I don't know if all the gypsies, no, that I don't know. The gypsies from the West, from the West: No. To the camps? To . . . to a ghetto, not to the camps. To a ghetto in Litzmannstadt. That happened in the beginning, before the French war, the German-French war, broke out in the summer of 1940, I think. Or was it later? I don't know.

LESS: Weren't the gypsies taken to Auschwitz later and gassed?

EICHMANN: Herr Hauptmann, at this late date I don't know. All we had to do was

Adolf Eichmann stands (in box) as his death sentence is pronounced on December 15, 1961, by the judges in his Jerusalem trial.

make the rolling stock available and draw up the schedules.

LESS: You didn't supply guidelines—

EICHMANN: No guidelines, no guidelines.

LESS: . . . covering the gypsies?

EICHMANN: The Reichsführer [Himmler] himself made the decisions about the gypsies. That's it, and the . . . the guidelines for the gypsies were simple. I know all about them. I mean, there weren't any. The Reichsführer handled everything. Because, you see, with the other guidelines it was always necessary to consult other departments. You've seen how it was, Herr Hauptmann: the Foreign Office butts in, and then various specifications of nationality have to be considered, and so on . . . With the gypsies, as far as I remember . . . nobody worried in the least about any specification whatever.

LESS: Why really did they exterminate all the gypsies?

EICHMANN: Herr Hauptmann, that was one of those . . . one of those things, I think . . . Führer . . . Reichsführer . . . I don't know . . . there were . . . all of a sudden it happened . . . and the order went out . . . I don't know. And as far as I know, they were never seriously studied by any branch of Reich Security Headquarters. I mean: their origins, where they came from, manners, customs. Let me put it this way: In their case, you can't speak of organized communities . . . larger units and so on. Where the centers are and that kind of thing. I don't know if anyone worked on that . . . Certainly, no one did in Section IV. Nothing of the kind was planned with the gypsies.

LESS: Did you keep card files of individual cases?

EICHMANN: The order about the gypsies, if I remember right . . . I really don't remember these things. They weren't turned over to my bureau until much later. And when I did get them, there were none left. There hadn't been very many in the first place. There can't have been very many, because none of the countries in the West were out-and-out gypsy countries. Like Hungary or Rumania, for instance. They had appreciably more gypsies than . . . let's say, the Greater German Reich, as it was then called. I don't believe there were more than five or six thousand in the Reich. I don't believe there were any more.

LESS: Weren't there somewhere between seven hundred thousand and a million gypsies in Poland, Russia, Rumania, and Hungary?

EICHMANN: I don't know, Herr Hauptmann, I don't know.

LESS: You remember that you've spoken here several times about your deputy Günther . . . how he once told you about this prussic . . . about that gas business.

EICHMANN: Yes, I do. At the very beginning . . . right here I . . .

LESS: Didn't you say to Günther: "How could you? . . . How could you do such a thing? Why do you involve yourself in such things?"

EICHMANN: Yes, of course.

LESS: "How am I, Eichmann, to justify this to [Gestapo chief Heinrich] Müller?"

EICHMANN: I'm sure I never said that to him.

LESS: You didn't?

EICHMANN: No! I can imagine that he may have said: "Look here. I have orders to do this and that."

LESS: Now I'm going to show you four pages of documents. Do you wish to comment?

EICHMANN: These are letters of October 25, 1941, from the Reich Minister for Occupied Eastern Territories to the Reich Commissioner for Ostland. This one says that "Oberdienstleiter Brack of the Führer's Office has declared his willingness to cooperate in the production of the necessary housing and gassing apparatus. Such apparatus is not at present available in sufficient quantity. It has still to be produced. Since in Brack's opinion it would be far more difficult to produce this apparatus in the Reich than on the spot, Brack thinks it advisable to send his men, and in particular his chemist Dr. Kallmayer, to Riga immediately . . . etc., etc. Accordingly, you are requested to communicate with Oberdienstleiter Brack at the Führer's Office through your SS and police commander, and ask him to dispatch Dr. Kallmayer and the necessary assistants. Permit me to state that this procedure meets with the approval of Sturmbannführer Eichmann, the specialist for Jewish questions at Reich Security Headquarters. We are informed by Sturmbannführer Eichmann that camps for Jews are to be set up in Riga and Minsk, and that Jews from the Old Reich [Germany] may possibly be sent to them."

I also have here a "Memorandum concerning consultations which our Amtsgerichtsrat collaborator"—name not given, probably Dr. Wetzel of the Reich Ministry for Occupied Eastern Territories—"has carried on with Oberdienstleiter Brack and the specialist Sturmbannführer Eichmann." I have no comment to make on that.

LESS: It's about the production of gas . . . of gassing apparatus, isn't it?

EICHMANN: Yes, but there's this to be said. I gather from this that the Führer's Office took charge of the procurement. Reich Security Headquarters was only asked for its consent, which consent was given through me. This convinces me that what I've just told you is just what I said to him. I wonder who instructed the Ministry for the East, or the people around Amtsgerichtsrat Dr. Wetzel, to do anything connected with gas machines. There must have been some prime mover. Maybe those Ministry of the East people said to themselves: "This has to be done more elegantly." They were no longer satisfied with shooting. Just now it occurred to me—because I didn't give Günther [a Gestapo subordinate] that order to buy a hundred kilos of prussic acid—it occurred to me that maybe my deputy Günther had a direct connection with Globocnik, so he supplied those people with the chemicals which . . . which maybe they themselves were originally supposed to procure.

LESS: But the crux of the matter is this: Could Günther have ordered that gas without your knowledge? You speak of a direct connection with Globocnik [SS Police leader in occupied Poland]. But the first connection was made by you. You went to see Globocnik.

EICHMANN: Yes, that's a fact. That is a fact.

LESS: You went to see Globocnik. You went to Lemberg, you inspected Auschwitz. You went to all those extermination points, you saw the methods being used. In some places people were being gassed with motors, in others they were being shot. So your report to Müller or Heydrich or Himmler—wherever the report ended up—showed that these methods were, to put it crudely, inefficient. Consequently, some way had to be found to speed up the killing. It was also taken into consideration that such methods must have had a bad psychological effect on the men charged with carrying out the extermination measures. You had to consider that your own men might suffer from having to shoot hundreds and thousands of people. They weren't all natural-born murderers. Maybe their consciences would bother them later on. So better do it in a less visible form. Why not with gas? Maybe that was the train of thought. So Günther, probably with your knowledge, was told to take action, and the gas was supplied.

EICHMANN: I don't believe it happened that way, Herr Hauptmann. There'd be some trace of it in my memory. It wasn't the job of the Security Police to procure this gas. It simply was not our job.

LESS: How do you account for the fact that gassing was being done and that all the persons involved in this gassing point their finger at Eichmann and Bureau IV B 4?

EICHMANN: Well, that is a . . . that's just the funny part of it. Because we had nothing to do with it, nothing whatever . . . We had nothing to do with it. Nothing! Nothing! Nothing!

LESS: And all these statements are—

EICHMANN: Officially I . . . officially I had . . . Officially we had nothing to do with it, and unofficially I wasn't interested. I had . . . I had nothing to do with these things, I can tell you truthfully. And nobody here will ever prove the contrary.

LESS: But did you have official knowledge that gassing was going on?

EICHMANN: I knew it, of course I knew.

LESS: What was your attitude toward the total physical destruction of the Jewish people in the framework of the final solution of the Jewish question?

EICHMANN: I've already told you, Herr Hauptmann, that then . . . when I heard for the first time that . . . that . . . that . . . I felt as if someone had hit me over the head. And when I saw those first things, I've told you that too, I went weak in the knees. That's, that is a fact, and I was very glad in all those years that I had nothing to do with the killing. I had nothing to do with the killing.

LESS: But didn't deportation amount to killing?

EICHMANN: Herr Hauptmann, I've already told you . . . it wasn't my job to decide who was drawn into the work process and who was not. I had orders to deport. And when my colleague Wisliceny writes in his confessions that there were ways of circumventing Hitler's orders, I'd be glad to know what those ways were. I say: There was one way and only one way: to take a pistol and shoot yourself. That's obvious. I didn't.

LESS: In other words, you weren't opposed?

EICHMANN: I obeyed. Regardless of what I was ordered to do, I would have obeyed. Certainly, I would have obeyed. I obeyed, I obeyed. I can't shed my skin, Herr Hauptmann. I . . . that was my attitude at the time, and that's the way it was. When I received an order, I obeyed. An oath is an oath. In the observance of that oath, I was uncompromising. Today I'd never take an oath. No one could make me, no judge for instance, could make me take a witness's oath. I refuse; I refuse on moral grounds. Because I've learned by experience that if you let yourself be bound by an oath, you'll have to take the consequences someday. I see that today we have to pay for it because we never forgot our oath and that made us obey. If I hadn't obeyed then, I'd have been punished then. So which . . . whichever way things turn out, it's always bad to take an oath.

LESS: Your friend and colleague Dieter Wisliceny writes: "The men who worked with Eichmann were accustomed to carry out orders blindly. Apart from myself, the only one to attempt resistance in Hungary was Obersturmbannführer Krumey. I often tried, by appealing to their reason, to get those men to engage in a little quiet sabotage or a slowdown. It was impossible. Most of those men were of a totally primitive type, and Eichmann's influence on them was too great."

EICHMANN: I never noticed any resistance, either on the part of Wisliceny or of Krumey. I noticed no resistance. None whatever. . . .

EICHMANN: When Wisliceny writes in his confession: "On the strength of my personal experience, I once again state that Eichmann played a decisive part in the decimation of the European Jews and that, although he was covered by the orders of Hitler and Himmler, he must be held fully responsible, because there were ways of circumventing Hitler's orders"—I can only say that no man is justified in circumventing an order.

LESS: You have spoken of "responsibility for carrying out orders . . ."

EICHMANN: That's right. I am responsible for what I . . . for the things my orders obliged me to do. I told you at the start, Herr Hauptmann, I have no desire to evade that responsibility in any way whatsoever. Because I can't. On the other hand, I refuse to take responsibility for things I had no orders for and which were not in my department. I am not one of the people who said in 1945 and still say today: "I was always against it"—who try to save their necks with that sort of—let's say—sort of tawdry explanation. It wouldn't be true.

See also Eichmann trial; Gypsies, persecution of; Lidice massacre, Vol. 1; Eichmann, Adolf, Vol. 3.

The First Gas Chambers

Nazi authorities first used gas chambers to kill Germany's mentally ill citizens during the so-called T-4 Program of 1939–1941. Many of the SS staff who administered and guarded these "euthanasia centers," such as Captain Christian Wirth, were later transferred to occupied Poland to help set up death camps there. In the following anonymous account, a man recounts being hired at a euthanasia center to help dispose of dead bodies.

In 1939 I worked for Lell & Co. in Freindorf near Ansfelden and earned 25 RM [Reichsmarks] per week. This was hardly enough to feed my wife and children. So I was always on the look out for ways to earn more money. At this point, my brother had returned from the Reich to Linz as an SA brigade leader. I asked him if he could find me a better job. Finally, in April 1939 he called me to his office . . . I was asked how much I earned. They laughed when they heard that I was only getting 25 RM. I and the others were then told that we were going to Hartheim and would earn more there. I began work at Hartheim on 2 April 1940 . . .

About a fortnight later, Captain [Christian] Wirth called us together—there were mainly men present—and made a speech:

'Comrades, I have called you together to explain to you what is going to happen in the palace. I have been ordered by the Reich Chancellery to take charge here in the palace. I, as Captain, am in overall command. We have got to build a crematorium here in order to burn the mentally ill from the *Ostmark* [Austria]. Five doctors have been assigned to examine the mentally ill in order to establish who is capable of being saved and who is not. Those who aren't will be put in the crematorium and burnt. The mentally ill are a burden on the state. Some men will be assigned to work in the crematorium. Above all, you will have to keep quiet about this or face the death penalty. Anyone who doesn't keep quiet will go to a concentration camp or be shot.

A short time after Captain Wirth's speech, work was started on the crematorium. I and others were given the job of 'burner'. I must emphasize that I did not apply for this job myself. For the job of burner I was promised an additional payment of 35 RM a month which was later paid. In addition, I got a bonus of 35 RM (for silence). This sum was to be paid later.

About six weeks after the 2 April 1940, the preparations and the buildings were ready and the plant began to operate. The mentally ill were, as far as I know, brought from the various asylums by train and bus to Hartheim at very different times of the day. Sometimes the numbers arriving were large, sometimes small. The numbers arriv-

ing varied between 40 and 150. First, they were taken to the undressing room. There they—men and women in different sections —had to undress or were undressed. Their clothes and luggage were put in a pile, labelled, registered and numbered. The people who had undressed then went along a passage into the so-called reception room. In this room there was a large table. A doctor was there together with a staff of 3–4 assistants. The doctor on duty there was either Dr Lonauer or Dr Renno. As far as I can judge as a layman, the doctors did not examine these people but only checked their files. Someone then stamped them. An orderly had to stamp them individually on the shoulder or the chest with a consecutive number. The number was approximately 3–4 cm in size. Those people who had gold teeth or a gold bridge were marked with a cross on their backs. After this procedure, the people were led into a nearby room and photographed. Then the people were led out of the photography room through a second exit back into the reception room and from there through a steel door into the gas chamber. The gas chamber had a very bare interior. It had a wooden floor and there were wooden benches in the chamber. Later, the floor was concreted and finally it and the walls were tiled. The ceiling and the other parts of the walls were painted with oil. The whole room was designed to give the impression that it was a bathroom. Three showers were fixed in the ceiling. The room was aired by ventilators. A window in the gas chamber was covered with a grill. A second steel door led into the room where the gassing apparatus was installed.

When the whole transport had been dealt with, i.e. when the registration had been carried out, the photographs taken, people's numbers stamped on them, and those with gold teeth marked, they all went into the bath-gas room. The steel doors were shut and the doctor on duty fed gas into the gas chamber. After a short time the people in the gas chamber were dead. After around an hour

J. Noakes and G. Pridham, eds., *Nazism 1919–1945,* Vol. 3, *Foreign Policy, War, and Racial Extermination: A Documentary Reader.* Exeter, England: University of Exeter Press, 1988.

and a half, the gas chamber was ventilated. At this point, we burners had to start work.

Before I deal with that, I would like to make a few more statements about the feeding of the gas into the gas chamber. Next to the gas chamber there was a small room in which there were a number of steel canisters. I cannot say what kind of gas was in these canisters or where it came from. The contents of these canisters was fed through a rubber pipe into a steel pipe. On the canister there was a pressure gauge. When the gas chamber was full the doctor went to the canisters, opened the tap and the gas poured through a 15–20 mm iron pipe into the gas chamber. As I have stated already, between the gas chamber and the gas canister room there was a steel door. A third door led from the gas chamber into the yard. These doors had a brick surround and there was a peephole into the gas chamber. Through this peephole one could see what went on in the gas chamber.

Once the room had been aired, we burners—we always had twelve hour shifts—had to get the corpses out of the gas chamber and bring them into the mortuary. The mortuary was next to the gas canister room. Getting the corpses out of the gas chamber into the mortuary was a difficult and nerve-racking task. It was not easy to disentangle the corpses, which were locked together, and drag them into the mortuary. This task was made even more difficult initially by the fact that the floor was uneven and when the floor was concreted it was rough. This made dragging the corpses into the mortuary difficult. Later when the floor was tiled we put water down. That made moving the dead much easier. The corpses were piled up in the mortuary. Next to the mortuary was the crematorium. The crematorium was equipped with a so-called pan which could be taken out of the oven. The dead were laid on this pan and were pushed in and left there just like with a baking oven. Depending on the number of corpses, we burnt 2–8 at a time. The oven was coke-fired. The work went on night and day as required. Before the corpses were burnt the burners pulled out the gold teeth of those who had been marked with a cross. They were taken to the administration. Because I cannot feel properly with my right hand because of the partial paralysis of my right side, I was unable to pull the teeth. Once I tried it and the gold tooth slipped down the dead person's gorge. Since I could no longer find the tooth, I was bawled out by Captain Wirth. After that I ceased to pull teeth. After the corpses had been burnt, the remnants of the bones which had fallen through the grid would be put into a bone mill and ground to powder. This bonemeal was then sent to the grieving relatives as the remains of their dead. We estimated roughly 3 kg of such meal for each corpse.

Since the work was very exhausting and, as I said, nerve-racking, we got about 1/4 liter of schnaps per day. I reckon that we burnt about 20,000 mentally ill people in this way.

In 1944 we also burnt concentration camp prisoners. In my opinion they were mostly people with serious illnesses but not mentally sick. Sick eastern workers were also burnt by us in Hartheim. By my reckoning in all about 30,000 people must have been killed.

Before Christmas 1944, the community plant was stopped and the oven dismantled. From this point on, no one else was burnt in Hartheim.

Now I will give a few more details of things which I can remember. On one occasion 150 people were gassed at one time. The gas chamber was so full that the people in there could hardly fall down and got so tangled together that we could hardly pull the corpses apart. Since gassings had already taken place, the mortuary was so full that the corpses at the bottom were already beginning to decay by the time we came to burn them. On another occasion, a transport came with women infected with typhus. On the orders of Captain Wirth four women were brought into the red room and shot in the back of the neck there by Captain Wirth. While I am on the subject of women, I would like to mention that they burnt more easily than the men. I think this was because they have more fat than men. They also have a lighter bone structure. The remains of the incineration were at first thrown into the Danube and then later on were buried. As far as the personality of Captain Wirth is concerned, I only want to say that he was a beast. He threatened everybody at every opportunity with concentration camp or with shooting. Now I think I have said all I know. I still suffer from bad dreams. On these occasions all the dead people appear to me in spirit and I sometimes think I will go mad.

See also euthanasia, Vol. 1; T-4 Program, Vol. 2.

Final Diary Entries

Just before the young Dutch girl Anne Frank and her family were captured by Gestapo agents and deported with other Jews to transit camps and ultimately Bergen-Belsen, the camp where Frank died in March 1945 of typhus, she entered her comments on the German resistance and on her growing identity in "Kitty," the diary she had faithfully kept during years in hiding.

Friday, 21 July, 1944
Dear Kitty,

Now I am getting really hopeful, now things are going well at last. Yes, really, they're going well! Super news! An attempt has been made on Hitler's life and not even by Jewish communists or English capitalists this time, but by a proud German general, and what's more, he's a count, and still quite young. The Führer's life was saved by Divine Providence and, unfortunately, he managed to get off with just a few scratches and burns. A few officers and generals who were with him have been killed and wounded. The chief culprit was shot.

Anyway, it certainly shows that there are lots of officers and generals who are sick of the war and would like to see Hitler descend into a bottomless pit. When they've disposed of Hitler, their aim is to establish a military dictator, who will make peace with the Allies, then they intend to rearm and start another war in about twenty years' time. Perhaps the Divine Power tarried on purpose in getting him out of the way, because it would be much easier and more advantageous to the Allies if the impeccable Germans kill each other off; it'll make less work for the Russians and the English and they'll be able to begin rebuilding their own towns all the sooner.

But still, we're not that far yet, and I don't want to anticipate the glorious events too soon. Still, you must have noticed, this is all sober reality and that I'm in quite a matter-of-fact mood today; for once, I'm not jabbering about high ideals. And what's more, Hitler has even been so kind as to announce to his faithful, devoted people that from now on everyone in the armed forces must obey the Gestapo, and that any soldier who knows that one of his superiors was involved in this low, cowardly attempt upon his life may shoot the same on the spot, without court-martial.

What a perfect shambles it's going to be. Little Johnnie's feet begin hurting him during a long march, he's snapped at by his boss, the officer, Johnnie grabs his rifle and

Anne Frank, *The Diary of a Young Girl*. Trans. B.M. Mooyaart-Doubleday. Garden City, NY: Doubleday, 1952.

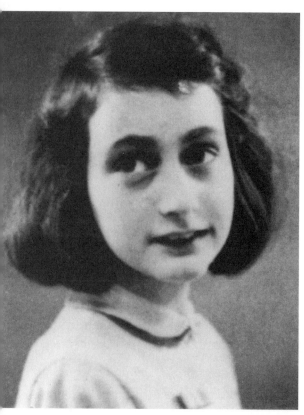

The diary of Anne Frank offers rare insight into the lives of Jews in hiding in Nazi-occupied Amsterdam during the Holocaust.

cries out: "You wanted to murder the Führer, so there's your reward." One bang and the proud chief who dared to tick off little Johnnie has passed into eternal life (or is it eternal death?). In the end, whenever an officer finds himself up against a soldier, or having to take the lead, he'll be wetting his pants from anxiety, because the soldiers will dare to say more than they do. Do you gather a bit what I mean, or have I been skipping too much from one subject to another? I can't help it; the prospect that I may be sitting on school benches next October makes me feel far too cheerful to be logical! Oh, dearie me, hadn't I just told you that I didn't want to be too hopeful? Forgive me, they haven't given me the name "little bundle of contradictions" all for nothing!

Yours, Anne

Tuesday, 1 August, 1944

Dear Kitty,

"Little bundle of contradictions." That's how I ended my last letter and that's how I'm going to begin this one. "A little bundle of contradictions," can you tell me exactly what it is? What does contradiction mean? Like so many words, it can mean two things, contradiction from without and contradiction from within.

The first is the ordinary "not giving in easily, always knowing best, getting in the last word," *enfin*, all the unpleasant qualities for which I'm renowned. The second nobody knows about, that's my own secret.

I've already told you before that I have, as it were, a dual personality. One half embodies my exuberant cheerfulness, making fun of everything, my high-spiritedness, and above all, the way I take everything lightly. This includes not taking offense at a flirtation, a kiss, an embrace, a dirty joke. This side is usually lying in wait and pushes away the other, which is much better, deeper and purer. You must realize that no one knows Anne's better side and that's why most people find me so insufferable.

Certainly I'm a giddy clown for one afternoon, but then everyone's had enough of me for another month. Really, it's just the same as a love film is for deep-thinking people, simply a diversion, amusing just for once, something which is soon forgotten, not bad, but certainly not good. I loathe having to tell you this, but why shouldn't I, if I know it's true anyway? My lighter superficial side will always be too quick for the deeper side of me and that's why it will always win. You can't imagine how often I've already tried to push this Anne away, to cripple her, to hide her, because after all, she's only half of what's called Anne: but it doesn't work and I know, too, why it doesn't work.

I'm awfully scared that everyone who knows me as I always am will discover that I have another side, a finer and better side.

I'm afraid they'll laugh at me, think I'm ridiculous and sentimental, not take me seriously. I'm used to not being taken seriously but it's only the "lighthearted" Anne that's used to it and can beat it; the "deeper" Anne is too frail for it. Sometimes, if I really compel the good Anne to take the stage for a quarter of an hour, she simply shrivels up as soon as she has to speak, and lets Anne number one take over, and before I realize it, she has disappeared.

Therefore, the nice Anne is never present in company, has not appeared one single time so far, but almost always predominates when we're alone. I know exactly how I'd like to be, how I am too . . . inside. But, alas, I'm only like that for myself. And perhaps that's why, no, I'm sure it's the reason why I say I've got a happy nature within and why other people think I've got a happy nature without. I am guided by the pure Anne within, but outside I'm nothing but a frolicsome little goat who's broken loose.

As I've already said, I never utter my real feelings about anything and that's how I've acquired the name of chaser-after-boys, flirt, know-all, reader of love stories. The cheerful Anne laughs about it, gives cheeky answers, shrugs her shoulders indifferently, behaves as if she doesn't care, but, oh dearie me, the quiet Anne's reactions are just the opposite. If I'm to be quite honest, then I must admit that it does hurt me, that I try terribly hard to change myself, but that I'm always fighting against a more powerful enemy.

A voice sobs within me: "There you are, that's what's become of you: you're uncharitable, you look supercilious and peevish, people dislike you and all because you won't listen to the advice given you by your own better half." Oh, I would like to listen, but it doesn't work; if I'm quiet and serious, everyone thinks it's a new comedy and then I have to get out of it by turning it into a joke, not to mention my own family, who are sure to think I'm ill, make me swallow pills for headaches and nerves, feel my neck and my head to see whether I'm running a temperature, ask if I'm constipated and criticize me for being in a bad mood. I can't keep that up: if I'm watched to that extent, I start by getting snappy, then unhappy, and finally I twist my heart round again, so that the bad is on the outside and the good is on the inside and keep on trying to find a way of becoming what I would so like to be, and what I could be, if . . . there weren't any other people living in the world.

Yours, Anne

See also deportation, Vol. 1; Frank, Anne, Vol. 3.

A Bishop Calls for an End to Euthanasia

By 1941 the Third Reich's program to administer euthanasia, or "mercy killing," to tens of thousands of mentally ill Germans had become known to the general public. August Graf von Galen, the bishop of Münster, made a public call to stop the practice, citing not only Christianity but German law *and the danger that the Nazis might not stop with the mentally ill.*

Fellow Christians! In the pastoral letter of the German bishops of 26 June 1941, which was read out in all the Catholic churches in Germany on 6 July 1941, it states among other things: It is true that there are definite commandments in Catholic moral doctrine which are no longer applicable if their fulfilment involves too many difficulties. However, there are sacred obligations of conscience from which no one has the power to release us and which we must fulfil even if it costs us our lives. Never under any circumstances may a human being kill an innocent person apart from war and legitimate self-defence. On 6 July, I already had cause to add to the pastoral letter the following explanation: for some months we have been hearing reports that, on the orders of Berlin, patients from mental asylums who have been ill for a long time and may appear incurable, are being compulsorily removed. Then, after a short time, the relatives are regularly informed that the corpse has been burnt and the ashes can be delivered. There is a general suspicion verging on certainty, that these numerous unexpected deaths of mentally ill people do not occur of themselves but are deliberately brought about, that the doctrine is being followed, according to which one may destroy so-called 'worthless life', that is kill innocent people if one considers that their lives are of no further value for the nation and the state.

I am reliably informed that lists are also being drawn up in the asylums of the province of Westphalia as well of those patients who are to be taken away as so-called 'unproductive national comrades' and shortly to be killed. The first transport left the Marienthal institution near Münster during this past week.

German men and women §211 of the Reich Penal Code is still valid. It states: 'he who deliberately kills another person will be punished by death for murder if the killing is premeditated.'

Those patients who are destined to be killed are transported away from home to a distant asylum presumably in order to protect those who deliberately kill those poor people, members of our families, from this legal punishment. Some illness is then given as the cause of death. Since the corpse has been burnt straight away the relatives and also the criminal police are unable to establish whether the illness really occurred and what the cause of death was. However, I have been assured that the Reich Interior Ministry and the office of the Reich Doctors' Leader, Dr. Conti, make no bones about the fact that in reality a large number of mentally ill people in Germany have been deliberately killed and more will be killed in the future.

The Penal Code lays down in §139: 'He who receives credible information concerning the intention to commit a crime against life and neglects to alert the authorities or the person who is threatened in time . . . will be punished'. When I learnt of the intention to transport patients from Marienthal in order to kill them, I brought a formal charge at the State Court in Münster and with the Police President in Münster by means of a registered letter which read as follows: 'According to information which I have received, in the course of this week a large number of patients from the Marienthal Provincal Asylum near Münster are to be transported to the Eichberg asylum as so-called "unproductive national comrades" and will then soon be deliberately killed, as is generally believed has occurred with such transports from other asylums. Since such an action is not only contrary to the moral laws of God and Nature but also is punishable with death as murder under §211 of the Penal Code, I hereby bring a charge in accordance with my duty under §139 of the Penal Code, and request you to provide immediate protection for the national comrades threatened in this way by taking action against those agencies who are intending their removal and murder, and that you inform me of the steps that have been taken'. I have received no news con-

J. Noakes and G. Pridham, eds., *Nazism 1919–1945,* Vol. 3, *Foreign Policy, War, and Racial Extermination: A Documentary Reader.* Exeter, England: University of Exeter Press, 1988.

cerning intervention by the Prosecutor's Office or by the police.

. . . Thus we must assume that the poor helpless patients will soon be killed. For what reason? Not because they have committed a crime worthy of death. Not because they attacked their nurses or orderlies so that the latter had no other choice but to use legitimate force to defend their lives against their attackers. Those are cases where, in addition to the killing of an armed enemy in a just war, the use of force to the point of killing is allowed and is often required. No, it is not for such reasons that these unfortunate patients must die but rather because, in the opinion of some department, on the testimony of some commission, they have become 'worthless life' because according to this testimony they are 'unproductive national comrades'. The argument goes: they can no longer produce commodities, they are like an old machine that no longer works, they are like an old horse which has become incurably lame, they are like a cow which no longer gives milk. What does one do with such an old machine? It is thrown on the scrap heap. What does one do with a lame horse, with such an unproductive cow? No, I do not want to continue the comparison to the end—however fearful the justification for it and the symbolic force of it are. We are not dealing with machines, horses and cows whose only function is to serve mankind, to produce goods for man. One may smash them, one may slaughter them as soon as they no longer fulfil this function. No, we are dealing with human beings, our fellow human beings, our brothers and sisters. With poor people, sick people, if you like unproductive people. But have they for that reason forfeited the right to life? Have you, have I the right to live only so long as we are productive, so long as we are recognised by others as productive? If you establish and apply the principle that you can kill 'unproductive' fellow human beings then woe betide us all when we become old and frail! If one is allowed to kill the unproduc-

tive people then woe betide the invalids who have used up, sacrificed and lost their health and strength in the productive process. If one is allowed forcibly to remove one's unproductive fellow human beings then woe betide loyal soldiers who return to the homeland seriously disabled, as cripples, as invalids. If it is once accepted that people have the right to kill 'unproductive' fellow humans—and even if initially it only affects the poor defenceless mentally ill—then as a *matter of principle* murder is permitted for all unproductive people, in other words for the incurably sick, the people who have become invalids through labour and war, for us all when we become old, frail and therefore unproductive.

Then, it is only necessary for some secret edict to order that the method developed for the mentally ill should be extended to other 'unproductive' people, that it should be applied to those suffering from incurable lung disease, to the elderly who are frail or invalids, to the severely disabled soldiers. Then none of our lives will be safe any more. Some commission can put us on the list of the 'unproductive', who in their opinion have become worthless life. And no police force will protect us and no court will investigate our murder and give the murderer the punishment he deserves. Who will be able to trust his doctor any more? He may report his patient as 'unproductive' and receive instructions to kill him. It is impossible to imagine the degree of moral depravity, of general mistrust that would then spread even through families if this dreadful doctrine is tolerated, accepted and followed. Woe to mankind, woe to our German nation if God's holy commandment 'Thou shalt not kill', which God proclaimed on Mount Sinai amidst thunder and lightning, which God our Creator inscribed in the conscience of mankind from the very beginning, is not only broken, but if this transgression is actually tolerated and permitted to go unpunished.

I'll give you an example of what is going on. In Marienthal there was a man of about

55, a peasant from a rural parish in the Münster area—I could give you his name—who for some years had been suffering from mental disturbance and who had therefore been put in the care of the Marienthal asylum. He was not really mentally ill, he could receive visitors and was very pleased whenever his relatives came to see him. Only a fortnight ago, he received a visit from his wife and from one of his sons who is a soldier at the front and had home leave. So the farewell was a sad one: who knows if the soldier will return, will see his father again, for after all he may die in the struggle on behalf of his national comrades. The son, the soldier, will almost certainly never see his father again here on earth because since then he has been put on the list of the 'unproductive'. A relative who wanted to visit the father in Marienthal last week was turned away with the news that the patient had been transported away from here on the orders of the Ministerial Council for the Defence of the Reich. Nobody could say where to; the relatives would be informed in a few days time. What will the news be? Will it be the same as in other cases? That the person has died, that the corpse has been burnt, that the ashes can be delivered after payment of a fee? In that case, the soldier who is at the front risking his life for his German national comrades, will not see his father again here on earth because German national comrades at home have killed him. . . .

See also euthanasia, Vol. 1; T-4 Program, Vol. 2; Bouhler, Philip; Galen, August Graf von, Vol. 3.

The Einsatzgruppen in Action

In postwar testimony Hermann Graebe, a German engineer, recounts his visit to a potential construction site in the German-occupied Ukraine. He arrived in time to witness an Einsatzgruppen shooting of local Jews.

From September 1941 until January 1944, I was the manager and chief engineer of a branch of the construction firm, Josef Jung of Solingen with its headquarters in Sdolbunow, Ukraine. In this capacity I had to visit the firm's building sites. The firm was contracted by an Army construction office to build grain silos on the former air field near Dubno in the Ukraine.

When I visited the site office on 5 October 1942 my foreman, Hubert Moennikes of Hamburg-Harburg, Aussenmühlenweg 21, told me that Jews from Dubno had been shot near the site in three large ditches which were about thirty metres long and three metres deep. Approximately 1,500 people a day had been killed. All of the approximately 5,000 Jews who had been living in Dubno up to the action were going to be killed. Since the shootings had taken place in his presence he was still very upset.

Whereupon I accompanied Moennikes to the building site and near it saw large mounds of earth about thirty metres long and two metres high. A few lorries were parked in front of the mounds from which people were being driven by armed Ukrainian militia under the supervision of an SS

J. Noakes and G. Pridham, eds., *Nazism 1919–1945*, Vol. 3, *Foreign Policy, War, and Racial Extermination: A Documentary Reader.* Exeter, England: University of Exeter Press, 1988.

man. The militia provided the guards on the lorries and drove them to and from the ditch. All these people wore the prescribed yellow patches on the front and back of their clothing so that they were identifiable as Jews.

Moennikes and I went straight to the ditches. We were not prevented from doing so. I could now hear a series of rifle shots from behind the mounds. The people who had got off the lorries—men, women, and children of all ages—had to undress on the orders of an SS man who was carrying a riding or dog whip in his hand. They had to place their clothing on separate piles for shoes, clothing and underwear. I saw a pile of shoes containing approximately 800–1,000 pairs, and great heaps of underwear and clothing.

Without weeping or crying out these people undressed and stood together in family groups, embracing each other and saying good-bye while waiting for a sign from another SS man who stood on the edge of the ditch and also had a whip. During the quarter of an hour in which I stood near the ditch, I did not hear a single complaint or a plea for mercy. I watched a family of about eight, a man and a woman, both about fifty-years-old with their children of about one, eight, and ten, as well as two grown-up daughters of about twenty and twenty-four. An old woman with snow-white hair held a one year old child in her arms singing to it and tickling it. The child squeaked with delight. The married couple looked on with tears in their eyes. The father held the ten-year-old boy by the hand speaking softly to him. The boy was struggling to hold back his tears. The father pointed a finger to the sky and stroked his head and seemed to be explaining something to him. At this moment, the SS man near the ditch called out something to his comrade. The latter counted off some about twenty people and ordered them behind the mound. The family of which I have just spoken was among them. I can still remember how a girl, slender and dark, pointed at herself as she went past me saying 'twenty three'.

I walked round the mound and stood in front of the huge grave. The bodies were lying so tightly packed together that only their heads showed, from almost all of which blood ran down over their shoulders. Some were still moving. Others raised their hands and turned their heads to show they were still alive. The ditch was already three quarters full. I estimate that it already held about a thousand bodies. I turned my eyes towards the man doing the shooting. He was an SS man; he sat, legs swinging, on the edge of the ditch. He had an automatic rifle resting on his knees and was smoking a cigarette. The people, completely naked, climbed down steps which had been cut into the clay wall of the ditch, stumbled over the heads of those lying there and stopped at the spot indicated by the SS man. They lay down on top of the dead or wounded; some stroked those still living and spoke quietly to them. Then I heard a series of rifle shots. I looked into the ditch and saw the bodies contorting or, the heads already inert, sinking on the corpses beneath. Blood flowed from the nape of their necks. I was surprised not to be ordered away, but I noticed three postmen in uniform standing nearby. Then the next batch came up, climbed down into the ditch, laid themselves next to the previous victims and were shot.

On the way back, as I rounded the mound, I saw another lorry load of people which had just arrived. This one included the sick and infirm. An old and very emaciated woman with frightfully thin legs was being undressed by others, already naked. She was being supported by two people and seemed paralysed. The naked people carried the woman round the mound. I left the place with Moennikes and went back to Dubno by car.

The next morning, returning to the building site, I saw some thirty naked bodies lying thirty to fifty metres from the ditch. Some were still alive; they stared into space with a fixed gaze and seemed not to feel the coolness of the morning nor be aware of the workers from my firm standing around. A girl of about twenty spoke to me and asked for clothes and to help her escape. At that moment, we heard the sound of a car approaching at speed; I saw that it was an SS Commando. I went back to my building site. Ten minutes later, we heard rifle shots coming from the ditch. The Jews who were still alive had been ordered to throw the bodies into the ditch; then they had to lie down themselves to receive a bullet in the back of the neck.

I am making the above statement in Wiesbaden, Germany on 10 November 1945. I swear to God that it is the whole truth.

See also Einsatzgruppen, Final Solution, Vol. 1; Heydrich, Reinhard; Ohlendorf, Otto, Vol. 3.

Hitler's Call for a War of Extermination

General Franz Halder records in minutes of a meeting with Hitler prior to the Third Reich's invasion of the Soviet Union in June 1941 that the Führer made it clear that the war between Germany and the U.S.S.R. was to be a brutal fight for survival, in which conventional rules of warfare would not apply.

Struggle between two *Weltanschauungen* [world views]. Devastating assessment of Bolshevism: it is the equivalent of social delinquency. Communism is a tremendous danger for the future. We must get away from the standpoint of soldierly comradeship. The Communist is from first to last no comrade. It is a war of extermination. If we do not regard it as such, we may defeat the enemy, but in thirty years' time we will again be confronted by the Communist enemy. We are not fighting a war in order to conserve the enemy.

Future State structure: North Russia belongs to Finland. Protectorates for the Baltic States, Ukraine, White Russia.

Fight against Russia: destruction of the Bolshevik commissars and the Communist intelligentsia. A new intelligentsia must be prevented from emerging. A primitive Socialist intelligentsia is sufficient there. The struggle must be fought against the poison of subversion. It is not a question of court martials. The leaders of the troops must know what is involved. They must take the lead in the struggle. The troops must defend themselves with the methods with which they are attacked. Commissars and G.P.U. people [Soviet political police] are criminals and must be treated as such. That does not mean that the troops need get out of hand. The leader must draw up his orders in accordance with the sentiment of his troops.

The struggle will be very different from that in the west. In the east toughness now means mildness in the future. The leaders must make sacrifices and overcome their scruples.

See also Barbarossa, Commissar Order, Einsatzgruppen, Vol. 1; Halder, Franz, Vol. 3.

Jeremy Noakes and Geoffrey Pridham, eds., *Documents on Nazism, 1919–1945.* New York: Viking, 1974.

Kristallnacht Report

The ambitious and brutal SS leader Reinhard Heydrich, head of the SD and RSHA, reports on the events of the nationwide attack on Jews staged November 9–10, 1938. His totals, it is now clear, were generally underestimated.

*R*e: Action Against the Jews. The reports so far received from the stations of the State Police give the following picture until November 11, 1938:

In numerous cities the plundering of Jewish shops and firms has taken place. In order to prevent further plundering, severe

Paul Mendes-Flohr and Jehuda Reinharz, eds., *The Jew in the Modern World: A Documentary History.* New York: Oxford University Press, 1995.

measures were taken everywhere. One hundred seventy-four plunderers were arrested.

The number of pillaged Jewish shops and apartment houses cannot yet be confirmed. The following numbers appearing in the reports—815 destroyed shops, 29 warehouses set on fire or otherwise destroyed, 171 apartment houses set on fire or otherwise destroyed—reflect only part of the actual damage. The urgency with which the reports had to be prepared made it necessary to restrict them to general statements, such as "numerous" or "most shops destroyed." The reported numbers, therefore, will greatly increase.

One hundred ninety-one synagogues were set on fire, another 76 completely demolished. Also, 11 community houses,

Berliners pass the smashed windows of a Jewish shop on November 10, 1938, the day after the Kristallnacht riots that destroyed Jewish businesses and synagogues across Germany.

cemetery chapels and the like were set on fire and another 3 completely destroyed.

About 20,000 Jews were arrested, also 7 Aryans and 3 foreigners. The latter were taken into protective custody.

Thirty-six fatalities were reported, as well as 36 seriously wounded. All fatalities and the seriously wounded are Jews. One Jew is still missing. Among the Jewish fatalities there was one Polish citizen; among the wounded there were 2 Polish citizens.

See also anti-Semitism, Jewish Question, Kristallnacht, Vol. 1; Heydrich, Reinhard, Vol. 3

Himmler Claims His Legacy

In this conversation among close associates in 1943, Himmler suggests that the SS has provided a great service to Germany's future by taking command of the "Jewish Question."

Y ou will accept it as self-evident and gratifying that in your districts there are no Jews any more. All German people—a few exceptions notwithstanding—have also understood that we could not have endured the Allied bombardment, nor the hardships of the fourth—and, perhaps, the coming fifth and sixth—war year with this destructive pestilence still in the body of our people. The sentence, "The Jews must be exterminated," is a short one, gentlemen, and is easily said. For the person who has to execute what this sentence implies, however, it is the most difficult and hardest thing in the world. Look, of course they are Jews, it is quite clear, they are only Jews, but consider how many people—members of the Party as well—have sent their famous petitions to me or to the authorities, declaring that all Jews, naturally, were pigs, but that so-and-so was a decent Jew and should not be touched. I dare say that, according to the number of petitions and opinions expressed in private, there were more decent Jews in Germany than the number of Jews that actually were to be found in the entire country. In Germany we have so many millions of people who have their famous decent Jew. . . . I am only saying this because, from your own experience within your districts, you will have learned that respectable and decent National Socialist people all know their decent Jew.

I must ask you only to listen and never to speak about what I am telling you in this intimate circle. We had to answer the question: What about the women and the children? Here, too, I had made up my mind, find a clear-cut solution. I did not feel that I had the right to exterminate the men—that is, to murder them, or have them murdered—and then allow their children to grow into avengers, threatening our sons and grandchildren. A fateful decision had to be made: This people had to vanish from the earth. For the organization in charge of the mission, it was the hardest decision we have had to make so far. It has been executed—as I believe I may say—without damage to the spirit and soul of our men and leaders. This danger was very real. The path between the two existing possibilities, either

Paul Mendes-Flohr and Jehuda Reinharz, eds., *The Jew in the Modern World: A Documentary History.* New York: Oxford University Press, 1995.

to become too brutal and to lose all respect for human life, or else to become too soft and dizzy and suffer from nervous break-downs—the path between this Scylla and Charybdis was frightfully narrow.

All Jewish fortunes that were confiscated —a property of infinite value—were trans-ferred, up to the last penny, to the Treasury of the Reich. I have always insisted on this: if we want to win the war we are obliged to our people and to our race—and obliged to our Führer who is now, once in 2,000 years, given to our people—not to be petty in these matters and to be consistent. From the outset I decided that should a member of the SS take only one single Mark, he would be sentenced to death. In recent days I have therefore signed a number of death war-rants—I might as well say it, approximately a dozen. Here one has to be relentless, less the Party and Nation suffer.

I feel most obliged to you—who are the highest commissioners, the highest digni-taries of the Party, of this Political Order, of this political instrument in the hands of our Führer. By the end of this year, the Jewish question in the countries occupied by us will be solved. There will only be remnants of isolated Jews who went into hiding. The question of the Jews married to Gentiles, and the question of half-Jews, will be inves-tigated logically and rationally, decided upon, and solved. . . .

With this I wish to conclude my remarks concerning the Jewish question. Now you know all about it, and you will keep quiet. In the distant future, perhaps, one might consider if the German people should be told anything more about it. I believe it is better that we—all of us—who have taken this upon ourselves for our people and have taken the responsibility (the responsibility for the deed, not merely for the idea), should take our secret to our graves. . . .

Reichsführer-SS Heinrich Himmler, as head of all Nazi police forces, ruled a vast state within a state in the Nazi hierarchy.

See also Auschwitz, extermination camps, Vol. 1; SS, Vol. 2; Himmler, Heinrich, Vol. 3.

Hitler Implies a Future Jewish Holocaust

Although Adolf Hitler never, at least in official documents, ordered the extermination of Europe's Jews, he made it clear in this speech, made on January 30, 1939, that they might face annihilation. In this speech Hitler blames Jews for the increasing tensions that were to lead to World War II.

We, therefore, owe it to the security of the Reich to bring home to the German people in good time the truth about these men. *The German nation has no feeling of hatred toward England, America or France.* All it wants is peace and quiet.

But these other nations are continually being stirred up to hatred of Germany and the German people by Jewish and non-Jewish agitators. And so, should the warmongers achieve what they are aiming at, our own people would be landed in a situation for which they would be psychologically quite unprepared and which they would thus fail to grasp. *I therefore consider it necessary that from now on our Propaganda Ministry and our press should always make a point of answering these attacks* and, above all, bring them to the notice of the German people. The German nation must know who the men are who want to bring about a war by hook or by crook.

It is my conviction that these people are mistaken in their calculations, for when once National Socialist propaganda is devoted to the answering of attacks, we shall succeed just as we succeeded inside Germany herself in overcoming, through the convincing power of our propaganda, the Jewish world enemy.

The nations will in a short time realize that National Socialist Germany wants no enmity with other nations, that all the assertions as to our intended attacks on other nations are lies—lies born out of morbid hysteria or of a mania for self-preservation on the part of certain politicians; and that in certain States these lies are being used by unscrupulous profiteers to salvage their own finances, that, above all, international Jewry may hope in this way to satisfy its thirst for revenge and gain, that on the other hand this is the grossest defamation that can be brought to bear on a great and peace-loving nation.

Never, for instance, have German soldiers fought on American soil unless it was in the cause of American independence and freedom; but American soldiers were brought to Europe to help strangle a great nation that was striving for its freedom. *Germany did not attack America, but America attacked Germany, as the committee of investigation of the American Senate concluded,* from purely capitalist motives, without any other cause. But there is one thing that every one should realize: These attempts cannot influence Germany in the slightest in the way in which she settles her Jewish problem. On the contrary, in connection with the Jewish question, I have this to say: *It is a shameful spectacle to see how the whole democratic world is oozing sympathy for the poor tormented Jewish people, but remains hard-hearted and obdurate when it comes to helping them, which is surely, in view of its attitude, an obvious duty.* The arguments that are brought up as an excuse for not helping them actually speak for us Germans and Italians.

Adolf Hitler, *My New Order.* Ed. Raoul de Roussy de Sales. New York: Reynal and Hitchcock, 1941.

For this is what they say:

First, 'We'—that is, the democracies—'are not in a position to take in the Jews.' Yet in these empires there are not even ten people to the square kilometer. While Germany with her 140 inhabitants to the square kilometer is supposed to have room for them!

Second, they assure us: 'We cannot take them unless Germany is prepared to allow them a certain amount of capital to bring with them as immigrants.'

For hundreds of years Germany was good enough to receive these elements, although they possessed nothing except infectious political and physical diseases. What they possess today, they have to by far the largest extent gained at the cost of the less astute German nation by the most reprehensible manipulations.

Today we are merely paying this people what they deserve. When the German nation was, thanks to the inflation instigated and carried through by Jews, deprived of the entire savings that it had accumulated in years of honest work, when the rest of the world took away the German nation's foreign investments, when we were divested of the whole of our colonial possessions, these philanthropic considerations evidently carried little noticeable weight with democratic statesmen.

Today I can only assure these gentlemen that, thanks to the brutal education with which the democracies favored us for fifteen years, we have completely hardened to all attacks of sentiment. After more than 800,000 children of the nation had died of hunger and undernourishment at the close of the war, we witnessed almost 1,000,000 head of milking cows being driven away from us in accordance with the cruel paragraphs of a dictate that the humane democratic apostles of the world forced upon us as a peace treaty.

We witnessed over 1,000,000 German prisoners of war being retained in confinement for no reason at all for a whole year after the war was ended. We witnessed over one and a half million Germans being torn away from all that they possessed in the territories lying on our frontiers, and being whipped out with practically only what they wore on their backs. We had to endure having millions of our fellow-countrymen torn from us without their consent, and without their being afforded the slightest possibility of existence. I could supplement these examples with dozens of the most cruel kind. For this reason we asked to be spared all sentimental talk.

The German nation does not wish its interests to be controlled by any foreign nation. France to the French, England to the English, America to the Americans, and Germany to the Germans. We are resolved to prevent the settlement in our country of a strange people that was capable of snatching for itself all the leading positions in the land, and to oust it. For it is our will to educate our own nation for these leading positions. We have hundreds of thousands of very intelligent children of peasants and of the working classes. We shall have them educated—in fact, we have already begun—and we wish that one day they, and not the representatives of an alien race, may hold the leading positions in the State altogether with our educated classes.

Above all, German culture, as its name alone shows, is German and not Jewish, and therefore its management and care will be entrusted to members of our own nation. If the rest of the world cries out with a hypocritical mien against this barbaric expulsion from Germany of such an irreplaceable and culturally eminently valuable element, we can only be astonished at this reaction. For how thankful they must be that we are releasing apostles of culture and placing them at the disposal of the rest of the world. In accordance with their own declarations they cannot find a single reason to excuse themselves for refusing to receive this most valuable race in their own countries. Nor can I see a reason why the members of this race should be imposed upon the German nation, while in the States that are so enthusiastic about these 'splendid people' their settlement should suddenly be refused with every imaginable excuse. I think the sooner this problem is solved the better, *for Europe cannot settle down until the Jewish question is cleared up. It may very well be possible that sooner or later an agreement on this problem may be reached in Europe, even between those nations that otherwise do not so easily come together.*

The world has sufficient space for settlement, but we must once and for all get rid of the opinion that the Jewish race was only created by God for the purpose of being in a certain percentage a parasite living on the body and the productive work of other nations. *The Jewish race will have to adapt itself to sound constructive activity as other nations do, or sooner or later it will succumb to a crisis of an inconceivable magnitude.*

One thing I should like to say on this day, which may be memorable for others as well as for us Germans: In the course of my life I have very often been a prophet and have usually been ridiculed for it. During the time of my struggle for power, it was in the first instance the Jewish race that only received my prophecies with laughter when I said that I would one day take over the leadership of the State and with it that of the whole nation and that I would then, among many other things, settle the Jewish problem. Their laughter was uproarious, but I think that for some time now they have been laughing on the other side of their face. Today *I will once more be a prophet. If the international Jewish financiers in and outside Europe should succeed in plunging the nations once more into a world war, then the result will not be the bolshevization of the earth, and thus the victory of Jewry, but the annihilation of the Jewish race in Europe!*

See also Final Solution, Vol. 1.

Hitler's Early Hatred of Jews

In Mein Kampf, *Hitler recalled his first encounters with Jews while a young man in Vienna. He asserted that these encounters brought him a true understanding of German nationalism, race, and politics. Recent research disputes Hitler's version of his actions in Vienna, suggesting that he sold his artwork to Jews and otherwise interacted with Jewish businesses.*

In the period of this bitter struggle between spiritual education and cold reasoning, the pictures that the streets of Vienna showed me rendered me invaluable services. The time came when I no longer walked blindly through the mighty city as I had done at first, but, with open eyes, looked at the people as well as the buildings.

One day when I was walking through the inner city, I suddenly came upon a being clad in a long caftan, with black curls.

Is this also a Jew? was my first thought.

At Linz they certainly did not look like that. Secretly and cautiously I watched the man, but the longer I stared at this strange face and scrutinized one feature after the other, the more my mind reshaped the first question into another form:

Is this also a German?

As was my custom in such cases, I tried to remove my doubts by reading. For the first time in my life I bought some anti-Semitic pamphlets for a few pennies. They all started with the supposition that the reader already knew the Jewish question in principle or understood it to a certain degree. Finally, the tone was such that I again had doubts because the assertions were supported by such extremely unscientific arguments.

I then suffered relapses for weeks, and once even for months.

The matter seemed so monstrous, the accusations so unbounded that the fear of committing an injustice tortured me and made me anxious and uncertain again.

However, even I could no longer actually doubt that they were not Germans with a special religion, but an entirely different race; since I had begun to think about this question, since my attention was drawn to the Jews, I began to see Vienna in a different light from before. Wherever I went I saw Jews, and the more I saw of them, the sharper I began to distinguish them from other people. The inner city especially and the districts north of the Danube Canal swarmed with a people which through its appearance alone had no resemblance to the German people.

Even if my doubts had continued, my hesitation was finally dispelled by the attitude of part of the Jews themselves.

A great movement amongst them, which was widely represented in Vienna, was determined to affirm the national character of Jewry: *the Zionists* [Jews who sought a national homeland in Palestine].

It appeared as though only part of the Jews approved of this attitude and the majority disagreed or even condemned it. The appearance, when closely examined, dis-

solved itself for reasons of expedience into an evil mist of excuses or even lies. For the so-called liberal Jews did not deny the Zionists for being non-Jewish, but for being Jews whose open acknowledgment of their Jewish nationality was impractical or even dangerous.

This did not alter their internal solidarity in the least.

Soon this apparent fight between Zionists and liberal Jews disgusted me; it was unreal throughout, based on lies, and little suited to the generally accepted high moral standard and purity of this race.

The moral and physical cleanliness of this race was a point in itself. It was externally apparent that these were not water-loving people, and unfortunately one could frequently tell that even with eyes closed. Later the smell of these caftan wearers often made me ill. Added to this were their dirty clothes and their none too heroic appearance.

Perhaps all this was not very attractive; aside from the physical uncleanliness, it was repelling suddenly to discover the moral blemishes of the chosen people.

Nothing gave me more cause for reflection than the gradually increased insight into the activities of Jews in certain fields.

Was there any form of filth or profligacy, above all in cultural life, in which at least one Jew did not participate?

When carefully cutting open such a growth, one could find a little Jew, blinded by the sudden light, like a maggot in a rotting corpse.

The Jews' activity in the press, in art, literature, and the theater, as I learned to know it, did not add to their credit in my eyes. All unctuous assertions were of little or no avail. It was sufficient to look at the bill-boards, to read the names of those who produced these awful works for theaters and movies if one wanted to become hardened for a long time. This was pestilence, spiritual pestilence with which the people were infected, worse than the Black Death of former times! And in what quantities this poison was produced

Adolf Hitler, *Mein Kampf.* New York: Reynal and Hitchcock, 1939.

and distributed! Of course, the lower the spiritual and the moral standard of such an art manufacturer, the greater his fertility, till such a fellow, like a centrifugal machine, splashes his dirt into the faces of others. Besides, one must remember their countless number; one must remember that for one Goethe, Nature plays a dirty trick upon mankind in producing ten thousand such scribblers who, as germ carriers of the worst sort, poison the minds of the world.

It could not be overlooked how terrible it was that the Jew above all was chosen in so great a number for this disgraceful task.

Was this to prove the fact that the Jews were the chosen people?

Carefully I began to examine the names of those who created these unclean products of artistic life. The result had a devastating influence on my previous attitude towards the Jews. No matter how much my feeling resisted, Reason had to draw its own conclusions.

The fact was not to be denied that ninety per cent of all literary and artistic rubbish and of theatrical humbug was due to a race which hardly amounted to one-hundredth of all inhabitants of the country. Yet it was so.

Now I also began to examine my beloved 'world press' from this point of view.

The deeper I probed, the more the subject of my former admiration diminished. I could no longer stand its style, I had to reject its contents on account of its shallowness, the objectivity of its presentation seemed untrue rather than honest truth; the authors, however, were—Jews.

Now I began to notice thousands of things which previously I had hardly seen, and I began to understand others which had already caused me reflection.

Now I saw the liberal attitude of the press in a different light; its dignified language, when answering attacks, or its completely ignoring them, was revealed to me as a trick as clever as it was mean; the glorified theatrical criticisms always dealt with Jewish authors, and never did they attack anyone except the German. The slight pinpricks against Wilhelm II proved in its consistence the methods, and so did the commendation of French culture and civilization. The trashy contents of the novel now became obscene, and the language contained tones of a foreign race; the general intention was obviously so detrimental to the German nationality that it could only have been intentional.

But who had an interest in this?

Was it all a mere accident?

Slowly I became uncertain.

This development was accelerated by my insight into a series of other events. This was the conception of manners and morality as it was openly shown and exercised by a great number of Jews.

Again the life in the street gave some really evil demonstrations.

In no other city of western Europe could the relationship between Jewry and prostitution, and even now the white slave traffic, be studied better than in Vienna, with the possible exception of the seaports of Southern France. When walking at night through the streets and alleys of the Leopoldsstadt, with every step one could witness things which were unknown to the greater part of the German nation until the war gave the soldiers on the Eastern Front an opportunity to see similar things, or rather forced them to see them.

An icy shudder ran down my spine when seeing for the first time the Jew as a cool, shameless, and calculating manager of this shocking vice, the outcome of the scum of the big city.

But then my indignation flared up.

Now I did not evade the discussion of the Jewish question any longer; no, I sought it out. As I learned to look for the Jew in every field of our cultural and artistic life, I suddenly bumped against him in a place where I had never suspected.

The scales dropped from my eyes when I found the Jew as the leader of Social Democracy. This put an end to a long internal struggle.

During my daily contact with my worker comrades, I was struck by the changeability with which they demonstrated different attitudes towards one and the same question, sometimes in the course of a few days, sometimes even after a few hours. I could hardly understand how people who expressed sensible opinions when talked to individually suddenly changed their minds when influenced by the spell of the masses. It often made me despair. After hours of talking I often thought that I had broken the ice or cleared up some nonsense and rejoiced at my success, only to find to my dismay on the following day that I had to start all over again; everything had been in vain. The madness of their ideas seemed to swing back and forth like a pendulum in perpetual motion.

I could still understand everything: that they were dissatisfied with their lot and cursed Fate for hitting them so hard; that they hated the employers whom they looked upon as the cruel executives of Fate; that they cursed the authorities who in their eyes had no understanding for their situation; that they demonstrated against the high cost of living and marched in the streets to make their demands; all this I could understand at least without recourse to reason. But what I never understood was their boundless hate towards their own nationality, how they despised their national greatness, soiled its history and abused its heroes.

The fight against one's own race, against one's own nest and homeland, was as senseless as it was incomprehensible. It was unnatural.

See also anti-Semitism, Vol. 1; *Mein Kampf,* Vol. 2; Hitler, Adolf, Vol. 3.

A Report from the Auschwitz Commandant

Rudolf Höss unflinchingly describes the gassing procedure at Auschwitz as well as his role in managing the largest and most deadly camp.

The gassing was carried out in the detention cells of Block 11. Protected by a gas-mask, I watched the killing myself. In the crowded cells death came instantaneously the moment the Cyclon B was thrown in. A short, almost smothered cry, and it was all over. During this first experience of gassing people, I did not fully realise what was happening, perhaps because I was too impressed by the whole procedure. I have a clearer recollection of the gassing of nine hundred Russians which took place shortly afterwards in the old crematorium, since the use of Block 11 for this purpose caused too much trouble. While the transport was detraining, holes were pierced in the earth and in the concrete ceiling of the mortuary. The Russians were ordered to undress in an anteroom; they then quietly entered the mortuary, for they had been told they were to be deloused. The whole transport exactly filled the mortuary to capacity. The doors were then sealed and the gas shaken down through the holes in

Paul Mendes-Flohr and Jehuda Reinharz, eds., *The Jew in the Modern World: A Documentary History.* New York: Oxford University Press, 1995.

the roof. I do not know how long this killing took. For a little while a humming sound could be heard. When the powder was thrown in, there were cries of "Gas!," then a great bellowing, and the trapped prisoners hurled themselves against both the doors. But the doors held. They were opened several hours later, so that the place might be aired. It was then that I saw, for the first time, gassed bodies in mass.

It made me feel uncomfortable and I shuddered, although I had imagined that death by gassing would be worse than it was. I had always thought that the victims would experience a terrible choking sensation. But the bodies, without exception, showed no signs of convulsion. The doctors explained to me that the prussic acid had a paralysing effect on the lungs, but its action was so quick and strong that death came before the convulsions could set in, and in this its effects differed from those produced by carbon monoxide or by a general oxygen deficiency.

The killing of these Russian prisoners-of-war did not cause me much concern at the time. The order had been given, and I had to carry it out. I must even admit that this gassing set my mind at rest, for the mass extermination of the Jews was to start soon and at that time neither Eichmann nor I was certain how these mass killings were to be carried out. It would be by gas, but we did not know which gas or how it was to be used. Now we had the gas, and we had established a procedure. I always shuddered at the prospect of carrying out exterminations by shooting, when I thought of the vast numbers concerned, and of the women and children. The shooting of hostages, and the group executions ordered by the Reichsführer SS or by the Reich Security Head Office had been enough for me. I was therefore relieved to think that we were to be spared all these blood-baths, and that the victims too would be spared suffering until their last moment came. It was precisely this which had caused me the greatest concern when I had heard Eichmann's description of Jews being mown down by the Special Squads [*Einsatzkommandos*] armed with machine-guns and machine-pistols. Many gruesome scenes are said to have taken place, people running away after being shot, the finishing off of the wounded and particularly of the women and children. Many members of the *Einsatzkommandos,* unable to endure wading through blood any longer, had committed suicide. Some had even gone mad. Most of the members of the *Kommandos* had to rely on alcohol when carrying out their horrible work. . . .

In the spring of 1942 the first transports of Jews, all earmarked for extermination, arrived from Upper Silesia.

They were taken from the detraining platform to the "Cottage"—to Bunker I—across the meadows where later Building Site II was located. The transport was conducted by Aumeier and Palitzsch and some of the block leaders. They talked with the Jews about general topics, enquiring concerning their qualifications and trades, with a view to misleading them. On arrival at the "Cottage," they were told to undress. At first they went calmly into the rooms where they were supposed to be disinfected. But some of them showed signs of alarm, and spoke of death by suffocation and of annihilation. A sort of panic set in at once. Immediately all the Jews still outside were pushed into the chambers, and the doors were screwed shut. With subsequent transports the difficult individuals were picked out early on and most carefully supervised. At the first signs of unrest, those responsible were unobtrusively led behind the building and killed with a small-calibre gun that was inaudible to the others. The presence and calm behaviour of the Special Detachment served to reassure those who were worried or who suspected what was about to happen. A further calming effect was obtained by members of the Special Detachment accompanying them into the rooms and remaining with them until the end.

The interior of a gas chamber at Auschwitz-Birkenau, the largest of the six Nazi extermination camps in occupied Poland.

It was most important that the whole business of arriving and undressing should take place in an atmosphere of the greatest possible calm. People reluctant to take off their clothes had to be helped by those of their companions who had already undressed, or by men of the Special Detachment.

The refractory ones were calmed down and encouraged to undress. The prisoners of the Special Detachment also saw to it that the process of undressing was carried out quickly, so that the victims would have little time to wonder what was happening.

The eager help given by the Special Detachment in encouraging them to undress and in conducting them into the gas-chambers was most remarkable. I have never known, nor heard, of any of its members giving these people who were about to be gassed the slightest hint of what lay ahead of them. On the contrary, they did everything in their power to deceive them and particularly to pacify the suspicious ones. Though they might refuse to believe the SS men, they had complete faith in these members of their own race, and to re-assure them and keep them calm the Special Detachments therefore always consisted of Jews who themselves came from the same districts as did the people on whom a particular action was to be carried out.

They would talk about life in the camp, and most of them asked for news of friends or relations who had arrived in earlier transports. It was interesting to hear the lies that the Special Detachment told them with such conviction, and to see the emphatic gestures with which they underlined them.

Many of the women hid their babies among the piles of clothing. The men of the Special Detachment were particularly on the lookout for this, and would speak words of encouragement to the woman until they had persuaded her to take the child with her. The women believed that the disinfectant might be bad for their smaller children, hence their efforts to conceal them.

The smaller children usually cried because of the strangeness of being undressed in this fashion, but when their mothers or members of the Special Detachment comforted them, they became calm and entered the gas chambers, playing or joking with one another and carrying their toys.

I noticed that women who either guessed or knew what awaited them nevertheless found the courage to joke with the children to encourage them, despite the mortal terror visible in their own eyes.

One woman approached me as she walked past and, pointing to her four children who were manfully helping the smallest ones over the rough ground, whispered:

"How can you bring yourself to kill such beautiful, darling children? Have you no heart at all?"

One old man, as he passed by me, hissed:

"Germany will pay a heavy penance for this mass murder of the Jews."

His eyes glowed with hatred as he said this. Nevertheless he walked calmly into the gas-chamber, without worrying about the others.

I remember, too, a woman who tried to throw her children out of the gas-chamber, just as the door was closing. Weeping she called out:

"At least let my precious children live."

There were many such shattering scenes, which affected all who witnessed them.

During the spring of 1942 hundreds of vigorous men and women walked all unsuspecting to their death in the gas-chambers, under the blossom-laden fruit trees of the "Cottage" orchard. This picture of death in the midst of life remains with me to this day. . . .

This mass extermination, with all its attendant circumstances, did not, as I know, fail to affect those who took a part in it.

With very few exceptions, nearly all of those detailed to do this monstrous "work," this "service," and who, like myself, have given sufficient thought to the matter, have been deeply marked by these events.

Many of the men involved approached me as I went my rounds through the extermination buildings, and poured out their anxieties and impressions to me, in the hope that I could allay them.

Again and again during these confidential conversations I was asked: is it necessary that we do all this? Is it necessary that hundreds of thousands of women and children be destroyed? And I, who in my innermost being only fought them off and attempted to console them by repeating that it was done on Hitler's order. I had to tell them that this extermination of Jewry had to be, so that Germany and our posterity might be freed for ever from their relentless adversaries.

There was no doubt in the mind of any of us that Hitler's order had to be obeyed regardless, and that it was the duty of the SS to carry it out. Nevertheless we were all tormented by secret doubts.

I myself dared not admit to such doubts. In order to make my subordinates carry on with their task, it was psychologically essential that I myself appear convinced of the necessity for this gruesomely harsh order.

Everyone watched me. They observed the impression produced upon me by the kind of scenes that I have described above, and my reactions. Every word I said on the subject was discussed. I had to exercise intense self-control in order to prevent my innermost doubts and feelings of oppression from becoming apparent.

I had to appear cold and indifferent to events that must have wrung the heart of anyone possessed of human feelings. I might not even look away when afraid lest my natural emotions get the upper hand. I had to watch coldly, while the mothers with laughing or crying children went into the gas-chambers.

On one occasion two small children were so absorbed in some game that they quite refused to let their mother tear them away from it. Even the Jews of the Special Detachment were reluctant to pick the children up. The imploring look in the eyes of the mother, who certainly knew what was happening, is something I shall never forget. The people were already in the gas-chamber and becoming restive, and I had to act. Everyone was looking at me. I nodded to the junior noncommissioned officer on duty and he picked up the screaming, struggling children in his arms and carried them into the gas-chamber, accompanied by their mother who was weeping in the most heart-rending fashion. My pity was so great that I longed to vanish from the scene; yet I might not show the slightest trace of emotions.

I had to see everything, I had to watch hour after hour, by day and by night, the removal and burning of the bodies, the extraction of the teeth, the cutting of hair, the whole grisly, interminable business. I had to stand for hours on end in the ghastly stench, while the mass graves were being opened and the bodies dragged out and burned.

I had to look through the peep-hole of the gas-chambers and watch the process of death itself, because the doctors wanted me to see it.

I had to do all this because I was the one to whom everyone looked, because I had to show them all that I did not merely issue the orders and make the regulations but was also prepared myself to be present at whatever task I had assigned to my subordinates.

The Reichsführer SS [Himmler] sent various high-ranking Party leaders and SS officers to Auschwitz so that they might see for themselves the process of extermination of the Jews. They were all deeply impressed by what they saw. Some who had previously spoken most loudly about the necessity for this extermination fell silent once they had actually seen the "final solution of the Jewish problem." I was repeatedly asked how I

and my men could go on watching these operations, and how we were able to stand it.

My invariable answer was that the iron determination with which we must carry out Hitler's orders could only be obtained by a stifling of all human emotions. Each of these gentlemen declared that he was glad the job had not been given to him.

I had many detailed discussions with Eichmann concerning all matters connected with the "final solution of the Jewish problem," but without ever disclosing my inner anxieties, I tried in every way to discover Eichmann's innermost and real convictions about the "solution."

Yes, every way. Yet even when we were quite alone together and the drink had been flowing freely so that he was in his most expansive mood, he showed that he was completely obsessed with the idea of destroying every single Jew that he could lay his hands on. Without pity and in cold blood we must complete this extermination as rapidly as possible. Any compromise, even the slightest, would have to be paid for bitterly at a later date.

In the face of such grim determination I was forced to bury all my human considerations as deeply as possible.

Indeed, I must freely confess that after these conversations with Eichmann I almost came to regard such emotions as a betrayal of the Führer.

There was no escape for me from this dilemma.

I had to go on with this process of extermination. I had to continue this mass murder and coldly to watch it, without regard for the doubts that were seething deep inside me.

I had to observe every happening with a cold indifference. Even those petty incidents that others might not notice I found hard to forget. In Auschwitz I truly had no reason to complain that I was bored.

See also Auschwitz, extermination camps, Vol. 1; Höss, Rudolf, Vol. 3.

Warsaw Jews Must Resist

In early 1943, a small group of Jews in the Warsaw ghetto took steps to ensure that, if they were to die, they would die with dignity. The Jewish Fighting Organization, formed to resist further German efforts to "liquidate" the ghetto, posted this message to remind other surviving Jews of the need for resistance.

On January 22, 1943, six months will have passed since the deportations from Warsaw began. We all remember well the days of terror during which 300,000 of our brothers and sisters were cruelly put to death in the death camp of Treblinka. Six months have passed of life in constant fear of death, not knowing what the next day may bring. We have received information from all sides about the destruction of the Jews in the Government-General, in Germany, in the occupied territories. When we listen to this bitter news we wait for our own hour to come, every day and every moment. Today we must understand that the Nazi murderers have let us live only because they want to make use of our capacity to work to our last drop of blood and sweat, to our last breath. We are slaves. And when the slaves are no longer profitable, they are killed. Everyone among us must understand that, and everyone among us must remember it always.

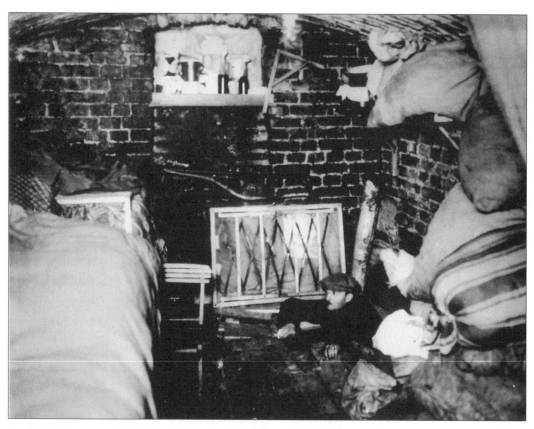

Jewish fighters readied this underground bunker in the Warsaw ghetto in preparation for the Jewish uprising of 1943.

During the past few weeks certain people have spread stories about letters that were said to have been received from Jews deported from Warsaw, who were said to be in labor camps near Minsk or Bobruisk. *Jews in your masses, do not believe these tales. They are spread by Jews who are working for the Gestapo.* The blood-stained murderers have a particular aim in doing this: to reassure the Jewish population in order that later the next deportation can be carried out without difficulty, with a minimum of force and without losses to the Germans. They want the Jews not to prepare hiding-places and not

to resist. Jews, do not repeat these lying [Nazi] agents. The Gestapo's dastardly people will get their just desserts. *Jews in your masses,* the hour is near. You must be prepared to resist, not to give yourselves up like sheep to slaughter. *Not even one Jew must go to the train. People who cannot resist actively must offer passive resistance, that is, by hiding.* We have now received information from Lvov that the Jewish Police there itself carried out the deportation of 3,000 Jews. Such things will not happen again in Warsaw. The killing of Lejkin proves it. Now our slogan must be: *Let everyone be ready to die like a human being!*

January 1943

See also Jewish Fighting Organization, Vol. 1; Warsaw ghetto uprising, Vol 2.

Paul Mendes-Flohr and Jehuda Reinharz, eds., *The Jew in the Modern World: A Documentary History.* New York: Oxford University Press, 1995.

Sent by a Brief Comment to Dachau

A young German woman remembers her arrest and detention in a concentration camp after uttering a small criticism of Adolf Hitler.

I had a job ironing shirts at Mueller's laundry in Karlsruhe on the day Adolf Hitler became Chancellor of Greater Germany. But I had few thoughts for this political upheaval, since I was madly in love and soon to be a bride.

Ten days later I was married. Kurt was foreman of Mueller's packing department. While Kurt and I were honeymooning in Berlin, I got a telegram from my mother telling me that my father had been arrested. He was a Social Democrat and an ardent

trade-union worker. When I returned to Karlsruhe a neighbor told me that the Gestapo had taken my mother too.

I have never heard of either of them again.

Mueller's assistant foreman in the packing department wanted Kurt's job. So he denounced my husband to the police as an enemy of the Reich. Four S.A. men came to our flat at midnight. They dragged Kurt from bed beside me and kicked him down the stairs to a car. It was the last time I saw him in Germany. Within three weeks of marriage I had lost my parents and my husband.

I left Karlsruhe, with not a penny left in the world, to become maid of all work to a schoolmaster and his wife in Munich. Frau Hornbach, my new mistress, did not know I was married until one day she found me crying in the kitchen. Desperate for a little

Allen Churchill, ed., *Eyewitness: Hitler.* New York: Walker, 1979.

sympathy, I told her everything. She was very sympathetic. She released in me all the pent-up emotion I had been concealing. I committed an irretrievable error. I cursed Adolf Hitler.

As soon as I had calmed down, Frau Hornbach sent me to bed. She was a good German citizen. She told her husband, with the result that he immediately reported me by telephone and, at midnight, two S.A. men came and arrested me.

I knew it was hopeless to protest or to struggle, so I dressed quietly and went down to the slick new limousine the two men had commandeered. My guards were not more than twenty years old. I am—or was—not unattractive, and I was twenty-three. The youths sat on either side of me in the back of the car. They began to exchange obscene remarks about my figure. I tried not to listen. Said one of them mockingly:

"Do you think those curves are real, Lutze? Or is it one of those French tricks?"

The other one replied, "Well, it's easy to find out. What's holding you back?"

I bit his hand.

Lutze struck me in the face with his fist. A huge gold ring on his finger cut me over the eye. I submitted to manhandling for the rest of the journey. When we reached the police headquarters I was taken before a young captain by the two S.A. men.

"What's the charge?" he asked.

"Slander of the Führer and intrigue with enemies of the Reich already under arrest."

"Take her to Koch."

I was hustled down a corridor to a small room filled with tobacco haze where a paunchy middle-aged man sat back in a swivel chair with his feet on the desk. His face was mottled with red splotches, and when he roared at my guards, I shuddered.

"What's she here for, black or white?" he growled.

"White," said Lutze's companion.

I discovered later that this meant I was merely under suspicion and not the object of any specific charge or the victim of any

Nazi's personal venom. It was lucky for me. Those arrested "for white" may be and often are released early from the concentration camps.

Sergeant Koch began to take an interest in me. "You'll be out in no time, little girl," he said. And then added, with a leer, "If you're a good girl and do as you're told."

I shivered again. He saw it and scowled. "You'll learn not to be so sensitive here, you little slut."

He picked up the telephone, pressed a button, and said, "Send Anna to me."

Anna, brown-smocked and so bulky that even Koch seemed slim beside her, came up two minutes later. Her face was as hard as flint. Koch filled in a form, handed it to her, and said, "Sign for the new pigeon, Anna."

Then he winked and said, "Look after her carefully as a favor to me. She's rather sensitive."

Anna seized my arm and jerked her thumb toward the door. I went meekly.

The women's section of the Munich police prison was fuller than ever in its history. The crimes of ninety percent of the women prisoners were simply that their husbands had incurred the hatred of the Nazis. Before I was allotted to a cell, I was taken for medical examination. This, I discovered, was an excuse for the young Nazi doctor in charge to compel any attractive girl to undress before him. Next I was given a bath—scrubbed with floor brushes by two burly wardresses.

One of my cell mates was a middle-aged housewife. Her name was Mittelmann, and she seemed overcome chiefly by the disgrace of going to prison. She wept continually. The other inmate of Cell 79 was more interesting. She was a Jewess, and was most hauntingly beautiful. She told me her name was Jetty, but I never found out her surname. She was the wife of a doctor who had already fallen a victim to the terror. Brown Shirts had shot him as he was trying to escape from his home after a friend had telephoned to warn him.

Jetty was always reproaching herself for his death. "Oh, Pauline," she choked, "he would have got away in time if I hadn't held him in my arms so long. I couldn't bear to let him go. I loved him too much. I killed him, Pauline, I killed him!"

She told me of the treatment in the prison, where she had been for three weeks. She warned me never to show my feelings at the sights I would see, and to submit to the obscene behavior of the S.A. men when I was called for examination. "If you do," she said, "you are much more likely not to be seriously bothered."

Most of the Nazi prison officials were cases of sex complexes, it seemed. Sadism, cruelty for its own sake, was the commonest kind. The first time I saw a girl stripped and flogged on the exercise ground I fainted from sheer horror; but I became hardened to worse sights than that. Meanwhile, we three cell mates had no uniforms, only the dresses we had been arrested in. My first meal made me sick. It consisted of a tin mug full of an evil-smelling stew, with a piece of dry bread and a mug of water. Jetty said, "You'd better eat it, my dear. The Nazis won't care in the least if you starve to death."

I finally forced myself to eat it.

At 5 A.M. a wardress opened the cell door and told Jetty to get dressed. She obeyed calmly, and before she went she kissed me and said, "I don't expect I shall see you again, Pauline. Good-bye, and be brave."

The wardress struck her across the face and dragged her out into the corridor. I wept until we were told to get up, at six o'clock.

That morning Frau Mittelmann told me that her husband had been manager of a department at the Munich gasworks. He had never taken any interest in politics, but one day he had told his assistant not to get mixed up with hoodlums who fought at street corners as the Nazis did. The assistant repeated these words to the Nazis and got his superior's job as a reward.

"But you?" I said. "Surely they have nothing against you?"

"I was so upset, I told my neighbor I thought Hitler was a blackguard," sobbed Frau Mittelmann, "and she told the Gestapo."

My first three days in the prison were fairly uneventful. The fourth morning we were all ordered to the exercise yard two hours earlier than usual. We were drawn up in two ranks. Four Brown Shirts appeared at the entrance gates. They dragged in a curious wooden contraption with armholes in side pillars.

It turned out to be a flogging block.

The governor of the prison, accompanied by the young doctor who had examined me, entered the yard. Behind him, held up by two wardresses, came a young woman prisoner. I discovered later that she was a new arrival who had been so outraged by the "medical examination" by the doctor that she had picked up an inkstand and cut open his head with it. I had noticed that he was wearing a strip of sticking plaster across his left temple.

The governor addressed us. "Prisoners," he said, "you are going to witness an example of the punishment meted out to those who attempt violence against the upholders of law and order."

He stood aside. The half-fainting girl was handed to the Brown Shirts, who held her by the arms while the doctor stripped her down to the waist. He then signed to them to fasten her to the block.

They fastened her ankles with small chains and thrust her limp arms through the holes.

For the first time she now seemed to become aware of what was happening to her. A heartrending groan escaped her lips. She looked at us with a wild appeal in her eyes. It was agonizing.

A Brown Shirt took a stand behind her and slashed the air with a many-tailed whip. Then the governor lifted a hand. The first blow fell. The victim's cries were drowned by involuntary screams from half a dozen of us. After the sixth stroke, she seemed to lose consciousness. After the twelfth, the governor ordered the man to stop and motioned to the doctor, who jerked back her drooping head and looked into her eyes. He made no attempt to examine her back, which was crimson with blood.

He nodded to two wardresses, who stood by while the men unshackled her. Before the women could grab her, she collapsed. One of the men emptied a bucket of water over her. It revived her and she began to groan. The wardresses dragged her away.

The governor addressed us again: "The penalty for attack on prison officials is death. This girl has been spared. Remember, if you try to do as she did, you may not be so lucky. Dismiss."

Lucky!

Anna gave us the signal to march back indoors, and we were quickly shepherded to our cells.

I have seen twenty-three women flogged in German prisons, but it was this first sight that affected me most deeply. I was almost unconscious as I walked into my cell, and when Frau Mittelmann began to weep and wail about how awful it had been, I fell in a dead faint on the floor. The good woman revived me with the few drops of water we had in the cell. She told me I had been "out" for nearly five minutes.

Two days after this, Anna came to my cell in the afternoon and said, "Follow me." I followed her with my heart pounding hard. Was I to be flogged?

I was taken to the young captain who had interviewed me the day I arrived. His name was Muegel. He stared at me for a minute, then ordered Anna out of the room. Then he opened a thin file of papers on his desk and read them. I was amazed at the details about me that the Nazis had dug up. At last he said:

"Did your father teach you to believe in trade-unionism and Social Democracy?"

I replied with perfect truth that I had never had any interest in politics, and neither had my husband.

"But your husband and your parents are under arrest, you know," he said. "What about that?"

I declared heatedly that they had been arrested on false evidence from people who had grudges against them.

He said, "There doesn't seem to be much evidence against you—except on the charge of defamation of the Führer. That is a very serious charge."

I tried to explain that I had not meant what I had said about the Führer; that I had been overwrought.

Muegel got up and came around to me. "I think you might get out pretty soon," he said with a smile.

I almost burst into tears of joy as I thanked him. But he had not finished.

"That is, if you behave yourself here. But I'm sure you will. I rather like you. And I have a little influence in this place." He came closer, breathing heavily. "In fact, you're a beautiful girl, Pauline."

I wanted to scream. Then I remembered what Jetty had told me about submitting instead of struggling. I tried to seem calm. I even forced a smile. He suddenly gathered me in his arms and began to kiss me. . . .

I was weeping when Anna was summoned to take me away. Her only comment to me was, "Straighten your dress. We won't have any sloppiness here."

In due course I was sent on to serve six months in the Dachau concentration camp. I was taken there with five other women, two of whom were Jewesses. We arrived at seven o'clock one November morning. I am bound to say for dreadful Dachau that the medical examination given me there was the genuine, decent thing.

This time I was allotted to a cell with three others. My stay, as it turned out, was to last only nine weeks. That, however, was quite long enough for me to see my full share of the horrors that so many writers have described. I will confine my account of Dachau to one appalling episode.

A Jewess named Berta Minauer was reported by a wardress for disobedience and was sent for by the camp commandant. I happened to be about ten yards behind her as she crossed the exercise yard between two S.A. men. I had been sent with a message to the camp kitchens.

Suddenly she screamed, snatched a knife from the belt of one man and plunged it into the other man's back. A sentry and I were the only witnesses. The uninjured man had knocked her down by the time the sentry opened the gate and rushed in. He sent the S.A. man for help and then began kicking the wretched Berta in the face. He roared curses. I think the girl must have become demented, for she was screaming back at him, and she managed to get to her feet and even tried to grapple with him. He felled her, and she lay writhing as he went on kicking her ferociously. Three S.A. men arrived with a stretcher and picked up the man she had stabbed.

Suddenly they and the sentry caught the Jewess up and dragged her to the wall of one of the huts. The sentry then plunged his bayonet through her stomach and pinned her writhing body to the wall.

Then the men tore at her clothes until she was half naked and began to kick her sys-tematically. The sentry tore handfuls of hair from her scalp. Before they had finished, she was dead.

They stood looking at her broken body for a few minutes. Then the sentry withdrew his bayonet, let the body fall, and wiped off the steel on her clothes. The S.A. man went off indoors and the sentry went back to his gate. Not one of them had paid the slightest attention to me. I crept indoors by myself.

When we were all out for exercise two hours later, there was no trace of the scene. . . .

On January 26, 1934, thanks to the good offices of a friendly official, I was released for good behavior. I was examined by a doctor (no one is allowed to leave bearing marks of punishment) and told to sign a document affirming that I had been justly treated and would never discuss anything seen or heard in the prison camp.

I was also given back my own clothes and told to report to the villa of one Herr Kastner, where I would go to work as a housemaid.

See also asocials, persecution of; concentration camps; Dachau, Vol. 1.

Working in a Factory at Auschwitz

Primo Levi, a young Italian Jew who had been trained as a chemist, was among the most articulate and eloquent survivors of Hitler's death camps. Able to acquire certain privileges in Auschwitz, he nonetheless faced continual reminders of his "subhuman" status, related in the following account.

How many months have gone by since we entered the camp? How many since the day I was dismissed from Ka-Be [the camp infirmary]? And since the day of the chemistry examination? And since the October selection?

Alberto and I often ask ourselves these questions, and many others as well. We were ninety-six when we arrived, we, the Italians of convoy 174,000; only twenty-nine of us survived until October, and of these, eight went in the selection. We are now twenty-one and the winter has hardly begun. How many of us will be alive at the new year? How many when spring begins?

There have been no air raids now for several weeks; the November rain has turned to snow, and the snow has covered the ruins. The Germans and Poles go to work in rubber jackboots, woollen ear-pads and padded overalls; the English prisoners have their wonderful fur-lined jackets. They have distributed no overcoats in our Lager [camp] except to a few of the privileged; we are a specialized Kommando, which—in theory—only works under shelter; so we are left in our summer outfits.

We are the chemists, 'therefore' we work at the phenylbeta sacks. We cleared out the warehouse after the first air raids in the height of the summer. The phenylbeta seeped under our clothes and stuck to our sweating limbs and chafed us like leprosy; the skin came off our faces in large burnt patches. Then the air raids temporarily stopped and we carried the sacks back into the warehouse. Then the warehouse was hit and we took the sacks into the cellar of the styrene department. Now the warehouse has been repaired and once again we have to pile up the sacks there. The caustic smell of the phenylbeta impregnates our only suit, and follows us day and night like our shadows. So far, the advantages of being in the Chemical Kommando have been limited to the following: the others have received overcoats while we have not; the others carry 100 pound cement sacks, while we carry 125 pound phenylbeta sacks. How can we still think about the chemistry examination and our illusions of that time? At least four times during the summer we have heard speak of Doktor Pannwitz's laboratory in Bau [building] 939, and the rumour spread that the analysts for the Polymerization Department would be chosen among us.

But now it is time to stop, it is all over now. This is the last act: the winter has begun, and with it our last battle. There is no longer any reason to doubt that it will be the last. Any time during the day when we happen to listen to the voice of our bodies, or ask our limbs, the answer is always the same: our strength will not last out. Everything around us speaks of a final decay and ruin. Half of Bau 939 is a heap of twisted metal and smashed concrete; large deformed blue icicles hang like pillars from the enormous tubings where the overheated steam used to roar. The Buna [chemical factory] is silent now, and when the wind is propitious, if one listens hard, one can hear the continuous dull underground rumbling of the front which is getting nearer. Three hundred prisoners have arrived in the Lager from the Lodz ghetto, transferred by the Germans before the Russian advance: they told us rumours about the legendary battle of the Warsaw ghetto, and they described how the Germans had liquidated the Lublin camp over a year ago: four machine-guns in the corners and the huts set on fire; the civilized world will never know about it. When will it be our turn?

This morning the Kapo [a camp supervisor] divided up the squads as usual. The Magnesium Chloride ten to the Magnesium Chloride: and they leave, dragging their feet, as slowly as possible, because the Magnesium Chloride is an extremely unpleasant job; you stand all day up to your ankles in cold, briny water, which soaks into your shoes, your clothes and your skin. The Kapo grabs hold of a brick and throws it among the group; they get clumsily out of the way, but do not quicken their pace. This is almost a custom, it happens every morning, and does not always mean that the Kapo has a definite intent to hurt.

The four of the *Scheisshaus* [latrine] to their work: and the four attached to the building of the new latrine leave. For when we exceeded the force of fifty Häftlinge with the arrival of the convoys from Lodz and Transylvania, the mysterious German bureaucrat who supervises these matters authorized us to build a *'Zweiplatziges Kommandoscheisshaus',* i.e. a two-seated closet reserved for our Kommando. We are not unaware of this mark of distinction, which makes ours one of the few Kommandos of which one can with reason boast one's membership: but it is evident that we will lose one of the simplest of pretexts to absent ourselves from work and arrange combinations with civilians. *'Noblesse oblige,'* says Henri, who has other strings to his bow.

The twelve for the bricks. Meister Dahm's five. The two for the tanks. How many absent? Three absent. Homolka gone into Ka-Be this morning, the ironsmith dead yesterday, François transferred who knows where or why. The roll-call is correct; the Kapo notes it down and is satisfied. There are only us eighteen of the phenylbeta left, beside the prominents of the Kommando. And now the unexpected happens.

The Kapo says:—Doktor Pannwitz has communicated to the *Arbeitsdienst* [work detail] that three Häftlinge have been chosen for the Laboratory: 169509, Brackier; 175633, Kandel; 174517, Levi—. For a moment my ears ring and the Buna whirls around me. There are three Levis in Kommando 98, but *Hundert Vierundsiebzig Fünf Hundert Siebzehn* [174517, the number tattooed on his wrist] is me, there is no possible doubt. I am one of the three chosen.

The Kapo looks us up and down with a twisted smile. A Belgian, a Russian and an Italian: three *'Franzosen'* [Frenchmen] in short. Is it possible that three *Franzosen* have really been chosen to enter the paradise of the Laboratory?

Many comrades congratulate us; Alberto first of all, with genuine joy, without a shadow of envy. Alberto holds nothing against my fortune, he is really very pleased, both because of our friendship and because he will also gain from it. In fact, by now we two are bound by a tight bond of alliance, by which every 'organized' scrap is divided into two strictly equal parts. He has no reason to envy me, as he neither hoped nor desired to enter the Laboratory. The blood in his veins is too free for this untamed friend of mine to think of relaxing in a system; his instinct leads him elsewhere, to other solutions, towards the unforeseen, the impromptu, the new. Without hesitating, Alberto prefers the uncertainties and battles of the 'free profession' to a good employment.

I have a ticket from the *Arbeitsdienst* in my pocket, on which it is written that Häftling 174517, as a specialized worker, has the right to a new shirt and underpants and must be shaved every Wednesday.

The ravaged Buna lies under the first snows, silent and stiff like an enormous corpse; every day the sirens of the *Fliegeralarm* [air-raid alarm] wail; the Russians are fifty miles away. The electric power station has stopped, the methanol rectification columns no longer exist, three of the four acetylene gasometers have been blown up. Prisoners 'reclaimed' from all the camps in east Poland pour into our Lager haphazardly; the minority are set to work, the majority leave immediately for Birkenau and the Chimney. The ration has been still further reduced. The Ka-Be is overflowing, the E-Häftlinge have brought scarlet fever, diphtheria and petechial typhus into the camp.

But Häftling 174517 has been promoted as a specialist and has the right to a new shirt and underpants and has to be shaved every Wednesday. No one can boast of understanding the Germans.

We entered the Laboratory timid, suspicious and bewildered like three wild beasts slinking into a large city. How clean and polished the floor is! It is a laboratory surprisingly like any other laboratory. Three long work-benches covered with hundreds of familiar objects. The glass instruments in a corner to drip, the precision balance, a Heraeus oven, a Höppler thermostat. The smell makes me start back as if from the blow of a whip: the weak aromatic smell of organic chemistry laboratories. For a moment the large semidark room at the university, my fourth year, the mild air of May in Italy comes back to me with brutal violence and immediately vanishes.

Herr Stawinoga gives us our work-places. Stawinoga is a German Pole, still young, with an energetic, but sad and tired face. He is also Doktor: not of chemistry, but *(ne pas chercherà comprendre* [it is not possible to comprehend]) of comparative philology; all the same, he is head of the laboratory. He does not speak to us willingly, but does not seem ill-disposed. He calls us 'Monsieur' which is ridiculous and disconcerting.

The temperature in the laboratory is wonderful; the thermometer reads 65°F. We agree that they can make us wash the glass instruments, sweep the floor, carry the hydrogen flasks, anything so as to remain here, and so solve the problem of the winter for us. And then, on a second examination, even the problem of hunger should not be difficult to solve. Will they really want to search us at the exit every day? And even if they want to, will they do it every time that we ask to go to the latrine? Obviously not. And there is soap, petrol, alcohol here. I will stitch a secret pocket inside my jacket, and combine with the Englishman who works in the repairs-yard and trades in petrol. We will see how strict the supervision is: but by now I have spent a year in the Lager and I know that if one wants to steal and seriously sets one's mind to it, no supervision and no searchings can prevent it.

So it would seem that fate, by a new unsuspected path, has arranged that we three, the object of envy of all the ten thousand condemned, suffer neither hunger nor cold this winter. This means a strong probability of not falling seriously ill, of not being frozen, of overcoming the selections. In these conditions, those less expert than us about things in the Lager might even be tempted by the hope of survival and by the thought of liberty. But we are not, we know how these matters go; all this is the gift of fortune, to be enjoyed as intensely as possi-

ble and at once; for there is no certainty about tomorrow. At the first glass I break, the first error in measurement, the first time my attention is distracted, I will go back to waste away in the snow and the winds until I am ready for the Chimney. And besides, who knows what will happen when the Russians come?

Because the Russians will come. The ground trembles day and night under our feet; the muffled dull rumbling of their artillery now bursts uninterrupted into the novel silence of the Buna. One breathes a tense air, an air of resolution. The Poles no longer work, the French again walk with their head high. The English wink at us and greet us on the aside with a 'V' sign; and not always on the aside.

But the Germans are deaf and blind, enclosed in an armour of obstinacy and of wilful ignorance. Once again they have named the date for the beginning of the production of synthetic rubber: it will be the first of February 1945. They construct shelters and trenches, they repair the damage, they build, they fight, they command, they organize and they kill. What else could they do? They are Germans. This way of behaviour is not meditated and deliberate, but follows from their nature and from the destiny they have chosen. They could not act differently: if you wound the body of a dying man, the wound will begin to heal, even if the whole body dies within a day.

Every morning now, when the squads are divided, the Kapo calls us three of the Laboratory before all the others, *'die drei Leute vom Labor'* [the three people for labor]. In camp, in the evenings and the mornings, nothing distinguishes me from the flock, but during the day, at work, I am under shelter and warm, and nobody beats me; I steal and sell soap and petrol without risk, and perhaps I will be given a coupon for a pair of leather shoes. Even more, can this be called work? To work is to push wagons, carry sleepers, break stones, dig earth, press one's bare hands against the iciness of the freezing iron. But I sit all day, I have a notebook and a pencil and they have even given me a book to refresh my memory about analytical methods. I have a drawer where I can put my beret and gloves, and when I want to go out I only have to tell Herr Stawinoga, who never says no and asks no questions if I delay; he has the air of suffering in his flesh for the ruin which surrounds him.

My comrades in the Kommando envy me, and they are right; should I not be contented? But in the morning, I hardly escape the raging wind and cross the doorstep of the laboratory when I find at my side the comrade of all my peaceful moments, of Ka-Be, of the rest-Sundays—the pain of remembering, the old ferocious suffering of feeling myself a man again, which attacks me like a dog the moment my conscience comes out of the gloom. Then I take my pencil and notebook and write what I would never dare tell anyone.

Then there are the women. How long is it since I have seen a woman? In Buna we quite often met the Polish and Ukrainian women workers, in trousers and leather jackets, huge and violent like their men. They were sweaty and dishevelled in the summer, padded out with thick clothes in the winter and worked with spades and pickaxes. We did not feel ourselves next to women.

It is different here. Faced with the girls of the laboratory, we three feel ourselves sink into the ground from shame and embarrassment. We know what we look like: we see each other and sometimes we happen to see our reflection in a clean window. We are ridiculous and repugnant. Our cranium is bald on Monday, and covered by a short brownish mould by Saturday. We have a swollen and yellow face, marked permanently by the cuts made by the hasty barber, and often by bruises and numbed sores; our neck is long and knobbly, like that of plucked chickens. Our clothes are incredibly dirty, stained by mud, grease and blood; Kandel's breeches only arrive half-

way down his calves, showing his bony, hairy ankles; my jacket runs off my shoulders as if off a wooden clothes-hanger. We are full of fleas, and we often scratch ourselves shamelessly; we have to ask permission to go to the latrines with humiliating frequency. Our wooden shoes are insupportably noisy and are plastered with alternate layers of mud and regulation grease.

Besides which, we are accustomed to our smell, but the girls are not and never miss a chance of showing it. It is not the generic smell of the badly washed, but the smell of the Häftling, faint and sweetish, which greeted us at our arrival in the Lager and which tenaciously pervades the dormitories, kitchens, washrooms and closets of the Lager. One acquires it at once and one never loses it: 'so young and already stinking!' is our way of greeting new arrivals.

To us the girls seem outside this world. There are three young German girls, Fräulein Liczba, the Polish store-keeper, and Frau Meyer, the secretary. They have smooth, rosy skin, beautiful attractive clothes, clean and warm, blond hair, long and well-set; they speak with grace and self-possession, and instead of keeping the laboratory clean and in order, as they ought to, they smoke in the corners, scandalously eat bread and jam, file their nails, break a lot of glass vessels and then try to put the blame on us; when they sweep, they sweep our feet. They never speak to us and turn up their noses when they see us shuffling across the laboratory, squalid and filthy, awkward and insecure in our shoes. I once asked Fräulein Liczba for some information, and she did not reply but turned with an annoyed face to Stawinoga and spoke to him quickly. I did not understand the sentence, but I clearly grasped 'Stink-jude' and my blood froze. Stawinoga told me that for anything to do with the work we should turn directly to him.

These girls sing, like girls sing in laboratories all over the world, and it makes us deeply unhappy. They talk among themselves:

CONCENTRATION CAMPS AND THE HOLOCAUST

they talk about the rationing, about their fiancés, about their homes, about the approaching holidays . . .

'Are you going home on Sunday? I am not, travelling is so uncomfortable!'

'I am going home for Christmas. Only two weeks and then it will be Christmas again; it hardly seems real, this year has gone by so quickly!'

. . . This year has gone by so quickly. This time last year I was a free man: an outlaw but free, I had a name and a family, I had an eager and restless mind, an agile and healthy body. I used to think of many, faraway things: of my work, of the end of the war, of good and evil, of the nature of things and of the laws which govern human actions; and also of the mountains, of singing and loving, of music, of poetry. I had an enormous, deep-rooted, foolish faith in the benevolence of fate; to kill and to die

seemed extraneous literary things to me. My days were both cheerful and sad, but I regretted them equally, they were all full and positive; the future stood before me as a great treasure. Today the only thing left of the life of those days is what one needs to suffer hunger and cold; I am not even alive enough to know how to kill myself.

If I spoke German better I could try to explain all this to Frau Meyer; but she would certainly not understand, or if she was so good and intelligent as to understand, she would be unable to bear my proximity, and would flee from me, as one flees from contact with an incurable invalid, or from a man condemned to death. Or perhaps she would give me a coupon for a pint of civilian soup.

This year has gone by so quickly.

See also Auschwitz, Vol. 1; slave labor, Vol. 2.

The Nuremberg Laws

The following two laws, announced by Adolf Hitler at the 1935 Nuremberg Nazi Party Congress, gave anti-Semitism a basis in German law, opening the door to a flood of specific restrictive measures.

Reich Citizenship Law September 15, 1935

The Reichstag has unanimously enacted the following law, which is promulgated herewith:

§1

1) A subject of the State is a person who enjoys the protection of the German Reich and who in consequence has specific obligations towards it.

2) The status of subject of the State is acquired in accordance with the provisions of the Reich and State Citizenship Law.

§2

1) A Reich citizen is a subject of the State who is of German or related blood, who proves by his conduct that he is willing and fit faithfully to serve the German people and Reich.

2) Reich citizenship is acquired through the granting of a Reich Citizenship Certificate.

3) The Reich citizen is the sole bearer of full political rights in accordance with the Law.

§3

The Reich Minister of the Interior, in coordination with the Deputy of the Führer, will issue the Legal and Administrative orders required to implement and complete this Law.

Rita Steinhardt Botwinick, ed., *A Holocaust Reader: From Ideology to Annihilation.* Upper Saddle River, NJ: Prentice-Hall, 1997.

Nuremberg, September 15, 1935
at the Reich Party Congress of Freedom
> *The Führer and Reich Chancellor*
> *Adolf Hitler*
> *The Reich Minister of the Interior*
> *Frick*

Law for the Protection of German Blood and German Honor
September 15, 1935

Moved by the understanding that purity of the German Blood is the essential condition for the continued existence of German people, and inspired by the inflexible determination to ensure the existence of the German Nation for all time, the Reichstag has unanimously adopted the following Law, which is promulgated herewith:

§1

1) Marriages between Jews and subjects of the state of German or related blood are forbidden. Marriages nevertheless concluded are invalid, even if concluded abroad to circumvent this law.

2) Annulment proceedings can be initiated only by the State Prosecutor.

§2

Extramarital intercourse between Jews and subjects of the state of German or related blood is forbidden.

§3

Jews may not employ in their households female subjects of the state of German or related blood who are under 45 years old.

§4

1) Jews are forbidden to fly the Reich or National flag or to display the Reich colors.

2) They are, on the other hand, permitted to display the Jewish colors. The exercise of this right is protected by the State.

§5

1) Any person who violates the prohibition under §1 will be punished by a prison sentence with hard labor.

2) A male who violates the prohibition under §2 will be punished with a prison sentence with or without hard labor.

3) Any person violating the provisions under §3 or 4 will be punished with a prison sentence of up to one year and a fine, or with one or the other of these penalties.

§6

The Reich Minister of the Interior, in coordination with the Deputy of the Führer and the Reich Minister of Justice, will issue the Legal and Administrative regulations required to implement and complete this Law.

§7

The Law takes effect on the day following promulgations except for §3, which goes into force on January 1, 1936.

Nuremberg, September 15, 1935
at the Reich Party Congress of Freedom
> *The Führer and Reich Chancellor*
> *Adolf Hitler*
> *The Reich Minister of the Interior*
> *Frick*
> *The Reich Minister of Justice*
> *Dr. Gürtner*
> *The Deputy of the Führer*
> *R. Hess*

See also anti-Semitism, Vol. 1; Nuremberg Laws, Vol. 2.

Surviving a Death March

Over the winter of 1944–1945, the SS closed and attempted to destroy the extermination camps in occupied Poland, withdrawing ahead of advancing Russian armies. German officials marched many of the surviving inmates to camps in Germany. Thousands died on these so-called death marches. One survivor recounts his experiences.

We were on a road leading north, in a column of five prisoners to a row, half a mile long. The SS guards were walking on both sides of the column, fingers on the triggers of their machine guns. Two or three were marching ahead of the column and a few behind it. An officer on a motorcycle was riding up and down the road making sure everything was in order. Many military vehicles of all kinds were driving past. Some of the German formations seemed still intact, while others looked like the remains of a fighting force that had taken a bad beating. There were many stalled or abandoned vehicles lying on the shoulder of the road. Civilians were walking along carrying bundles; some had horse carts packed with their belongings. Allied planes and a few Russian ones flew continuously over our heads, but we didn't see a single German plane. From time to time, when one of the Allied planes spotted a group of German military vehicles, the pilot would dive down and strafe them. It did my heart good to see Germans jump and dive for cover. Somehow we weren't much concerned for our own safety; our column was very visible from the air, and our striped uniforms made it obvious that we were prisoners. Whenever the planes flew low over us, the guards stepped up to the column, feeling safer from air attack when closer to us.

Rita Steinhardt Botwinick, ed., *A Holocaust Reader: From Ideology to Annihilation.* Upper Saddle River, NJ: Prentice-Hall, 1997.

After a while they led us onto a secondary road parallel to the main one, where things were much quieter. The peasants in the fields, almost all of them old men, women, and children, looked with curiosity but no surprise at the endless column of prisoners in their striped uniforms. I now weighed less than a hundred pounds, Sam, about eighty-five or ninety, and most of the others were in a similar state. But the guards kept us marching at a brisk pace.

It was not yet noon when an elderly Pole marching a couple of rows ahead of us suddenly tripped and fell. He got up again with the help of the others around him, but he must have sprained or twisted an ankle, because he continued walking only with great difficulty, heavily favoring one leg. For a mile or so his neighbors on both sides supported him, but he was in constant pain and after a while couldn't walk at all—he had to be literally carried. An SS guard saw that he was holding up the column, and with his gun motioned to him to step out of the ranks. When one of the prisoners who was carrying him wanted to stay with him, the guard pointed his machine gun at him in turn, and ordered him to keep moving. The guard then pushed the man over to the side of the road and raised his machine gun. Realizing that he was going to be killed, the man fell on his knees and joined his hands together in a gesture of prayer. The SS guard, his gun about two feet from the man's head, let loose with a burst of fire, and the Pole keeled over and lay still on the ground. Seeing that the other prisoners were slowing down, their heads turning to look at the man lying on the ground, the guard ran back to the column and started hitting the marchers within his reach to hurry them along.

Our mood changed abruptly. Conversation stopped, and all of us walked carefully, making sure not to stumble. Sam and I took turns holding each other's arm. The incident had driven home to us that we were all still in mortal danger. Even though the war was in its last days, the SS obviously had orders not to let a single prisoner out of their control. The rules for this march were: Walk or die.

We continued walking nonstop for several more hours. Some of the weaker prisoners, unable to keep up the pace, began to fall back toward the end of the column. This, we knew, meant a bullet in the head. The stragglers at the end of the column were using their last drop of strength in a desperate effort not to get separated from the rest. Some were wheezing, gasping for air, others stumbled on until finally, all strength gone, they fell one by one to their knees, or simply dropped. Like angels of death the SS men at the rear of the column were looking for stragglers and shot them where they fell as if it were the most routine thing in the world. Their faces were blank. There was no hate in them, no pity, just business as usual. By the time they ordered us to stop for our first break, five or six prisoners from our column were gone, their bodies left behind on the side of the road, riddled with bullets.

Strangely, even though it was now clear that the march was going to be a murderous affair, I still felt far safer than I ever had in the camp. Here they didn't know I was a Jew, and if they were going to kill me it would be only because I couldn't walk, not simply because I was a Jew. To my mind, killing a man because he could not keep up the pace in a forced march somehow wasn't as bad as killing him because he had been born a Jew. Such reasoning may seem lunatic, but under the circumstances it made perfect sense to me. Having lived for so many years under the gun, when any one of the guards had the clear and unquestioned right to murder me at any moment, at a whim, even for fun, even though I had done nothing to provoke it, for the sole reason

that I was born a Jew, I had grown to yearn to have my right to live judged by some other criterion, any other—even by whether or not I was able to walk.

Sam and I divided our food rations carefully into twelve portions, and we ate one portion during our brief rest. We knew that our lives depended on making it last as long as possible, on conserving every last bit of energy. However, we saw many other prisoners, no hungrier than we, consume their entire three or four days' ration in a few minutes.

There was another Jewish prisoner in our column, Warshawski, and when the guards ordered us to resume our march, Warshawski walked alongside Sam and me. Despite the shooting of the stragglers, I was more optimistic than ever about our chances to make it. The odds seemed good that the SS would not kill so many people, especially since as far as they knew there were no Jews among us. Besides, even if they had planned to execute us all, it would have been almost impossible for them to manage it. They couldn't mow us all down at once out there in the open; thousands would escape, and their own lives would be greatly endangered. I even overheard some of the Poles discussing the possibility of suddenly jumping the guards, but they had their machine guns at the ready; whoever attacked them first would surely be killed, and no one was willing to die moments before liberation, to save the others. Besides, even if a substantial number of prisoners managed to escape, the SS might still have time to hunt down many of them.

As the sun began to sink slowly in the west, the guards led us off the road to a large farm, which was to be our resting place for the night. They pushed perhaps a thousand of us into a large barn. There wasn't enough room for all of us to lie down, and some had to lay their legs over others' bodies. Sam and I were especially cautious with our food, waiting until it was completely dark before we ate our next portion, and being very quiet about it. We were afraid that some of the prisoners who had no food left might jump us and take ours by force.

The hay in the barn smelled good, and even though we were packed in so tight, I had a good night's sleep. Early in the morning the guards ordered us out, and we were once more on the march. Fortunately, it wasn't raining and the weather was mild. We turned into another road, on which we could tell another column was marching ahead of us; every few hundred feet we saw bullet-ridden bodies of prisoners lying at the side of the road.

All day long the SS played their deadly game of march or die, with the killings increasing every hour. Some of the prisoners' shoes were either too big for them or too small, and they were beginning to develop painful blisters; many walked barefoot, carrying their shoes tied together around their necks. Occasionally we heard the rumble of artillery, but now it seemed more remote and sporadic than it had just before we left the camp. I didn't feel as hungry as I had in the camp either, perhaps because I was so absorbed in the life-and-death game with the SS. We were marching now on winding country roads; evidently the SS wanted to stay away from the highways. I felt good, and Sam was holding up fairly well too. We were on the north German plain, which was sparsely populated, and, luckily for us, very flat. The roads would have been much more thickly strewn with our bodies had the terrain been hilly. That night the guards again brought us to a large farm, but this time they let all of us sleep outside, so at least we had plenty of room to stretch our legs.

This went on day after day, except that the number of victims kept increasing hourly. Sam and I had enough food for four days, but many of the others had had nothing to eat since the first rest stop, and more and more were unable to continue the march. The pace was slowing, which helped a little, but still many prisoners, especially the older ones, were unable to keep up and were shot down in cold blood. The lack of any visible emotion in the killers continued to amaze me. Many of the victims fought for their lives until the very last minute, pleading in vain with their executioners for mercy, while others, having witnessed too many earlier killings with no mercy shown, accepted their deaths with resignation. Some prisoners were so hungry they started eating roots and even grass, which caused many of them to develop dysentery, weakening them still further. Most had started the march in fairly good spirits, but now many were losing hope. The battlefront seemed more remote, and we had no idea whatever as to what was going on.

By the sixth or seventh day, Sam was weakening; he had to hold on to my arm most of the time. If we didn't get some food very soon, we wouldn't be able to make it. We were marching in a heavily wooded area, and at night the guards were letting us rest on the edge of these woods.

The killings became very frequent now, as more and more people were collapsing from exhaustion. At least seven hundred in our column were shot to death in two days. We could see hundreds of other corpses alongside the road, left by columns marching ahead of us. The countryside was beautiful, spring was in full bloom. The incongruity between the radiance of the nature around us and the slaughter of innocent people was hard to reconcile.

It was still broad daylight at the end of the seventh day, April 26, and we were lying on the ground, exhausted and hungry, in a corner formed by the country road and a narrow cow path, when suddenly a small white truck appeared and turned into the path. More trucks just like it, perhaps eight or nine in all, followed and stopped, lined up next to each other. They all had red crosses painted on their sides. It seemed like a mirage. A wild thought struck me; maybe they had brought food for us! But that could only be my hunger talking. It was too incredible even to contemplate. Why would the Germans want to feed us now? It was totally inconsistent with all their other actions, and, anyway, they themselves were short of food. Besides, why white trucks with red crosses? We saw a few civilians from the convoy talking to the SS officer in charge. Then the guards ordered some of the stronger prisoners to open the back doors of the trucks, and to my astonishment they started unloading corrugated white boxes marked with red crosses.

A surge of joy rushed through our ranks. Food! It looked like food! And in seconds we heard that it was, as the prisoners unloading the trucks passed the word along to the others. Most of us had risen to our feet. They were piling the boxes up. Hundreds of them were being unloaded, so it couldn't all be for just the SS; it had to be for us!

The guards ordered us to line up, and soon the prisoners at the head of the line were receiving one box for every four people. The guards warned us that the prisoners themselves were responsible for dividing the food evenly, and that anyone who started a fight would be immediately shot. Sam and I were standing far down the line, but it was moving fast. We heard shouts of joy from the prisoners as they tore the boxes open, and cries of "Chocolate! Cheese! Meat!"

I was dizzy from excitement. It was a miracle, a real miracle was happening before our eyes. Someone wanted to save us! Having known for so long nothing but brutality, hardened by the daily inhumanity of the camps, the thousands of deaths, it was hard to take it in, this evidence of some good in man. What did it mean? Who had sent this food? How had they found us in the middle of nowhere? Warshawski, Sam, a friendly Pole, and I received our box, and when we opened it we saw that it came from America. It was neatly packed with two different kinds of cheese, a can of sardines, three or four packages of crackers, including Ritz, a bar of Hershey's chocolate, a can of Spam, a can of powdered milk, and a long package of small, square slices of pumpernickel. We could not believe our eyes. I suggested that I divide everything in the box into four parts,

and we would then alternate choosing our shares. Everyone agreed, and so I set to work, conscious of my heavy responsibility to make sure each share was exactly even.

I divided the crackers first, so we could get something inside us immediately. Next came the sardines, because we had no way to store them. We tried not to cram the food into our mouths, but it was hard to hold back. Our bodies were starved, every cell aching for nourishment. The sardines tasted fantastically good. Each morsel was a little piece of heaven, and every part of my body was crying out, "Thank you! Thank you!" to the food as it traveled through.

I used a spoon which I sharpened on a stone to divide the cheese and the Spam. We had never heard of Spam. It was delicious. How clever of the Americans to invent such a wonderful new kind of food! The chocolate was difficult to divide because it was very hard and crumbly, but I finally managed to cut it up into four equal parts. The powdered milk presented a storage problem, but we had some of it mixed with water, and saved the rest. I kept the chocolate for last. It was so good I was longing to eat my whole share at once, but Sam and I had decided that this food had to last us at least three days, and we each divided our share into little bits.

Since I was stronger than Sam at this point, when the march resumed the following morning I offered to carry his food as well as my own. As we walked along we could talk of nothing but the "miracle." No one told us how the food had got to us, so we could only speculate. Something very unusual must be going on; never before had the SS permitted anything like it. Maybe Hitler was dead; were he still alive, he would never permit anything like that. Or perhaps the war was over. But if so, why were the guards still here? Perhaps the International Red Cross had arranged this, and if so it was a sign that a crack had appeared in the wall with which the SS had isolated us from the rest of the world. Whatever its source, the food not only fed our starving bodies, it gave a lift to our spirits as well. We had not yet reached the end of the road, but at least there was someone out there who cared. Knowing this, I felt more at peace than I had in a long time, and I fell sound asleep. . . .

The march continued, and so did the killings. The distribution of the Red Cross boxes evidently hadn't changed the SS's standing order: Any prisoner who couldn't keep up with the pace was to be shot to death. They were not letting anyone out of their hands alive. However, the shootings weren't quite as frequent now as they had been the day before the food arrived. Those parcels had given us a life-saving infusion of energy and hope. Now once more, as at the beginning, it was legs giving out or injuries to them rather than failing strength that were the main cause of the killings. The column was moving more slowly now, too, and the guards were not hurrying us so much.

Again we stopped for the night at the edge of a forest. The moment of liberation was very close, and we had some food again. If only our legs would hold up, we had a good chance of making it. I slept well that night, and the next morning, April 28, I felt better than I had in a long time. That day went by uneventfully. Sam, Warshawski, and I stayed close together. We ate a little more of the food from the Red Cross, and it was heavenly.

The next morning, after we had marched for an hour or so, we saw a number of dead horses lying on the road, evidently victims of Allied strafing. Frenziedly the prisoners ahead of us were throwing themselves on the carcasses and cutting off hunks of flesh with their stone-sharpened spoons. Some were even trying to tear off pieces with their fingers and teeth. As long as the prisoners stayed on the road, the guards didn't interfere. When the crowd around the carcasses had thinned out a little, Sam and I and some of the other prisoners toward the end of the column cut off some meat for ourselves. It was a grisly business and our spoons weren't sharp enough, but we persisted and got at least a couple of pounds. None of us had anything to put it in, so we stuffed our jackets inside our pants, tightened the pants, and carried the meat inside the jackets above the waist. The meat was bloody, and soon our jackets were soaked with blood. The column looked like a bunch of butchers on the march.

Still there was no relief from the killings; prisoner after prisoner was shot down. It seemed utterly senseless. By now we couldn't be far from the North Sea, and a mad thought struck me: Perhaps the Red Cross had boats waiting to take us to Sweden.

That night we stopped near another forest. A few of the prisoners had brought matches with them from Sachsenhausen, and soon there were hundreds of little fires going. We all sat around them cooking our horsemeat, using the sharpened ends of wooden sticks to hold chunks of it over the flames. This was the first meat I had tasted in almost two years. It was very tough, but I kept at it doggedly chewing each piece as long as I could, knowing that this extra energy could mean the difference between life and death. We ate only part of the meat, saving the rest, for it was still impossible even to guess how much longer we would have to hold out. Why was it taking the Allies so long to reach us? Most of the prisoners were very subdued, as if the long march had dulled our senses; the last few days we had been shuffling along in a sort of stupor.

On the morning of April 30, we were about to resume our march when the little white Red Cross trucks appeared again on the road. Sam and I still had some food left from the first parcel, but many of the others had long since eaten all their share. We greeted the trucks with cheers, not only because of the food, but also because their arrival meant that someone on the outside knew we were alive, cared about us, and was in touch with the SS on our behalf. This time each box had to be shared among five prisoners, so the portions were a little smaller.

But with the horsemeat and what was left over from the first box, our food reserve was building up and Sam and I could afford the luxury of eating a larger part of our portion.

Once again Allied planes appeared, in large numbers and flying very low. We could see them diving in and out over a wide road not far from us that had on it a heavy concentration of German tanks, armored cars, and trucks. They could see us very well, and were clearly taking pains not to hit the column—which was no help to the unfortunate ones who couldn't keep up, and who were still being executed with the same cold, mechanical ruthlessness as before.

When we stopped again for the night, fires soon started up again to cook more of the horsemeat. I didn't eat much of it this time, since I preferred the food from the Red Cross box. Again I slept well in the open air; it was quite warm for that time of year. When the morning of May 1 came, someone suggested that maybe the Russians had been holding off until today, their big national holiday, to liberate us. We marched off once again, still surrounded by the guards. This evacuation, if it could still be called that, was taking much longer than anyone had anticipated. Prisoner after prisoner was killed, the bodies still littering the road. I knew that if it hadn't been for the Red Cross food, it would have been far worse; many more prisoners would have been dead by now.

I looked around. We were all filthy, unshaven, our striped suits soaked with blood from the horsemeat. Many were stumbling along, unable to walk. I occupied my mind with wondering how those food parcels had reached us, but could arrive at no explanation. We came upon more dead horses lying on the road and replenished our supply of meat, throwing away what had been left from before; it had started to go bad.

In the evening we stopped at the edge of another forest, and the SS guards stationed themselves as usual around us to make sure no one escaped. Now that we had a fresh supply of meat, hundreds of fires started again. A Pole who had been walking along with Sam, Warshawski, and me during the last few days, who had been a truck driver before the war, ate prodigious quantities of the horsemeat with relish, but I had to force myself. That truck driver was a good-natured fellow who probably suspected that we were Jews but never asked outright, and we of course volunteered nothing. For dessert I ate a little more of the chocolate I had left, promising myself that if I survived, I would eat nothing else for the rest of my life.

Night fell, the fires were extinguished, and we went to sleep. From time to time I woke up at the noise from the military vehicles moving along the road. Early next morning, before we had to set out on the march again, the fires were started up to cook some more of the horsemeat. We were all sitting around our fires, holding chunks of the meat on sticks over the flames, when a voice came from the edge of the forest: "The guards are gone."

See also death marches, Vol. 1.

Jews Are, for Now, a Necessary Evil

In this 1928 polemic, Nazi philosopher Alfred Rosenberg describes Jews as materialistic, antispiritual, and a force for disorder and lawlessness. Yet, he continues, they serve as a continual reminder of Germany's mission to save the world.

L et us repeat once more, and again and again, the most important point that has been made up to now: the Jewish religion completely lacks the belief in a supra-sensible Beyond. Indeed, one even gets an almost positive impression that, in the course of time, everything that in the least could foster a belief in an incorporeal life after death was intentionally eliminated. The Jews, with their religion oriented to purely earthly affairs, stand alone in the world! This should not be forgotten for a single moment; it is highly significant. For it is this exceptional situation which explains why a "shady nation" such as that of the Jews has survived the greatest and most glorious nations, and will continue to survive, until the end of all time, until the hour of salvation strikes for all mankind. The Jewish nation will not perish before this hour strikes. The world is preserved, as we shall see, only by a positive yea-saying to the world. Among the Jewish people this world-affirmation is totally pure, without any admixture of world-denial. All other nations that have ever existed, and exist today, had, or have, such an admixture, characterized by the idea of a Hereafter, even if only a trace of it. This mere trace would have sufficed, or would suffice, to provide the necessary counterweight to the unadulterated yea-saying to

the world, as embodied in the Jewish people. For the inner light—and belief in immortality is the inner light—does not need always to shine with the brightest glow in order to produce an effect; it must simply be there, it must not be allowed to be snuffed out, or otherwise mankind would be lost forever to the terrestrial world. Everything takes its own time, however, a fact which is all too often overlooked. The denial of the world needs a still longer time in order to grow so that it will acquire a lasting predominance over affirmation of the world. At this time it seems again to have sunk to a zero point; its opposite, symbolized by the Jewish people, is triumphant as never before. It seems as if the inner light has completely vanished from this earth. But, to anticipate, it merely seems that way. Denial of the world cannot perish because it is part of the soul of mankind and the soul is immortal. Where the idea of the immortal dwells, the longing for the eternal or the withdrawal from temporality must always emerge again; hence a denial of the world will always reappear. And this is the meaning of the non-Jewish peoples: they are the custodians of world-negation, of the idea of the Hereafter, even if they maintain it in the poorest way. Hence, one or another of them can quietly go under, but what really matters lives on in their descendants. If, however, the Jewish people were to perish, no nation would be left which would hold world-affirmation in high esteem—the end of all time would be here.

This would also be the case if the Zionist idea were to become a reality, namely, if the entire Jewish people would unite to become a national entity in Palestine or somewhere else. Such a unification of Jews has never ex-

George L. Mosse, ed., *Nazi Culture.* New York: Schocken, 1981.

isted before: this must be stressed not twice but three times, inasmuch as it is little known. Long before the destruction of the Temple in Jerusalem [ca. A.D. 81] a large part of the Jews lived in the diaspora, that is, dispersed among the "heathen" people. And, as every schoolboy knows, at the beginning of their history they were "guests" among the Egyptians. What arose afterward in Palestine was anything but a state structure. At best it was an attempt to build one, when it was not a preparatory school for the exploitation or the destruction of foreign peoples. To the Jew Weininger [an early-twentieth-century writer] his own nation is like an invisible cohesive web of slime fungus (*plasmodium*), existing since time immemorial and spread over the entire earth; and this expansionism, as he correctly observes (without, of course, proving it), is an essential component of the idea, of the nature of Judaism. This immediately becomes clear if we again regard the Jewish people as the embodiment of world-affirmation. Without it, nothing of a terrestrial character, and thus no nation, is conceivable. Hence, the Jew, the only consistent and consequently the only viable yea-sayer to the world, must be found wherever other men bear in themselves—if only in the tiniest degree—a compulsion to overcome the world. The Jew represents the still necessary counterweight to them; otherwise that urgent craving would be fulfilled immediately and thereby would not usher in the salvation of the world (since the Jewish people would still remain in existence), but would destroy it in a different way through the elimination of the spiritual power without which it cannot exist either. I will discuss this idea more fully later on; here I wish merely to demonstrate that the world could not exist if the Jews were living by themselves. This is why an old prophecy proclaims that the end of the world will arrive on the day when the Jews will have established the state of Palestine . . .

From all this it follows that Judaism is part of the organism of mankind just as, let

The racist ideology of Alfred Rosenberg was the basis of many of the Third Reich's anti-Semitic policies.

us say, certain bacteria are part of man's body, and indeed the Jews are as necessary as bacteria. The body contains, as we know, a host of tiny organisms without which it would perish, even though they feed on it. Similarly, mankind needs the Jewish strain in order to preserve its vitality until its earthly mission is fulfilled. In other words, the world-affirmation exemplified by Judaism in its purest form, though disastrous in itself, is a condition of man's earthly being—as long as men exist—and we cannot even imagine its nonexistence. It will collapse only when all mankind is redeemed.

Thus, we are obliged to accept the Jews among us as a necessary evil, for who knows how many thousands of years to come. But just as the body would become stunted if the bacteria increased beyond a salutary number, our nation too—to describe a more limited circle—would gradually succumb to a spiritual malady if the Jew were to become too much for it. Were he to leave us entirely (this is the aim of Zionism, or at least what it pretends to be) it would be just as disastrous as if he were to dominate us. The mission of the German nation will come to an end—and this is my firm conviction—with the last hour of mankind. But we could never reach it if we lost world-affirmation, the Jew among us, because no life is possible without world-affirmation. On the other hand, if the Jew were continually to stifle us, we would never be able to fulfill our mission, which is the salvation of the world, but would, to be frank, succumb to insanity, for pure world-affirmation, the unrestrained will for a vain existence, leads to no other goal. It would literally lead to a void, to the destruction not only of the illusory earthly world but also of the truly existent, the spiritual. Considered in himself the Jew represents nothing else but this blind will for destruction, the insanity of mankind. It is known

that Jewish people are especially prone to mental disease. "Dominated by delusions," said [German philosopher Arthur] Schopenhauer about the Jew. . . . To strip the world of its soul, that and nothing else is what Judaism wants. This, however, would be tantamount to the world's destruction.

Even now, while the Jews still live among us, all their undertakings reveal this aim, and necessarily so. Their aim is to strip mankind of its soul. This is why they endeavor to break any form behind which the living soul is operative. For as arch-materialists it is their insane opinion that it is precisely the spiritual, which they sense only obscurely, that is connected with the form as a matter of life and death and must perish with it. Hence they are also, all and sundry, anarchists, consciously or unconsciously. In fact, they cannot be anything else but opponents of order and law, because order and law, in a unique way, bear the radiant imprint of a purer world. [German poet Friedrich] Schiller calls order "the daughter of heaven," and for the divine origin of law we find much evidence in Schiller and still more in [poet and writer Johann Wolfgang von] Goethe.

Without order and law no conception of state can be actualized, since they are the indispensable foundation for it. For this very reason, the Jew, the mortal enemy of order and law, can never create a viable state in Palestine. The result would again be chaos. For this word, correctly translated, means an infinite void, nothingness.

See also anti-Semitism, Vol. 1; racial science, Vol. 2; Rosenberg, Alfred, Vol. 3.

Life in the Warsaw Ghetto

A Jewish chronicler describes the over-crowding and squalor of the Warsaw ghetto, where between 1940 and 1942 hundreds of thousands of Jews were packed into a few city blocks.

On the streets children are crying in vain, children who are dying of hunger. They howl, beg, sing, moan, shiver with cold, without underwear, without clothing, without shoes, in rags, sacks, flannel which are bound in strips round the emaciated skeletons, children swollen with hunger, disfigured, half conscious, already completely grown-up at the age of five, gloomy and weary of life. They are like old people and are only conscious of one thing: 'I'm cold'. 'I'm hungry'. They have become aware of the most important things in life that quickly. Through their innocent sacrifice and their frightening helplessness the thousands upon thousands of these little beggars level the main accusation against the proud civilization of today. Ten per cent of the new generation have already perished: every day and every night hundreds of these children die and there is no hope that anybody will put a stop to it.

There are not only children. Young and old people, men and women, bourgeois and proletarians, intelligentsia and business people are all being declassed and degraded . . . They are being gobbled up by the streets on to which they are brutally and ruthlessly thrown. They beg for one month, for two months, for three months—but they all go down-hill and die on the street or in hospitals from cold, or hunger, or sickness, or depression. Former human beings whom no

one needs fall by the wayside: former citizens, former 'useful members of human society.'

I no longer look at people; when I hear groaning and sobbing I go over to the other side of the road; when I see something wrapped in rags shivering with cold, stretched out on the ground I turn away and do not want to look . . . I can't. It's become too much for me. And yet only an hour has passed . . .

For various reasons standards of hygiene are terribly poor. Above all, the fearful population density in the streets with which nowhere in Europe can be remotely compared. The fatal over-population is particularly apparent in the streets: people literally rub against each other, it is impossible to pass unhindered through the streets. And then the lack of light, gas, and heating materials. Water consumption is also much reduced; people wash themselves much less and do not have baths or hot water. There are no green spaces, gardens, parks: no clumps of trees and no lawns to be seen. For a year no one has seen a village, a wood, a field, a river or a mountain: no one has breathed slightly better air for even a few days this year. Bedding and clothing are changed very rarely because of the lack of soap. To speak of food hygiene would be a provocation and would be regarded as mockery. People eat what is available, however much is available and when it is available. Other principles of nutrition are unknown here. Having said all this, one can easily draw one's own conclusions as to the consequences: stomach typhus and typhus, dysentery, tuberculosis, pneumonia, influenza, metabolic disturbances, the most common digestive illnesses, lack of vitamins and all other illnesses associated with the lack of bread, fresh air, clothing, and heating materials. Typhus is systematically

J. Noakes and G. Pridham, eds., *Nazism 1919–1945,* Vol.3, *Foreign Policy, War, and Racial Extermination: A Documentary Reader.* Exeter, England: University of Exeter Press, 1988.

and continually destroying the population. There are victims in every family. On average up to a thousand people are dying each month. In the early morning the corpses of beggars, children, old people, young people and women are lying in every street—the victims of the hunger and the cold. The hospitals are so terribly overcrowded that there are 2–3 patients lying in every bed. Those who do not find a place in a bed lie on the floor in rooms and corridors. The shortage of the necessary medicines in sufficient quantities makes it impossible to treat the sick. Moreover, there is a shortage of food for the sick. There is only soup and tea . . .

While this cruel struggle for a little bit of bread, for a few metres of living space, for the maintenance of health, energy and life is going on, people are incapable of devot-

ing much energy and strength to intellectual matters. In any case, there are German restrictions and bans. Nothing can be printed, taught or learnt. People are not allowed to organize themselves or exchange cultural possessions. We are cut off from the world and from books. It is not permitted to open libraries and sort out books from other printed materials. We are not allowed to print anything, neither books nor newspapers; schools, academic institutions etc. are not permitted to open. There are no cinemas, radio, no contacts with world culture. Nothing reaches us, no products of the human spirit reach us. We have to smuggle in not only food stuffs and manufactured goods, but also cultural products.

See also ghettos, Final Solution, Vol. 1; Warsaw ghetto uprising, Vol. 2.

Rules at Dachau

Dachau was the first major concentration camp administered by the SS. Opened near Munich in 1933, it became the model for camp structure and administration for the duration of the Third Reich. Its regulations made it clear that both prisoners and guards could expect harsh treatment if they fail to obey.

*I*ntroduction. The following regulations on punishment are issued for the maintenance of discipline and order within the area of the Dachau Concentration Camp as part of the existing camp regulations.

All internees of the Dachau Concentration Camp are subject to these regulations from the time of their imprisonment to the hour of their release.

Jeremy Noakes and Geoffrey Pridham, eds., *Documents on Nazism, 1919–1945*. New York: Viking, 1974.

Authority for ordering punishments lies in the hands of the camp commander, who is personally responsible to the political police commander for the carrying out of the camp regulations.

Tolerance means weakness. In the light of this conception, punishment will be mercilessly handed out whenever the interests of the fatherland warrant it. The fellow countryman who is decent but misled will never be affected by these regulations. But let it be a warning both to the inciting politicians and to intellectual agitators, no matter which: watch out that you are not caught, for otherwise it will be your neck and you will be dealt with according to your own methods. . . .

Article 6. The following are punishable with eight days' solitary confinement, and twenty-five strokes to be administered before and after the serving of the sentence:

Young prisoners at Dachau, the first Nazi concentration camp, cheer as the U.S. Army liberates the camp on April 29, 1945.

1. Anyone making depreciatory or ironical remarks to a member of the SS, deliberately omitting the prescribed marks of respect, or in any other way demonstrating unwillingness to submit himself to disciplinary measures.

2. Prisoner-sergeants and prisoner squad leaders or foremen who exceed their authority as orderlies, assume the privileges of a superior over other prisoners, accord like-minded prisoners special privileges in work or in any other way, tyrannize over fellow prisoners who have political views different from their own, make false reports on them, or prejudice them in any other way.

Article 7. The following are punishable with two weeks' solitary confinement:

1. Anyone exchanging by his own volition, without being authorized by the company commander, the quarters to which he is assigned, or instigating or inducing his fellow prisoners to do so.

2. Anyone enclosing or hiding forbidden articles or articles produced in the camp in outgoing laundry bundles, or sewing them into pieces of laundry, etc.

3. Anyone entering or leaving barracks, shelters, or other building by other than authorized entrances, or creeping through windows or other openings.

4. Anyone smoking in shelters, toilets and places which are fire hazards, or keeping or depositing inflammable objects in such places. If a fire results from neglect of

this prohibition, it will be considered as an act of sabotage.

Article 8. The following are punishable with two weeks' solitary confinement and twenty-five strokes to be administered before and after the serving of the sentence:

1. Anyone leaving or entering the internment camp without an escort or who joins an outgoing work detail without proper authority.

2. Anyone making depreciatory remarks in letters or other documents about National Socialist leaders, the State and Government, authorities and institutions, glorifying Marxist or liberal leaders or November [Weimar] parties, or reporting on occurrences in the concentration camp.

3. Anyone keeping forbidden articles, tools, or weapons in his quarters or in palliasses. . . .

Article 11. In accordance with the law on revolutionaries, the following offenders, considered as agitators, will be hanged. Anyone who, for the purpose of agitating, does the following in the camp, at work, in the sleeping quarters, in the kitchens and workshops, toilets and places of rest: discusses politics, carries on controversial talks and meetings, forms cliques, loiters around with others; who, for the purpose of supplying the propaganda of the opposition with atrocity stories, collects true or false information about the concentration camp; receives such information, buries it, talks about it to others, smuggles it out of the camp into the hands of foreign visitors or others by clandestine or other means, passes it on in writing or by word of month to released prisoners or prisoners who are placed over them, conceals it in clothing or other articles, throws stones and other objects over the camp wall containing such information; or produces secret documents; or, for the purpose of agitating, climbs on barrack roofs or trees, seeks contact with the outside world by giving light or other signals, or induces others to escape or commit a crime, gives

them advice to that effect or supports such undertakings in any way whatsoever. . . .

Article 19. Confinement will be in a cell, with a hard bed, and with bread and water. The prisoner will receive warm food every four days. Punitive work consists of severe physical or particularly dirty work, performed under close supervision. Incidental punishments are: drilling, beatings, withholding of mail and food, hard rest, tying to stakes, reprimands and warnings.

All punishments will be recorded on files.

Confinement and punitive labour prolong the term of internment by at least eight weeks, an incidental punishment by four weeks. Prisoners in solitary confinement will not be released for a considerable time. . . .

Anyone letting a prisoner escape will be arrested and handed over to the Bavarian Political Police for liberating prisoners through negligence.

If a prisoner attempts to escape, he is to be shot without warning. The guard who has shot an escaping prisoner in the line of duty will not be punished.

If a prisoner attacks a guard, the latter is to resist the attack not by physical force but by the use of his weapons. A guard disregarding this regulation must expect his immediate dismissal. In any case anyone who keeps his back covered will seldom have to worry about an attack.

If a unit of prisoners mutinies or revolts, it is to be shot at by all supervising guards. Warning shots are forbidden on principle.

The work time is determined by the camp commander. A guard who brings his prisoners back too early is guilty of serious dereliction of duty and can be dismissed.

Should a work detachment be obliged to stop its work prematurely for some reason or other, then the work detachment leader must have the reason certified on the back of the work service slip by either the construction division or the requisitioning office.

See also concentration camps, Dachau, Vol. 1; SS, Vol. 2.

The Wannsee Conference Protocols

On January 20, 1942, SS police and security chief Reinhard Heydrich met with a number of Third Reich officials at a villa in the Berlin suburb of Wannsee. In the following record of the infamous meeting, he announces that Hitler, Göring, and Himmler have decided on a "Final Solution to the Jewish Question" and that the SS is going to carry it out. Acting secretary and recorder of the proceedings is SS lieutenant colonel Adolf Eichmann.

P ROTOCOL OF CONFERENCE
I. The following took part in the conference on the final solution of the Jewish question held on January 20, 1942, in Berlin, Am Grossen Wannsee No. 56–58:

> *Gauleiter* Dr. Meyer and Reich,
>   Office Director Dr. Leibbrandt
> Secretary of State Dr. Stuckart
> Secretary of State Neumann
> Secretary of State Dr. Freisler
> Secretary of State Dr. Bühler
> Undersecretary of State Dr. Luther
> SS *Oberführer* Klopfer
> Ministerial Director Kritzinger
> SS *Gruppenführer* Hofmann
> SS *Gruppenführer* Müller
> SS *Obersturmbanifführer* Eichmann
> SS *Oberführer* Dr. Schöngarth,
>   Commander of the Security Police
>   and the SD in the Government-
>   General
> Reich Ministry for the Occupied
>   Eastern Territories
> Reich Ministry of the Interior
> Plenipotentiary for the Four Year Plan

Rita Steinhardt Botwinick, ed., *A Holocaust Reader: From Ideology to Annihilation.* Upper Saddle River, NJ: Prentice-Hall, 1997.

> Reich Ministry of Justice
> Office of the Governor General
> Foreign Ministry
> Party Chancellery
> Reich Chancellery
> Race and Settlement Main Office
> Reich Security Main Office
> Reich Security Main Office
> Security Police and SD
> SS *Sturmbannführer* Dr. Lange,
>   Commander of the Security Police
>   and the SD in the [Latvian
>   Jurisdiction] as Representative
>   of the Commander of the Security
>   Police and the SD for the
>   *Reichskommissariat* for the
>   *Ostland*
> Security Police and SD

II. The meeting opened with the announcement by the Chief of the Security Police and the SD, SS *Obergruppenführer* Heydrich, of his appointment by the Reich Marshal [Göring] as Plenipotentiary for the Preparation of the Final Solution of the European Jewish Question. He noted that this Conference had been called in order to obtain clarity on questions of principle. The Reich Marshal's request for a draft plan concerning the organizational, practical and economic aspects of the final solution of the European Jewish question required prior joint consideration by all central agencies directly involved in these questions, with a view to maintaining parallel policy lines.

Responsibility for the handling of the final solution of the Jewish question, he said, would lie centrally with the *Reichsführer* SS [Himmler] and the Chief of the German Police (Chief of the Security Police and the SD), without regard to geographic boundaries.

The Chief of the Security Police and the SD then gave brief review of the struggle conducted up to now against this foe.

The most important elements are:

a) Forcing the Jews out of the various areas of life of the German people.
b) Forcing the Jews out of the living space of the German people.

In pursuit of these aims, the accelerated emigration of the Jews from the area of the Reich, as the only possible provisional solution, was pressed forward and carried out according to plan.

On instructions by the Reich Marshal, a Reich Central Office for Jewish Emigration was set up in January 1939, and its direction entrusted to the Chief of the Security Police and the SD. Its tasks were, in particular:

a) To take all measures for the *preparation* of increased emigration of the Jews;
b) To *direct* the flow of emigration;
c) To speed up emigration in *individual* cases.

The aim of this task was to cleanse the German living space of Jews in a legal manner.

The disadvantages engendered by such forced pressing of emigration were clear to all the authorities. But in the absence of other possible solutions, they had to be accepted for the time being.

In the period that followed, the handling of emigration was not a German problem alone, but one with which the authorities of the countries of destination or immigration also had to deal. Financial difficulties—such as increases ordered by the various foreign governments in the sums of money that immigrants were required to have and in landing fees—as well as lack of berths on ships and continually tightening restrictions or bans on immigration, hampered emigration efforts very greatly. Despite these difficulties a total of approximately 537,000 Jews were caused to emigrate between the assumption of power and up to October 31, 1941.

These consisted of the following:

From January 30, 1933: from the *Altreich* [Germany before 1938], Approx. 360,000

From March 15, 1938: from the *Ostmark* [Austria], Approx. 147,000

From March 15, 1939: from the Protectorate of Bohemia and Moravia, Approx. 30,000

The financing of the emigration was carried out by the Jews or Jewish political organizations themselves. To prevent the remaining behind of proletarianized Jews, the principle was observed that wealthy Jews must finance the emigration of the Jews without means; to this end, a special assessment or emigration levy, in accordance with wealth owned, was imposed, the proceeds being used to meet the financial obligations of the emigration of destitute Jews.

In addition to the funds raised in German marks, foreign currency was needed for the monies which emigrants were required to show on arrival abroad and for landing fees. To conserve the German holdings of foreign currency, Jewish financial institutions abroad were persuaded by Jewish organizations in this country to make themselves responsible for finding the required sums in foreign currency. A total of about $9,500,000 was provided by these foreign Jews as gifts up to October 30, 1941.

In the meantime, in view of the dangers of emigration in war-time, and the possibilities in the East, the *Reichsführer* SS and Chief of the German Police has forbidden the emigration of Jews.

III. Emigration has now been replaced by evacuation of the Jews to the East, as a further possible solution, with the appropriate prior authorization by the Führer.

However, this operation should be regarded only as a provisional option; but it is already supplying practical experience of great significance in view of the coming final solution of the Jewish question.

In the course of this final solution of the European Jewish question approximately 11 million Jews may be taken into consideration, distributed over the individual countries as follows:

Country	Number
A. *Altreich*	131,800
Ostmark	43,700
Eastern Territories	420,000
Government-General	2,284,000
Bialystok	400,000
Protectorate of Bohemia and Moravia	74,200
Estonia—free of Jews	
Latvia	3,500
Lithuania	34,000
Belgium	43,000
Denmark	5,600
France: Occupied territory	165,000
France: Unoccupied territory	700.000
Greece	69,600
Netherlands	160,800
Norway	1,300
B. Bulgaria	48,000
England	330,000
Finland	2,300
Ireland	4,000
Italy, including Sardinia	58,000
Albania	200
Croatia	40,000
Portugal	3,000
Rumania, including Bessarabia	342,000
Sweden	8,000
Switzerland	18,000
Serbia	10,000
Slovakia	88,000
Spain	6,000
Turkey (in Europe)	55,000
Hungary	742,800
U.S.S.R.	5,000,000
Ukraine	2,994,684
Byelorussia, without Bialystok	446,484
Total:	over 11,000,000

As far as the figures for Jews of the various foreign countries are concerned, the numbers given include only Jews by religion since the definition of Jews according to racial principles is in part still lacking there. Owing to the prevailing attitudes and concepts, the handling of this problem in the individual countries will encounter certain difficulties, especially in Hungary and Rumania. For instance, in Rumania the Jew can still obtain, for money, documents officially certifying that he holds foreign citizenship.

The influence of the Jews in all spheres of life in the U.S.S.R. is well known. There are about 5 million Jews in European Russia, and barely another 250,000 in Asiatic Russia.

Under appropriate direction the Jews are to be utilized for work in the East in an expedient manner in the course of final solution. In large columns, with the sexes separated, Jews capable of work will be moved into these areas as they build roads, during which a large proportion will no doubt drop out through natural reduction. The remnant that eventually remains will require suitable treatment; because it will without doubt represent the most resistant part, it consists of a natural selection that could, on its release, become the germ cell of a new Jewish revival. (Witness the experience of history.)

Europe is to be combed through from West to East in the course of the practical implementation of the final solution. The area of the Reich, including the Protectorate of Bohemia and Moravia, will have to be handled in advance, if only because of the housing problem and other socio-political needs.

The evacuated Jews will first be taken, group by group, to so-called transit ghettos, in order to be transported further east from there.

An important precondition, SS *Obergruppenführer* Heydrich noted further, for the carrying out of the evacuation in general is the precise determination of the groups of persons involved. It is intended not to evacuate Jews over 65 years old, but to place them in an old-age ghetto—Theresienstadt is being considered.

In addition to these age groups—about 30% of the 280,000 Jews who were present in the *Altreich* and the *Ostmark* October 31, 1941, were over 65 years old—Jews with severe war injuries and Jews with war decorations (Iron Cross, First Class) will be admitted to the Jewish old-age ghetto. This suitable solution will eliminate at one blow the many applications for exceptions.

The start of the individual major evacuation *Aktionen* [Action] will depend largely on military developments. With regard to the handling of the final solution in the European areas occupied by us and under our influence, it was proposed that the officials dealing with this subject in the Foreign Ministry should confer with the appropriate experts in the Security Police and the SD.

In Slovakia and Croatia the matter is no longer too difficult, as the most essential, central problems in this respect have already been brought to a solution there. In Rumania the government has in the meantime also appointed a Plenipotentiary for Jewish Affairs. In order to settle the problem in Hungary, it will be necessary in the near future to impose an adviser for Jewish questions on the Hungarian Government.

With regard to setting in motion preparations for the settling of the problem in Italy, SS *Obergruppenführer* Heydrich considers liaison with the Police Chief in these matters would be in place.

In occupied and unoccupied France the rounding-up of the Jews for evacuation will, in all probability, be carried out without great difficulties.

On this point, Undersecretary of State Luther stated that far-reaching treatment of this problem would meet with difficulties in some countries, such as the Nordic States, and that it was therefore advisable to postpone action in these countries for the present. In view of the small number of Jews involved there, the postponement will in any case not occasion any significant curtailment. On the other hand, the Foreign Ministry foresees no great difficulties for the south-east and west of Europe.

SS *Gruppenführer* Hofmann intends to send a specialist from the Main Office for Race and Settlement to Hungary for general orientation when the subject is taken in hand there by the Chief of the Security Police and the SD. It was decided that this specialist from the Race and Settlement Main Office, who is not to take an active part, will temporarily be designated officially as Assistant to the Police Attaché.

IV. In the implementation of the plan for the final solution, the Nuremberg Laws are to form the basis, as it were; a precondition for the total clearing up of the problem will also require solutions for the question of mixed marriages and *Mischlinge* [people of part-Jewish heritage].

SS *Gruppenführer* Hofmann is of the opinion that extensive use must be made of sterilization, as the *Mischling,* given the choice of evacuation or sterilization, would prefer to accept sterilization.

Secretary of State Dr. Stuckart noted that in this form the practical aspects of the possible solutions proposed above for settling of the problems of mixed marriages and *Mischlinge* would entail endless administrative work. In order to take the biological realities into account, at any rate, Secretary of State Dr. Stuckart proposed a move in the direction of compulsory sterilization.

To simplify the problem of the *Mischlinge* further possibilities should be considered, with the aim that the Legislator should rule something like: "These marriages are dissolved."

As to the question of the effect of the evacuation of the Jews on the economy, Secretary of State Neumann stated that Jews employed in essential war industries could not be evacuated for the present, as long as no replacements were available.

SS *Obergruppenführer* Heydrich pointed out that those Jews would not be evacuated in any case, in accordance with the directives approved by him for the implementation of the current evacuation *Aktion.*

Secretary of State Dr. Bühler put on record that the Government-General would welcome it if the final solution of this problem *was begun in the Government-General,* as, on the one hand, the question of transport there played no major role and considerations of labor supply would not hinder the course of this *Aktion.* Jews must be removed as fast as possible from the Government-General, because it was there in particular that the Jew as carrier of epidemics spelled a great danger, and, at the same time, he caused constant disorder in the economic structure of the country by his continuous black-market dealings. Furthermore, of the approximately 2 1/2 million Jews under consideration, the majority were in any case *unfit for work.*

Secretary of State Dr. Bühler further states that the solution of the Jewish question in the Government-General was pri-marily the responsibility of the Chief of the Security Police and the SD and that his work would have the support of the authorities of the Government-General. He had only one request: that the Jewish question in this area be solved as quickly as possible.

In conclusion, there was a discussion of the various possible forms which the solution might take, and here both *Gauleiter* Dr. Meyer and Secretary of State Dr. Bühler were of the opinion that certain preparatory work for the final solution should be carried out locally in the area concerned, but that in doing so, alarm among the population must be avoided.

The conference concluded with the request of the Chief of the Security Police and the SD to the participants at the conference to give him the necessary support in carrying out the tasks of the [final] solution.

See also Final Solution, Vol. 1; Wannsee Conference, Vol. 2; Eichmann, Adolf; Heydrich, Reinhard, Vol. 3.

CHAPTER FOUR

EVERYDAY LIFE IN THE THIRD REICH

In addition to the Third Reich's legacies of war and Holocaust, modern research has focused increasingly on the way ordinary people lived under Adolf Hitler and his regime. Historians and psychologists examine accounts of the period to understand the Nazis' attempts to intimidate and brainwash their fellow Germans as well as the ways people responded to those attempts.

One of the major efforts of the Nazi regime during the 1930s was to connect all aspects of German life to Nazi goals and beliefs through the process known as Gleichschaltung, or "coordination." Nazi officials and policy makers tried to establish control over education, the churches, and the arts, and they also established special organizations for workers, for women, and for young people. Many leading Nazis truly believed that these organizations worked for the good of individuals as well as the good of the state, and many Germans shared this belief. For a few years, at least, Adolf Hitler brought Germany an energy and dynamism that had been lacking for years. Many Ger-

mans found this exciting enough to ignore the regime's excesses. Moreover, the Nazis consciously tried to ensure ordinary Germans that the regime cared about them. Workers were provided with cheap vacations; women, whom Hitler believed should remain in the home, with inexpensive domestic help and other benefits, and all Germans could take advantage of the Third Reich's many festivals, outings, holidays, and rallies. Even popular songs drummed home the Nazi messages of devotion, sacrifice, and reverence for Adolf Hitler.

Again, most Germans reconciled themselves to the regime. Those who rejected it often claimed that it brought dishonor to Germany and to Germans. If they complained too loudly, however, like the White Rose student protest movement of 1942 and 1943, they were subjected to brutal punishments. Nazi leaders wanted ordinary Germans to believe that they were working for the people, but they were ready to take extreme measures against those Germans who disagreed.

Christianity and Nazism Are Incompatible

One of Hitler's closest advisers, Martin Bormann, argues in 1941 that Christianity, because it is "unscientific" and supports disunity and diversity, is opposed to the Nazi system.

The concepts of National Socialism and Christianity are irreconcilable. The Christian Churches build on people's ignorance and attempt to preserve the ignorance of as wide a section of the population as possible. National Socialism, on the other hand, is based on scientific foundations. Christianity has immutable tenets, laid down nearly 2000 years ago, which have increasingly petrified into dogmas incompatible with reality. National Socialism, on the other hand, if it is to continue to fulfil its task, must always be in accordance with the latest findings of scientific research.

The Christian Churches have always recognized the dangers which threaten their existence in the form of exact scientific knowledge. They have therefore endeavoured by means of pseudo-science, which is what theology is, to suppress or falsify scientific research with their dogma. Our National Socialist ideology is far loftier than the concepts of Christianity, which in their essential points have been taken over from Jewry. For this reason also we have no need of Christianity.

No human being would know anything of Christianity if it had not been drilled into him in his childhood by pastors. The so-called 'dear God' does not by any means give young people advance notice of his existence. Astonishingly, for all his omnipotence, he leaves this to the efforts of the pastors. If, therefore, in the future our youth learns nothing of this Christianity, whose doctrines are far inferior to ours, Christianity will disappear of its own accord.

It is also surprising that before the beginning of the present era nothing was known of this Christian God. Further, since that point in time the vast majority of the earth's inhabitants have never learned anything about this Christianity; so, according to the arrogant but Christian doctrine, they were damned from the start.

If we National Socialists speak of belief in God, we do not understand by God, as the naive Christians and their spiritual camp followers do, a human-type being sitting around somewhere in space. Rather must we open people's eyes to the fact that, apart from our small planet which is very unimportant in the universe, there are an inconceivably large number of other bodies, innumerable additional bodies, which like the sun are surrounded by planets and these in turn by smaller bodies, the moons. The natural force by which all these innumerable planets move in the universe we call 'the Almighty' or 'God'. The claim that this world force is concerned about the fate of every single being, of the tiniest earth bacillus, or can be influenced by so-called prayers or other astonishing things, is based on a proper dose of *naiveté* or else on a calculating shamelessness.

As opposed to that, we National Socialists set ourselves the task of living as naturally as

Jeremy Noakes and Geoffrey Pridham, eds., *Documents on Nazism 1919–1945*. New York: Viking, 1974.

possible, that is to say, biologically. The more accurately we recognize and observe the laws of nature and of life, and the more we adhere to them, so much the more do we conform to the will of the Almighty. The more insight we have into the will of the Almighty, the greater will be our successes.

It follows from the irreconcilability of National Socialist and Christian concepts the we must reject any strengthening of existing denominations or any demand by Christian denominations in the process of emerging. We should not differentiate here between the various Christian denominations. For this reason too the thought of establishing a Reich Evangelical Church by merging the various Evangelical Churches

Hitler deputy Martin Bormann asserted that the government, not the church, should hold ultimate authority over the German people.

has been definitely given up because the Evangelical Church is just as hostile to us as the Catholic Church. Any strengthening of the Evangelical Church would merely redound to our disadvantage.

It was a historical mistake on the part of the German emperors of the Middle Ages that they repeatedly created order at the Vatican in Rome. It is always an error, into which we Germans unfortunately fall too often, to attempt to create order where we ought to have an interest in disunity and separation. . . .

In former generations the leadership of the people lay exclusively in the hands of the Church. The State limited itself to issuing laws and decrees and primarily to administration. The real leadership of the people lay not with the State but with the Churches. The latter exerted through the priest the strongest influence on the life of the individual human being, on families and on the community as a whole. . . . The State was dependent on the aid of the Church. . . .

The ideological dependence of the State on the Church, the yielding of the leadership of the people to the Church, had become a matter of course, so that nobody dared oppose it seriously. To refuse to accept this as an incontrovertible fact from the beginning was considered absurb stupidity until just before the take-over of power.

For the first time in German history, the Führer has the leadership of the people consciously and completely in his own hands. In the Party, its components and its affiliated organizations the Führer has created for himself, and thereby for the German Reich, an instrument which makes him independent of the Church. All influences which might impair or damage the leadership of the people exercised by the Führer with the help of the NSDAP must be eliminated. More and more the people must be separated from the Churches and their organs, the pastors. Of course, from their own viewpoint, the Churches must and will defend themselves against this loss of power.

But never again must influence over the leadership of the people be yielded to the Churches. This influence must be broken finally and completely.

Only the Reich Government and under its direction the Party, its components and affiliated organizations, have the right to the leadership of the people. Just as the deleterious influences of astrologers, seers and other quacks are eliminated and suppressed by the State, so must the possibility of Church influence also be totally removed. Not until this has happened does the leadership of the State have real influence over its individual citizens. Not until then are people and Reich secure in their existence for the future.

It would only repeat the fatal mistakes of past centuries if we were to contribute in any way to the strengthening of one of the various Churches, in view of our knowledge of their ideological hostility towards us. The interest of the Reich lies not in conquering but in preserving and strengthening ecclesiastical particularism.

See also religion in the Third Reich, völkisch state, Vol. 2; Bormann, Martin, Vol. 3.

Brainwashing the Young

This selection from an elementary school reading text used during the Third Reich era suggests that Adolf Hitler, even as a small child, was a leader of men who dreamed of a Greater German Reich.

On the border between Bavaria and Austria lies the small town of Braunau, in which Adolf Hitler was born on 20 April 1889. Braunau belonged to Austria; Hitler's father was an Austrian customs official. There was a lot to see for the little boy at the border. However, he could not understand one thing; the same men lived on either side, they spoke the same language and they had the same appearance, however, on the other side of the River Inn another emperor ruled; here the eagle had two heads on the shield and over there only one. That was really strange.

The boy learned well in school. But he rather played around with the other boys in the meadows and forests. They liked to obey him, and he frequently was the gang leader in their games.

During history classes, his eyes shone with enthusiasm during the teaching periods. That was something for him, to hear about war and heroes. After he had been at home a long time, he still thought about everything he learned in school. Even today he remembers the history teacher with pleasure. He wanted to know more and more of Germany's past. He could not find out enough, and soon he was not satisfied anymore with what he heard in school. He searched for books and read them.

Then one day he found in his home a volume with the heading "The German-French war." He read it through and was glad that he was a boy and could also become a soldier one day. When reading and looking at the pictures, he thought a great deal and could not figure it out:

"Father, on these pictures there aren't any Austrian uniforms; how come?"

"We did not fight then."

"Why not?"

Benjamin C. Sax and Dieter Kuntz, eds., *Inside Hitler's Germany: A Documentary History of Life in the Third Reich.* Lexington, MA: D.C. Heath, 1992.

"We do not belong to Germany, but to Austria."

"But we are also Germans."

"Certainly—but not Reich Germans."

From now on this word would not leave him alone.

"I rather would belong to the German Reich," he answered his father then. The longing awoke in his young heart for one big Reich, which includes all Germans.

See also education in the Third Reich, Vol. 1; Hitler, Adolf, Vol. 3.

Growing Up in Nazi Germany

A German music critic, Werner Burckhardt, tells an interviewer what it was like to be young during the era of the Third Reich.

During the war I started high school in Hamburg. We were lucky. We had a teacher in Latin and Greek who was a pathological democrat. He took dangerous risks in his lectures, this Dr. Drude. When we translated sentences from Latin into German, he wrote on the blackboard: Dr. Gobelius. It was quite obvious to everybody in the class that he was referring to Dr. Goebbels. We had two shaped sentences in Latin: Somebody is lying. Dr. Gobelius is always lying. He was playing with his life.

When there was this strong axis of Rome and Berlin, Dr. Drude came into class one morning with an axle in his hand. He would ride a motorcycle to school. He was a hippie before his time. He pulled this axle from his motorcycle and held it up before the class: "You see, boys? Even an axis can break." We all knew what he meant, of course. Don't you think it was rather daring at the time?

There were twenty-seven of us in class. Fourteen, fifteen years old. It was a miracle

that nothing happened. I'm sure the students told their parents. I know quite well that at least three of the fathers of my friends were Nazis. One was the director of a big insurance firm owned by the Nazis. Nobody betrayed him. I think it was the respect for this man. Maybe they guessed that the end was not too far away for the Hitler regime. That Dr. Drude gave us something that would help us endure. Some kind of humanity.

My father had a dry-cleaning shop in the center of Hamburg's Jewish community. On one side lived the lawyers and doctors. They were assimilated Germans. You did not think of them as Jews. On the other side lived the purer Jews. And the poorer. They owned little shops and lived in small, not so well-looking houses. They were all customers of my father.

When Crystal Night [Kristallnacht] came, I was a small boy. This was 1935 [actually 1938], I was seven. This was the night Nazi anti-Semitism broke out in a big way. My father took me by the hand, Sunday morning, and he showed me the broken windows of the Jewish department stores. All the valuable clothes, silk and all these things, were lying in the dirt of the street or thrown into the water of the Alster River.

My father never talked politics. He was not a sophisticated man. He didn't talk

Studs Terkel, *The Good War: An Oral History of World War II.* New York: Ballantine, 1984.

highbrow or intellectual things. He showed me all this debris and he said this is crazy. You must remember, also, my father was a merchant and he didn't like to see all this destruction of goods.

My father and I didn't talk too much together. There was a silent agreement. We knew these things were wrong. They wanted him to join the Nazi Party. Recruiters very often came into the shop. He said no, he didn't want to. He said he just doesn't have time for these things. He has so much work to do in the shop. He is not interested in politics. He was just evading. No, he didn't defy them. My father hasn't been a hero. He just didn't want to have anything to do with these people for whom he had such contempt. He very clearly saw it as opportunism and that they didn't believe it themselves. He knew some of them personally. These weren't the idealistic type of Nazis. So they felt it was just a waste of time talking to him, and left.

I felt funny when all the Jews were leaving. The richer Jews left for the Netherlands and France. These very big cars stopped before the shop to pick up their wardrobes, cleaned and pressed. The poor Jews picked up whatever they had. They all left and nobody talked about it.

It was just too dangerous to be too frank. Dr. Drude's survival is a miracle. I know that the owner of the café around the corner vanished for a long time. He would talk a lot. Maybe he had been a bit too frank. He came back, but he was now a silent man. It was understood.

Hamburg, you must remember, had a strong democratic tradition. Social democratic, even communist. Because of the port, working people from all over the world came through here. Hitler hated Hamburg. He was only here two times. I even think he was afraid of Hamburg.

When I was at the *Gymnasium* [high school], I had to attend Hitler *Jugend* [Youth] classes, also. We all had to wear a uniform, and every Wednesday we got the life of the Führer told to us and had to repeat it word by word. Not omitting anything, not adding anything. Just as it was. Every Saturday we had to go to the suburbs and play war games. Sort of child play, like hide-and-seek. But there was always this background of war behind it.

When the bombings began in Hamburg, they took all the young boys and girls away to the southern part of Germany and even to Czechoslovakia, to a *Kinderland* [children's camp]. When I came back in '43, I had to go to the Luftwaffe. I was in the flak brigade, to shoot at Allied planes. I was fifteen. . . .

We had to get out of bed every night at eleven o'clock and stay up till two o'clock in the morning. We still had our school lectures. Every morning a teacher would come out in the snow and ice to our camp and give us Latin and Greek. One day that, another day German and history. A third day, mathematics and chemistry. All this and flak brigade.

In '44 I was now sixteen. They wanted to send me to the eastern front. I was caught by the British and became a prisoner of war. I was in this camp till June of '45. They took our watches and we got a little bit beaten, too. They were angry and far away from home.

With the war over, I went back to school. It was in the fall of '45. We had to get the stones out of the ruins and rebuild. I went to the university, Hamburg, and the rest is now.

The old are trying to deny. But in the people who were very young in the Hitler regime and caught a glimpse of the horrors, and in the young today, maybe there is reason for a little bit of hope.

The Narrowing of German Life and Culture

Martha Dodd lived in the Third Reich during the 1930s with her father, William E. Dodd, the American ambassador to Germany. In 1939 she wrote of the dullness and restrictions of German life and culture and the stupid oppression of the Nazi regime.

There is nothing left of German art and science, so absolute is the dictatorship and so devastating the terror and enforcement of it. Before Hitler came to power many writers fled with their families, many of them leaving possessions behind them. Later, the others who could not get out, were put in prison, several tortured to death, as, for instance, the poet Erich Mühsam, or sent to concentration camps. These of course included the writers who were pacifist, liberal, social-democratic, Jewish or Marxist, or in any other way opposed to the reign of the fanatic Hitler. And as it turned out there was not a really good writer left in Germany, with the exception of the rather talented Fallada and aged Hauptmann. Those who by some quirk escaped Hitler's heavy hand are either silenced by capitulation or must write books censored and approved by the Propaganda Ministry.

The theatre and the cinema, relieved of all brilliant Jewish talent, is a trivial thing compared to its former glory. Naturally, all the actors and actresses must be acceptable to the Nazis, must be Aryan, and must conform to Nazi ideals. They must act in plays that have been passed upon or written, if they are modern, by Nazis, and must be directed by the proper people. Occasionally there are revivals of old plays—German classics written by Aryans and glorifying German history, or Shakespeare. One revival in Berlin was withdrawn after the clamor and applause of the audience during the recitation of a passage extolling human freedom. For the most part the theatre season in Berlin is so dull few people do more than laugh at the appearance of a new play. Once there was a dramatic version of the life of Thomas Paine. It had been so perverted to fit into the Nazi conception of the character that my father left in the middle of the second act. Production and staging jog along in a heavy boring rhythm of mediocrity. None of the brilliance, innovation, and imagination that existed before Hitler and in the Reinhardt days can be found in the contemporary theatre.

In the movies the situation is even worse—if that is possible. German comedy is at best a pathetically heavy-handed slapstick affair. A sense of humor is not a noted German trait and, under Nazism, when the nominal humor the Germans do have must be so restricted, it is especially conspicuous by its absence. The movies of a more serious nature are so dull and so devoted to the extolling of Nazi and national virtues that it is a bore to have to see one. It is a tragic state of affairs when one remembers that the German cinema before Hitler was known over the world for its daring and artistic experimentation. Emil Jannings was perhaps Germany's best actor, but the recent movies he has been forced to appear in are slowly ruining even his reputation.

One would think that the Nazis, realizing the lamentable quality of their movies and the lack of box-office success, might try to import good foreign pictures. On the contrary, however, the same kind of rules and

Martha Dodd, *Through Embassy Eyes*. New York: Harcourt, Brace, 1939.

regulations apply to all movies. Charlie Chaplin is forbidden in Germany because he is Jewish, the same applies to the Marx brothers and many other—both comic and seriously dramatic—American movie stars. Once the Germans were in love with Sylvia Sidney; her pictures were on Kurfürstendamm and her photos in the papers. Unfortunately one day a bright young man found out she was Jewish and from that time on there was a boycott of Sylvia Sidney in Germany. Not only is the Jewish boycott considered in censorship of foreign importations but also the type of picture. If the foreign movies were pacifistic or too flippant or in other ways failed to meet the standards of pure Aryan elevation they were not shown. Yet whenever a foreign picture does come to town it usually outlasts the local productions by weeks and often months.

Since Furtwängler has agreed to knuckle under to the Nazis (after a few minor squabbles), for which Toscanini branded him publicly as irresponsible, one can still attend fine concerts and hear good music. There were other great German conductors and composers who were evicted from Germany or who left of their own accord. Erich Kleiber, co-conductor of the Berlin Philharmonic, a conscientious, excellent, and progressive man with fine musical knowledge and restraint, not specializing in Furtwängler's displays of personality, was removed from his post and found a place in Vienna temporarily.

Naturally jazz of any type is loathed and feared by Hitler. It represents to him the International Marxist-Jewish conspiracy. It is not based solely upon the Germanic rhythms, as he demands of all music, but rather on rhythms that are deep in every human being. Consequently, "swing" or any other variation of jazz is primitive, depraved—in the "sub-human world spirit" class of music. Only a few night clubs attempt to play jazz and they are very bad. Hitler allows two or three such places to stay open in Berlin for the sake of the for-eigners and diplomats living in and visiting the German capital—foreigners who pay heavily into Nazi coffers. The permission is reluctantly given and may cease at any moment. One never hears jazz among the true Germanic crowds.

Fritz Kreisler, though not Jewish according to all reports, a Viennese of world-wide fame, is not allowed to play in Germany though he resides there with his American wife. He is a gentle, non-political soul, though once he expressed his fervent admiration for Mussolini. Hitler, however, doesn't like him. A good friend of [Putzi] Hanfstaengl's, who was always a welcome guest at their home, one sees him usually at diplomatic homes, among Germans and foreigners not connected with the government, and hardly ever at a Nazi function of any sort. Perhaps they have traced a touch of Jewish blood in his or his wife's veins—I don't know—perhaps he once expressed himself against Hitler, perhaps he is a pacifist, or perhaps the Nazis think him inferior to their non-existent musical talent. In any case, Hanfstaengl used to rant at length about how "when once he got his dear Fuehrer to see or hear Kreisler," he was sure the Leader would agree to his appearing in Germany. It may be also that Kreisler himself, the fine and beautiful spirit that he is, would not play, even if he could, in Nazi Germany.

Many foreign musicians still come to Germany; on the other hand, there are many who refuse to set their foot in Nazi-land even though they are not Jewish, as, for instance, Toscanini. By restricting their native and foreign artists to pure Aryans, the Nazis have eliminated from the cultural life of their nation many of the greatest musicians, interpretative and creative, in the world.

Of course, in the realm of painting, sculpture, and architecture the same conditions of sterility exist. Hitler has announced both privately and publicly that he will have none of the "new-fangled notions" in art. In his Munich art show in 1937 he collected what he and his friends thought were the best examples of German art. The general impression of the exhibit was one of colored photography. Among the black list were many extraordinary and creative talents. If his criticism of art were applied to foreign art as well, by the logic of his choices for the Munich Gallery, he would be forced to eliminate artists like Cézanne, Gauguin, Renoir, Van Gogh, and most of the great French modern school which represents the only revolution in art in centuries. All of these geniuses he would have to throw to the dust can. In their stead he would idealize and glorify to a degree of uncontrolled and passionate approval, all art that is naturalistic and unimaginative—any tribute to Germanic culture and Teutonic giants. Most such pictures would actually be photographs tinted as paintings. His favorite picture of himself, which caused hilarious amusement all over Germany, except with worshipful and artistically ignorant Nazis, is such an absurd and horrible caricature of painting, it can serve as graphic symbol of Hitler's bad taste.

Hitler's antagonism to modern architecture is as intense as that to modern painting. He disapproves heartily of such structures as Columbus Haus and Shell Haus in Berlin, two stunning and effective examples of steel and glass made into office buildings. It was constantly rumored that he planned to tear them down. Whenever a new building is constructed its architect and his plans have to pass the rigid censorship of the Nazis. And all new party buildings represent what Hitler believes to be art and they can be seen all over Germany and especially in Munich where a new Nazi city is being constructed, so to speak, on the ashes of the old Munich.

It is obvious that his ideals of art stem from his own frustrated ambitions as a painter and an architect. It is equally obvious that the enforcement of his ideals in this particular line would be as strict and ruthless as other enforcements, especially because he believes he knows this field better than others and because he was formerly denied the right to realize his "genius." Now he can run rampant with no one to stop him, designate the type of art to be produced in Germany, and even design the buildings himself. It is not surprising then that the suppression of artistic talent not in conformance to his vision is drastic. It is more difficult for artists to express in their art any opposition to Hitler than it is for writers. They cannot subtly imply sarcasm in the construction of a building, or paint a picture which, if interpreted in reverse, would reveal a denunciation.

The fashionable sculptor of the moment is a Scandinavian named Thorak whom I saw on many occasions and who was a dear friend of Hanfstaengl's. He has done busts of many of the great and near-great in the world. He has a tremendous, heavy, and heroic style. He is liked by Hitler because no matter what sort of face he does he will instill it with a brute strength, a power and vitality striking to the eye—whether it is there in the face or not. He told me once he thought Hitler's bust—for which he was commissioned—would be a difficult task indeed. He compared it to Mussolini's, and if I am not mistaken Mustafa Kemal's, and deplored the lack of sculptural line in it and the labor necessary to make it appear as compellingly powerful as Hitler wanted it to be. He was commissioned to do the Berlin Exhibit in Paris last summer. In front of the buildings was a group of men and women which took away your breath with its sheer strength and brute force. The heads were the size of enlarged peas and the bodies huge hulking blobs of stone formalized into a synthetic Teutonic beauty. Thorak, a little man somewhat over five feet, with a homely, attractive, and twisted face, has been lashed to the wheel of Nazi art which crushed under its weight all of the delicate, subtle, and genius-torn creations of art and labeled them neurotic, Jewish, Marxist, or sub-human.

The state of German universities is well known throughout the world. The three best historians in Germany were either retired or dismissed at the time my brother was taking his degree in Berlin. There has been a continuous stream of intellectual emigrants to America and England since Hitler came to power. It is exciting to know that we have so profited by the Nazi dictatorship but it is tragic for German youth. There is no university in Germany now that can honorably bear that name. They are all elevated institutions of Nazi propaganda. The number of students has decreased, and especially of women students—who can be at most ten per cent of the matriculated student body—almost to the extent of satisfying Hitler, who believes, perhaps because of his own lack of intellectual ability or training, that young people have had too much education in the past. History, not to mention all the other relevant subjects, must be interpreted from the Nazi racial and historical point of view. The rectors of the universities are, if possible, Nazis, either by membership or by policy, and the professors must take oaths of loyalty to the regime. When they come into the classroom and when they leave, they must Heil Hitler. They cannot say or write anything derogatory to Hitler or to the past of Germany as it has been molded to Hitler's taste. Of course, contemporary history—that from the World War to the present—must be treated with infinite care. Stresemann and the Weimar Republic, all the statesmen and officials of the Democratic era, are either ignored or calumniated disgracefully. There can be no real research in subjects that impinge upon any of the Nazi theories, and these theories exist in and dominate every field of intellectual life, from anthropology to English literature. Thousands of professors, including naturally some Jews, have emigrated to other countries, hundreds have been retired or dismissed, many have been quietly put away somewhere, and innumerable courageous men must hold their tongues forever or answer with their freedom and safety.

Students are not encouraged to go to universities—there are too many other careers open for young men and women who accept the Nazi tenets of faith. If they do resist going into the army or into the Party work and insist on a university education, they must first go through a year's training in a labor camp. Here they are taught Nazi propaganda and are forced to live as peasants for the period of time they are there. This accords with the Nazi theory of *blut und boden*, the sacredness of Germanic blood and soil, which all good Germans must experience. After this rigorous training, they are allowed to attend a university in restricted numbers which are passed upon, either by the Nazis themselves or their agents in the universities, and must not forget to Heil Hitler and live and think according to Nazi standards. Hitler's plan is that if his education scheme works, from the cradle up, it will not matter what sort of material the student gets his hands on in a university. By that time he will be so conditioned to Nazi theories and ways of life that he will not be influenced by anything else. One only has to read the "Nazi Primer" to see what is in store for young people who may or may not decide to enter the university much later in their lives.

Brawn, not brain, is the ultimate end of university training for both men and women. If a student reveals himself to be proficient at sports and military training, if he can recite the catechism of Nazi faith, if he shows himself to be a disciplined soldier and potential party member, it makes little difference to the Nazis whether he has acquired learning or not. In fact, the intellectual is so sneered at, heaped with such searing contempt and hate, it is better for the student not to reveal intellectual qualities or to show curiosity and objectivity of the sort respected and encouraged in our universities.

If the student wants to be an instructor, he must again be rigorously tested by the Nazis and must prove himself adept in Nazi ideology and present himself as a fine example of Nordic superiority, both physically and mentally.

All branches of practical and theoretical science have been subordinated to war research. The talent and resources they now have left have been concentrated on the perfecting of the war machine, including chemical warfare.

Thus, in art, in science, in the professions, in general intellectual and cultural life, the Nazis have made inroads of destruction which may take generations to repair. For the glory of the past, for the incomparable gifts Germany made to the world, there has been substituted a propaganda and technique of superstition, a perfect organization of sterility, false legends, and sadism upon which every country in the world, except Italy and Japan, looks with horror.

My father was so shocked and sickened at what had happened to the culture and civilization he used to know as a young student in Leipzig, he dreaded even passing through a university town. Several times, before speaking at universities throughout Germany—he thought that by lecturing in his objective, critical, and implicative way he might arouse some sleeping ambitions and ideals in his audience—he made it known as indirectly and subtly as possible that no honorary degree must be offered him. I am sure that nothing would have pleased him more, had conditions been different, than the award of an honorary degree from some of the German universities he used to visit and study in as a young man, but he would have been compelled to refuse a university degree awarded while Hitler was in power.

See also arts and architecture in the Third Reich, literature in the Third Reich, Vol. 1; universities in the Third Reich, Vol. 2.

The Purpose of Art

In this exchange of letters from 1933, famed German conductor Wilhelm Furtwängler tries to defend musical freedom while Nazi propaganda minister Joseph Goebbels reminds him that the truly creative artist must serve the national interest.

Dear Reich Minister,
In view of my work over many years with the German public and my inner bond with German music I take the liberty of drawing your attention to events within the world of music which in my opinion need not necessarily follow from the restoration of our national dignity which we all welcome with joy and gratitude. My feelings in this are purely those of an artist. The function of art and artists is to bring together, not to separate. In the final analysis, I recognize only one line of division—that between good and bad art. But while the line of division between Jews and non-Jews is being drawn with a relentless, even a doctrinaire, sharpness, even where the political attitude of the person concerned gives no grounds for complaint, the other line of division, extremely important, if not decisive, in the long run—that between good and bad —is being far too much neglected.

Musical life today, weakened anyway by the world crisis, radio, etc., cannot take any more experiments. One cannot fix the quota for music as with other things necessary for life like potatoes and bread. If nothing is offered in concerts, nobody goes to them. So that for music the question of quality is not simply an idealistic one, but a question of

Jeremy Noakes and Geoffrey Pridham, eds., *Documents on Nazism, 1919–1945*. New York: Viking, 1974.

Conductor Wilhelm Furtwängler acknowledges the applause of Hitler and other Nazi high officials after a Berlin Philharmonic concert.

life and death. If the fight against Jews is mainly directed against those artists who, lacking roots themselves and being destructive, try to achieve an effect through kitsch, dry virtuosity and similar things, then this is quite all right. The fight against them and the spirit they embody cannot be pursued emphatically and consistently enough. But if this fight is directed against *real* artists as well, this will not be in the interests of cultural life, particularly because artists anywhere are much too rare for any country to be able to dispense with their work without loss to culture.

It should therefore be stated clearly that men like Walter, Klemperer, Reinhardt [all conductors], etc. must be allowed in future to express their art in Germany.

Once again, then, let our fight be directed against the rootless, subversive, levelling, *destructive* spirit, but not against the real artist who is always creative and therefore constructive, however one may judge his art.

In this sense I appeal to you in the name of German art to prevent things from happening which it may not be possible to put right again.

Very respectfully yours,
[signed] WILHELM FURTWÄNGLER

Goebbels's Response

I am grateful for the opportunity given me by your letter to enlighten you about the attitude of the nationally-inclined forces in German life to art in general and to music in particular. In this connexion, I am particularly pleased that, right at the beginning of your letter, you emphasize in the name of German artists that you gladly and gratefully welcome the restoration of our national dignity.

I never assumed that this could be anything other than the case, for I believe that the struggle we wage for Germany's reconstruction concerns the German artist not only in a passive but in an active way. I refer to something the Reich Chancellor said publicly three years ago, before our seizure of power: 'If German artists knew what we shall do for them one day, they would not fight against us but with us.'

It is your right to feel as an artist and to see things from an artist's point of view. But that need not mean that you regard the whole development in Germany in an unpolitical way. Politics too is an art, perhaps the highest and most comprehensive there is, and we who shape modern German policy feel ourselves in this to be artists who have been given the responsible task of forming, out of the raw material of the mass, the firm concrete structure of a people. It is not only the task of art and the artist to bring together, but beyond this it is their task to form, to give shape, to remove the diseased and create freedom for the healthy. Thus, as a German politician, I am unable to recognize only the single line of division which you see—that between good and bad art. Art must not only be good, it must also appear to be connected with the people, or rather, only an art which draws on the people itself can in the final analysis be good and mean something to the people for whom it is created.

There must be no art in the absolute sense as known by liberal democracy. The attempt to serve it would result in the people no longer having any inner relationship to art and in the artist himself isolating and cutting himself off from the driving forces of the time in the vacuum of the *'l'art pour l'art'* [art for art's sake] point of view. Art must be good; but beyond this it must be responsible, professional, popular and aggressive. I readily admit that it cannot take any more experiments. But it would have been more suitable to protest against artistic experiments at a time when the whole world of German art was almost exclusively dominated by the love of experiments on the part of elements alien to the people and of the race who tainted and compromised the reputation of German art.

I am sure you are quite right to say that for music quality is not only an idealistic question but a matter of life and death. You are even more right to join our struggle against the rootlessly destructive artistic style, corrupted by kitsch and dry virtuosity. I readily admit that even Germanic representatives took part in these evil goings-on, but that only proves how deeply the roots of these dangers had penetrated into the German people and how necessary it has seemed, therefore, to oppose them. Real artists are rare. Accordingly they must be promoted and supported. But in that case they must be real artists.

You will always be able to express your art in Germany—in the future too. To complain about the fact that now and then men like Walter, Klemperer, Reinhardt etc. have had to cancel concerts seems to me to be particularly inappropriate at the moment, since on many occasions real German artists were condemned to silence during the past fourteen years; and the events of the past weeks, not approved of by us either, represent only a natural reaction to those facts. At any rate, I am of the opinion that *every real artist* should be given room for free creativity. But in that case, he must, as you say yourself, be a *constructive creative person*. . . .

See also arts and architecture in the Third Reich, Vol. 1; music in the Third Reich, Vol. 2.

The Third Reich Must Maintain Family and Racial Purity

In a 1938 publication, a Nazi doctor describes measures taken by the state to ensure that families have the healthiest and most racially pure children possible, thereby to ensure the "improvement" of the German race.

The nation and the race must be regarded as the pivot upon which all State activity hinges. "The nation as such," Herr Hitler has said, "is the eternal fountain from which new life is always emanating; and this fountain must be kept in a healthy state." Hence, our struggle is concerned with the preservation of racial health and the encouragement of large-sized families. Measures aiming at the reduction of unemployment, the protection of the home soil, the provision of small holdings and settlements near the outskirts of large cities, and a suitable readjustment of our fiscal and population policies, have already been introduced; and others will follow.

The results achieved, however, can only be of practical value and of a lasting character when the change of attitude is complete and makes itself felt in every branch of State activity. Moreover, there must be a uniformly directed administrative apparatus to assist in carrying out the necessary hygienic reforms.

In spite of the unsatisfactory economic and financial conditions ruling in 1933, the Ministry of the Interior succeeded in unifying the public health system of the country and in doing away with the wasteful decentralisation previously existing. By the Act passed on July 3rd, 1934, the various boards of health established by the subordinate public authorities were given over to central administration, and a new department—that for racial hygiene—was added. The new boards of health set up in every municipality or district are directed by a State-appointed physician, assisted by an efficient staff. The scope of the work done by the Public Health Department has been extended by the addition to it of the Advisory Offices for Racial Culture and Heredity. Their functions are: to watch the natural growth (or otherwise) of the population, to safeguard the nation's inherited assets, and to enlighten persons intending to marry.

The progress of racial science has been very considerable in recent years; and much benefit to the community has been derived from it. Although it is not possible to influence the course of the racial development by direct methods, it can be done indirectly. Darwin explained the upward development in the animal and vegetable kingdoms by pointing out that those animals and plants which are capable of assimilating themselves to their surroundings more successfully than others are best fitted to survive in the struggle for existence and to pass their characteristic features on to their descendants. This is called "natural selection," and its opposite (in the domain of human development) is the artificial selection brought about by the influences of civilisation. The very progress of human knowledge produces an increasing amount of artificial interference with the influences that are at

Arthur Gütt, "Population Policy," in *Germany Speaks, by Twenty-One Leading Members of Party and State.* London: Thornton Butterworth, 1938.

work naturally. The weaker elements—which, if Nature alone were at work, would soon be eliminated—are kept alive and are even specially cared for by the skill of our physicians and by the improved conditions of life. In the realm of Nature and among the uncivilised peoples, everything that is unhealthy speedily perishes. Among civilised nations, the opposite development takes place. The healthy and valuable individuals either refuse to marry or, if they do, largely practise family limitation.

During the Liberalist and Marxist régime [the Weimar Republic] in Germany, it was also believed that the human race could be improved by artificial means. It was thought that the characteristics thus acquired were hereditable; and this view is still largely advocated. But, we may ask, what useful purpose can be served by the constant extension of public welfare work, so long as the efforts in that direction fail to deal with the real causes of a nation's decay? It has been proved that the unhealthy traits are usually reproduced to a larger extent than the healthy ones; and [racial scientist Francis] Galton has already emphasised that this circumstance tends to increase the danger of racial degeneration.

We know that we cannot restore the natural conditions of life, and we do not intend to do so or to throw overboard the blessings of a higher civilisation. But as we are aware of the causes of degeneration, we can counteract the effects of an artificial environment by an artificial selection of the right kind, i.e., by promoting racial culture; and the final outcome will correspond to our intentions. If we facilitate the propagation of healthy stock by systematic selection and by the elimination of the unhealthy elements, we shall be able to improve the physical standards not, perhaps, of the present generation, out of those that will succeed us. Credit is due to the National Socialist Government for perceiving the danger of degeneration and for issuing legislation dealing with it, e.g., the Acts for the Prevention of Hereditarily Diseased Offspring, for the Restoration of Professionalism in the Public Services, for dealing with Habitual Offenders and Immoral Offences, and many others.

It goes without saying that the medical activities carried out by physicians on behalf of individuals and on that of the community will continue to go on along the lines universally adopted in conformity with the researches of Koch, Lister, Pasteur, and other celebrated scientists.

It was a great achievement on the part of Robert Koch when he succeeded, many years ago, in discovering that various micro-organisms are the cause of anthrax, tuberculosis, cholera, etc. The result was that a systematic campaign against these infectious diseases was organised throughout the civilised world. Acts were passed by which the State was given the right to interfere with the private life of individuals, on the ground that such interference, although restricting individual liberty, would benefit the nation as a whole. It can hardly be denied that—in pursuance of such legislation—the State was not only entitled, but compelled, to issue regulations governing the duty of individuals to report all cases of infection, providing for the isolation of the patients concerned, and so on. The same right must therefore be claimed by the State for its activities in the wider domain of racial hygiene.

Germany has taken the lead in these endeavours by taking practical steps towards the initiation of a systematic population policy. The Advisory Offices already referred to are required, among other matters, to administer the Act for the Prevention of Hereditarily Diseased Offspring. Whenever it may be assumed, with a fair measure of probability, that a serious hereditary disease will be propagated, sterilisation may be resorted to. The scope of the Act is limited to the most important diseases, e.g., congenital imbecility or insanity, epilepsy, hereditary deafness or blindness, etc., and stringent regulations have been issued to prevent any misuse.

Special courts have been created to decide whether, in any given instance, the provisions of the Act are to be applied to it. They are composed of physicians and judges. Prior to making their decision, they carefully examine the circumstances of the case in question. It must be remembered, in this connection, that sterilisation is by no means identical with castration. It may be effected by means of X-rays or radium treatment, so that an operation is not necessarily required. The work performed by the courts is of a highly responsible nature, its ultimate object being to stamp out all hereditary diseases.

A clearly defined legal position has been created in every domain of racial biology. The interception of pregnancy for hygienic reasons—a difficult problem in every civilised country—has been dealt with in a satisfactory way by giving the necessary discretionary powers to commissions composed of medical men.

Additional safeguards are provided by the Act dealing with Habitual Offenders and Immoral Offences, passed on November 24th, 1936. It empowers the ordinary courts to inflict adequate punishment upon habitual offenders and upon persons committing immoral offences against women and children.

It is obvious that the measures hitherto discussed are of a negative character only. Their chief aim is to remove the dangers that have arisen as the result of many decades of neglect. They must, of course, be supplemented by others intended to ensure a healthy offspring and the economic safeguarding of the family. . . .

In the course of the past thousand years or so, people had quite forgotten that they are the result of heredity and environment. Marriages, therefore, were frequently brought about by purely external reasons, such as the desire for a dowry, for social preferment, etc. Men of good physique did not hesitate to marry girls suffering from grave physical or mental defects; and healthy girls often regarded it as a work of Christian charity to choose for their partner in life a sick and unhealthy man for whom they could care and to whose needs they could administer.

No one seemed to mind that marriages thus contracted would tend to produce an offspring liable to the same grave defects. A mistaken sense of charity prompted people to commit acts of ruthless cruelty towards those who—being racially inferior or suffering from an incurable disease—furnished visible evidence of "the sin against the race." Statistical evidence of the great danger to which such an attitude must lead is by no means lacking. Up to now people have failed to see that the ultimate outcome of this development must be the decay and the utter ruin of our civilisation. They are still governed by too strong a faith in the doctrines with which they were conversant throughout their lives, without realising all their implications. It was therefore an event of the utmost historical importance when the National Socialist Government proceeded to enact the various legislative measures by which the evil could be tackled at its root.

The racial purity of a nation and its freedom from hereditary disease are just as closely related to one another as body and soul. The former is mainly concerned with the preservation of that which is good and healthy. To ensure the latter, the Act prohibiting marriages between persons suffering from hereditary disease makes it incumbent upon registrars to refuse a marriage licence if one or other of the following conditions obtains:

(*a*) If either the man or the woman is suffering from an infectious disease likely to inflict grave injury upon the other party or their issue.

(*b*) If either party is under restraint or tutelage.

(*c*) If either party, although not under restraint, is yet suffering from a mental disability which makes it undesirable in the national interest that he or she should marry.

(*d*) If either party is suffering from one of the congenital diseases specified in the Act governing the Prevention of Hereditarily Diseased Offspring.

Clause (*d*) will not be considered an obstacle to marriage if the other party is sterile.

Thus, the contraction of a marriage can now be legally prohibited if its consummation would be certain to cause grave damage to the parties concerned. In drawing up these regulations, the legislator has wisely limited the scope of his interference to a minimum and has carefully defined their exact meaning. Even the most uncompromising opponents of National Socialism will probably admit that the prohibitions cover those circumstances only in which a citizen conscious of his responsibilities would abstain from marrying in any case. Foreign critics, indeed, have not found fault with any of them, well knowing that the propagation of infectious diseases and mental defects is bound to undermine the health of any nation. . . .

Marriages detrimental to the racial purity of the German stock have been made illegal by the Nuremberg Law for the Protection of the German Race and German Honour (September 15th, 1935). In the preamble, a concise statement is given of the objects aimed at by the National Socialist Government in the domain of racial policy. It begins as follows:

> Fully convinced that the purity of the German stock is indispensable to the continued existence of the German nation and animated by the inflexible determination to safeguard its existence for all times, the Reichstag has unanimously resolved upon the following law.

The law prohibits all marriages between Jews and any German nationals who are of German stock or of kindred ancestry. Any marriages contracted abroad in order to evade this prohibition are illegal. Proceedings to have them annulled can only be instituted by the public prosecutor. The same prohibition applies to illicit sexual intercourse between the persons named. Any infringement of the law will be punished.

It stands to reason, however, that all these measures—if isolated—will still fail in their objective unless steps are also taken to protect the vital rights of all healthy families by due recognition of their economic needs.

The political and social future of our country can only be definitely safeguarded on condition that the middle classes, the employees and the workers have their proper share in the national assets. The State is required to make it possible for all citizens to carry out their appointed tasks and to become part-owners of the means of production. Economic and social legislation will be needed to enable prolific families to purchase the means of subsistence. This can only be achieved by an adjustment of the burdens each family has to carry; and this, in turn, can be brought about by tax remission, by educational assistance, or other measures.

The problem we have to solve is this. How can we provide financial aid to all prolific and biologically healthy families by way of uniform and comprehensive action? It is evident that such assistance—if it is to benefit racial health—must be graded according to the income of the persons concerned. Its precise form will therefore vary, although the general principle underlying it will be the same. In the upper middle classes, the object aimed at may be attained by tax reform; those who are employed in the public services may have their salaries increased; the masses of workers and employees in private undertakings may be assisted by creating a "national family adjustment fund," whilst an altogether different method may have to be adopted in connection with the farming community, handicraftsmen, and others. In no case will this involve additional taxation. All that will happen will be a re-distribution of incomes in conformity with the principles of a sound population policy. Owing to the economic difficulties caused by the Versailles Treaty and the incompetency of previous governments, it has been impossible so far to provide the adjustment fund referred to. Its creation, however, is a vitally important necessity, which must overrule all other considerations, even though it may involve increased social charges for families with few children or no children at all. This necessity can now be explained to workers and employees far more convincingly than could have been done in the past; and there is no doubt that they will grasp its significance. If we succeed in convincing all classes of the vital importance of this task, they will continue to be content with the present modest level of the provision made against the vicissitudes of life, because, in doing so, they will help to attain the higher aims before us, viz., the maintenance of our national existence and the safeguarding of our national future.

The conviction must become universal that the problems in the domain of our population policy cannot be solved unless we have the courage to adjust the whole of our financial, social and economic policy to the principles already set forth. We can no longer carry on social policy in this country without, at the same time, combating unemployment and carrying on a healthy population policy. Unemployment, however, can only be definitely overcome if we succeed in finding a satisfactory solution of the problem concerning the position of women and in safeguarding the vital rights of the family.

The German nation has now realised, just before it was too late, that a breach with its past and a neglect of its racial ideals is bound to inflict grave injury upon everyone. Houston Stewart Chamberlain has somewhere referred to the nineteenth century as "the age of irreverence," thus foreseeing the development that took place during the past thirty years. A man's actions are not determined, in the last resort, by his education, his intelligence or his surroundings, but by the racial traits bequeathed to him by his remote ancestors. Just as a nation's past history can be a source of strength to it, the history of our family can be an inspiration to us throughout our lives. A study of it can teach us where our ancestors came from, what work they were doing, what was their worth or worthlessness, and what characteristics they may have passed on to us. When every individual realises that he is only a link in the long chain that connects him with his ancestors and that he has the same obligations towards the future as they had, it will be time to dismiss our apprehensions regarding the continued existence of our people. Thus, it will always be necessary to cultivate the family sense. Women, especially, must again become the custodians of the family traditions. It is therefore very gratifying to see that the various women's organisations make it their special business to teach young girls to be conscious of their responsibilities, just as the corresponding men's organisations endeavour to foster the same spirit in men and youths.

The increased attention given by Germany to racial hygiene has resulted in a widening of the scope covered by the activities of the public health authorities. Numerous foreign scientists and also foreign nations are prepared to follow the lead thus given by us. It is not intended to replace the existing system of public hygienic services by a different one, but rather to supplement the one by the other. The work already done to combat disease will be continued as usual, in close collaboration with medical science. The introduction of a practical system of biological and racial culture, however, is certain to increase the public's appreciation of its duties towards the family and towards future generations, and will therefore raise the physical and intellectual standards of our people. Beyond that, it strengthens our desire for the preservation of peace.

For all these reasons we consider it our duty to direct the attention of the European nations, and of the white race in general, towards the dangers threatening our common civilisation from Russia in the east and from Africa—by way of large armies composed of races of non-European stock specially trained by France—in the south.

If there were another war, valuable national assets would be destroyed not only at the front, but also at home. Thus, racial hygiene and war will always be irreconcilable enemies. The Chancellor wants peace not only for his own country's sake, but also because a European war would be the end of the white races and of white civilisation. Not only Central Europe, but France, Italy and Great Britain also, would perish, whilst Bolshevism would be the real victor.

I firmly believe that the recognition of this danger will bring the highly civilised nations closer together and will strengthen the feeling of solidarity.

See also eugenics, Vol. 1; racial science, Vol. 2.

On the Nature of Women

In one of his random dinnertime conversations, transcribed by an anonymous guest, Hitler explains his views on how women and men are fundamentally different.

In woman, jealousy is a defensive reaction. It surely has an ancestral origin, and must go back to the time when woman simply couldn't do without the protection of a man. First of all, it's the reaction of a pregnant woman, who as such has all the more need of protection. She feels so weak in those circumstances, so timid—for herself and for the child she's carrying. And this child itself, how many years will it take to gain its independence! Without the protection of a man, woman would feel exposed to all perils. So it's natural that she should be quite particularly attached to the hero, to the man who gives her the most security. Once this security is obtained, it's comprehensible that she should bitterly defend her property—hence the origin of jealousy.

Man is inspired by a similar feeling towards the woman he loves, but the realm of feminine jealousy is infinitely vaster. A mother is jealous of her daughter-in-law, a sister of her sister-in-law.

I was present one day at a scene that Eva Chamberlain [wife of author Houston Stewart Chamberlain] made at the expense of her brother, Siegfried Wagner [son of composer Richard Wagner]. It was absolutely incredible, the more so as they were both married. Siegfried's young wife, Winifried, was, so to speak, tolerated by her sisters-in-law. Nevertheless, on the day of the catastrophe, her presence was thought particularly opportune. She was a woman of irreproachable behaviour. Siegfried owes her four handsome children, all of them obviously his—all of them Wagners!

One day I detected an unexpected reaction even in Frau Bruckmann [a Munich socialite]. She had invited to her house, at the same time as myself, a very pretty woman of Munich society. As we were taking our leave, Frau Bruckmann perceived in her female guest's manner a sign of an interest that she doubtless deemed untimely. The consequence was that she never again invited us both at once. As I've said, the woman was beautiful, and perhaps she felt some interest in me—nothing more.

H.R. Trevor-Roper, ed., *Hitler's Secret Conversations, 1941–1944*. Trans. Norman Cameron and R.H. Stevens. New York: Farrar, Straus, and Young, 1958.

I knew a woman whose voice became raucous with emotion when I spoke in her presence to another woman.

Man's universe is vast compared with that of woman. Man is taken up with his ideas, his preoccupations. It's only incidental if he devotes all his thoughts to a woman. Woman's universe, on the other hand, is man. She sees nothing else, so to speak, and that's why she's capable of loving so deeply.

Intelligence, in a woman, is not an essential thing. My mother, for example, would have cut a poor figure in the society of our cultivated women. She lived strictly for her husband and children. They were her entire universe. But she gave a son to Germany.

Marriages that originate only in sensual infatuation are usually somewhat shaky. Such bonds are easily untied. Separations are particularly painful when there has been a genuine comradeship between man and wife.

I think it improper that a woman should be liable to be called upon to give evidence in Court on intimate matters. I've had that abolished. I detest prying and espionage.

That reminds me of a characteristic of Frederick the Great. He was complaining one day to his Chief of Police that he was the worst informed monarch in Europe concerning what went on inside his kingdom. "Nothing would be easier, Sire. Put at my disposal the methods that my colleagues have use of, and I shall certainly do as well as they." "At that price," said the King, "I won't take it." I myself never used such methods, and I shall never give audience to a sneak. There's something utterly repugnant about such a person. As for female spies, let's not speak of them! Not only are these women prostitutes, but they make the

Adolf Hitler believed that women should devote themselves to the home and the family, claiming, "Woman's universe . . . is man."

man whom they are preparing to betray the victim of the obscenest sort of play-acting.

In the days of my youth, I was something of a solitary, and I got along very easily without society. I've changed a lot, for nowadays I can no longer bear solitude. What I like best is to dine with a pretty woman. And rather than be left at home by myself, I'd go and dine at the *Osteria*.

See also women in the Third Reich, Vol. 2; Hitler, Adolf, Vol. 3.

The State Must Dominate the Churches

In a 1933 radio broadcast, Hitler explains why Germany's Evangelical (Protestant) churches must submit to National Socialist authority for the sake of cultural unity.

"If I take up any position towards the elections in the Evangelical Church I do this solely from the standpoint of the political leader, that is to say that I am not moved to do so by questions of faith, dogmatics, or doctrine. These are purely internal church affairs. But over and above these questions there are problems which compel the politician and the responsible leader of a people publicly to make known his position. They embrace [völkisch] and State interests in their relation to the Confessions.

"National Socialism has always affirmed that it is determined to take the Christian Churches under the protection of the State. For their part the churches cannot for a second doubt that they need the protection of the State, and that only through the State can they be enabled to fulfill their religious mission. Indeed, the churches demand this protection from the State. On the other hand, in consideration for this protection, the State must require from the churches that they in their turn should render to it that support which it needs to secure its permanence. Churches which fail to render to the State any positive support in this sense are for the State just as worthless as is for a church the State which is incapable of fulfilling its duties to the Church. The decisive factor which can justify the existence alike of church and State is the maintenance of men's spiritual and bodily health, for if that health were destroyed it would mean the end of the State and also the end of the Church. Therefore the State cannot afford to be indifferent to the religious affairs of its day and neither can, on the other hand, the churches be indifferent to the [völkisch]-political events and changes. Just as formerly Christianity and later the Reformation had their gigantic political effects, so with every political-[völkisch] upheaval affect also the destiny of the churches. Only a fool can imagine that, for example, the victory of bolshevism could be irrelevant for the Catholic or the Evangelical Church and that therefore it would not disturb or even prevent the former activities of bishops or superintendents. The assertion that such dangers could be overcome through the action of the churches alone is untenable; it is contradicted by the facts. Neither the Catholic Church nor the Evangelical, nor the Russian-Uniate Church has been able or would be able to stay the advance of bolshevism. Wherever there has not been created [völkisch]-political defense to counter that advance, there the victory of communism is already won, or at least the battle is still undecided.

"It is thus clear that the churches themselves must take up a definite position towards such [völkisch]-political revolutionary movements. This the Roman Church in the Lateran Treaties has done for the first time in a clear and unequivocal form toward fascism. The German Concordat which has now been signed is the second equally clear step in this sphere. It is my sincere hope that thereby for Germany, too, through free agreement there has been produced a final clarification of spheres in the functions of the State and of one Church.

Adolf Hitler, *My New Order.* Ed. Raoul de Roussy de Sales. New York: Reynal and Hitchcock, 1941.

As a National Socialist I have the most earnest wish that it may be possible to reach with the Evangelical Church also a no less clear settlement.

But this presupposes that, if it is at all possible, the place of the many Evangelical Churches should be taken by a united Reichskirche [Reich Church]. The State has no interest in negotiating with twenty-five or thirty churches, all the more since it is convinced that in face of the gigantic tasks of the present time here, too, it is only a concentration of all forces which can be regarded as effective. The powerful State can only wish to extend its protection to such religious organizations as can in their turn become of use to it.

"And in fact amongst the congregations of the Evangelical Confessions there has arisen in the 'German Christians' a Movement which is filled with the determination to do justice to the great tasks of the day and has aimed at a union of the Evangelical Churches of the German States and at a union of Confessions. If this question is now really on the way toward solution, in the judgment of history no false or stupid objections will be able to dispute the fact that this service was rendered by the [völkisch]-political revolution in Germany and by the Movement within the Evangelical Confessions which clearly and unequivocally professed its allegiance to this national and [völkisch] Movement at a time when unfortunately, just as in the Roman Church, many pastors and superintendents without reason opposed the national uprising in the most violent, indeed often in a fanatical, way.

"In the interest of the recovery of the German nation which I regard as indissolubly bound up with the National Socialist Movement I naturally wish that the new church elections should in their result support our new policy for People and State."

See also Confessing Church, German Christians, Vol. 1; religion in the Third Reich, Vol. 2; Bonhoeffer, Dietrich, Vol. 3.

Program for a Hitler Youth Campout

As this daily plan for a Hitler Youth outing makes clear, Reich youth leaders took every opportunity to remind young people of both German greatness and their obligations to the state. Even the daily passwords commemorate great events or people from German history as well as the important qualities of Nazi youth.

What is outlined below is only to be regarded as an example of how various material should be evenly distributed. The 9th of July is used as the day of arrival, the 23rd of July as the day of departure.

Friday 10 July
Password: Adolf Hitler
Motto for the day: Hitler is Germany and Germany is Hitler.
Words: We owe to our leader Adolf Hitler the fact that we can open our camp today.
Song: Onward, onward . . .
Community hour: is omitted since the group is still very tired.

Jeremy Noakes and Geoffrey Pridham, eds., *Documents on Nazism, 1919–1945.* New York: Viking, 1974.

Saturday 11 July

Password: Baldur von Schirach

Motto for the day: Anything that under-
mines our unity must go on the pyre!

Song: We are no civilian, peasant, workman
. . .

Community hour: What do I want in the
Hitler Youth? (Reich Youth Leadership
folder)

Sunday 12 July

Password: Germany

Motto for the day: Germany, Germany
above all!

Words for the morning celebration: We are
not in the Hitler Youth to be provided for
life, to receive perhaps a position or office later on, but we want to serve Germany unselfishly, as is spoken of in the
song: 'We carry in our beating hearts
faith in Germany.'

Song: On, raise our flags . . .

Community hour: is omitted on account of
Sunday duties, i.e. sports contests etc.

Monday 13 July

Password: Widukind

Motto for the day: To be one nation is the
religion of our time.

Words: If we fight to create a united youth
organization and for all young men to be
in it, we serve our nation, because the
youth of today will become the nation of
tomorrow.

Song: Holy fatherland . . .

Community hour: We commit ourselves to
the ideal of our ancestors. (Reich Youth
Leadership folder)

Tuesday 14 July

Password: Frederick the Great

Motto for the day: It is not necessary for me
to live, but certainly necessary for me to
do my duty!

Words: We speak of the principle of volun-
teering, on which basis we have met.

Song: The marching of the column sounds . . .

Community hour: Prussianism, our ideal.

Wednesday 15 July

Password: Schill

Motto for the day: Germany's defence—
Germany's honour.

Words: Schill revolted against a Prussia
without defences and therefore without
honour. Adolf Hitler restored honour to
Germany when he gave the German nation back her weapons. We want to make
ourselves strong so that we never again
lose our honour.

Song: Now we must march . . .

Community hour: The soldier protects German work. (Reich Youth Leadership
folder)

Thursday 16 July

Password: Langemarck

Motto of the day: You have not fallen in
vain!

Words: The camp leader speaks of the respect the whole youth should have for
the two million dead who were killed in
the world war. They died for Germany;
we strengthen ourselves also for Germany. Therefore we are the heirs of the
front. Once the soldiers of the Great War
were dragged through the dirt (they were
called murderers!); today the whole of
German youth goes on a pilgrimage to
the places where they were killed and
lowers its flags in memory of their holy
sacrifice.

Song: Wild geese rush through the night . . .

Community hour: Out of the World War
grew the Third Reich. (Reich Youth
Leadership folder)

Friday 17 July

Password: Richthofen

Motto for the day: Nation, fly again!

Words: The camp leader tells about the determined sacrifice which the few German
combat aviators had to make during the
world war. Names like Immelmann,
Boelcke, Richthofen are not forgotten.
Today we possess a strong air fleet which
has continued the tradition of those few

who accomplished the impossible with technically imperfect planes.

Song: Soldiers carry rifles . . .

Community hour: Letters and some excerpts are read from the numerous good books about aviation.

Saturday 18 July

Password: Schlageter

Motto for the day: Let struggle be the highest aim of youth!

Words: The camp leader speaks about the fact that we all have to become fighters, that we have to accept as slogans for our life everything which requires from us a manly, heroic attitude: That which does not kill me makes me only the stronger! One does not beg for a right, one fights for it! What is good?—To be brave is good! He who fights has right on his side; he who does not fight has lost all rights! What we can do ourselves, we must not leave to God. . . . Therefore pray, when we have to pray: Lord, let us never be cowardly!

Song: Unroll the blood-red flags . . .

Community hour: Germans in the world—Versailles is a burden on us. (Reich Youth Leadership folders)

Sunday 19 July

Password: Herbert Norkus

Motto for the day: Our service to Germany is divine service!

Song: Now let the flags fly . . .

Morning celebration: On this morning a bigger morning celebration takes place.

Fundamental thought: We cannot be called heretics and pagans, if we have made a Herbert Norkus's readiness for sacrifice the motto of our lives.

Community hour: is omitted because of Sunday duties, i.e. parents' day, contests, etc.

Monday 20 July

Password: Blood

Motto for the day: To remain pure and become mature.

Words: The camp leader talks about this motto by Walter Flex and demands from the boys clean, decent thinking and action. The sentence, 'Service is service and liquor is liquor' is not valid for us; but: 'All or nothing!'

Song: Young nation, step forward, for your hour has come . . .

Community hour: Ideological examination for the Hitler Youth and German Young People efficiency medal.

Tuesday 21 July

Password: Honour

Motto of the day: For a member of the youth organization his honour is the greatest thing!

Words: The camp leader speaks about this motto.

Song: Behind the flag we march . . .

Community hour: see 20 July.

Wednesday 22 July

Password: Old Guard

Motto of the day: Germany must live, even if we have to die!

Song: Through Greater-Berlin we march . . .

Final celebration: On this evening the final celebration takes place, at which the camp leader speaks for the last time. Adolf Hitler, Baldur von Schirach, Widukind, Frederick the Great, Schill, Langemarck, Richthofen, Schlageter, Herbert Norkus, Blood, Honour, Old Guard have been the passwords. All commit themselves to the one word 'Germany' which shall also prevail over the whole life of the Cub.

See also education in the Third Reich, Hitler Youth, Vol. 1.

Strength Through Joy: Taking Care of the German Worker

Robert Ley, leader of the German Labor Front, describes the various benefits of the Strength Through Joy program, designed to convince German workers that Hitler's regime had their interests and welfare at heart.

The social rebuilding of Germany is unthinkable without the NS association "Strength Through Joy," and we are proud that the Führer himself has called it one of the greatest social organizations of all time. "Strength Through Joy" is not merely a leisure-time organization; it is a National Socialist community involved in creating a new life-style and in establishing the new social order. Beauty of Labor is a necessary component of Strength Through Joy; it forms the basis on which planned recreation must be established.

The improvements that were reported to this organization come to a total of 109 million marks this year. These funds were spent exclusively on factory improvements carried out in the spirit of "Beauty of Labor." But we can confidently state that the actual figure is much higher because today improvements are often not reported to us as they are commonly regarded as a matter of course. The total expenditures for Beauty of Labor come to approximately 600 million marks.

The campaign "Good Illumination— Good Light" conducted last year was repeated this year, and the success of this

Benjamin C. Sax and Dieter Kuntz, eds., *Inside Hitler's Germany: A Documentary History of the Third Reich.* Lexington, MA: D.C. Heath, 1992.

lighting campaign can be seen in the tremendous sales increase achieved by the electrical industry as a result of good modern lighting.

An equally great success was the campaign "Clean People—Tidy Factory." . . .

From the development of the workplace as the basis of communal life and communal culture, the road leads to the development of the time after working hours, leisure time. We not only want to expose you to the diverse number of possibilities of spending your leisure time, but we also want to direct you toward a meaningful life. . . .

The greatest activity was undertaken in the area of theater, which was even expanded this year. For the 1937–38 season, approximately 7,000 performances have been scheduled.

The Special Campaign for Reich Superhighways was expanded this year. During 1937 a total of 110,000 working comrades were registered and living in 550 work camps. In each of these camps we organized the showing of two or three movies a month. The grand total comes to 4,000 concerts and 3,000 entertainment evenings for the camps altogether.

Another newly established organization, founded this year, is the Soldier's Theater, which is part of "Strength Through Joy" but performs only in army garrisons and in places where the army is on maneuvers. This first Soldier's Theater was so successful that for the coming year a new series of similar theaters is planned.

A further important measure of our cultural-political theater activity is the Reich Theater Campaign of "Strength Through

Joy," which is employed primarily in the border areas of the Reich.

The cultivation of concert activity in general was given a further boost this year. Aside from the master concerts, the factory concerts were also carefully cultivated. Here symphony orchestras as well as the factories' own orchestras were engaged.

The agency After Working Hours has to a large extent undertaken the task of carrying out art exhibitions in businesses and factories. Up to now, the total number of these exhibits comes to 1,273, of which 602 —almost half—were organized this year alone.

The grand total of all those participating in the cultural and entertainment events of the agency After Working Hours comes to a figure of roughly 34 million for this accounting year.

The activity of the German educational/cultural enterprise "Strength Through Joy" shows us to what extent the individual countryman today strives to coordinate himself with a National Socialist life-style. The number of countrymen who have become involved in Strength Through Joy since the inception of the educational/cultural activity totals 10,180,000.

Cultural activity in the area of music has been anchored in the Reich Music Chamber division Youth and *Volk* Music. The singing and musical associations directed by "Strength Through Joy," in cooperation with the Hitler Youth and other formations, held 4,400 "public singings" and other musical events during the past year. There were 800,000 German countrymen who witnessed these events. . . .

An area just as important as the proper use of leisure time is the promotion of bodily exercise. The past year signaled the introduction and energetic advancement of sports in the factory. With this, we tackled a new field of activity of immense proportions and meaning.

The continuing extension of the activity of the sports department and particularly

the development of sports in the factory has led to a noticeable lack of qualified exercise instructors and exercise facilities. The number of available gymnasiums, sports fields, and swimming pools is insufficient, particularly in winter. The sports department of "Strength Through Joy" has therefore undertaken a large-scale training program for honorary exercise directors. On the other side of the coin, many factories have begun construction of their own sports facilities. Sports facilities at 900 factories are already finished and another 235 are currently being built. . . .

The crowning, so to speak, of the efforts of Strength Through Joy to provide dignified and meaningful utilization of the leisure time of German working people is the organization of vacations.

Nowhere in the world do people work so much and so diligently as here in Germany. Those that work, however, need equally complete rest and relaxation. The more you work, the better should be your vacation! Sensibly organized vacations are of great importance in maintaining the vitality and productivity of our people.

The KdF [Strength Through Joy] trips have become so popular with our people because all has been planned for them, even to the smallest detail. The KdF vacationer travels without cares. Each one has his place reserved on the train; his room and board, sightseeing, excursions—all have been prepared ahead of time.

The number of trip participants has this year again experienced a significant increase. The previous year saw the number of KdF travelers rise from three to six million, and this time we saw another increase of three million. This year, then, there were nine million KdF travelers. One-third of these have taken extended vacations of one to three weeks. Almost two million took part in KdF hikes and 180,000 have traveled to Norway, Madeira, or Italy aboard ships from our KdF fleet. This ship traffic dominates the harbors of Hamburg and

Robert Ley, leader of the German Labor Front, administered the Nazi Strength Through Joy program.

Bremen and exceeds by far the total of all other cruise travel in all German harbors together.

We created something else new: what are called the Exchange-Trains. They are the fruit of our accord with Italy. . . . At the beginning of October, 425 *Dopolavora* [Italian workers] came across the border bound for Munich, Nuremberg, and Berlin. A short time later, a long express train with first- and second-class carriages left Berlin and took 425 workers from the Reich capital across the Brenner [Pass] to Rome and Florence. Two organizations with the same goal, "Strength Through Joy" and *"Dopolavora,"* have found each other through

their common activities and are now strengthening the political axis between Rome and Berlin because they are improving the practical relations between the peoples of the two nations.

For the last three years we have been traveling to Portugal as regularly as we have to Norway. It won't be long before our KdF fleet leaves Europe in search of different parts of the earth. As soon as next year we will visit Africa, where we will provide experiences for our German workers which will far surpass those hitherto. . . .

In Rügen we are constructing a giant KdF seaside swimming facility, which is looking more and more as though it will be the most beautiful seaside facility in the world. Four others are soon to be built.

This year we will begin construction of winter hostels in the mountains for the KdF vacationers in order to further winter vacations and winter sports, which are the healthiest and most beautiful one can imagine.

The village beautification activity, which was extended this year and in which more than 5,000 villages were involved, goes a long way in beautifying the overall image of German villages and, above all, improves housing conditions.

Everything we are creating has but one great goal: the formation of a just social order based on our racial ancestry and our German character, and the creation of the highest standard of living for our people. What the German people have accomplished in four years on poor soil and in limited space has no equal in the world. It was accomplished with unity of purpose in order to ensure the existence, future, and joy of life of the German people. . . .

See also German Labor Front, Vol. 1; Strength Through Joy, Volkswagen, Vol. 2; Ley, Robert, Vol. 3.

An Official Statement from the Reich Women's Leader

In a 1938 book, Gertrude Scholtz-Klink describes how all significant German women's associations have been incorporated into the Nazi regime because, as she puts it, women's duty as much as men's is to serve the state. She also points out how the state provides women with work and child-care opportunities.

When National Socialism became the ruling power in Germany we women realized that it was our duty to contribute our share to the Leader's reconstruction programme side by side with men. We did not say much about it, but started to work at once. Our first concern was to help all those mothers who had suffered great hardships during the War and the postwar period and all those other women who—as mothers—have now to adjust themselves to the demands of the new age.

Acting in accordance with the recognition of these facts, we first created the Reich Mothers' Service, the functions of which are set forth in Article I of the regulations governing it:

> The training of mothers is animated by the spirit of national solidarity and by the conviction that they can be of very great service to the nation and the State. The object of such training is to develop the physical and intellectual efficiency of mothers, to make them appreciate the great duties incumbent upon them, to instruct them in the up-bringing and education of their chil-

dren, and to qualify them for their domestic and economic tasks.

In order to provide such training, several courses of instruction have been drawn up, each of which deals with one particular subject only, e.g., infant care, general hygiene, sick nursing at home, children's education, cooking, sewing, etc. These courses are fixtures in all towns with a population exceeding 50,000, whilst itinerant teachers conduct similar ones in the smaller towns and in the country. Every German woman over 18 can join them, irrespective of her religious, political or other views. The maximum number of members has been limited to 25 for each course, because the instruction given does not consist of theoretical lectures, but takes the form of practical teaching to working groups, where questions will be asked and answered. Since the establishment of the [Reich Mother's Service], i.e., between April 1st, 1934, and October 1st, 1937, some 1,179,000 married and unmarried women have been thus instructed in 56,400 courses, conducted by over 3,000 teachers of whom about 1,200 are employed full-time, whilst the remaining 2,300 (also possessing the necessary qualifications) act in an honorary capacity or in that of part-time instructresses.

Our next concern was with those millions of German women who, day after day, attend to their heavy duties in factories. We look upon it as most important to make them realise that they, too, are the representatives of their nation. They, too, must take pride in their work and must be able to say: "I have a useful duty to fulfil; and the work I do is an essential part of the work performed by the whole nation."

Gertrude Scholtz-Klink, "The Place of Women in the New Germany," in *Germany Speaks, by Twenty-One Leading Members of Party and State.* London: Thornton Butterworth, 1938.

With this end in view, we have created the Women's Section of the German Labour Front, which has now a membership of over 8,000,000. Foreign critics have frequently stated that German women have no chance of earning their livelihood by working in industrial or other undertakings. I therefore take this opportunity of emphasising that more than 11,500,000 women are employed in the various professions and occupations; the Women's Section of the German Labour Front attending to their interests. Moreover, we are of the opinion that a woman will always find it possible to secure paid employment provided that she is strong enough to do the work demanded of her. This applies to women workers of all categories, irrespective of whether the work is of the physical or intellectual kind. It is therefore the business of the [Women's Section] to ensure that women are not employed in any capacity that might prove detrimental to their womanhood and to give them all the protection to which they are specifically entitled. In order to translate these ideas into practice, the [Women's Section] has proceeded to appoint a "social industrial woman worker" for every undertaking in which a considerable number of women are employed. The functions to be exercised by these [women social workers] are of a general and a special kind. They have to see to it that all women employed in the same undertaking look upon their own interests as identical with those of the latter and that a proper spirit of comradeship grows up among them. They are assisted in their task by the works' leader and the confidential council, and they are in a position to gain the confidence of the other women workers because all of them are comrades of one another. They have to prevent strife, jealousy, and irresponsible talk from poisoning the social atmosphere of the works, to help those of their fellow-workers who may be oppressed by domestic worries, and to assist in rendering the conditions of work as dignified as possible. To that end, they have

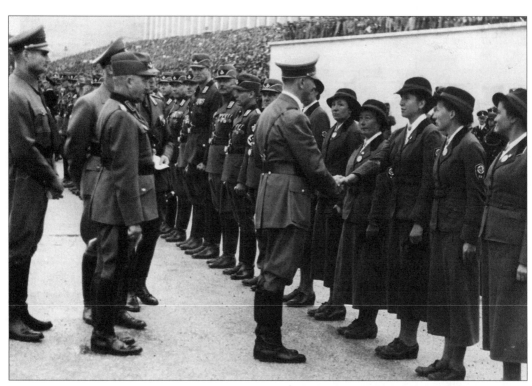

Hitler greets German women's leaders at the 1938 Reich Party Day rally in Nuremberg.

to furnish the works' leader with suggestions for any measures that may be required to adapt the processes of work—in conformity with the technical peculiarities of the undertaking—to the natural capacities of women. Finally, they have to assist in the transfer of women workers to other places of employment, in the task of making the aspect of the working premises as pleasing as possible, etc. This enumeration of their functions shows that they must not only be experienced social workers, but must also be familiar with the actual work. For this latter reason, they are required to devote several months to such work before they are appointed to the post of social workers. During that time they receive the same wages as the other women workers and are subject to the same regulations as they. Similar arrangements, although on a more modest scale, are made in connection with smaller works, i.e., those where the number of women workers is less than 200.

Special care is devoted by our organisation to married women workers with children and to those expecting to be confined. In this domain of social work we provide assistance, in conjunction with the National Socialist Welfare Organisation, exceeding the standards set by the existing legislation. Such supplementary assistance consists in money, food, linen, etc.

I must not omit to add a few words in reference to the women students who spend part of their holidays for the benefit of those women workers—notably those who have large families—who are in need of a week's relaxation in addition to their regular holidays. The students generously attend to the factory work of these women during their absence; and as they demand no wages, the workers suffer no pecuniary loss whatever. In many instances free quarters are provided for the students by the National Socialist Women's Organisation [NSWO] whilst the Welfare Organisation grants special facilities to the women on holiday, such as additional food parcels, board and lodging in

one of their mothers' hostels and so on. During the first few years of the operation of the scheme, the students relieved the workers to the extent of 57,700 days' work. Large numbers of letters are received by us every day, in which workers and students alike tell us how grateful they are for their unforgettable experience. Works' leaders, too, continually inform us of the beneficial results achieved.

After completing the inauguration of the above schemes, we continued our work in a different direction, i.e., by organising ourselves. We have now co-ordinated the previously existing women's associations and thus created the German Women's Association [GWA], which is sub-divided into sections along the lines laid down by the NSWO.

The GWA consists, apart from the Mothers' Service already mentioned, of the following sections: National and domestic economy; cultural and educational matters; assistance, and a foreign section. In addition, there are four large administrative departments, viz., general administration; finances; organisation and staff; the Press and propaganda matters, which latter also deals with the radio, films, and exhibitions.

In the section for national and domestic economy, women and girls are trained to apply the principles of national solidarity. They are taught that, in every household, the mother is responsible for the health of the whole family by providing good food and by generally exercising her duties with skill and efficiency.

The cultural and educational section makes the nation's cultural assets available to women; women artists are assisted in their work, and particular attention is paid to the achievements of women in the realm of science.

The assistance section deals with the work done by female nurses, the Red Cross, and the air defence society.

The foreign section establishes contact with women's associations abroad, supplies information to foreigners, exchanges experiences with foreign organisations, makes arrangements for seeing the institutions in connection with the work of the GWA, etc.

All these groups are under the general direction of the NSWO, which may therefore be regarded as the leading organisation, whilst the GWA and the [Women's Section] constitute the joint foundation for the work done by women throughout the country.

Foreigners have repeatedly asked me about the kind of compulsion exercised to make women take part in all this work. I wish to assure inquirers that we know of no compulsion whatever. Those who want to join us, must do so absolutely voluntarily;

and I can only say that all of them are joyfully devoted to their work.

Let me conclude by quoting a remark which I made on the occasion of the Women's Congress held at the time of the Nuremberg party rally (1935): "All the work done by us as a matter of course, which is now so comprehensive that we cannot any longer describe it in detail, is only a means to an end. It is the expression of the determination of German women to assist in solving the great problems of our age. A spirit of comradeship animates all of us; and our devotion to our nation guides all our efforts."

See also women in the Third Reich, Vol . 2; Scholtz-Klink, Gertrude, Vol. 3.

The Hitler Youth

Reich youth leader Baldur von Shirach explains how the Hitler Youth prepares young Germans for national leadership and provides a necessary supplement to their education. He also notes that the young are a central part of the Nazi Party's plans for Germany's future.

The Hitler Youth knows no superiors, only leaders.

The leader is not a private individual who just happens to direct a youth organization from eight to six. His is more than an occupation; it is a calling. He cannot leave his task in the evening like an office worker, for he himself is a part of the task. He is committed far beyond his office hours. National Socialist leadership consists not in insignia, stars, and braids worn on the uniform, but rather in the constant dedication to that accomplishment for which stars

George L. Mosse, ed., *Nazi Culture.* New York: Schocken, 1981.

and braid are only a token of recognition. The HJ (Hitler-Jugend [German for Hitler Youth]) leader owes it to his followers to set them an example; he must lead a National Socialist life. He does not need to be physically stronger than the youths he leads, but he should be the strongest of his unit in terms of spiritual and character values. The structure of the HJ is such that the HJ leader cannot simply sit on a throne; he must be a comrade among comrades. His followers should look up to him not because his authority comes from above, but because it is based on the quiet superiority that derives from self-restraint.

A single will leads the Hitler Youth. The HJ leader, from the smallest to the largest unit, enjoys absolute authority. This means that he has the unrestricted right to command because he also has unrestricted responsibility. He knows that greater responsibility takes precedence over the lesser one. Therefore he silently subjects himself to the commands of his leaders, even if they are directed against himself. For him, as well as for the whole of young Germany, the history of the Hitler Youth is proof that even a fellowship of young people can be a success only when it unconditionally recognizes the authority of leadership. The success of National Socialism is the success of discipline; the edifice of the National Socialist youth is likewise erected on the foundation of discipline and obedience. The lesson of the period of the time of persecution likewise applies to the time of our victory and power. Thus the Jungvole [the organization for boys aged ten to fourteen] youngster who at the age of ten enters the movement of Adolf Hitler soon learns to subordinate his own petty will to the laws which have built states and made whole nations happy, but the violation of which results in the loss of freedom and the collapse of the Volk. As he grows older, he learns that discipline and subordination are not arbitrary inventions called into being by a few power-hungry men to safeguard their own personal position, but that they are, rather, the premises for his own and his nation's existence.

The great value of organization for a youth rests on this fact. Among those of his own age, and even in play, he acquires knowledge that will serve above all as a setting for adult life. And as he is instructed in discipline in a form in keeping with his mental faculties, he begins to understand that his own blind obedience gives the will of the group the possibility of success. Thus what is learned in early years by struggling with small tasks will later benefit the state in the fulfillment of its larger tasks. . . .

Everywhere now new youth hostels of the National Socialist type have come into being. The HJ is aware not only of the great influence of education, but especially of the practical experience of life. If German youth today takes hikes, it does not do so with a false and gushing sentimentality intoxicated with Nature, but even here it subordinates its action to a political purpose.

German youth roams the countryside in order to know its fatherland and, above all, comrades in other parts of the Reich. Anyone who has experienced the German Volk community and has learned to appreciate his fatherland in this way, in terms of the National Socialist ideology, will be able, if called upon to do so, to defend this state with his life.

The deeper meaning underlying the idea of hostels is to get the youth of large cities away from the morally corrosive dangers of its environment and to show that there is a form of recreation which is more satisfying than movies and beer joints and which costs less money. Through the youth hostel movement, even the poorest children of our people are given a chance to know the homeland for which they may be called upon to stake their lives. They need no expensive hotel accommodations and for only a few pennies they can be housed in a beautiful and practical building in the most beautiful regions of their homeland. A youth which has learned to know its great fatherland in such a way will in later life have a much wider political horizon than that of the beer hall. . . .

There are above all three forces which, in combination, determine the correct development of youth: the parental home, the school, and the Hitler Youth. The family is the smallest and at the same time the most important unit of our Volk community. It can never be the task of the HJ to interfere with the life of the family and with the work of the parents in bringing up their children. But neither should the parental home interfere with the work of the HJ. The HJ leader, however, should consider it his duty not only to maintain the best relations with the parents of the youngsters entrusted to him, but also to allow them every possible insight into the work of the organization. He must be ready to answer questions put to him by the parents of his young charges and should try to become the confidant of the family. Only that leader knows his young charges who also knows their fathers and mothers, their living conditions, their home, their joys and sorrows.

Every youth movement needs the spiritual cooperation of the parental home. If both parties attempt to undermine each other's authority, then there are wrong leaders at work. The parental home is in an even better position to give unqualified recognition to the service of the Hitler Youth, since this service supports the authority of the parents and does not impair it.

The HJ, especially in the last two years, has suffered from the fact that it did not have sufficient time for the fulfillment of its prescribed tasks. It is impossible for young workers to attend HJ service before eight in the evening. Thus students could not be assembled before this time either, since an earlier and separate assembly of students would have violated the spirit of the whole. But inasmuch as their service could not be continued into the early-morning hours, it was necessary to utilize every weekday evening and every Sunday. Such a situation is intolerable for two reasons: (1) the daily-attendance requirement disrupted family life and was the cause of inferior performances on the part of the youngsters during the day; (2) despite its efforts, the HJ did not have all the time it needed. On Sundays, consideration for the church frequently made it impossible to march out before noon. Further, in line with the agreement with the Evangelical Church, one evening a week and two Sundays each month had to be reserved. A decree of the Ministry of the Interior which stated that all juveniles had to be home by 8 P.M. could not be complied with because most employed youths were unable to do so, especially in localities where it took a young worker an hour or more to reach home after quitting work at 7 P.M. The decree was nullified by reality, coupled with the fact that the HJ in particular did not and could not abandon its principle that in some way time had to be found for the educational work of the

state. No police regulations, however well-meaning, could change this situation. This could be done only by a new arrangement —namely, the reservation of a full weekday for the purposes of the HJ. The plan for a State Youth Day provides for five work (or school) days for juveniles; a sixth day will be devoted exclusively to the HJ and its political education; and the seventh day, also exclusively, shall belong to the family. This arrangement, espoused by Reich Minister of Education Bernhard Rust, settled many difficulties which a continuation of the former situation would have created, particularly since the Reich youth leadership on its own decided that with the introduction of the State Youth Day, all weekday evenings, with the exception of Wednesday, should be exempt from service. Wednesday evening, which is traditionally the den evening of the HJ, will be an educational evening with a unified program prepared by the Reich youth leadership.

Thus the parental home can finally count on a definite division of service. The youth, however, has its own day, the day of the HJ, which it can devote to hiking and sports, a day in which it is led away from the school-bench and workshop so that it may renew the living experience of its own time, the experience of comradeship.

Thus the relationship between youth organization and family is balanced to some degree. Jointly, both are helping to clarify for German youth its task and mission—the parents by transmitting the lessons of their own lives to their children and by imbuing youthful hearts with the unique experience of German family life; the youth leadership by proclaiming and formulating the demands which National Socialism makes on Young Germany.

The school is education from above; the HJ that from below. In the school it is the teaching staff which educates; in the HJ it is the youth leadership. Obviously, within the school the authority of the teacher must be the highest authority. Equally obvious is the fact that the authority of the HJ leader is the highest authority outside of the school. If both parties scrupulously observe this distinction there can be no friction, particularly if both are also clearly aware that youth education is a unified whole in which both have to integrate themselves meaningfully. Without intending any criticism of the teaching profession, it must be said that a teacher, as such, should not, at the same time, also be an HJ leader. The fact that we also have several hundred teachers in the ranks of the HJ does not contradict this requirement. The HJ leadership comes from all walks of life; hence it also includes members of the teaching profession. But the Reich youth leadership does not as a matter of course recognize in any given teacher a greater aptitude for the office of youth leader than it does in any other Volk comrade. A teacher with special aptitude for youth work has the same possibilities for advancement within the HJ that are open to every other Volk comrade. His profession, however, does not give him a claim to youth leadership. Teaching and leadership are two fundamental different matters. Even the most experienced and successful schoolmaster may be a complete failure in the leadership of a youth group, just as, on the other hand, an able HJ leader may be incapable of giving regular school instruction. The prerequisites of teaching, in addition to a natural calling, include a definite, planned training routine supervised by the state. The youth leader also is subjected to a certain educational routine, which must, above all, include practical activity within the youth movement. Beyond that, he must possess an ability that no teacher's seminar, no university, and no ministry of public education can give him—namely, the ability to lead, which is inborn. This innate gift of leadership is crucial for the calling of youth leader. Whoever possesses it, whether teacher, peasant, or factory worker, can be employed in youth work. Unfortunately, many a teacher is of the opinion, among other things, that the right to youth leadership was bestowed on him along with his teacher's certificate, as it were. A fateful error! If by some oversight such a teacher should take over the leadership of a youth group, he would unconsciously falsify the meaning of the youth movement, because he would conceive of the youth organization simply as a continuation of scholastic instruction by different means. What for the youngsters is intended as marching and a serious hike then becomes a school outing, etc. All too easily, an office that obligates him to work with youth seduces a teacher into an erroneous self-estimation. He is apt to confound the authority bestowed on him as a teacher by the government with the other, innate authority of the leader. The end result is that the teacher and the youth are both disappointed; the teacher loses faith in himself and the youth loses faith in the idea. Such mistakes are hard to overcome, especially in the field of youth leadership. Hence it is far better to prevent such failures from the outset. Moreover, many a teacher has confirmed to me that a teacher who has a serious conception of the teaching profession would seldom be able to cope simultaneously with the responsibilities of educator and youth leader, since the work load would be much too great.

Moreover, the sociological structure of the Hitler Youth, in which the overwhelming majority are working youths, would confront a teacher who is an HJ leader with a social group altogether different from that which he had imagined from his work at school. The pedagogical qualifications which enable him to deal successfully with his own students within the HJ have no validity as soon as he is surrounded by apprentices from a wide variety of trades who have dropped out of school. And if at first he had presumed that he had to deal only with a school class dressed in uniform, he now becomes fully aware of the fact that the HJ, down to its smallest cell, represents the whole people.

The line of demarcation between school and the HJ cannot be drawn clearly enough. To be sure, the cooperation between youth leaders and teachers must be based on mutual confidence and comradeship. The more frequently that teacher and youth leader discuss the problems of the youths entrusted to their care, the better it will be not only for the school but also for the youth organization. A lazy student (and there are lazy students even in the HJ!) may frequently be more strongly motivated to do better work if his youth leader, after a conference with the teacher, exhorts him to do better, than would be the case if a warning came directly from the teacher. In this connection the following must be given special consideration: with the rise of the National Socialist youth movement, all schools today have classes that include leaders of the JV [Jungvolk] and the Hitler Youth as well as of the BDM [Bund Deutscher Mädel, the League of German Girls] among its students. The teacher must exercise a great deal of tact in order to find the right tone in dealing with them. Naturally they are pupils just as much as the others in the class. Nevertheless, it is a different thing to reprimand a student who leads a youth group outside of school than to reprimand one who is nothing but a student. Here the teacher must always strive not to reduce unnecessarily the authority of a youth leader in front of his comrades. He should tell him privately what must be said to him in the interest of his education. And if he is unsuccessful, he should get in touch with the superiors of the particular youth leader rather than engage in a disputation with him before the whole class, which frequently will lead only to the psychologically understandable consequence that the Hitler Youth will close ranks against the teacher, because they are unable to distinguish clearly between a reprimand to the pupil and one to their youth-group leader. And if in the excitement of the moment a word should be uttered against the HJ, the confidence of the student body in the teaching staff is destroyed, and it is not eas-ily re-established. But the more a teacher strives to enter into the spirit and structure of the HJ, the more success will he have. In my opinion, a teacher today must be willing to make the truly small sacrifice of attending this or that affair of the HJ, to show that he takes an interest in what his pupils are doing outside of school. So many teachers in Germany have in this way known how to establish psychological bonds between themselves and their students! But how many have made the mistake of turning their backs on the youth! The latter simply forget that in a higher sense youth is always right because youth carries within itself the new life. The inflexible adherence of such teachers to the olden times will only place them outside the new times, and they no longer will have any contact with youth and life.

In these times, the teacher is more necessary than ever. Like the youth leader, he has a great and magnificent task to perform for the sake of the young generation. Less than ever before should he be satisfied to close his books with the final bell and call it a day.

To be sure, youth has no particular respect for knowledge. It respects only the man. Whoever is a real man among the teachers will be able to make an exciting experience even out of the musty classroom. He who is not is beyond help. We can only hope that the breed which looked upon teaching only as a comfortable berth, and saw in the pupil only an unpleasant material that had to be worked, will soon die out. We all know men of this type, called "kettle-drummers" in popular usage. There are fewer of them every day. They can't stand the fresh air of the Third Reich, and as they vanish, the stalwart figures of our young teachers take their places. They, however, stand with both feet in the present, march in rank and file with their comrades in SA and PO [Political Organization], and, like them, are the older comrades of the Hitler Youth.

The liberalistic era invented the horrible title of Head Director of Studies. National Socialism will show us what a schoolmaster is.

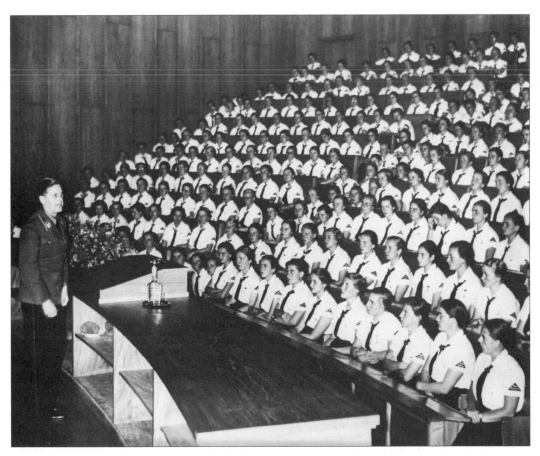

Baldur von Schirach, leader of the Hitler Youth, speaks to uniformed members of the League of German Girls in Berlin in 1934.

The HJ is a corporate component of the NSDAP. Its task is to see that new members of the National Socialist movement will grow up in the same spirit through which the Party achieved greatness. Every movement that finds itself in the possession of political power runs the danger of being corrupted by opportunists. Even the National Socialist movement has had its difficulties with these "knights of expediency." In popular usage they are known as the "hundred-and-ten percenters." These are people who for years have joined whatever political party was dominant, only to leave it at once when the star of political expediency began to wane. They have no interest in a world view nor the slightest spiritual impulse for their political decisions. Their only interest is the possibility of personal

profit and advantage. It is obvious that on January 30, 1933, such types also thought they saw opportunities for personal gain in National Socialism. Aware as they are of their own inferiority, these people are always examining the actions of National Socialist leaders to see whether they might not perhaps glimpse a betrayal of the National Socialist idea. Such "followers" of National Socialism are a greater danger to the movement than its real enemies. The NSDAP protects itself from these creatures primarily through its youth organizations. Whoever at the age of ten or twelve joined the JV and until his eighteenth year belonged to the HJ has served such a long probation period that the National Socialist party can be certain of him as an utterly reliable fighter. The party has no other way of safeguarding its inner strength. In the period of struggle, every NSDAP member, by the very fact of belonging to the party, was subjected to sacrifice and persecution; whoever came to us in those years was motivated by his faith. Today membership in the NSDAP carries with it a certain prestige. Rightfully this prestige is even greater the longer the membership has lasted. Today everyone knows that the insignia of the Old Guard of the party are symbols of willing sacrifice and loyal collaboration in the National Socialist movement.

It may well be that our movement, even after January 30, 1933, won hundreds of thousands of loyal and indefatigable members—but none of them, however eager, could any longer subject themselves to the probation of the period of struggle. It would be unjust to doubt whether any of them could prove his mettle if put to the test. The fact remains, however, that the old members, as lonely men, aligned themselves with a lonely Leader, while the new ones, in a chorus of millions, hailed the legal Commander-in-Chief of a nation. And it remains true that there are still men who would like to exploit a great, selfless idea for their personal advantage and to misuse the German freedom movement for their selfish purposes.

Thus, the National Socialist party seeks to increase its ranks from among our youth—from the mass of those who, like the old fighters of National Socialism, have in their early years sworn themselves to follow the flag out of faith and enthusiasm. Membership over a period of years in the HJ provides an opportunity for rightly judging a youngster's inclination and his worth to the community. Not every Hitler Youth necessarily becomes a member of the National Socialist party; membership in the HJ constitutes no title to later membership in the higher "order" of the movement. But

whoever in his youth has unfailingly fulfilled his duty to the movement can be sure that on the day of the solemn and ceremonial graduation of youth into the NSDAP, on the ninth of November, the portals of the party will be opened to him.

It is hardly necessary to point out that harmonious cooperation between the NSDAP and the HJ is especially indispensable. The relations between the top leadership of the youth organization and the Reich leadership, as well as those of the regional leadership to the respective provincial National Socialist administration, are imbued by the common will to further and strengthen the movement. Wherever difficulties arise, they will be quickly overcome by joint discussions. The close connection between the HJ and the political organization is clearly expressed in a regulation enacted by Dr. Ley [German Labor Front leader] making it compulsory for political leaders to appoint a suitable HJ leader as their aide. Through this measure the PO purposes to acquaint a greater circle of HJ leaders, while they are still active in the HJ, with the scope of duties of political leaders and thereby secure a pool of candidates for political leadership. Thus thousands of HJ members have been ordered to serve as aides to political leaders for a one-year period. Even if they should later on devote themselves exclusively to youth work, the knowledge that they will have acquired in the course of their political activity will be of great and essential value for the relationship between youth and the party. On the whole, the Reich youth leadership strives to bring the individual HJ leader into the closest possible contact with other branches of the movement.

See also education in the Third Reich, Hitler Youth, League of German Girls, Vol. 1; Shirach, Baldur von, Vol. 3.

An American on Hitler's Charisma

William L. Shirer was an American corre-spondent and broadcaster who reported on the Third Reich until forced to leave Ger-many in 1941. In this diary entry he specu-lates on the amazing appeal of Adolf Hitler to ordinary Germans.

NUREMBERG, *September 4, 1934*
Like a Roman emperor Hitler rode into this mediæval town at sundown today past solid phalanxes of wildly cheering Nazis who packed the narrow streets that once saw Hans Sachs and the *Meistersinger* [a figure from medieval German history who inspired an opera by Mozart]. Tens of thousands of Swastika flags blot out the Gothic beauties of the place, the façades of the old houses, the gabled roofs. The streets, hardly wider than alleys, are a sea of brown and black uniforms. I got my first glimpse of Hitler as he drove by our hotel, the Württemberger Hof, to his headquarters down the street at the Deutscher Hof, a favourite old hotel of his, which has been remodelled for him. He fumbled his cap with his left hand as he stood in his car acknowledging the delirious welcome with somewhat feeble Nazi salutes from his right arm. He was clad in a rather worn gaberdine trench-coat, his face had no particular expression at all—I expected it to be stronger—and for the life of me I could not quite comprehend what hidden springs he undoubtedly unloosed in the hysterical mob which was greeting him so wildly. He does not stand before the crowd with that theatrical imperiousness which I have seen Mussolini use. I was glad to see that he did not poke out his chin and throw his head back as does the Duce nor make his eyes

glassy—though there *is* something glassy in his eyes, the strongest thing in his face. He almost seemed to be affecting a modesty in his bearing. I doubt if it's genuine.

This evening at the beautiful old Rathaus [town hall] Hitler formally opened this, the fourth party rally. He spoke for only three minutes, probably thinking to save his voice for the six big speeches he is scheduled to make during the next five days. Putzi Hanf-stängl, an immense, high-strung, incoherent clown who does not often fail to remind us that he is part American and graduated from Harvard, made the main speech of the day in his capacity of foreign press chief of the party. Obviously trying to please his boss, he had the crust to ask us to "report on affairs in Germany without attempting to interpret them." "History alone," Putzi shouted, "can evaluate the events now taking place under Hitler." What he meant, and what Goebbels and Rosenberg mean, is that we should jump on the bandwagon of Nazi propaganda. I fear Putzi's words fell on deaf, if good-humoured, ears among the American and British correspondents, who rather like him despite his clownish stupidity.

About ten o'clock tonight I got caught in a mob of ten thousand hysterics who jammed the moat in front of Hitler's hotel, shouting: "We want our Führer." I was a lit-tle shocked at the faces, especially those of the women, when Hitler finally appeared on the balcony for a moment. They reminded me of the crazed expressions I saw once in the back country of Louisiana on the faces of some Holy Rollers who were about to hit the trail. They looked up at him as if he were a Messiah, their faces transformed into something positively inhuman. If he had remained in sight for more than a few

William L. Shirer, *Berlin Diary.* New York: Knopf, 1941.

Hitler's personal charisma and mastery of propaganda inspired near-hysterical devotion in many Germans.

moments, I think many of the women would have swooned from excitement.

Later I pushed my way into the lobby of the Deutscher Hof [a plush hotel]. I recognized Julius Streicher, whom they call here the Uncrowned Czar of Franconia. In Berlin he is known more as the number-one Jew-baiter and editor of the vulgar and pornographic anti-Semitic sheet the *Stürmer*. His head was shaved, and this seemed to augment the sadism of his face. As he walked about, he brandished a short whip.

NUREMBERG, *September 5, 1934*

I'm beginning to comprehend, I think, some of the reasons for Hitler's astounding success. Borrowing a chapter from the Roman church, he is restoring pageantry and colour and mysticism to the drab lives of twentieth-century Germans. This morning's opening meeting in the Luitpold Hall on the outskirts of Nuremberg was more than a gorgeous show; it also had something of the mysticism and religious fervour of an Easter or Christmas Mass in a great Gothic cathedral. The hall was a sea of brightly coloured flags. Even Hitler's arrival was made dramatic. The band stopped playing. There was a hush over the thirty thousand people packed in the hall. Then the band struck up the *Badenweiler March,* a very catchy tune, and used only, I'm told, when Hitler makes his big entries. Hitler appeared in the back of the auditorium, and followed by his aides, Göring, Goebbels, Hess, Himmler, and the others, he strode slowly down the long centre aisle while thirty thousand hands were raised in salute. It is a ritual, the old-timers say, which is always followed. Then an immense symphony orchestra played Beethoven's *Egmont* Overture. Great Klieg lights played on the stage, where Hitler sat surrounded by a hundred party officials and officers of the army and navy. Behind them the "blood flag," the one carried down the streets of Munich in the ill-fated putsch. Behind this, four or five hundred S.A. standards. When the music was over, Rudolf Hess, Hitler's closest confidant, rose and slowly read the names of the Nazi "martyrs"—brown-shirts who had been killed in the struggle for power—a roll-call of the dead, and the thirty thousand seemed very moved.

In such an atmosphere no wonder, then, that every word dropped by Hitler seemed like an inspired Word from on high. Man's —or at least the German's—critical faculty is swept away at such moments, and every lie pronounced is accepted as high truth itself. It was while the crowd—all Nazi officials—were in this mood that the Führer's proclamation was sprung on them. He did not read it himself. It was read by *Gauleiter* Wagner of Bavaria, who, curiously, has a voice and manner of speaking

so like Hitler's that some of the correspondents who were listening back at the hotel on the radio thought it was Hitler.

As to the proclamation, it contained such statements as these, all wildly applauded as if they were new truths: "The German form of life is definitely determined for the next thousand years. For us, the nervous nineteenth century has finally ended. There will be no revolution in Germany for the next one thousand years!"

Or: "Germany has done everything possible to assure world peace. If war comes to Europe it will come only because of Communist chaos." Later before a *"Kultur"* [culture] meeting he added: "Only brainless dwarfs cannot realize that Germany has been the breakwater against Communist floods which would have drowned Europe and its culture."

See also Führer cult, Vol. 1; Nuremberg rallies, Vol. 2.

Songs of the Third Reich

The following is a selection of the marches, folk songs, and popular songs sung at Nazi Party rallies, Hitler Youth outings, and by German army and SS units. Many consist of new lyrics set to old tunes from the German folk or classical traditions. German-language versions are provided to give a sense of the original rhythm.

"**D**eutschland Über Alles" ("Germany Above All")

The German national anthem dating from before the Nazi era. The words were written by the poet Heinrich Hoffman in 1841 and set to a melody by the great classical

composer Franz Haydn. Today only the third of the verses below is sung, and there are movements to ban the song entirely.

English:
1. Germany, Germany above all
   Above all in the world
   When, always for protection and
      defense,
   Brothers stand together
   From the Maas to the Memel
   From the Etsch to the Belt
   Germany, Germany above all
2. German women, German loyalty
   German wine and German song
   Shall retain throughout the
      world
   Their old respected fame,

Third Reich Factbook, www.skalman.nu/third-reich. Translations by the author.

To inspire us to noble deeds
For the entire length of our lives.
German women, German loyalty
German wine and German song.

3. Unity, rights, and freedom
For the German fatherland
Let us all strive to this goal,
Brotherly, with heart and hand.
Unity, rights and freedom
Are the pledges of grand fortune.
Prosper in fortune's glory,
Prosper, German fatherland.

German:

1. Deutschland, Deutschland über alles,
Über alles in der Welt,
Wenn es stets zu Schutz und Trutze
Brüderlich zusammenhält,
Von der Maas bis an die Memel,
Von der Etsch bis an den Belt-
Deutschland, Deutschland über alles,
Über alles in der Welt.

2. Deutsche Frauen, deutsche Treue,
Deutscher Wein und deutscher Sang
Sollen in der Welt behalten
Ihren alten schänen Klang,
Uns zu edler Tat begeistern
Unser ganzes Leben lang.
Deutsche Frauen, deutsche Treue,
Deutscher Wein und deutscher Sang.

3. Einigkeit und Recht und Freiheit
Für das deutsche Vaterland!
Danach lasst uns unser Streben,
Brüderlich mit Herz und Hand.
Einigkeit und Recht und Freiheit
Sind des glückes unterpfand.
Blüh' im Glanzes dieses Glückes,
Blühe, deutsches Vaterland!

"The Horst Wessel Song"

The unofficial national anthem of the Third
Reich and its number-one marching song,
composed by a young storm trooper named
Horst Wessel. He died in dubious circumstances involving a prostitute and Communist thugs in Berlin in 1929, but Joseph
Goebbels and his propaganda machine
turned him into a Nazi martyr. The song is

also known as *"Hold the Banner High!"*
("Die Fahne Hoch!")

English:

1. Hold high the banner! Close the ranks!
The SA marches on with steady stride
Comrades killed by the Red Front
(communists) or reaction
(conservatives) are buried,
But their spirit marches on with us.

2. Free the streets for the Brown battalions!
Free the streets for the Storm troopers!
The Swastika gives hope to our
entranced millions,
That the day of freedom and bread
is at hand.

3. For the last time the trumpet will blow!
We all stand ready for the fight!
Soon Hitler's banners will wave over
all the streets!
And our slavery will soon be over!

1. Hold high the banner! Close the ranks!
The SA marches on with steady stride
Comrades killed by the Red Front
(communists) or reaction
(conservatives) are buried,
But their spirit marches on with us.

German:

1. Die Fahne hoch die Reihen fest
geschlossen!
S.A. marschiert mit ruhig festem Schritt,
Kam'raden die Rotfront und Reaktion
erschossen,
Marschier'n im Geist in unsern
Reihen mit.

2. Die Strasse frei den braunen
Batallionen,
Die Strasse frei dem Sturmab-
teilungsmann,
Es schau'n auf's Hakenkreutz voll
Hoffnung schon Millionen,
Der Tag für Freiheit und für Brot
bricht an.

3. Zum letzten Mal wird nun Appell
geblasen,
Zum Kampfe steh'n wir alle
schon bereit,

Bald flattern Hitler-fahnen über
   allen Strassen
Die Knechtschaft dauert nur mehr
   kurze Zeit.
1. Die Fahne hoch die Reihen fest
   geschlossen!
   S.A. marschiert mit ruhig festem Schritt,
   Kam'raden die Rotfront und Reaktion
      erschossen,
   Marschier'n im Geist in unsern
      Reihen mit.

"Ich Hatt' Einen Kameraden"
("I Had a Comrade")

A popular song reminding Germans to be
willing to fight on despite the loss of their
comrades in arms.

English:
1. I had a comrade,
   You'll never find a better one
   The drum beat to the struggle
   And he walked by my side
   In the same step and stride
   In the same step and stride.
2. A bullet came flying,
   "Is it meant for me or for you?"
   It struck him down.
   He lay at my feet,
   As if he were a part of me,
   As if he were a part of me.
3. He tries to reach out to me
   As I am loading.
   "I cannot give you my hand.
   May you have eternal life,
   My good Comrade!
   My good Comrade!"

German:
1. Ich hatt' einen Kameraden,
   Einen bessern findst du nit.
   Die Trommel schlug zum Streite,
   Er ging an meiner Seite
   Im gleichen Schritt und Tritt.
   Im gleichen Schritt und Tritt.
2. Eine Kugel kam geflogen:
   Gilt's mir oder gilt es dir?
   Ihn hat es weggerissen,

Er liegt mir vor den Füssen
Als wär's ein Stück von mir.
Als wär's ein Stück von mir.
3. Will mir die Hand noch reichen,
   Derweil ich eben lad'.
   "Kann dir die Hand nicht geben,
   Bleib du im ew'gen Leben
   Mein guter Kamerad!
   Mein guter Kamerad!"

"Hitlerleute" ("Hitler People")

One of many songs devoted to the Führer
cult, a worshipful hymn to Adolf Hitler, and
yet another reminder of the need for struggle and sacrifice.

English:
1. In the struggle for the homeland,
   Many Hitler people died.
   But none thought to complain,
   Each wants to take this brave chance.
   We all want to struggle around
      the clock
   For the one who brings us bread and
      freedom!
   They line up and succeed
   In breaking forth from heaven with
      their loud and resounding cry.
Chorus:
   Hitler People, Hitler People,
   The chains of slavery can be heard
      in the land.
   But soon comes the day they will
      be broken,
   We are not cowardly slaves!
2. From the spiritual seducers,
   We will set our brothers free!
   From the madness of Marxism,
   Through National Socialism,
   A native land to build,
   Where the German people can be free!
   Onward! Fresh for the struggle!
   Adolf Hitler will find us ready for
      the fight! (repeat chorus)

German:
1. In dem Kampfe um die Heimat
   Starben viele Hitlerleute.

Aber keiner denkt ans Klagen,
Jeder will es mutig wagen.
Ringen woll'n wir um die Stunde,
Die uns Brot und Freiheit bringt
    (Freiheit bringt).
Reiht euch ein, es gelingt,
Laut und drohend schon der Ruf zum
    Himmel dringt.
Chorus:
    Hitlerleute, Hitlerleute,
    Es klirrt die Sklavenkette heute noch
        im Land.
    Es kommt der Tag, da sie zerbricht,
    Feige Knechte sind wir nicht!
2. Von der geistigen Verführung
    Unsre Brüder zu befreien,
    Von dem Wahnsinn des Marxismus
    Durch den deutschen Sozialismus!
    Eine Heimat zu erringen,
    Die die deutschen einst befreit
        (einst befreit).
    Vorwärts, frisch in den Streit!
    Adolf Hitler findet uns zum Kampf
        bereit.
    (repeat chorus)

"Heil Hitler Dir"
Another song devoted to Hitler worship,
this one is directed to the Führer himself. In
addition to the usual pledges of loyalty and
uncritical admiration for the Nazi cause,
this song offers the promise that the German people will help Hitler purify the Fatherland by getting rid of the Jews.

(English)
1. Germany awake to your better
        dream!
    Give foreign Jews no place in your
        Reich!
    We want to fight for your resurrection!
    Aryan blood will not be sullied!
2. All of these hypocrites, we will toss
        them out,
    Jews must escape from our German
        house!
    First the earth must be made clean,
    For us to be united and happy!

3. We are the fighters of the Nazi Party,
    Loyally German in our hearts, and
        in battle strong and tough.
    We are devoted to the Swastika,
    Hail our Führer, Heil Hitler to you.

German:
1. Deutschland erwache aus deinem
        bessen Traum!
    Gib fremden Juden in deinem Reich
        nicht Raum!
    Wir wollen kämpfen für dein
        Auferstehn!
    Arisches Blut soll nicht untergehn!
2. All diese Heuchler, wir werfen
        sie hinaus,
    Juda entweiche aus unserm deutschen
        Haus!
    Ist erst die Scholle gesäubert und rein,
    Werden wir einig und glücklich sein!
3. Wir sind die Kämpfer der N.S.D.A.P.:
    Treudeutsch im Herzen, im Kampfe
        fest und zäh.
    Dem Hakenkreuze ergeben sind wir
    Heil unserm Führer, Heil Hitler dir!

"Von Finland bis Zum Schwarzen Meer"
("From Finland down to the Black Sea")
Some Nazi songs were calls to military
readiness and heroism. This one calls for
the German armed forces to storm across
the eastern front in their war with the Soviet Union.

English:
1. We stand our post for Germany.
    And hold the great watch
    Now the sun rises in the east,
    And calls the millions to battle.
Chorus:
    From Finland down to the Black Sea,
    Onward! Onward!
    Forward to the east, you thundering
        host!
    Freedom the aim, victory the prize,
    Führer, command. We will follow.
2. The march that began with Horst
        Wessel,

In the brown uniform of the SA,
Is followed by the grey columns
   (of the army)
The great hour is now!
(repeat chorus)

German:
1. Wir standen für Deutschland auf Posten
   Und hielten die grosse Wacht.
   Nun hebt sich die Sonne im Osten
   Und ruft die Millionen zur Schlacht.
Chorus:
   Von Finnland bis zum Schwarzen
      Meer:
   Vorwärts, vorwärts!
   Vorwärts nach Osten, du stürmend'
      Heer!
   Freiheit das Ziel, Sieg das Panier!
   Führer, befiehl! Wir folgen dir!
2. Den Marsch von Horst Wessel
      begonnen
   Im braunen Gewand der SA
   Vollenden die grauen Kolonnen:
   Die grosse Stunde ist da!
   (repeat chorus)

"Gegen Briten und Franzosen"
("Against the British and the French")
Another war song, this one directed toward
the Third Reich's main enemies on the
western front. It is maudlin and sentimental
rather than rousing.

English:
1. To the soldiers of Adolf Hitler,
   Let's move out for the battle,
   Against the British and the French.
   No one stays at home, at home!
   Against the British and the French,
   No one stays at home
Chorus:
   Live well, my child,
   Because the wind howls in the
      west,
   Live well, dear mother,
   Today we must part!
2. Load your keenest weapons,
   And do not close your eyes,

The enemy wants to rise victorious
   over us,
And the world is quiet, is quiet
The enemy wants to rise victorious
   over us,
And the world is quiet.
(repeat chorus)
3. When we have exterminated the brood,
   According to good German custom,
   On the graves of our comrades,
   We will plant a green laurel bush!
   On the graves of our comrades,
   A green laurel bush.

German:
1. Als Soldaten Adolf Hitlers,
   Ziehen wir zum Kampfe aus,
   Gegen Briten und Franzosen,
   Niemand bleibt zu Haus, zu Haus!
   Gegen Briten und Franzosen,
   Niemand bleibt zu Haus!
Chorus:
   Lebe wohl mein Kind,
   Denn im Westen pfeift der Wind,
      der Wind.
   Leb' wohl Mütterlein,
   Heute muss geschieden sein!
2. Ladet eure schärfsten Waffen,
   Drückt auch nicht ein Auge zu,
   Siegreich woll'n den Feind wir
      schlagen,
   Und die Welt hat Ruh, hat Ruh.
   Siegreich woll'n den Feind wir
      schlagen,
   Und die Welt hat Ruh.
   (repeat chorus)
3. Haben wir die Brut vernichte
   Pflanzt nach gutem deutschen Brauch
   Auf das Grab der Kameraden,
   Einen grünen Lorbeerstrauch!
   Auf das Grab der Kameraden,
   Einen Lorbeerstrauch!

"Lied der Hitler Jugend"
("Song of the Hitler Youth")
The main marching song for the various
Hitler Youth contingents, sung at meetings,
rallies, and on outdoor excursions.

English:
1. Do you hear the drums pound?
   They call you all together
   Timidity is now past.
   They sound clearly from valley to
      valley.
2. We are the Hitler Youth,
   And help to set each other free,
   We stand with our young blood
   For the German people and our
      native land!
3. We know no social classes,
   Only loyalty is only for Germany.
   The world's enemies, whom we hate,
   Are not the German kind.

German:
1. Hört ihr die Trommel schlagen?
   Sie ruft euch allzumal!
   Vorbei das bange Zagen,
   Hell braust's von Tal zu Tal.
2. Wir sind die Hitlerjugend
   Und helfen euch befrei'n,
   Wir stehn mit unserm jungen Blut
   Für Volk und Heimat ein!
3. Wir kennen keine Klassen,
   Nur Deutsche treu geschart,
   Der Weltfeind, den wir hassen,
   Ist nicht von deutscher Art.
   See also music in the Third Reich, propaganda in the Third Reich, Vol. 2.

SS Marriage Requirements

As the purest of the pure, SS men were to be allowed to marry only under the strictest of racial guidelines and only with the approval of Reichsführer-SS Heinrich Himmler.

1. The SS is a band of definitely Nordic German men selected according to certain principles.

2. In accordance with the National Socialist ideology and with the realization that the future of our nation rests on the preservation of the race through selection and on the inheritance of good blood, I hereby institute from 1 January 1932 the 'Marriage Certificate' for all unmarried members of the SS.

3. The aim is to create a hereditarily healthy clan of a definitely Nordic German type.

4. The marriage certificate will be awarded or refused solely on the basis of racial health and heredity.

Jeremy Noakes and Geoffrey Pridham, eds., *Documents on Nazism, 1919–1945.* New York: Viking, 1974.

5. Every SS man intending to get married must procure for this purpose the marriage certificate of the Reichsführer SS.

6. SS members who marry despite having been denied marriage certificates will be removed from the SS; they will be given the chance of resignation.

7. It is the task of the SS 'Race Office' to work out the details of marriage petitions.

8. The SS Race Office is in charge of the 'Clan Book of the SS' in which the families of SS members will be entered after being awarded the marriage certificate or after acceptance of the petition to enter into marriage.

9. The Reichsführer SS, the director of the Race Office, and the specialists of this office are pledged to secrecy on their word of honour.

10. The SS is convinced that with this order it has taken a step of great significance. Derision, scorn, and incomprehension will not move us; the future is ours!

See also SS, Vol. 2; Himmler, Heinrich, Vol. 3.

Student Protest Leaflets: The White Rose

As World War II progressed, voices of protest were raised in Germany against their nation's brutality and loss of honor, though their protest was brutally suppressed. One came from students at the University of Munich and came to be known as the White Rose. The small group's leaders, and the authors of the following leaflets, included Hans Scholl, a medical student who had also served on the eastern front.

The First Leaflet

Nothing is so unworthy of a civilized nation as allowing itself to be "governed" without opposition by an irresponsible clique that has yielded to base instinct. It is certain that today every honest German is ashamed of his government. Who among us has any conception of the dimensions of shame that will befall us and our children when one day the veil has fallen from our eyes and the most horrible of crimes—crimes that infinitely outdistance every human measure—reach the light of day? If the German people are already so corrupted and spiritually crushed that they do not raise a hand, frivolously trusting in a questionable faith in lawful order in history; if they surrender man's highest principle, that which raises him above all other God's creatures, his free will; if they abandon the will to take decisive action and turn the wheel of history and thus subject it to their own rational decision; if they are so devoid of all individuality, have already gone so far along the road toward turning into a spiritless and cowardly mass—then, yes, they deserve their downfall. [German writer Johann Wolfang von] Goethe speaks of the Germans as a tragic people, like the Jews and the Greeks, but today it would appear rather that they are a spineless, will-less herd of hangers-on, who now—the marrow sucked out of their bones, robbed of their center of stability—are waiting to be hounded to their destruction. So it seems—but it is not so. Rather, by means of gradual, treacherous, systematic abuse, the system has put every man into a spiritual prison. Only now, finding himself lying in fetters, has he become aware of his fate. Only a few recognized the threat of ruin, and the reward for their heroic warning was death. We will have more to say about the fate of these persons. If everyone waits until the other man makes a start, the messengers of avenging Nemesis will come steadily closer; then even the last victim will have been cast senselessly into the maw of the insatiable demon. Therefore every individual, conscious of his responsibility as a member of Christian and Western civilization, must defend himself as best he can at this late hour, he must work against the scourges of mankind, against fascism and any similar system of totalitarianism. Offer passive resistance—*resistance*—wherever you may be, forestall the spread of this atheistic war machine before it is too late, before the last cities, like Cologne, have been reduced to rubble, and before the nation's last young man has given his blood on some battlefield for the *hubris* of a sub-human. Do not forget that every people deserves the regime it is willing to endure.". . . .

Leaflet of the Resistance

A Call to All Germans!

The war is approaching its destined end.

As in the year 1918, the German government is trying to focus attention exclusively on the growing threat of submarine warfare, while in the East the armies are constantly in retreat and invasion is imminent in the West. Mobilization in the United States has not yet reached its climax, but already it exceeds anything that the world has ever seen. It has become a mathematical certainty that Hitler is leading the German people into the abyss. *Hitler cannot win the war; he can only prolong it.* The guilt of Hitler and his minions goes beyond all measure. Retribution comes closer and closer.

But what are the German people doing? They will not see and will not listen. Blindly they follow their seducers into ruin. *Victory at any price!* is inscribed on their banner. "I will fight to the last man," says Hitler—but in the meantime the war has already been lost.

Germans! Do you and your children want to suffer the same fate that befell the Jews? Do you want to be judged by the same standards as your traducers? Are we to be forever the nation which is hated and rejected by all mankind? No. Dissociate yourselves from National Socialist gangsterism. Prove by your deeds that you think otherwise. A new war of liberation is about to begin. The better part of the nation will fight on our side. Cast off the cloak of indifference you have wrapped around you. Make the decision *before it is too late!* Do not believe the National Socialist propaganda which has driven the fear of Bolshevism into your bones. Do not believe that Germany's welfare is linked to the victory of National Socialism for good or ill. A criminal regime cannot achieve a German victory. Separate yourselves *in time* from everything connected with National Socialism. In the aftermath a terrible but just judgment will be meted out to those who stayed in hiding, who were cowardly and hesitant.

What can we learn from the outcome of this war—this war that never was a national war?

The imperialist ideology of force, from whatever side it comes, must be shattered for all time. A one-sided Prussian militarism must never again be allowed to assume power. Only in large-scale cooperation among the nations of Europe can the ground be prepared for reconstruction. Centralized hegemony, such as the Prussian state has tried to exercise in Germany and in Europe, must be cut down at its inception. The Germany of the future must be a federal state. At this juncture only a sound federal system can imbue a weakened Europe with a new life. The workers must be liberated from their condition of downtrodden slavery under National Socialism. The illusory structure of autonomous national industry must disappear. Every nation and each man have a right to the goods of the whole world!

Freedom of speech, freedom of religion, the protection of individual citizens from the arbitrary will of criminal regimes of violence—these will be the bases of the New Europe.

Support the resistance. Distribute the leaflets! . . .

The Last Leaflet

Fellow Fighters in the Resistance!

Shaken and broken, our people behold the loss of the men of Stalingrad. Three hundred and thirty thousand German men have been senselessly and irresponsibly driven to death and destruction by the inspired strategy of our World War I Private First Class. Führer, we thank you!

The German people are in ferment. Will we continue to entrust the fate of our armies to a dilettante? Do we want to sacrifice the rest of German youth to the base ambitions of a Party clique? No, never! The day of reckoning has come—the reckoning of German youth with the most abominable tyrant our people have ever been forced to endure. In the name of German youth we demand restitution by Adolf Hitler's state of our personal freedom, the most precious treasure that we have, out of which he has swindled us in the most miserable way.

We grew up in a state in which all free expression of opinion is unscrupulously suppressed. The Hitler Youth, the SA, the SS have tried to drug us, to revolutionize us, to regiment us in the most promising young years of our lives. "Philosophical training" is the name given to the despicable method by which our budding intellectual development is muffled in a fog of empty phrases. A system of selection of leaders at once unimaginably devilish and narrow-minded trains up its future party bigwigs in the "Castles of the Knightly Order" to become Godless, impudent, and conscienceless exploiters and executioners—blind, stupid hangers-on of the Führer. We "Intellectual Workers" are the ones who should put obstacles in the path of this caste of overlords. Soldiers at the front are regimented like schoolboys by student leaders and trainees for the post of Gauleiter, and the lewd jokes of the Gauleiters insult the honor of the women students. German women students at the university in Munich have given a dignified reply to the besmirching of their honor, and German students have defended the women in the universities and have stood firm. . . . That is a beginning of the struggle for our free self-determination—without which intellectual and spiritual values cannot be created. We thank the brave comrades, both men and women, who have set us a brilliant example.

For us there is but one slogan: fight against the party! Get out of the party organizations, which are used to keep our mouths sealed and hold us in political bondage! Get out of the lecture rooms of the SS corporals and sergeants and the party bootlickers! We want genuine learning and real freedom of opinion. No threat can terrorize us, not even the shutting down of the institutions of higher learning. This is the struggle of each and every one of us for our future, our freedom, and our honor under a regime conscious of its moral responsibility.

Freedom and honor! For ten long years Hitler and his coadjutors have manhandled, squeezed, twisted, and debased these two splendid German words to the point of nausea, as only dilettantes can, casting the highest values of a nation before swine. They have sufficiently demonstrated in the ten years of destruction of all material and intellectual freedom, of all moral substance among the German people, what they understand by freedom and honor. The frightful bloodbath has opened the eyes of even the stupidest German—it is a slaughter which they arranged in the name of "freedom and honor of the German nation" throughout Europe, and which they daily start anew. The name of Germany is dishonored for all time if German youth does not finally rise, take revenge, and atone, smash its tormentors, and set up a new Europe of the spirit. Students! The German people look to us. As in 1813 the people expected us to shake off the Napoleonic yoke, so in 1943 they look to us to break the National Socialist terror through the power of the spirit. Beresina and Stalingrad are burning in the East. The dead of Stalingrad implore us to take action.

"Up, up, my people, let smoke and flame be our sign!"

Our people stand ready to rebel against the National Socialist enslavement of Europe in a fervent new breakthrough of freedom and honor.

See also resistance movements, Germany; White Rose, Vol. 2; Scholl, Hans and Scholl, Sophie, Vol. 3.

The Verdict of the People's Court on Rebels

The Third Reich's so-called People's Court met to condemn those Germans who acted against the will of Hitler's state. During much of World War II its leading judge was the notorious Roland Freisler. Here, he summarizes the offenses of and pronounces "people's judgment" on the leaders of the White Rose student resistance movement.

February 21, 1943
Berlin

Reich Attorney General
to the People's Court

H = Regular Volume
S = Supplementary Volume

Indictment

S v. 2

1. *Hans* Fritz *Scholl* of Munich, born September 22, 1918, in Ingersheim, single, no previous convictions, taken into investigative custody on February 18, 1943;

S v. 1

2. *Sophia* Magdalena *Scholl* of Munich, born on May 9, 1921, in Forchtenberg, single, no previous convictions, taken into investigative custody on February 18, 1943; and

3. *Christoph* Hermann *Probst* of Aldrans bei Innsbruck, born on November 6, 1919, in Murnau, married, no previous convictions, taken into investigative custody February 20, 1943; all at present in the jail of the headquarters, State Police (Gestapo), Munich, all at present not represented by counsel;

are accused:

in 1942 and 1943 in Munich, Augsburg, Salzburg, Vienna, Stuttgart, and Linz, committing together the same acts:

I. with attempted high treason, namely by force to change the constitution of the Reich, and acting with intent:

    1. to organize a conspiracy for the preparation of high treason,

    2. to render the armed forces unfit for the performance of their duty of protecting the German Reich against internal and external attack,

    3. to influence the masses through the preparation and distribution of writings; and

II. with having attempted, in the internal area of the Reich, during time of war, to give aid to the enemy against the Reich, injuring the war potential of the Reich; and

III. with having attempted to cripple and weaken the will of the German people to take measures toward their defense and self-determination,

Crimes according to Par. 80, Sec. 2; Par 83, Secs. 2 and 3, No. 1, 2, 3; Pars. 91b, 47, 73 of the Reich Criminal Code (St GB), and Par. 5 of the Special War Criminal Decree.

In the summer of 1942 and in January and February of 1943 the accused Hans *Scholl* prepared and distributed leaflets containing the demand for a settlement of accounts with National Socialism, for disaffection from the National Socialist "gangsterism," and for passive resistance and sabotage. In addition, in Munich he adorned walls with the defamatory slogan "Down With Hitler" and with canceled swastikas. The accused Sophie *Scholl* participated in the preparation and distribution of the seditious materials. The accused *Probst* composed the first draft of a leaflet.

I

Summary of Results of Investigations
S I 4—R

1. To the year 1930 the father of the accused Hans and Sophie Scholl was mayor of Forchtenberg. Later he was Economic Adviser in Ulm on the Danube. The accused Scholls have two sisters and a brother, who is now serving in the armed forces. Against the accused Hans Scholl, as well as against his brother Werner and his sister Inge, charges had previously been brought on the part of the Reich Police Headquarters, Stuttgart, concerning conspiratorial acts, which led to the temporary arrest of the above-named. Hans Scholl attended the local secondary school and in 1937 he enlisted in the army. In 1939 he began his studies in medicine, which he continued during his period of active service in the army in April, 1941. He was last assigned to the Student Company in Munich with the rank of sergeant. He covered the cost of tuition out of his army pay and out of an allowance from his father. In 1933 Scholl joined the *Hitler Jungvolk* [for boys aged 10–14] and was later transferred to the *Hitler Jugend* [Hitler Youth].

2. The accused Sophia Scholl worked first as kindergarten teacher and since the summer of 1942 has been studying science and philosophy at the University of Munich. Until 1941 she belonged to the *Bund deutscher Mädel* [League of German Girls], serving finally as Group Leader.

3. The accused Probst attended the Gymnasium [high school] in Nuremberg and, after finishing his Labor Service, volunteered for the army. Later he became a medical student and most recently belonged to the Student Company in Innsbruck with the rank of sergeant in the medical service.

II

In the summer of 1942 the so-called Leaflets of the White Rose were distributed through the mails. These seditious pamphlets contain attacks on National Socialism and on its cultural-political policies in particular; further, they contain statements concerning the alleged atrocities of National Socialism, namely the alleged murder of the Jews and the alleged forced deportation of the Poles. In addition, the leaflets contain the demand "to obstruct the continued functioning of the atheistic war machine" by passive resistance, before it is too late and before the last of the German cities, like Cologne, become heaps of ruins and German youth has bled to death for the "*hubris* of a subhuman." According to Leaflet No. II, a wave of unrest must go through the land. If "it is in the air," if many participate, then in a great final effort this system can be shaken off. An end with terror, the leaflet stated, is preferable to terror without end. In Leaflet No. III the idea is developed that it is the intent and goal of passive resistance to bring down National Socialism. In this struggle one should not hesitate to take any course, to do any deed. At all points National Socialism must be attacked, wherever it may be vulnerable. Not military victory should be the first concern of every German, but rather the defeat of National Socialism. Every committed opponent of National Socialism must therefore ask himself how he can most effectively struggle against the present "state" and deal it the most telling blows. To this end sabotage in armament plants and war industry, the obstruction of the smooth functioning of the war machine, and sabotage of all National Socialist functions, as well as in all areas of scientific and intellectual life, is demanded.

A total of four separate leaflets of this sort were distributed in Munich at that time.

In January and February of 1943 two separate seditious leaflets were distributed by means of random scattering and through the mails. One of these bears the heading "Leaflets of the Resistance Movement in Germany" and the other "Fellow Fighters in the Resistance!" or "German Students!" The first leaflet states that the war is approaching its sure and certain end. However, the German government is trying to direct all attention to the growing submarine threat, while in the East the armies are falling back ceaselessly in retreat, in the West the invasion is expected, and the armament of America is said to exceed anything that history has heretofore recorded. Hitler (it states) cannot win the war; he can only prolong it. The German people, who have blindly followed their seducers into ruin, should now dissociate themselves from National Socialist sub-humanity and through their deeds demonstrate that they do not agree. National Socialist propaganda, which has terrorized the people by fostering a fear of Bolshevism, should not be given credence, and people should not believe that Germany's future is tied to the victory of National Socialism for better or for worse.

The second leaflet, referring to the battle of the Sixth Army at Stalingrad, states that there is a ferment among the German people, and the question is raised whether the fate of our armies should be entrusted to a dilettante. The breaking of National Socialist terror, the leaflet expects, will be the work of students—to whom the German people are looking for guidance and who will achieve their goal through the power of the intellect.

III

1. The accused Hans *Scholl* occupied his thoughts for a long time with the political situation. He arrived at the conclusion that just as in 1918, so also after the seizure of power by the National Socialists in 1933, it was not the majority of the German masses but the intellectuals in particular who had failed politically. This is the only explanation, in his opinion, why mass movements with simplistic slogans had succeeded in drowning out all thought that was more profound. Accordingly, he felt it his duty to remind the middle-class intellectuals of their political obligations, one of which was to take up the struggle against National So-

Sophie Scholl, one of the founders of the White Rose student protest movement, was executed on February 22, 1943, at the age of twenty-two.

cialism. He therefore decided to prepare and distribute leaflets intended to carry his ideas to the broad masses of the people. He bought a duplicating machine, and with the help of a friend, Alexander *Schmorell,* with whom he had often discussed his political views, he acquired a typewriter. He then drafted the first leaflet of the "White Rose" and claims singlehandedly to have prepared about a hundred copies and to have mailed them to addresses chosen from the Munich telephone directory. In so doing, he selected people in academic circles particularly, but also restaurant owners who, he hoped, would spread the contents of the leaflets by word of mouth. Subsequently he prepared three additional leaflets of the "White Rose," which were likewise written by him. The contents of these leaflets are reproduced above, in Part II of this indictment. Again these were distributed through the mails.

He was prevented from issuing more writings by his assignment to active duty on the eastern front in July 1942. He claims that in part he himself paid for the materials used in preparing the leaflets; some portion of the costs were given to him, he claims, by his friend Schmorell.

The name "The White Rose," according to the statements of the accused Hans Scholl, was chosen arbitrarily and took its inception from his reading of a Spanish novel with this title. The accused claims that at first he did not plan an organization; only later, namely early in 1943, did he draw up the plan for an organization which was to propagate his ideas. He claims that he has not yet attempted to bring together a group of like-minded persons.

Early in 1943 the accused Hans Scholl—who in the meantime had been given leave from army service for the purpose of studying at the University of Munich, came to the conclusion—as he relates—that there was only one means of saving Europe, namely by shortening the war. To publicize this idea, he drafted two more leaflets, in editions totaling about 7,000, and with the titles mentioned above in Part II of this indictment. Of these he scattered about 5,000 copies in the inner city of Munich, and in addition he mailed numerous other copies. At the end of January he traveled to Salzburg, and from the railway post office he posted some 100 to 150 letters containing the leaflets he had prepared. In addition, about 1,500 of the seditious papers were distributed through the mails in Linz and Vienna by Schmorell, who at Scholl's behest traveled to these cities. Scholl contributed to the cost of train tickets. Finally Scholl had his sister Sophia take about 1,000 letters containing seditious leaflets to Augsburg and Stuttgart, where she put them in the mails. After the news of the reverses in the East, Hans Scholl again prepared leaflets in which he reproduced the text of his student leaflet under a new title. Of these he sent several hundred through the mails. He took the addresses from a directory of the University of Munich. On February 18, 1943, he and his sister also scattered more seditious papers. On this occasion he was observed by the witness *Schmied* and placed under arrest.

Early in 1943 the accused Hans Scholl requested his friend, the accused Probst (with whom he had for a long time exchanged ideas about the political situation), to write down his ideas on current developments. Probst then sent him a draft, which without doubt was to be duplicated and distributed, though there was no time for such action. This draft was found in Scholl's pocket at the time of his arrest.

At the end of January 1943 the accused Hans Scholl, at the suggestion of Schmorell, decided to make propaganda by painting defamatory slogans on walls. Schmorell prepared a stencil for him with the text "Down With Hitler" and with a swastika which was canceled through, and he furnished paint and brush. In early February 1943 Hans Scholl, together with Schmorell, painted such slogans in black tar on several houses in Munich, on the columns in front of the University, on the buildings of the National Theater and the Ministry of Economics, the Schauspielhaus Theater, and elsewhere.

2. The accused Sophia *Scholl* as early as the summer of 1942 took part in political discussions, in which she and her brother, Hans Scholl, came to the conclusion that Germany had lost the war. Thus she shared with her brother the view that agitation against the war should be carried out through leaflets. She claims to be unable to remember whether the idea of the preparation of leaflets had its inception with her or with her brother. She claims that she had no part in the preparation and distribution of the leaflets with the title "The White Rose" and that she did not become aware of them until a friend showed her a copy. On the other hand, she admits to having taken part in preparing and distributing the leaflets in 1943. Together with her brother she drafted

the text of the seditious "Leaflets of the Resistance in Germany." In addition, she had a part in the purchasing of paper, envelopes, and stencils, and together with her brother she actually prepared the duplicated copies of this leaflet. She also helped her brother address the envelopes for mailing. Furthermore, at the request of her brother she traveled by express train to Augsburg and Stuttgart and put the prepared letters into various mailboxes, and she took part in the distribution of the leaflets in Munich by depositing them in telephone booths and parked automobiles.

The accused Sophia Scholl was also implicated in the preparation and distribution of the student leaflets. She accompanied her brother to the university, was observed there in the act of scattering the leaflets, and was arrested when he was taken into custody.

The accused Sophia Scholl was not involved in the act of defacement of buildings, though when she learned about it, she offered to assist on future occasions. She even expressed the view to her brother that it might be a good form of concealment to have a woman taking part in this activity.

The accused Sophia Scholl knew that her brother spent considerable sums of money in the preparation of the seditious papers. In fact, she took charge of her brother's finances, since he was little concerned about money matters; she kept financial records and issued to him the sums he needed for these purposes.

3. The accused Probst, who was often in the company of brother and sister Scholl and who shared their ideas, wrote at the request of the accused Hans Scholl the draft, mentioned above, of his estimate of the current political scene. He claims, to be sure, that he did not know that Scholl intended to use the draft for a leaflet, but he did admit that he was aware that it might be used for illegal propaganda.

IV

The accused were on the whole willing to admit to their acts.

Testimony and Exhibits

I. The statements of the accused in the Supplementary Volumes I–III;

II. The Judge of the Police Praesidium of Munich: H 9 R;

III. The witnesses:
   1. Custodian Jakob Schmied, Munich, Türkenstrasse 33/I,
   2. and
   3. Officials of the Police yet to be named;

IV. Exhibits:
   1. The confiscated typewriters, duplicating machine, duplicating master, paint, and brushes;
   2. the leaflets and photographs in the appended volume of exhibits.

With the concurrence of the Chief of Staff of the Supreme Command of the Armed Services and the Reich Minister of Justice, the case is transferred to the People's Court for action and decision.

DOCUMENT 2. Transcript of the Sentence of Hans and Sophie Scholl and Christoph Probst, February 22, 1943.

Transcript
I H 47/43

In the Name of the German People
In the action against

1. *Hans* Fritz *Scholl,* Munich, born at Ingersheim, September 22, 1918,

2. *Sophia* Magdalena *Scholl,* Munich, born at Forchtenberg, May 9, 1921, and

2. *Christoph* Hermann *Probst,* of Aldrans bei Innsbruck, born at Murnau, November 6, 1919, now in investigative custody regarding treasonous assistance to the enemy, preparing to commit high treason, and weakening of the nation's armed security,

the People's Court, first Senate, pursuant to the trial held on February 22, 1943, in which the officers were:

President of the People's Court Dr. Freisler, Presiding,

Director of the Regional (Bavarian) Judiciary Stier,

SS *Group Leader* Breithaupt,
SA *Group Leader* Bunge,
State Secretary and SA *Group Leader* Köglmaier, and, representing the Attorney General to the Supreme Court of the Reich, Reich Attorney Weyersberg,
find:

That the accused have in time of war by means of leaflets called for the sabotage of the war effort and armaments and for the overthrow of the National Socialist way of life of our people, have propagated defeatist ideas, and have most vulgarly defamed the Führer, thereby giving aid to the enemy of the Reich and weakening the armed security of the nation.

On this account they are to be punished by

Death.

Their honor and rights as citizens are forfeited for all time.

See also People's Court, White Rose, Vol. 2; Freisler, Roland; Scholl, Hans and Scholl, Sophie, Vol. 3.

CHRONOLOGY

1889
April 20
Adolf Hitler is born in Braunau am Inn, a village in upper Austria near the Austria–Germany border.

1893
January 12
Hermann Göring is born in the Bavarian town of Rosenheim.

1897
October 29
Joseph Goebbels is born in Rheydt in the Rhineland.

1900
October 7
Heinrich Himmler is born near Munich.

1904
March 7
Reinhard Heydrich is born in Halle, Saxony.

1914
June 28
Austrian heir to the throne Archduke Franz Ferdinand is assassinated in Sarajevo, beginning the spiral of events that would start World War I.
August 3
Hitler joins the Bavarian infantry.

1918
November 9
Kaiser Wilhelm II, emperor of Imperial Germany, abdicates.
November 11
World War I ends with an armistice signed at Compiègne, in France.

November 12
Friedrich Ebert announces a new, democratic government for Germany, later known as the Weimar Republic.

1919
January 5
The German Workers' Party is founded in Munich by Anton Drexler and Karl Harrer; a Communist uprising by Spartacists begins.
January 15
Rosa Luxembourg and Karl Liebknecht, leaders of the Spartacists, are killed by right-wing, nationalist Freikorps.
April 4
Communists establish a Soviet republic in Munich known as the Räterepublik.
May 2
The Räterepublik is crushed by Freikorps in combination with the regular German army.
June 28
German representatives unwillingly sign the Treaty of Versailles, which greatly reduces Germany's armed forces and requires the nation to pay huge sums in war reparations.
July 31
The Weimar Constitution takes effect.
September 16
Hitler, at that point an informant for the German army in Munich, joins the German Workers' Party. He quickly learns that he has great skill in public speaking and organization.

1920
February 24
At a large meeting in a Munich beer hall, Hitler announces that the German Workers' Party is now the National Socialist German Workers' Party, or the Nazi Party for short.

He also announces the party's Twenty-Five Points.

1921
July 29
Hitler, as the result of conflicts among Nazi Party leaders, demands that he be recognized as chairman of the party. Realizing his leadership skills, other party leaders give in to his demands.
November 4
The SA, or Nazi storm troopers, is officially founded and placed under the authority of Ernst Röhm.

1923
January 11
The French army occupies the Ruhr in response to Germany's failure to pay war reparations. German reaction helps inspire a massive inflation of the German mark, and by November, one American dollar buys over 800 million marks.
January 28
The first Nazi Party day, a sign of rallies, pageantry, and propaganda to come, takes place in Munich. A second is held in Weimar in 1926, and subsequent mass rallies take place in Nuremberg in 1927, 1929, and annually from 1933 to 1938.
May 26
Albert Leo Schlageter, later turned into the first martyr for the Nazi cause, is executed by the French for spying and other antiocupation activities.
November 8–9
The Beer Hall Putsch, Hitler and the Nazis' first attempt to seize power. It fails and Hitler is arrested on November 11.
November 15
The inflation ends with the establishment of the Rentenmark.

1924
February 26
Hitler is placed on trial for treason. He uses the occasion to defend himself by justifying the Nazi program and attacking those who "humiliated" Germany by accepting the World War I armistice and the Treaty of Versailles. The trial brings him attention across Germany.
April 1
Hitler is sentenced to a term of five years in Munich's Landsberg Prison. With his faithful deputy Rudolf Hess at his side, he soon begins his autobiographical work, *Mein Kampf.*
December 20
Hitler is released from prison for good behavior.

1925
February 24
Hitler reclaims control of the Nazi Party, an organization that had fallen into disarray during his months in prison.
December 8
Mein Kampf is published.

1926
February 14
Hitler meets other Nazi leaders, including Gregor Strasser, leader of the northern German "left" wing, at a party conference in Bamberg. There he cements his domination of the party. Joseph Goebbels switches his allegiance from Strasser to Hitler.
December 1
Hitler names Goebbels Gauleiter of Berlin.

1927
August 19
The first Nuremberg Party rally.

1929
January 6
Heinrich Himmler, a young agriculturist and longtime Nazi, becomes head of the SS, a small corps of bodyguards and security men.
June 7
The Young Plan to reorganize reparations payments is announced. It inspires an uproar among conservative Germans, inspiring Alfred Hugenberg, leader of the German National People's Party, to sound out Adolf

Hitler as a possible coalition partner. It is Hitler's first true entrance into mainstream, respectable politics.

1930

January 30
The Nazi Party achieves its first major political appointment when Wilhelm Frick is named minister of the interior in the state of Thuringia.

February 23
Horst Wessel, a storm trooper of dubious associations, dies in Berlin. His "Horst Wessel Song" becomes the unofficial national anthem of the Third Reich.

September 14
In elections to the Reichstag, the Nazi Party receives 18 percent of the vote, their best showing yet. It entitles them to 107 seats out of a total of 577.

1931

May 11
The Kreditanstalt, a major Viennese bank, declares insolvency. Its failure sparks a banking and financial crisis across Europe and especially in Germany. Within one year more than 6 million Germans are unemployed.

1932

February 25
Hitler is granted German citizenship, clearing the way for him to run for president.

March 13
Hitler receives 13.7 million votes in a presidential election. The showing entitles him to a place in a runoff.

April 10
In a runoff election for president, Field Marshal Paul von Hindenburg is reelected.

April 14
On the orders of Chancellor Heinrich Brüning, the SA and SS are banned for their involvement in street violence. Hitler asks party members to observe the ban.

June 1
Franz von Papen replaces Brüning as chancellor and lifts the ban on the SA and SS.

July 31
The Nazi Party becomes the largest political party in Germany by winning 230 of 608 Reichstag seats. It is their best ever showing in a free election.

December 3
Kurt von Schleicher replaces Papen as chancellor.

1933

January 4
Hitler meets Papen to discuss a possible right-wing government.

January 30
Hitler is named chancellor of Germany by Hindenburg, who accepts the Hitler-Papen government.

February 27
The Reichstag fire, an event the Nazis quickly blame on Communists.

February 28
The Reichstag fire decree gives Hitler special powers to preserve order.

March 9
Himmler becomes police president of Munich.

March 13
Hitler opens the Reich Ministry of Public Enlightenment and Propaganda, naming Joseph Goebbels his minister.

March 20
Dachau, the first true concentration camp, is established.

March 24
The Enabling Act, passed by a Reichstag thrown into a new balance by a Communist ban, gives Hitler the power to act outside the Weimar Constitution.

April 1
Hitler declares a national boycott on Jewish businesses. It is a resounding failure.

April 7
The Law for the Restoration of the Civil Service removes Jews from government jobs and teaching positions and replaces them with loyal Nazis.

April 26
The Gestapo is formed out of the former Prussian State Police.

May 10
The Burning of the Books announces a new period of restrictions in German thought and culture.
July 20
A Concordat is signed between the Third Reich and the Roman Catholic Church recognizing religious freedoms.

1934
April 11
In a secret agreement with German military leaders, Hitler promises to contain the increasingly troublesome SA if the generals support him in his bid to become president as well as chancellor of Germany.
June 30
The Blood Purge; SS agents murder Ernst Röhm, Gregor Strasser, Kurt von Schleicher, and others who oppose the sole dictatorship of Hitler.
August 2
Hindenburg dies; Hitler combines the offices of president and chancellor to become the sole Führer of the Third Reich.
September
The now massive Nuremberg Party rally; the event is filmed by Leni Riefenstahl as a celebration of Hitler's new power and status. The film is released under the title *Triumph of the Will*.

1935
June 18
The Anglo-German Naval Accord makes it clear that neither Britain nor France will oppose German rearmament.
September 15
Hitler announces the Nuremberg Laws, which deprive German Jews of their right to citizenship and open the door to further restrictions.
October 3
Fascist Italy invades Ethiopia.

1936
March 7
Hitler sends German troops into the Rhine-land in defiance of the Treaty of Versailles and the Locarno Pact.
June 17
Heinrich Himmler is named head of all German police forces.
August 1
The Olympic Games open in Berlin.
August 23
German Protestant leaders issue the Barmen Declaration denouncing the Third Reich's attempt to nazify the church.
September 9
Nazi officials announce the Four-Year Plan for rearmament under the control of Hermann Göring.
October 25
Nazi Germany and Fascist Italy become allies with the Rome-Berlin Axis.
November 25
Germany and Japan enter into the Anti-Comintern Pact.

1937
April 27
The Spanish city of Guernica is bombed by the German Condor Legion, sent to Spain by Göring as head of the Luftwaffe to support right-wing forces in the Spanish Civil War.
November 5
The Hossbach Conference, in which Hitler announces his war aims to top military and diplomatic officials.

1938
February 4
Hitler reorganizes the German military in the aftermath of scandals that force the resignations of Minister of War Werner von Blomberg and commander in chief of the army Werner Freiherr von Fritsch. He creates the Oberkommando der Wehrmacht (OKW), or High Command of the armed forces. Hitler becomes supreme commander while General Wilhelm Keitel becomes operations chief and therefore highest-ranking officer.
February 4
Joachim von Ribbentrop is named foreign minister.

March 12

The Anschluss, or annexation of Austria by the Third Reich.

September 30

The Munich Conference, in which Britain and France effectively give in to Hitler's territorial demands in Czechoslovakia. The annexation of the Sudetenland quickly follows.

November 9–10

The Kristallnacht pogrom, a nationwide attack on German Jews. Hundreds are killed while innumerable homes, buildings, and synagogues are destroyed. Over the next days thousands of Jews are rounded up and sent to concentration camps while laws removing Jewish children from schools and Jewish managers and workers from businesses are passed.

1939

January 24

The SS opens the Office for Jewish Emigration with branches in Vienna and Prague.

January 30

In a speech before the Reichstag, Hitler announces that the "annihilation of the Jewish race in Europe" is a possible effect of a broad European war begun, he claims, by Jews.

March 15

Germany occupies the remainder of Czechoslovakia.

March 31

Britain and France pledge their assistance if Germany invades Poland.

August 23

The Nazi-Soviet Pact is signed. It guarantees that the Soviet Union will not interfere in a German invasion of Poland. A secret protocol grants the Soviets, in return, a wide sphere of influence in eastern Europe.

September 1

World War II begins when the Third Reich invades Poland.

September 3

Great Britain and France declare war on Germany.

September 17

Soviet forces sweep into eastern Poland and the Baltic states as a result of the secret protocol of August 23.

September 21

Reinhard Heydrich announces his plan to place all Polish Jews in ghettos. He also announces the formation of Einsatzgruppen, special squads to eliminate Polish civilian resistance.

September 27

Poland falls with the surrender of Warsaw; Himmler announces the organization of the Reich Central Security Office (RSHA) with jurisdiction over all police and security forces in Greater Germany and the occupied territories. Heydrich is named its chief.

October

The T-4 euthanasia program begins in Germany.

October 7

Hitler names Himmler Reich Commissioner for the Strengthening of Ethnic Germandom, granting him broad powers in eastern Europe.

October 12

Hans Frank, a Nazi legal official, is named governor-general of occupied Poland.

December 17

The *Graf Spee,* a German battleship, is sunk after a battle with British ships off of Montevideo, Uruguay.

1940

January 25

Himmler selects the southern Polish town of Auschwitz to be the site for a new concentration camp.

February 12

The first deportations of German Jews to Poland.

April 9

The Third Reich launches its invasions of Denmark and Norway.

May 10

The Third Reich invades the Netherlands, Belgium, Luxembourg, and France.

May 26

The evacuation of Allied troops from Dunkirk begins.

June 10
Italy declares war on Britain and France.
June 16
A new French government, led by Henri-Philippe Pétain, sues for peace with Germany. The armistice is signed on June 22 at Compiègne, in the exact location where Germany surrendered to France in 1918.
August 13
The Battle of Britain, ostensibly the preliminary phase of Germany's invasion of Great Britain, begins with massive air attacks.
August 15
Discussions over the "Jewish Question" in eastern Europe continue among SS officials with the presentation of the Madagascar Plan.
September 17
Hitler calls off the invasion of Britain, Luftwaffe planes having been unable to clear the way.
October 16
The establishment of the Warsaw ghetto begins.

1941

January 6
U.S. president Franklin D. Roosevelt calls for peace and announces the Four Freedoms.
February 12
General Erwin Rommel becomes head of the Afrika Korps.
early March
Hitler issues the Commissar Order, making it known to top military commanders that the coming war between the Third Reich and the Soviet Union will be a war for survival in which any brutal measure is justified, including the summary killing of Russian civilians.
March 24
President Roosevelt signs the Lend-Lease Act, making it possible for the United States to provide military aid and supplies to Great Britain.
April 6
Germany invades Yugoslavia and Greece.

May 10
Rudolf Hess makes his solo flight to Britain in the insane hope of negotiating a peace.
May 27
Roosevelt declares a state of national emergency because of German U-boat threats to American shipping in the Atlantic.
June 22
Operation Barbarossa, the German invasion of the Soviet Union, begins. The largest military operation in history, the invasion front stretches from the Baltic to the Black Sea.
July 31
Göring authorizes Heydrich to seek a "complete solution to the Jewish Question" in German-occupied Europe.
September 3
SS officials test the effectiveness of Zyklon B gas at Auschwitz.
September 6
The Vilna ghetto is established.
September 17
The beginning of the deportation of all remaining German Jews to the Polish ghettos.
September 28–29
The Einsatzgruppen massacres at Babi Yar near Kiev in the Ukraine. Over two days SS killing squads shoot up to thirty-four thousand victims.
December 7
The Japanese bomb the American naval base at Pearl Harbor, starting war between the two countries; Hitler issues the Night and Fog Decree.
December 11
Adolf Hitler declares war between Germany and the United States.
December 19
German armies are forced to pull back from their assault on Moscow. Hitler dismisses General Walther von Brauchitsch as commander in chief of the Wehrmacht and takes the post himself.

1942

January 1
Twenty-six nations sign a declaration to

form a United Nations when the global conflict ends.

January 20
At the Wannsee Conference, Heydrich makes it plain to selected officials that the "Final Solution to the Jewish Question" is to be death by gassing.

February 9
Albert Speer becomes Reich Minister for Armaments and War Production.

March
The beginning of Operation Reinhard, the killings of Polish Jews at the death camps of Belzec, Sobibor, and Treblinka.

March 28
Fritz Sauckel is named Plenipotentiary for the Allocation of Labor. His job is to collect, import, and allocate slave labor for German industries.

May 29
Heydrich is attacked by Czech nationalists in Prague. He dies of his wounds on June 4, inspiring a broad and brutal vengeance by the SS.

June 21
The first gassings in Auschwitz.

July 22
Himmler orders the "liquidation" of the Warsaw ghetto. Soon after, the Jewish Fighting Organization forms to plan resistance to the deportations.

August 23
The German attack on Stalingrad begins.

November 5
Allied forces conclusively defeat Rommel's Afrika Korps at El Alamein. Extensive Allied landings in North Africa soon follow.

1943

January 18
The Jewish Fighting Organization mounts its first attack in the Warsaw ghetto.

January 24
The Allies announce their policy of unconditional surrender.

January 29
The Germans order all Gypsies to be sent to concentration camps.

January 30
Ernst Kaltenbrunner becomes head of the RSHA.

February 2
Soviet forces accept the surrender of Field Marshal Paulus's Sixth Army in Stalingrad.

February 18
Hans Scholl, Sophie Scholl, and the other leaders of the White Rose student movement in Munich are arrested for anti-Nazi activities.

March 13
Operation Flash, General Henning von Tresckow's attempt to kill Hitler by placing a bomb on his plane, fails.

April 19
The beginning of the main phase of the Warsaw ghetto uprising.

May 16
The Warsaw ghetto uprising ends when SS general Jürgen Stroop cables Berlin with the message, "The Jewish Quarter in Warsaw is no more."

July 10
The Allies make successful landings on the Italian island of Sicily.

July 25
Mussolini is forced to step down as Fascist leader of Italy. He is replaced by Pietro Badoglio, who wants a peace with the Allies.

August 25
Himmler replaces Frick as minister of the interior.

September 3
Allied forces land on the Italian mainland.

September 8
Italy surrenders unconditionally to the Allies; German forces occupy the northern part of the country, taking Rome on September 10.

September 13
Mussolini is rescued from captivity by SS adventurer Otto Skorzeny.

October 2
The call for the deportation of Jews from Denmark. Thanks to the efforts of the Danish underground as well as dozens of ordinary

citizens, most of them are instead moved to safety in Sweden.

October 14

An uprising at Sobibor results in the escape of several hundred inmates.

November 4

The Erntefest, or Harvest Festival massacres in Poland, in which Himmler virtually completed the liquidation of Polish Jews. Soon after the extermination camps at Treblinka, Sobibor, and Belzec are closed.

November 6

Soviet forces retake Kiev.

November 28–December 1

Roosevelt, British prime minister Winston Churchill, and Soviet premier Joseph Stalin meet at Tehran.

December 24

General Dwight D. Eisenhower is named chief of the Supreme Headquarters of the Allied Expeditionary Force (SHAEF) as the Allies prepare to open a second front in western Europe.

1944

January 3

Soviet forces reach Poland.

January 19

The siege of Leningrad is lifted.

April 5

General Charles de Gaulle is officially recognized as the head of the French Committee of National Liberation.

May 15

Deportations of Jews from Hungary begin; despite the efforts of a number of international organizations and local rescuers, more than four hundred thousand Hungarian Jews are sent to their deaths at Auschwitz over the next two months.

June 4

American forces occupy Rome.

June 6

D-Day; the Allied invasion of western Europe begins with massive landings on the beaches of Normandy.

June 12

The first V-1 rockets fall on England.

July 20

Lieutenant Colonel Claus Graf von Stauffenberg places a bomb in Hitler's eastern headquarters at Rastenburg; the bomb goes off, but fails to kill the Nazi leader. Back in Berlin plotters fail to seize their advantage, and the last effort of the German resistance movement fails.

July 22

Hitler names Goebbels Plenipotentiary for Total War.

August 4

Anne Frank and her family are arrested in Amsterdam; Hitler sets up a special military court of honor to try and disgrace those military officials accused of being involved in the July 1944 Plot.

August 8

The first executions of July 20 conspirators; hundreds more follow.

August 25

De Gaulle liberates Paris.

September 8

The first V-2 rocket is fired on England.

September 12

Allied forces cross the German border in the west.

October 14

Rather than face Hitler's honor court or endanger his family, Rommel commits suicide.

November 2

Himmler orders gassings at Auschwitz halted.

November 26

Himmler orders the killing facilities at Auschwitz to be destroyed.

December 16

The Battle of the Bulge, the last German offensive in the west, begins.

1945

January 14

Soviet forces enter Germany from the east.

January 17

Soviet troops enter Warsaw; Auschwitz is evacuated, as those inmates able to walk are sent on forced death marches to Germany.

January 27

Soviet forces reach Auschwitz.

February 4–11
Roosevelt, Churchill, and Stalin meet at Yalta.

March 7
American forces successfully cross the Rhine River at the Remagen Bridge.

April 10
The Buchenwald concentration camp is liberated.

April 12
President Roosevelt dies and is succeeded by Harry S. Truman.

April 15
Bergen-Belsen is liberated.

April 23
Soviet forces reach Berlin and begin a vicious street-by-street battle.

April 25
Allied leaders refuse to negotiate a peace with Himmler.

April 25
Negotiations on the establishment of the United Nations get under way in San Francisco; American and Russian troops meet at the Elbe River.

April 28
Mussolini is killed by Italian partisans.

April 29
American troops liberate Dachau.

April 30
Hitler commits suicide in the Berlin Führerbunker after issuing his last will and political testament. He names Grand Admiral Karl Dönitz his successor.

May 1
Goebbels commits suicide.

May 2
German forces in Italy surrender unconditionally. Dönitz seeks to maintain a government at Flensburg in northern Germany, mainly in the hopes that as many Germans as possible can escape from Soviet-conquered areas. Soviet forces take Berlin and loot the Führerbunker.

May 5
German forces in Denmark, the Netherlands, and northern Germany surrender.

May 7
On the orders of Dönitz, General Alfred Jodl signs the Third Reich's unconditional surrender to the Allies at Reims in France.

May 8
The unconditional surrender takes effect, and World War II in Europe is over.

May 9
Soviet general Georgi Zhukov signs the unconditional surrender in Berlin.

June 26
The United Nations Charter is approved by fifty nations in San Francisco.

July 17–August 2
Stalin, Truman, and new British prime minister Clement Attlee meet at Potsdam.

August 6
Americans drop an atomic bomb on the Japanese city of Hiroshima.

August 9
A second atomic bomb is dropped on Nagasaki.

August 15
The Japanese surrender ends World War II in the Pacific.

FOR FURTHER RESEARCH

Books

Theodor Abel, *Why Hitler Came into Power*. Cambridge, MA: Harvard University Press, 1986.

William Sheridan Allen, *The Nazi Seizure of Power: The Experience of a Single German Town 1922–1945*. New York: Franklin Watts, 1984.

Per Anger, *With Raoul Wallenberg in Budapest: Memories of the War Years in Hungary*. New York: Holocaust Library, 1996.

Yitzhak Arad, *Belzec, Sobibor, Treblinka: The Operation Reinhard Death Camps*. Bloomington: Indiana University Press, 1987.

Hannah Arendt, *Eichmann in Jerusalem: A Report on the Banality of Evil*. New York: Penguin, 1965.

Pierre Aycoberry, *The Social History of the Third Reich*. Trans. Janet Lloyd. New York: New Press, 2000.

Mitchell G. Bard, ed., *The Complete History of the Holocaust*. San Diego: Greenhaven Press, 2001.

Yehuda Bauer, *A History of the Holocaust*. New York: Franklin Watts, 1982.

Werner Baumbach, *The Life and Death of the Luftwaffe*. New York: Coward McCann, 1960.

Michael Berenbaum, ed., *Witness to the Holocaust*. New York: HarperCollins, 1997.

Doris L. Bergen, *Twisted Cross: The German Christian Movement in the Third Reich*. Chapel Hill: University of North Carolina Press, 1985.

Richard Bessell, *Life in the Third Reich*. New York: Oxford University Press, 1987.

Nicholas Bethell, *The War Hitler Won: The Fall of Poland, September 1939*. New York: Holt, Rinehart, and Winston, 1973.

Charles Bewley, *Hermann Goering and the Third Reich*. New York: Devin-Adair, 1962.

Hans Peter Bluel, *Sex and Society in Nazi Germany*. Trans. J. Maxwell Brownjohn. Philadelphia: Lippincott, 1973.

Joseph Borkin, *The Crime and Punishment of IG Farben*. New York: Free Press, 1979.

Rita Steinhardt Botwinick, *A History of the Holocaust*. 2nd ed. Upper Saddle River, NJ: Prentice-Hall, 1996.

Eva Braun, *The Diary of Eva Braun*. Ed. Alan Bartlett. Bristol, England: Spectrum, 2000.

Elinor Brecher, *Schindler's Legacy: True Stories of the List Survivors*. New York: Plume, 1994.

Richard Breitman, *The Architect of Genocide: Himmler and the Final Solution*. Hanover, NH: University Press of New England, 1992.

Christopher Browning, *Ordinary Men*. New York: HarperCollins, 1992.

Alan Bullock, *Hitler and Stalin: Parallel Lives*. New York: Knopf, 1992.

———, *Hitler: A Study in Tyranny*. New York: HarperCollins, 1994.

Michael Burleigh, *The Racial State: Germany 1933–1945*. Cambridge, England: Cambridge University Press, 1992.

———, *The Third Reich*. New York: Hill and Wang, 2000.

William Carr, *A History of Germany 1815–1990*. London: Edward Arnold, 1991.

Robert Cecil, *The Myth of the Master Race: Alfred Rosenberg and Nazi Ideology.* New York: Dodd, Mead, 1972.

Houston Stewart Chamberlain, *The Foundations of the Nineteenth Century.* New York: Howard Fertig, 1968.

Allen Churchill, ed., *Eyewitness: Hitler.* New York: Walker, 1979.

Winston Churchill, *The Second World War.* 6 vols. London: Cassell, 1948–1954.

Alan Clark, *Barbarossa.* New York: William Morrow, 1965.

James V. Compton, *The Swastika and the Eagle.* Boston: Houghton Mifflin, 1967.

Robert E. Conot, *Justice at Nuremberg.* New York: Harper and Row, 1983.

James Cornwell, *Hitler's Pope: The Secret History of Pius XII.* New York: Viking Press, 1999.

Gordon Craig, *The Germans.* New York: Putnam, 1982.

———, *Germany 1866–1945.* New York: Oxford University Press, 1980.

Lucy Dawidowicz, *The War Against the Jews 1933–1945.* Philadelphia: Jewish Publications Society, 1975.

Otto Dietrich, *The Hitler I Knew.* Trans. Richard and Clara Winston. London: Methuen, 1957.

Leonard Dinnerstein, *America and the Survivors of the Holocaust.* New York: Columbia University Press, 1982.

Alexander Donat, *The Holocaust Kingdom: A Memoir.* New York: Holocaust Library, 1978.

Eichmann Interrogated: Transcripts from the Archives of the Israeli Police. Trans. Ralph Manheim. London: Bodley Head, 1983.

Dwight D. Eisenhower, *Crusade in Europe.* Baltimore: Johns Hopkins University Press, 1997.

Bert Engelmann, *In Hitler's Germany: Daily Life in the Third Reich.* Trans. Krishna Winston. New York: Pantheon, 1986.

David Faber with James D. Kitchen, *Because of Romek.* San Diego: Granite Hills Press, 1993.

Joachim C. Fest, *The Face of the Third Reich.* New York: Pantheon, 1970.

Norman G. Finkelstein, *The Holocaust Industry.* London: Verso, 2000.

Anne Frank, *The Diary of a Young Girl.* Trans. B.M. Mooyaart-Doubleday. Garden City, NY: Doubleday, 1952.

Henry Friedlander, *The Origins of Nazi Genocide: From Euthanasia to the Final Solution.* Chapel Hill: University of North Carolina Press, 1995.

Saul Freidlander, *Nazi Germany and the Jews.* New York: HarperCollins, 1997.

Hans Fritsche and Hildegard Springer, *The Sword in the Scales.* Trans. Diana Pyke and Heinrich Fraenkel. London: Allan Wingate, 1953.

Max Gallo, *The Night of Long Knives.* Trans. Lili Emmet. New York: Harper and Row, 1972.

Peter Gay, *Weimar Culture.* New York: Harper Torchbooks, 1968.

Germany Speaks, by Twenty-One Leading Members of Party and State. London: Thornton Butterworth, 1938.

Martin Gilbert, *Atlas of the Holocaust.* New York: William Morrow, 1993.

———, *Auschwitz and the Allies.* New York: Holt, Rinehart and Winston, 1981.

———, *The Second World War: A Complete History.* New York: Henry Holt, 1992.

Joseph Goebbels, *Final Entries 1945: The Diaries of Joseph Goebbels.* Ed. H.R. Trevor-Roper. New York: G.P. Putnam's Sons, 1978.

———, *The Goebbels Diaries 1942–1943.* Ed. and trans. Louis P. Lochner. Garden City, NY: Doubleday, 1948.

Daniel Goldhagen, *Hitler's Willing Executioners: Ordinary Germans and the Holocaust.* New York: Knopf, 1996.

Hermann Göring, *The Political Testament of Hermann Göring.* Arr. and trans. H.W. Blood-Ryan. London: John Long, 1939.

G.S. Graber, *Stauffenberg: Resistance Movement Within the General Staff.* New York: Ballantine, 1973.

Nathaniel Greene, ed., *Fascism: An Anthology*. New York: Thomas Y. Crowell, 1968.

Israel Gutman, *Resistance: The Warsaw Ghetto Uprising*. Boston: Mariner/Houghton Mifflin. Published in association with the American Holocaust Museum, 1994.

S. William Halperin, *Germany Tried Democracy*. New York: Thomas Y. Crowell, 1946.

Konrad Heiden, *A History of National Socialism*. New York: Knopf, 1935.

Raul Hilberg, *The Destruction of the European Jews*. Chicago: Quadrangle, 1961.

Adolf Hitler, *Mein Kampf*. Trans. Ralph Manheim. Boston: Houghton Mifflin, 1943.

———, *My New Order*. Ed. Raoul de Roussy de Sales. New York: Reynal and Hitchcock, 1941.

———, *The Speeches of Adolf Hitler, April 1922–August 1939*. Trans. and ed. Norman H. Baynes. New York: Howard Fertig, 1969.

Peter Hoffman, *The History of the German Resistance 1933–1945*. Montreal: McGill/Queens University Press, 1996.

Heinz Höhne, *The Order of the Death's Head: The Story of Hitler's SS*. Trans. Richard Barry. New York: Ballantine, 1969.

Rudolf Höss, *Death Dealer: The Memoirs of the SS Kommandant at Auschwitz*. Buffalo, NY: Prometheus, 1992.

Matthew Hughes and Chris Mann, *Inside Hitler's Germany: Life Under the Third Reich*. Dulles, VA: Brassey's, 2000.

Robert H. Jackson et al., *The Case Against the Nazi War Criminals*. New York: Knopf, 1946.

William Jenks, *Vienna and the Young Hitler*. New York: Columbia University Press, 1960.

Eric A. Johnson, *Nazi Terror: The Gestapo, Jews, and Ordinary Germans*. New York: Basic, 2000.

John Keegan, *Barbarossa: The Invasion of Russia 1941*. New York: Ballantine, 1970.

Thomas Keneally, *Schindler's List*. New York: Simon and Schuster, 1994.

Ian Kershaw, *Hitler 1889–1936: Hubris*. New York: Norton, 1999.

———, *Hitler 1936–1945: Nemesis*. New York: Norton, 2000.

———, *Hitler: Profiles in Power*. New York: Longman, 1991.

———, *The Nazi Dictatorship*. London: E. Arnold, 1993.

Tim Kirk, *The Longman Companion to Nazi Germany*. London: Longman, 1995.

Eugen Kogon, *The Theory and Practice of Hell*. New York: Octagon, 1976.

Claudia Koonz, *Mothers in the Fatherland: Women, the Family, and Nazi Politics*. New York: St. Martin's, 1988.

Helmut Krausnick and Marti Brozsat, *Anatomy of the SS State*. London: William Collins Sons, 1968.

August Kubizek, *The Young Hitler I Knew*. Trans. E.V. Anderson. Boston: Houghton Mifflin, 1955.

Walter Laqueur, *Generation Exodus*. Hanover, NH: Brandeis University Press/The University Press of New England, 2001.

———, *The Terrible Secret: Suppression of the Truth About Hitler's Final Solution*. New York: Viking, 1982.

———, *Young Germany: A History of the German Youth Movement*. London: Routledge and Kegan Paul, 1962.

Vera Laska, ed., *Women in the Resistance and in the Holocaust: The Voices of Eyewitnesses*. Westport, CT: Greenwood Press, 1983.

John K. Lattimer, *Hitler and the Nazi Leaders: A Unique Insight into Evil*. New York: Hippocrene, 2001.

Primo Levi, *The Drowned and the Saved*. New York: Vintage Books, 1989.

———, *Survival in Auschwitz*. New York: Touchstone Press/Simon and Schuster, 1958.

Günther Lewy, *The Catholic Church and Nazi Germany*. New York: McGraw-Hill, 1962.

Robert J. Lifton, *The Nazi Doctors*. New York: Basic, 1986.

Deborah E. Lipstadt, *Denying the Holocaust: The Growing Assault on Truth and Memory*. New York: Free Press, 1993.

Michael Marrus, *Vichy France and the Jews*. New York: Basic, 1981.

David Mason, *U-Boat: The Secret Menace*. London: Ballantine, 1972.

[Stanley McClatchie?], *See the Heart of Europe! [Sieh das Herz Europas!]*. Berlin: Verlag Heinrich Hoffman, 1938.

Paul Mendes-Flohr and Jehuda Reinharz, eds., *The Jew in the Modern World: A Documentary History*. New York: Oxford University Press, 1995.

Johanna M. Meskill, *Hitler and Japan: The Hollow Alliance*. New York: Atherton Press, 1966.

Leonard Mosley, *The Reich Marshal*. Garden City, NY: Doubleday, 1974.

George L. Mosse, *The Crisis of German Ideology: Intellectual Origins of the Third Reich*. New York: Grosset & Dunlap, 1964.

———, ed., *Nazi Culture: Intellectual, Cultural, and Social Life in the Third Reich*. New York: Schocken, 1966.

———, *Toward the Final Solution: A History of European Racism*. New York: Howard Fertig, 1997.

A.J. Nicholls, *Weimar and the Rise of Hitler*. New York: Macmillan, 1968.

Jeremy Noakes and Geoffrey Pridham, eds., *Documents on Nazism, 1919–1945*. New York: Viking Press, 1974.

———, *Nazism 1919–1945*. Vol. 3, *Foreign Policy, War, and Racial Extermination: A Documentary Reader*. Exeter, England: University of Exeter Press, 1988.

Emil Nolte, *Three Faces of Fascism*. Trans. Leila Vennewitz. New York: Holt, Rinehart and Winston, 1966.

Peter Novick, *The Holocaust in American Life*. Boston: Houghton Mifflin, 1999.

Miklos Nyiszli, *Auschwitz: A Doctor's Eyewitness Account*. Greenwich, CT: Fawcett Press, 1960.

Robert J. O'Neill, *The German Army and the Nazi Party 1933–1939*. London: Cassell, 1966.

Richard J. Overy, *War and Economy in the Third Reich*. New York: Oxford University Press, 1995.

Franz von Papen, *Memoirs*. Trans. Brian Connell. New York: E.P. Dutton, 1953.

Jonathan Petropoulos, *Art as Politics in the Third Reich*. Chapel Hill: University of North Carolina Press, 1996.

James Pool, *Hitler and His Secret Partners: Contributions, Loot, and Rewards 1933–1945*. New York: Pocket, 1997.

Gerald Posner, *Mengele: The Complete Story*. New York: Dell, 1987.

Bruce Quarrie, *Hitler's Samurai: The Waffen-SS in Action*. Wellingborough, England: Patrick Stephens, 1983.

Lawrence Rees, *The Nazis: A Warning from History*. New York: New Press, 1997.

Gerald Reitlinger, *The SS: Alibi of a Nation*. London: William Heinemann, 1957.

Abraham Resnick, *The Holocaust*. San Diego: Lucent, 1991.

Norman Rich, *Hitler's War Aims: The Establishment of the New Order*. New York: Norton, 1974.

Alfred Rosenberg, *The Myth of the Twentieth Century*. 1930. Reprint, Newport Beach, CA: Noontide, 1982.

H. Rosenfeld, *The Swedish Angel of Rescue: The Heroism and Torment of Raoul Wallenberg*. Buffalo, NY: Prometheus, 1982.

Arnold P. Rubin, *The Evil That Men Do: The Story of the Nazis*. New York: J. Messner, 1981.

Benjamin C. Sax and Dieter Kuntz, eds., *Inside Hitler's Germany: A Documentary History of Life in the Third Reich*. Lexington, MA: D.C. Heath, 1992.

Walter Schellenberg, *The Labyrinth: Memoirs of Walter Schellenberg, Hitler's Chief of Counterintelligence*. New York: Da Capo, 2000.

Fabian von Schlabrendorff, *The Secret War Against Hitler*. Trans. Hilda Simon. New York: Pitman, 1965.

Matthias Schmidt, *Albert Speer: The End of a Myth.* New York: St. Martin's, 1984.

Paul Schmidt, *Hitler's Interpreter: The Secret History of German Diplomacy 1936–1945.* New York: Macmillan, 1951.

Franz Schneider and Charles Gullans, trans., *Last Letters from Stalingrad.* New York: William Morrow, 1962.

David Schoenbaum, *Hitler's Social Revolution: Class and Status in Nazi Germany.* New York: Norton, 1997.

Inge Scholl, *The White Rose: Munich 1942–1943.* 2nd ed. Middletown, CT: Wesleyan University Press, 1970.

Michael Selzer, *Deliverance Day: The Last Hours at Dachau.* Philadelphia: Lippincott, 1978.

Gitta Sereny, *Into That Darkness: From Mercy Killing to Mass Murder.* New York: McGraw-Hill, 1974.

William Shirer, *Berlin Diary.* New York: Knopf, 1943.

———, *The Rise and Fall of the Third Reich.* New York: Fawcett Crest, 1950.

Ann Maria Sigmund, *Women of the Third Reich.* Richmond Hill, Ontario, Canada: NDE, 2000.

Howard K. Smith, *Last Train from Berlin.* New York: Knopf, 1962.

Albert Speer, *Inside the Third Reich.* Trans. Richard and Clara Winston. New York: Macmillan, 1970.

Art Spiegelman, *Maus: A Survivor's Tale.* 2 vols. New York: Pantheon, 1986, 1992.

Jackson J. Spielvogel, *Hitler and Nazi Germany.* Upper Saddle River, NJ: Prentice-Hall, 1992.

Jill Stephenson, *Women in Nazi Society.* London: Barnes and Noble, 1975.

Otto Strasser and Michael Stern, *Flight from Terror.* New York: Robert M. McBride, 1943.

A.J.P. Taylor, *The Origins of the Second World War.* London: Hamish Hamilton, 1961.

Telford Taylor, *The Anatomy of the Nuremberg Trials.* New York: Knopf, 1992.

Studs Terkel, *The Good War: An Oral History of World War II.* New York: Ballantine, 1984.

Rita Thalmann and Emanuel Fienerman, *Crystal Night: 9–10 November 1938.* Trans. Gilles Cremonesi. New York: Holocaust Library, 1974.

Michael C. Thomsett, *The German Opposition to Hitler.* Jefferson, NC: McFarland, 1997.

John Toland, *The Last 100 Days.* New York: Random House, 1965.

H.R. Trevor-Roper, ed., *Hitler's Secret Conversations, 1941–1944.* Trans. Norman Cameron and R.H. Stevens. New York: Farrar, Straus, and Young, 1958.

———, *The Last Days of Hitler.* New York: Macmillan, 1947.

Henry Ashby Turner, *German Big Business and the Rise of Hitler.* New York: Oxford University Press, 1985.

Robert L. Waite, The Psychopathic God: Adolf Hitler. New York: Basic, 1977.

Charles Whiting, *Massacre at Malmedy.* New York: Combined, 1996.

———, *Skorzeny: The Most Dangerous Man in Europe.* New York: Combined, 1998.

Elie Wiesel, *Night.* Trans. S. Rodway. New York: Bantam, 1960.

Simon Wiesenthal, *Justice Not Vengeance.* Trans. Ewald Osners. New York: Grove, 1989.

Charles Wighton, *Heydrich: Hitler's Most Evil Henchman.* London: Odham's Press, 1962.

Robert S. Wistrich, *Who's Who in Nazi Germany.* 2nd ed. New York: Routledge, 1995.

Desmond Young, *Rommel: The Desert Fox.* New York: Harper and Brothers, 1950.

Peter Young, ed., *The World Almanac Book of World War II.* Englewood Cliffs, NJ: Prentice-Hall, 1981.

Z.A.B. Zeman, *Nazi Propaganda.* London: Oxford University Press, 1973.

Yitzhak Zuckerman, *Surplus of Memory: Chronicle of the Warsaw Ghetto Uprising.*

Trans. Barbara Harshav. Berkeley and Los Angeles: University of California Press, 1993.

Websites

The Anne Frank House, www.annefrank.nl. The official website of the Anne Frank Museum, housed in the business annex where Anne and her family hid from the Gestapo. The site contains photos and stories.

Arsenal of Dictatorship, www.geocities.com/pentagon/2833. An interactive site describing the Third Reich's army, navy, and air force with a section on "secret weapons" and "weapons of reprisal."

Art of the Third Reich, http://fcit.coedu.usf.edu/holocaust/arts/artReich.htm. Biographies of Nazi artists, photos, paintings, even political cartoons. The site also contains links to a wealth of general material on the Third Reich.

The Avalon Project, www.yale.edu/lawweb/avalon/avalon.htm. A broad collection of World War II documents, including the twenty-two volume proceedings of the trial of the major war criminals by the International Military Tribunal at Nuremberg.

Concentration Camps: A Traveler's Guide to World War II Sites, www.concentrationcampguide.com. Accounts and photos from the author's visits to thirty-nine concentration camps and World War II sites.

The Einsatzgruppen, www.einsatzgruppenarchives.com/einsatz.html. Photos, stories, and links on the SS killing squads that killed millions on the eastern front.

The German Armed Forces in World War II, www.feldgrau.com. A detailed site on the regular German armed forces as well as the Waffen-SS.

The Himmler-Heydrich Duo, www.megspace.com/education/trp/hey.drich2.htm. The story of the two most reviled henchmen of the Third Reich.

The History Place, www.historyplace.com. Stories and links on virtually all aspects of the Third Reich from biographies of Nazi leaders to World War II battles to the Holocaust.

Medical Experiments of the Holocaust and Nazi Medicine, www.remember.org/educated/medexp.html. Materials on Nazi doctors and their experiments both before and during World War II.

Modern World History: The Rise of Hitler, www.bbc.co.uk/html. Educational site on the Nazi dictator with many useful links to Third Reich and World War II materials.

The Nazi Olympics, www.ushmm.org/olympics. An online museum exhibition created by the U.S. Holocaust Memorial Museum on the 1936 Olympics in Berlin. Links to the Memorial Museum's homepage.

The Nizkor Project, www.nizkor.org. A thorough site containing documents on the Third Reich and the Holocaust.

Propaganda in Nazi Germany, www.historylearningsite.co.uk/htm. Samples of propaganda posters, films, and speeches as well as links.

The Simon Wiesenthal Center, www.wiesenthal.com. Much material on the Holocaust and on the most famous of postwar Nazi hunters.

The Third Reich, www.history1900s.about.com. Many links to sites with articles about specific events during the Third Reich as well as primary documents and photos.

Third Reich Factbook, www.skalman.nu/third-reich. Devoted mostly to a thorough description of the Third Reich's armed forces. Contains material on military regalia and songs. Lots of unusual trivia.

Third Reich Historical Photo Archive, http://community-2.webtv.net/kloobengeep. Many photos on various aspects of the Third Reich.

Third Reich Roundtable, www.thirdreich.net. Biographies, photos, and links to material on most aspects of the Third Reich.

The Trial of Adolf Eichmann, www.pbs.org/eichmann. The website devoted to the

PBS special. Contains historical material, photos, exercises, and links.

World War II: War Crimes, www.louisville. edu/library/ekstrom/govpubs/subjects/war/ wcrimes.html. A links site covering the various war crimes trials.

Yad Vashem, www.yad-vashem.org. The website of Israel's Holocaust memorial and information center. Offers samples of primary documents as well as historical material and online museum exhibitions.

INDEX

COMPREHENSIVE INDEX

Note: The boldface numbers preceding the colons indicate volume number. The page numbers in boldface indicate the main entry for the subject.

PICTURE CREDITS

ABOUT THE EDITOR

Jeff T. Hay received a Ph.D. in European history from the University of California, San Diego, and now teaches European and world history, including a course on the Holocaust, at San Diego State University. He is the editor of a number of historical anthologies, including Greenhaven's *The Renaissance* and *Europe Rules the World.* He lives in Del Mar, California.

ABOUT THE CONSULTING EDITOR

Christopher R. Browning is Frank Porter Graham Professor of History at the University of North Carolina, Chapel Hill. He holds a Ph.D. from the University of Wisconsin, Madison, and an honorary doctorate from Hebrew Union College. A distinguished historian of the Holocaust, he delivered the George Macaulay Trevelyan Lectures at Cambridge University in 1999. He is the author of six books on the subject, including *Ordinary Men: Reserve Police Battalion 101 and the Final Solution in Poland* (1992), and is currently writing a two-volume study of Nazi Jewish policy during World War II as part of Yad Vashem's multivolume comprehensive history of the Holocaust.